Georg Brandes

William Shakespeare, a critical study

Vol. I

Georg Brandes

William Shakespeare, a critical study
Vol. I

ISBN/EAN: 9783337055653

Printed in Europe, USA, Canada, Australia, Japan

Cover: Foto ©ninafisch / pixelio.de

More available books at **www.hansebooks.com**

WILLIAM
SHAKESPEARE

WILLIAM SHAKESPEARE

A CRITICAL STUDY

BY

GEORGE BRANDES

IN TWO VOLUMES
VOL. I.

LONDON
WILLIAM HEINEMANN
1898

[All rights reserved]

CONTENTS

BOOK FIRST

CHAP.		PAGE
I.	A BIOGRAPHY OF SHAKESPEARE DIFFICULT BUT NOT IMPOSSIBLE	3
II.	STRATFORD—PARENTAGE—BOYHOOD	7
III.	MARRIAGE—SIR THOMAS LUCY—DEPARTURE FROM STRATFORD	13
IV.	LONDON—BUILDINGS, COSTUMES, MANNERS	16
V.	POLITICAL AND RELIGIOUS CONDITIONS—ENGLAND'S GROWING GREATNESS	20
VI.	SHAKESPEARE AS ACTOR AND RETOUCHER OF OLD PLAYS—GREENE'S ATTACK	23
VII.	THE "HENRY VI." TRILOGY	27
VIII.	CHRISTOPHER MARLOWE AND HIS LIFE-WORK — TITUS ANDRONICUS	34
IX.	SHAKESPEARE'S CONCEPTION OF THE RELATIONS OF THE SEXES—HIS MARRIAGE VIEWED IN THIS LIGHT—LOVE'S LABOUR'S LOST—ITS MATTER AND STYLE—JOHN LYLY AND EUPHUISM—THE PERSONAL ELEMENT	42
X.	LOVE'S LABOUR'S WON: THE FIRST SKETCH OF ALL'S WELL THAT ENDS WELL—THE COMEDY OF ERRORS—THE TWO GENTLEMEN OF VERONA	57
XI.	VENUS AND ADONIS: DESCRIPTIONS OF NATURE—THE RAPE OF LUCRECE: RELATION TO PAINTING	67
XII.	A MIDSUMMER NIGHT'S DREAM—ITS HISTORICAL CIRCUMSTANCES—ITS ARISTOCRATIC, POPULAR, COMIC, AND SUPERNATURAL ELEMENTS	76
XIII.	ROMEO AND JULIET—THE TWO QUARTOS—ITS ROMANESQUE STRUCTURE—THE USE OF OLD MOTIVES—THE CONCEPTION OF LOVE	87

CONTENTS

CHAP.   PAGE

XIV. LATTER-DAY ATTACKS UPON SHAKESPEARE—THE BACONIAN THEORY—SHAKESPEARE'S KNOWLEDGE, PHYSICAL AND PHILOSOPHICAL 104

XV. THE THEATRES—THEIR SITUATION AND ARRANGEMENTS—THE PLAYERS—THE POETS—POPULAR AUDIENCES—THE ARISTOCRATIC PUBLIC—SHAKESPEARE'S ARISTOCRATIC PRINCIPLES 117

XVI. THE THEATRES CLOSED ON ACCOUNT OF THE PLAGUE—DID SHAKESPEARE VISIT ITALY?—PASSAGES WHICH FAVOUR THIS CONJECTURE 134

XVII. SHAKESPEARE TURNS TO HISTORIC DRAMA—HIS RICHARD II. AND MARLOWE'S EDWARD II.—LACK OF HUMOUR AND OF CONSISTENCY OF STYLE—ENGLISH NATIONAL PRIDE 141

XVIII. RICHARD III. PSYCHOLOGY AND MONOLOGUES—SHAKESPEARE'S POWER OF SELF-TRANSFORMATION—CONTEMPT FOR WOMEN—THE PRINCIPAL SCENES—THE CLASSIC TENDENCY OF THE TRAGEDY 150

XIX. SHAKESPEARE LOSES HIS SON—TRACES OF HIS GRIEF IN KING JOHN—THE OLD PLAY OF THE SAME NAME—DISPLACEMENT OF ITS CENTRE OF GRAVITY—ELIMINATION OF RELIGIOUS POLEMICS—RETENTION OF THE NATIONAL BASIS—PATRIOTIC SPIRIT—SHAKESPEARE KNOWS NOTHING OF THE DISTINCTION BETWEEN NORMANS AND ANGLO-SAXONS, AND IGNORES THE MAGNA CHARTA 166

XX. "THE TAMING OF THE SHREW" AND "THE MERCHANT OF VENICE"—SHAKESPEARE'S PREOCCUPATION WITH THOUGHTS OF PROPERTY AND GAIN—HIS GROWING PROSPERITY—HIS ADMISSION TO THE RANKS OF THE "GENTRY"—HIS PURCHASE OF HOUSES AND LAND—MONEY TRANSACTIONS AND LAWSUITS 178

XXI. THE MERCHANT OF VENICE—ITS SOURCES—ITS CHARACTERS, ANTONIO, PORTIA, SHYLOCK—MOONLIGHT AND MUSIC—SHAKESPEARE'S RELATION TO MUSIC . . . 186

CONTENTS

CHAP.   PAGE

XXII. "EDWARD III." AND "ARDEN OF FEVERSHAM"—SHAKESPEARE'S DICTION—THE FIRST PART OF "HENRY IV."—FIRST INTRODUCTION OF HIS OWN EXPERIENCES OF LIFE IN THE HISTORIC DRAMA — WHY THE SUBJECT APPEALED TO HIM — TAVERN LIFE — SHAKESPEARE'S CIRCLE — SIR JOHN FALSTAFF — FALSTAFF AND THE GRACIOSO OF THE SPANISH DRAMA — RABELAIS AND SHAKESPEARE—PANURGE AND FALSTAFF 203

XXIII. HENRY PERCY—THE MASTERY OF THE CHARACTER DRAWING—HOTSPUR AND ACHILLES 220

XXIV. PRINCE HENRY—THE POINT OF DEPARTURE FOR SHAKESPEARE'S IMAGINATION—A TYPICAL ENGLISH NATIONAL HERO—THE FRESHNESS AND PERFECTION OF THE PLAY 229

XXV. "KING HENRY IV.," SECOND PART—OLD AND NEW CHARACTERS IN IT—DETAILS—"HENRY V.," A NATIONAL DRAMA—PATRIOTISM AND CHAUVINISM—THE VISION OF A GREATER ENGLAND 237

XXVI. ELIZABETH AND FALSTAFF — "THE MERRY WIVES OF WINDSOR"—THE PROSAIC AND BOURGEOIS TONE OF THE PIECE—THE FAIRY SCENES 244

XXVII. SHAKESPEARE'S MOST BRILLIANT PERIOD—THE FEMININE TYPES BELONGING TO IT—WITTY AND HIGHBORN YOUNG WOMEN—MUCH ADO ABOUT NOTHING—SLAVISH FAITHFULNESS TO HIS SOURCES—BENEDICK AND BEATRICE—SPIRITUAL DEVELOPMENT—THE LOW-COMEDY FIGURES . 249

XXVIII. THE INTERVAL OF SERENITY—AS YOU LIKE IT—THE ROVING SPIRIT—THE LONGING FOR NATURE—JAQUES AND SHAKESPEARE—THE PLAY A FEAST OF WIT . . 258

XXIX. CONSUMMATE SPIRITUAL HARMONY—TWELFTH NIGHT—JIBES AT PURITANISM—THE LANGUISHING CHARACTERS—VIOLA'S INSINUATING GRACE—FAREWELL TO MIRTH . 270

XXX. THE REVOLUTION IN SHAKESPEARE'S SOUL—THE GROWING MELANCHOLY OF THE FOLLOWING PERIOD—PESSIMISM, MISANTHROPY .   .   . 280

CONTENTS

BOOK SECOND

CHAP.		PAGE
I.	INTRODUCTION—THE ENGLAND OF ELIZABETH IN SHAKE-SPEARE'S YOUTH	284
II.	ELIZABETH'S OLD AGE	289
III.	ELIZABETH, ESSEX, AND BACON	295
IV.	THE FATE OF ESSEX AND SOUTHAMPTON	303
V.	THE YEAR 1601—THE SONNETS AND PEMBROKE	313
VI.	THE "DARK LADY" OF THE SONNETS—MARY FITTON	327
VII.	PLATONISM IN SHAKESPEARE'S AND MICHAEL ANGELO'S SONNETS—THE TECHNIQUE OF THE SONNETS	341
VIII.	JULIUS CÆSAR—ITS FUNDAMENTAL DEFECT	357
IX.	THE MERITS OF JULIUS CÆSAR—BRUTUS	372
X.	BEN JONSON AND HIS ROMAN PLAYS	384

WILLIAM SHAKESPEARE

BOOK FIRST

THE same year which saw the death of Michael Angelo in Rome, saw the birth of William Shakespeare at Stratford-on-Avon. The great artist of the Italian Renaissance, the man who painted the ceiling of the Sistine Chapel, was replaced, as it were, by the great artist of the English Renaissance, the man who wrote *King Lear*.

Death overtook Shakespeare in his native place on the same date on which Cervantes died in Madrid. The two great creative artists of the Spanish and the English Renaissance, the men to whom we owe Don Quixote and Hamlet, Sancho Panza and Falstaff, were simultaneously snatched away.

Michael Angelo has depicted mighty and suffering demigods in solitary grandeur. No Italian has rivalled him in sombre lyrism or tragic sublimity.

The finest creations of Cervantes stand as monuments of a humour so exalted that it marks an epoch in the literature of the world. No Spaniard has rivalled him in type-creating comic force.

Shakespeare stands co-equal with Michael Angelo in pathos and with Cervantes in humour. This of itself gives us a certain standard for measuring the height and range of his powers.

It is three hundred years since his genius [attained its full development, yet Europe is still busied with him as though with a contemporary. His dramas are acted and read wherever civilisation extends. Perhaps, however, he exercises the strongest fascination upon the reader whose natural bent of mind leads him to delight in searching out the human spirit concealed and revealed in a great artist's work. "I will not let you go until you have confessed to me the secret of your being"—these are the words that rise to the lips of such a reader of Shakespeare. Ranging the plays in their probable order of production, and reviewing the poet's life-work as a whole, he feels constrained to form for himself some image of the spiritual experience of which it is the expression.

I

A BIOGRAPHY OF SHAKESPEARE DIFFICULT BUT NOT IMPOSSIBLE

WHEN we pass from the notabilities of the nineteenth century to Shakespeare, all our ordinary critical methods leave us in the lurch. We have, as a rule, no lack of trustworthy information as to the productive spirits of our own day and of the past two centuries. We know the lives of authors and poets from their own accounts or those of their contemporaries; in many cases we have their letters; and we possess not only works attributed to them, but works which they themselves gave to the press. We not only know with certainty their authentic writings, but are assured that we possess them in authentic form. If disconcerting errors occur in their works, they are only misprints, which they themselves or others happen to have overlooked. Insidious though they may be, there is no particular difficulty in correcting them. Bernays, for example, has weeded out not a few from the text of Goethe.

It is otherwise with Shakespeare and his fellow-dramatists of Elizabethan England. He died in 1616, and the first biography of him, a few pages in length, dates from 1709. This is as though the first sketch of Goethe's life were not to be written till the year 1925. We possess no letters of Shakespeare's, and only one (a business letter) addressed to him. Of the manuscripts of his works not a single line is extant. Our sole specimens of his handwriting consist of five or six signatures, three appended to his will, two to contracts, and one, of very doubtful authenticity, on the copy of Florio's translation of Montaigne, which is shown at the British Museum. We do not know exactly how far several of the works attributed to Shakespeare are really his. In the case of such plays as *Titus Andronicus*, the trilogy of *Henry VI.*, *Pericles*, and *Henry VIII.*, the question of authorship presents great and manifold difficulties. In his youth Shakespeare had to adapt or retouch the plays of others; in later life he sometimes collaborated with younger men. And worse than this, with the exception of two short narrative poems, which Shakespeare himself gave to the press, not one of his works is known to have been published under his own supervision. He seems never to have sanctioned any publication, or to have read a single proof-sheet. The 1623 folio of his plays, issued after his death by two of his actor-friends, purports to be printed "according to the True Originall Copies;" but this assertion is demonstrably false in numerous instances in which we can test it—where the folio, that is to say, presents a simple reprint, often with additional blunders, of the old pirated quartos, which must have been based either on the surreptitious notes of stenographers or on "prompt copies" dishonestly acquired.

It has become the fashion to say, not without some show of justice, that we know next to nothing of Shakespeare's life. We do not know for certain either when he left Stratford or when he returned to Stratford from London. We do not know for certain whether he ever went abroad, ever visited Italy. We do not know the name of a single woman whom he loved during all his years in London. We do not know for certain to whom his Sonnets are addressed. We can see that as he advanced in life his prevailing mood became gloomier, but we do not know the reason. Later on, his temper seems to grow more serene, but we cannot tell why. We can form but tentative conjectures as to the order in which his works were produced, and can only with the greatest difficulty determine their approximate dates. We do not know what made him so careless of his fame as he seems to have been. We only know that he himself did not publish his dramatic works, and that he does not even mention them in his will.

On the other hand, enthusiastic and indefatigable research has gradually brought to light a great number of indubitable facts, which furnish us with points of departure and of guidance for an outline of the poet's life. We possess documents, contracts, legal records; we can cite utterances of contemporaries, allusions to works of Shakespeare's and to passages in them, quotations, fierce attacks, outbursts of spite and hatred, touching testimonies to his worth as a man and to the lovableness of his nature, evidence of the early recognition of his talent as an actor, of his

repute as a narrative poet, and of his popularity as a dramatist.
We have, moreover, one or two diaries kept by contemporaries,
and among others the account-book of an old theatrical manager
and pawnbroker, who supplied the players with money and
dresses, and who has carefully dated the production of many
plays.

To these contemporary evidences we must add that of
tradition. In 1662 a clergyman named John Ward, Vicar of
Stratford, took some notes of information gathered from the inhabitants of the district; and in 1693 a Mr. Dowdall recorded
some details which he had learnt from the octogenarian sexton
and verger of Stratford Church. But tradition is mainly represented by Rowe, Shakespeare's first tardy biographer. He refers
in particular to three sources of information. The earliest is Sir
William Davenant, Poet Laureate, who did nothing to discoun-
tenance the rumour which gave him out to be an illegitimate son
of Shakespeare. His contributions, however, can have reached
Rowe only at second hand, since he died before Rowe was born.
Naturally enough, then, the greater part of what is related on his
authority proves to be questionable. Rowe's second source of
information was Aubrey, an antiquary after the fashion of his
day, who, half a century after Shakespeare's death, visited Stratford on one of his riding-tours. He wrote numerous short
biographies, all of which contain gross and demonstrable errors,
so that we can scarcely put implicit faith in the insignificant
anecdotes about Shakespeare preserved in his manuscript of
1680. Rowe's most important source of information, however,
is Betterton the actor, who, about 1690, made a journey to
Warwickshire for the express purpose of collecting whatever
oral traditions with regard to Shakespeare might linger in the
district. His gleanings form the most valuable part of Rowe's
biography; contemporary documents subsequently discovered
have in several instances lent them curious confirmation.

We owe it, then, to a little group of worthy but by no means
brilliant men that we are able to sketch the outline of Shakespeare's career. They have preserved for us anecdotes of little
worth, even if they are true, while leaving us entirely in the
dark as to important points in his outward history, and throwing
little or no light upon the course of his inner life.

It is true that we possess in Shakespeare's Sonnets a group of poems which bring us more directly into touch with his personality than any of his other works. But to determine the value of the Sonnets as autobiographical documents requires not only historical knowledge but critical instinct and tact, since it is by no means self-evident that the poet is, in a literal sense, speaking in his own name.

II

STRATFORD—PARENTAGE—BOYHOOD

WILLIAM SHAKESPEARE was a child of the country. He was born in Stratford-on-Avon, a little town of fourteen or fifteen hundred inhabitants, lying in a pleasant and undulating tract of country, rich in green meadows and trees and leafy hedges, the natural features of which Shakespeare seems to have had in his mind's eye when he wrote the descriptions of scenery in *A Midsummer Night's Dream, As You Like It,* and *A Winter's Tale.* His first and deepest impressions of nature he received from this scenery; and he associated with it his earliest poetical impressions, gathered from the folk-songs of the peasantry, so often alluded to and reproduced in his plays. The town of Stratford lies upon the ancient high-road from London to Ireland, which here crosses the river Avon. To this circumstance it owes its name (Street-ford). A handsome bridge spanned the river. The picturesque houses, with their gable-roofs, were either wooden or frame-built. There were two handsome public buildings, which still remain: the fine old church close to the river, and the Guildhall, with its chapel and Grammar School. In the chapel, which possessed a pleasant peal of bells, there was a set of frescoes —probably the first and for long the only paintings known to Shakespeare.

For the rest, Stratford-on-Avon was an insanitary place of residence. There was no sort of underground drainage, and street-sweepers and scavengers were unknown. The waste water from the houses flowed out into badly kept gutters; the streets were full of evil-smelling pools, in which pigs and geese freely disported themselves; and dunghills skirted the highway. The first thing we learn about Shakespeare's father is that, in April 1552, he was fined twelvepence for having formed a great midden outside his house in Henley Street—a circumstance which on the one hand proves that he kept sheep and cattle, and on the other indicates his scant care for cleanliness, since the common dunghill lay only a stone's-throw from his house. At the time of his highest prosperity, in 1558, he, along with some other citizens, is again fined fourpence for the same misdemeanour.

The matter is not without interest, since it is in all probability to these defects of sanitation that Shakespeare's early death is to be ascribed.

Both on his father's and his mother's side, the poet was descended from yeoman families of Warwickshire. His grandfather, Richard Shakespeare, lived at Snitterfield, where he rented a small property. Richard's second son, John Shakespeare, removed to Stratford about 1551, and went into business in Henley Street as a tanner and glover. In the year 1557 his circumstances were considerably improved by his marriage with Mary Arden, the youngest daughter of Robert Arden, a well-to-do yeoman in the neighbourhood, who had died a few months before. On his death she had inherited his property of Asbies at Wilmecote; and she had, besides, a reversionary interest in a larger property at Snitterfield. Asbies was valued at £224, and brought in a rental of £28, or about £140 of our modern money. The inventory appended to her father's will gives us a good insight into the domestic economy of a rich yeoman's family of those days: a single bed with two mattresses, five sheets, three towels, &c. Garments of linen they do not seem to have possessed. The eating utensils were of no value: wooden spoons and wooden platters. Yet the home of Shakespeare's mother was, according to the standard of that day, distinctly well-to-do.

His marriage enabled John Shakespeare to extend his business. He had large transactions in wool, and also dealt, as occasion offered, in corn and other commodities. Aubrey's statement that he was a butcher seems to mean no more than that he himself fattened and killed the animals whose skins he used in his trade. But in those days the different occupations in a small English country town were not at all strictly discriminated; the man who produced the raw material would generally work it up as well.

John Shakespeare gradually rose to an influential position in the little town in which he had settled. He first (in 1557) became one of the ale-tasters, sworn to look to the quality of bread and

STRATFORD—PARENTAGE—BOYHOOD

beer; in the following year he was one of the four "petty constables" of the town. In 1561 he was Chamberlain, in 1565 Alderman, and finally, in 1568, High Bailiff.

William Shakespeare was his parents' third child. Two sisters, who died in infancy, preceded him. He was baptized on the 26th of April 1564; we do not know his birthday precisely. Tradition gives it as the 23rd of April; more probably it was the 22nd (in the new style the 4th of May), since, if Shakespeare had died upon his birthday, his epitaph would doubtless have mentioned the circumstance, and would not have stated that he died in his fifty-third year [*Ætatis* 53].

Neither of Shakespeare's parents possessed any school education; neither of them seems to have been able to write his or her own name. They desired, however, that their eldest son should not lack the education they themselves had been denied, and therefore sent the boy to the Free School or Grammar School of Stratford, where children from the age of seven upwards were grounded in Latin grammar, learned to construe out of a schoolbook called *Sententiæ Pueriles*, and afterwards read Ovid, Virgil, and Cicero. The school-hours, both in summer and winter, occupied the whole day, with the necessary intervals for meals and recreation. An obvious reminiscence of Shakespeare's schooldays is preserved for us in *The Merry Wives of Windsor* (iv. 1), where the schoolmaster, Sir Hugh Evans, hears little William his *Hic, Hæc, Hoc*, and assures himself of his knowledge that *pulcher* means fair, and *lapis* a stone. It even appears that his teacher was in fact a Welshman.

The district in which the child grew up was rich in historical memories and monuments. Warwick, with its castle, renowned since the Wars of the Roses, was in the immediate neighbourhood. It had been the residence, in his day, of the Earl of Warwick who distinguished himself at the battle of Shrewsbury and negotiated the marriage of Henry V. The district was, however, divided during the Wars of the Roses. Warwick for some time sided with York, Coventry with Lancaster. With Coventry, too, a town rich in memories of the period which he was afterwards to summon to life on the stage, Shakespeare must have been acquainted in his boyhood. It was in Coventry that the two adversaries who appear in his *Richard II.*, Henry Bolingbroke and the Duke of Norfolk, had their famous encounter. But in another respect as well Coventry must have had great attractions for the boy. It was the scene of regular theatrical representations, which, at first organised by the Church, afterwards passed into the hands of the guilds. Shakespeare must doubtless have seen the half-mediæval religious dramas sometimes alluded to in his works—plays which placed before the eyes of the audience Herod and the Massacre of the Innocents, souls burning in hell, and other startling scenes of a like nature[1] (*Henry V.*, ii. 3 and iii. 3).

Of royal and princely splendour Shakespeare had probably certain glimpses even in his childhood. When he was eight years old Elizabeth paid a visit to Sir Thomas Lucy of Charlecote, in the immediate neighbourhood of Stratford — the Sir Thomas Lucy who was to have such a determining influence upon Shakespeare's career. In any case, he must doubtless have visited the neighbouring castle of Kenilworth, and seen something of the great festivities organised by Leicester in Elizabeth's honour, during her visit to the castle in 1575. We know that the Shakespeare family possessed a near and influential kinsman in Leicester's trusted attendant, Edward Arden, who soon afterwards, apparently on account of the strained relations which arose between the Queen and Leicester after the fêtes, incurred the suspicion or displeasure of his master, and was ultimately executed.

Nor was it only mediæval mysteries that the future poet, during his boyhood, had opportunities of seeing. The town of Stratford showed a marked taste for secular theatricals. The first travelling company of players came to Stratford in the year when Shakespeare's father was High Bailiff, and between 1569 and 1587 no fewer than twenty-four strolling troupes visited the town. The companies who came most frequently were the Queen's Men and the servants of Lord Worcester, Lord Leicester, and Lord Warwick. Custom directed that they should first wait upon the High Bailiff to inform him in what nobleman's service they were enrolled; and their first performance took place before the Town Council alone. A writer named Willis, born in the same year as Shakespeare, has described how he was present at such a

---

[1] We find reminiscences of these scenes in Hamlet's expression, "He out-herods Herod," and in the comparison of a flea on Bardolph's nose to a black soul burning in hell-fire.

representation in the neighbouring town of Gloucester, standing between his father's knees; and we can thus picture to ourselves the way in which the glories of the theatre were for the first time revealed to the future poet.

As a boy and youth, then, he no doubt had opportunities of making himself familiar with the bulk of the old English repertory, partly composed of such pieces as he afterwards ridicules— for instance, the *Cambyses*, whose rant Falstaff parodies—partly of pieces which subsequently became the foundation of his own plays, such as *The Supposes*, which he used in *The Taming of the Shrew*, or *The Troublesome Raigne of King John*, or the *Famous Victories of Henry the Fifth*, which supplied some of the material for his *Henry IV*.

Probably Shakespeare, as a boy and youth, was not content with seeing the performances, but sought out the players in the different taverns where they took up their quarters, the "Swan," the "Crown," or the "Bear."

The school course was generally over when a boy reached his fourteenth year. It appears that when Shakespeare was at this age his father removed him from the school, having need of him in his business. His father's prosperity was by this time on the wane.

In the year 1578 John Shakespeare mortgaged his wife's property, Asbies, for a sum of £40, which he seems to have engaged to repay within two years, though this he himself denied. In the same year the Town Council agrees that he shall be required to pay only one-half of a tax (6s. 8d. in all) for the equipment of soldiers, and absolves him altogether from payment of a poor-rate levied on the other Aldermen. In the following year he cannot pay even his half of the pikemen-tax. In 1579 he sold the reversion of a piece of land falling to him on his mother-in-law's death. In the following year he wanted to pay off the mortgage on Asbies; but the mortgagee, a certain Edmund Lambert, declined to receive the money, for the reason, or under the pretext, that it had not been tendered within the stipulated time, and that Shakespeare had, moreover, borrowed other sums of him. In the course of the consequent lawsuit, John Shakespeare described himself as a person of "small wealthe, and verey fewe frends and alyance in the countie." The result of this lawsuit is unknown, but it seems as though the father, and the son after him, took it much to heart, and felt that a great injustice had been done them. In the Induction to *The Taming of the Shrew*, Christopher Sly calls himself "Old Sly's son of Burton Heath." But Barton-on-the-Heath was precisely the place where lived Edmund Lambert and his son John, who, after his death in 1587, carried on the litigation. And this utterance of the chief character in the Induction is, significantly enough, one of the few which Shakespeare added to the Induction to the old play he was here adapting.

From this time forward John Shakespeare's position goes from bad to worse. In the year 1586, when his son was probably already in London, his goods are distrained upon, and no fewer than three warrants are issued for his arrest; he seems for a time to have been imprisoned for debt. He is removed from his position as Alderman because he has not for a long time attended the meetings at the Guildhall. He probably dared not put in an appearance for fear of being arrested by his creditors. He seems to have lost a considerable sum of money by standing surety for his brother Henry. There was, moreover, a commercial crisis in Stratford. The cloth and yarn trade, in which most of the citizens were engaged, had become much less remunerative than before.

We find evidence of the painful position in which John Shakespeare remained so late as the year 1592, in Sir Thomas Lucy's report with reference to the inhabitants of Stratford who did not obey her Majesty's order that they should attend church once a month. He is mentioned as one of those who "coom not to Churche for fear of processe for debtte."

It is probable that the young William, when his father removed him from the Grammar School, assisted him in his trade; and it is not impossible that, as a somewhat dubious allusion in a contemporary seems to imply, he was for some time a clerk in an attorney's office. His great powers, at any rate, doubtless revealed themselves very early; he must have taken early to writing verses, and, like most men of genius, must have ripened early in every respect.

III

MARRIAGE—SIR THOMAS LUCY—DEPARTURE FROM STRATFORD

IN December 1582, being then only eighteen, William Shakespeare married Anne Hathaway, daughter of a well-to-do yeoman, recently deceased, in a neighbouring hamlet of the same parish. The marriage of a boy not yet out of his teens, whose father was in embarrassed circumstances, while he himself had probably nothing to live on but such scanty wages as he could earn in his father's service, seems on the face of it somewhat precipitate; and the arrangements for it, moreover, were unusually hurried. In a document dated November 28, 1582, two friends of the Hathaway family give a bond to the Bishop of Worcester's Court, declaring, under relatively heavy penalties, that there is no legal impediment to the solemnisation of the marriage after one publication of the banns, instead of the statutory three. So far as we can gather, it was the bride's family that hurried on the marriage, while the bridegroom's held back, and perhaps even opposed it. This haste is the less surprising when we find that the first child, a daughter named Susanna, was born in May 1583, only five months and three weeks after the wedding. It is probable, however, that a formal betrothal, which at that time was regarded as the essential part of the contract, had preceded the marriage.

In 1585 twins were born, a girl, Judith, and a boy, Hamnet (the name is also written Hamlet), no doubt called after a friend of the family, Hamnet Sadler, a baker in Stratford, who is mentioned in Shakespeare's will. This son died at the age of eleven.

It was probably soon after the birth of the twins that Shakespeare was forced to quit Stratford. According to Rowe he had "fallen into ill company," and taken part in more than one deer-stealing raid upon Sir Thomas Lucy's park at Charlecote. "For this he was prosecuted by that gentleman, as he thought, somewhat too severely, and in order to revenge that ill-usage he made a ballad upon him. . . . It is said to have been so very bitter that it redoubled the prosecution against him to that degree that he was obliged to leave his business and family in Warwickshire for some time and shelter himself in London." Rowe believed this ballad to be lost, but what purports to be the first verse of it has been preserved by Oldys, on the authority of a very old man who lived in the neighbourhood of Stratford. It may possibly be genuine. The coincidence between it and an unquestionable gibe at Sir Thomas Lucy in *The Merry Wives of Windsor* renders it probable that it has been more or less correctly remembered.[1] Although poaching was at that time regarded as a comparatively innocent and pardonable misdemeanour of youth, to which the Oxford students, for example, were for many generations greatly addicted, yet Sir Thomas Lucy, who seems to have newly and not over-plentifully stocked his park, deeply resented the depredations of young Stratford. He was, it would appear, no favourite in the town. He never, like the other landowners of the district, requited with a present of game the offerings of salt and sugar which, as we learn from the town accounts, the burgesses were in the habit of sending him. Shakespeare's misdeeds were not at that time punishable by law; but, as a great landowner and justice of the peace, Sir Thomas had the young fellow in his power, and there is every probability in favour of the tradition, preserved by the Rev. Richard Davies, who died in 1708, that he "had him oft whipt and sometimes imprisoned." It is confirmed by the substantial correctness of Davies' further statement: "His revenge was so great, that he is his Justice Clodpate [Shallow], . . . that in allusion to his name bore three louses rampant for his arms." We find, in fact, that in the opening scene of *The Merry Wives*, Justice Shallow, who accuses Falstaff of having shot his deer,

[1] It runs :—

"A parliament member, a justice of peace,
At home a poor scare-crow, at London an asse ;
If lowsie is Lucy, as some volke miscalle it,
Then Lucy is lowsie, whatever befall it ;
    He thinkes himself greate|
    Yet an asse in his state
We allowe by his eares but with asses to mate.
If Lucy is lowsie, as some volke miscalle it,
Sing lowsie Lucy, whatever befalle it.

DEPARTURE FROM STRATFORD 15

has, according to Slender's account, a dozen white luces (pikes) in his coat-of-arms, which, in the mouth of the Welshman, Sir Hugh Evans, become a dozen white louses—the word-play being exactly the same as that in the ballad. Three luces argent were the cognisance of the Lucy family.

The attempt to cast doubt upon this old tradition of Shakespeare's poaching exploits becomes doubly unreasonable in face of the fact that precisely in 1585 Sir Thomas Lucy spoke in Parliament in favour of more stringent game-laws.

The essential point, however, is simply this, that at about the age of twenty-one Shakespeare leaves his native town, not to return to it permanently until his life's course is nearly run. Even if he had not been forced to bid it farewell, the impulse to develop his talents and energies must ere long have driven him forth. Young and inexperienced as he was, at all events, he had now to betake himself to the capital to seek his fortune.

Whether he left any great happiness behind him we cannot tell; but it is scarcely probable. There is nothing to show that in the peasant girl, almost eight years older than himself, whom he married at the age of eighteen, Shakespeare found the woman who, even for a few years, could fill his life. Everything, indeed, points in the opposite direction. She and the children remained behind in Stratford, and he saw her only when he revisited his native place, as he did at long intervals, probably, at first, but afterwards annually. Tradition and the internal evidence of his writings prove that he lived, in London, the free Bohemian life of an actor and playwright. We know, too, that he was soon plunged in the business cares of a theatrical manager and part-proprietor. The woman's part in this life was not played by Anne Hathaway. On the other hand, there can be no doubt that Shakespeare never for a moment lost sight of Stratford, and that he had no sooner made a footing for himself in London than he set to work with the definite aim of acquiring land and property in the town from which he had gone forth penniless and humiliated. His father should hold up his head again, and the family honour be re-established.

IV

LONDON—BUILDINGS, COSTUMES, MANNERS

So the young man rode from Stratford to London. He probably, according to the custom of the poorer travellers of that time, sold his horse on his arrival at Smithfield; and, as Halliwell-Phillips ingeniously suggests, he may have sold it to James Burbage, who kept a livery stable in the neighbourhood. It may have been this man, the father of Richard Burbage, afterwards Shakespeare's most famous fellow-actor, who employed Shakespeare to take charge of the horses which his customers of the Smithfield district hired to ride to the play. James Burbage had built, and now owned, the first playhouse erected in London (1576), known as *The Theatre;* and a well-known tradition, which can be traced to Sir William Davenant, relates that Shakespeare was driven by dire necessity to hang about the doors of the theatre and hold the horses of those who had ridden to the play. The district was a remote and disreputable one, and swarmed with horse-thieves. Shakespeare won such favour as a horse-holder, and was in such general demand, that he had to engage boys as assistants, who announced themselves as "Shakespeare's boys," a style and title, it is said, which long clung to them. A fact which speaks in favour of this much-ridiculed legend is that, at the time to which it can be traced back, well on in the seventeenth century, the practice of riding to the theatres had entirely fallen into disuse. People then went to the play by water.

A Stratford tradition represents that Shakespeare first entered the theatre in the character of "servitor" to the actors, and Malone reports "a stage tradition that his first office in the theatre was that of prompter's attendant," whose business was to give the players notice of the time for their entrance. It is evident, however, that he soon rose above these menial stations.

The London to which Shakespeare came was a town of about

300,000 inhabitants. Its main streets had quite recently been paved, but were not yet lighted; it was surrounded with trenches, walls, and gates; it had high-gabled, red-roofed, two-story wooden houses, distinguished by means of projecting signs, from which they took their names—houses in which benches did duty for chairs, and the floors were carpeted with rushes. The streets were usually thronged, not with wheel-traffic, for the first carriage was imported into England in this very reign, but with people on foot, on horseback, or in litters; while the Thames, still blue and clear, in spite of the already large consumption of coal, was alive with thousands of boats threading their way, amid the watermen's shrill cries of "Eastward hoe!" or "Westward hoe!" through bevies of swans which put forth from, and returned to, the green meadows and beautiful gardens bordering the steam.

There was as yet only one bridge over the Thames, the mighty London Bridge, situated not far from that which now bears the name. It was broad, and lined with buildings; while on the tall gate-towers heads which had fallen on the block were almost always displayed. In its neighbourhood lay Eastcheap, the street in which stood Falstaff's tavern.

The central points of London were at that time the newly erected Exchange and St. Paul's Church, which was regarded not only as the Cathedral of the city, but as a meeting-place and promenade for idlers, a sort of club where the news of the day was to be heard, a hiring-fair for servants, and a sanctuary for debtors, who were there secure from arrest. The streets, still full of the many-coloured life of the Renaissance, rang with the cries of 'prentices inviting custom and hawkers proclaiming their wares; while through them passed many a procession, civil, ecclesiastical, or military, bridal companies, pageants, and troops of crossbow-men and men-at-arms.

Elizabeth might be met in the streets, driving in her huge State carriage, when she did not prefer to sail on the Thames in her magnificent gondola, followed by a crowd of gaily decorated boats.

In the City itself no theatres were tolerated. The civic authorities regarded them with an unfriendly eye, and had banished them to the outskirts and across the Thames, together with the rough amusements with which they had to compete: cock-fighting and bear-baiting with dogs.

The handsome, parti-coloured, extravagant costumes of the period are well known. The puffed sleeves of the men, the women's stiff ruffs, and the fantastic shapes of their hooped skirts, are still to be seen in stage presentations of plays of the time. The Queen and her Court set the example of great and unreasonable luxury with respect to the number and material of costumes. The ladies rouged their faces, and often dyed their hair. Auburn, as the Queen's colour, was the most fashionable. The conveniences of daily life were very meagre. Only of late had fireplaces begun to be substituted for the open hearths. Only of late had proper bedsteads come into general use; when Shakespeare's well-to-do grandfather, Richard Arden, made his will, in the year 1556, there was only one bedstead in the house where he lived with his seven daughters. People slept on straw mattresses, with a billet of wood under their heads and a fur rug over them. The only decoration of the rooms of the wealthier classes was the tapestry on the walls, behind which people so often conceal themselves in Shakespeare's plays.

The dinner-hour was at that time eleven in the morning, and it was reckoned fashionable to dine early. Those who could afford it ate rich and heavy dishes; the repasts would often last an inordinate time, and no regard whatever was paid to the minor decencies of life. Domestic utensils were very mean. So late as 1592, wooden trenchers, wooden platters, and wooden spoons were in common use. It was just about this time that tin and silver began to supplant wood. Table-knives had been in general use since about 1563; but forks were still unknown in Shakespeare's time—fingers supplied their place. In a description of five months' travels on the Continent, published by Coryat in 1611, he tells how surprised he was to find the use of forks quite common in Italy :—

"I obserued a custome in all those Italian Cities and Townes through which I passed, that is not vsed in any other country that I saw in my trauels, neither doe I thinke that any other nation of Christendome doth vse it, but only Italy. The Italian and also most strangers that are commorant in Italy doe alwaies at their meales vse a little forke when they cut their meate. For while with their knife which they hold in one hand they cut the meate out of the dish, they fasten their forke which they hold in their other hand vpon the same dish, so that whatsoeuer he be that sitting in the company of any others at

MANNERS AND CUSTOMS

meale, should vnaduisedly touch the dish of meate with his fingers from which all at the table doe cut, he will giue occasion of offence vnto the company, as hauing transgressed the lawes of good manners, in so much that for his error he shall be at the least brow-beaten, if not reprehended in wordes. . . . The reason of this their curiosity is, because the Italian cannot by any means indure to haue his dish touched with fingers, seing all men's fingers are not alike cleane." [1]

We see, too, that Coryat was the first to introduce the new appliance into his native land. He tells us that he thought it best to imitate the Italian fashion not only in Italy and Germany, but "often in England" after his return; and he relates how a learned and jocular gentleman of his acquaintance rallied him on that account and called him "Furcifer." In one of Ben Jonson's plays, *The Devil is an Ass*, dating from 1614, the use of forks is mentioned as lately imported from Italy, in order to save napkins. We must conceive, then, that Shakespeare was as unfamiliar with the use of the fork as a Bedouin Arab of to-day.

He does not seem to have smoked. Tobacco is never mentioned in his works, although the people of his day gathered in tobacco-shops where instruction was given in the new art of smoking, and although the gallants actually smoked as they sat on the stage of the theatre.

[1] *Coryat's Crudities*, ed. 1776, vol. i. p. 106.

V

POLITICAL AND RELIGIOUS CONDITIONS—
ENGLAND'S GROWING GREATNESS

THE period of Shakespeare's arrival in London was momentous both in politics and religion. It is the period of England's development into a great Protestant power. Under Bloody Mary, the wife of Philip II. of Spain, the government had been Spanish-Catholic; the persecutions directed against heresy brought many victims, and among them some of the most distinguished men in England, to the scaffold, and even to the stake. Spain made a cat's-paw of England in her contest with France, and reaped all the benefit of the alliance, while England paid the penalty. Calais, her last foothold on the Continent, was lost.

With Elizabeth, Protestantism ascended the throne and became a power in the world. She rejected Philip's courtship; she knew how unpopular the Spanish marriage had made her sister. In the struggle with the Papal power she had the Parliament on her side. Parliament had at once recognised her as Queen by the law of God and the country, whilst the Pope, on her accession, denied her right to the throne. The Catholic world took his part against her; first France, then Spain. England supported Protestant Scotland against its Catholic Queen and her Scottish-French army, and the Reformation triumphed in Scotland. Afterwards, when Mary Stuart had ceased to rule over Scotland and taken refuge in England, in the hope of there finding help, it was no longer France but Philip of Spain who stood by her. He saw his despotism in the Netherlands threatened by the victory of Protestantism in England.

Political interest led Elizabeth's Government to throw Mary into prison. The Pope excommunicated Elizabeth, absolved her subjects from their oath of allegiance, and declared her a usurper in her own kingdom. Whoever should obey her commands was

POLITICAL AND RELIGIOUS CONDITIONS 21

excommunicated along with her, and for twenty years on end one Catholic conspiracy against Elizabeth treads on another's heels, Mary Stuart being involved in almost all of them.

In 1585 Elizabeth opened the war with Spain by sending her fleet to the Netherlands, with her favourite, Leicester, in command of the troops. In the beginning of the following year, Francis Drake, who in 1577–80 had for the first time circumnavigated the world, surprised and took San Domingo and Carthagena. The ship in which he had achieved his great voyage lay at anchor in the Thames as a memorial of the feat; it was often visited by Londoners, and no doubt by Shakespeare among them.

In the years immediately following, the springtide of the national spirit burst into full bloom. Let us try to picture to ourselves the impression it must have made upon Shakespeare in the year 1587. On the 8th of February 1587 Mary Stuart was executed at Fotheringay, and the breach between England and the Catholic world was thus made irreparable. On the 16th of February, England's noblest knight and the flower of her chivalry, Sir Philip Sidney, the hero of Zutphen, and the chief of the Anglo-Italian school of poets, was buried in St. Paul's Cathedral, with a pomp which gave to the event the character of a national solemnity. Sidney was an ideal representative of the aristocracy of the day. He possessed the widest humanistic culture, had studied Aristotle and Plato no less than geometry and astronomy, had travelled and seen the world, had read and thought and written, and was not only a scholar but a soldier to boot. As a cavalry officer he had saved the English army at Gravelines, and he had been the friend and patron of Giordano Bruno, the freest thinker of his time. The Queen herself was present at his funeral, and so, no doubt, was Shakespeare.

In the following year Spain fitted out her great Armada and despatched it against England. As regards the size of the ships and the number of the troops they carried, it was the largest fleet that had ever been seen in European waters. And in the Netherlands, at Antwerp and Dunkerque, transports were in readiness for the conveyance of a second vast army to complete the destruction of England. But England was equal to the occasion. Elizabeth's Government demanded fifteen ships of the city of London; it fitted out thirty, besides raising a land force of 30,000 men and lending the Government £52,000 in ready money.

The Spanish fleet numbered one hundred and thirty huge galleons, the English only sixty sail, of lighter and less cumbrous build. The young English noblemen competed for the privilege of serving in it. The great Armada was ill designed for defying wind and weather in the English Channel. It manœuvred awkwardly, and, in the first encounters, proved itself powerless against the lighter ships of the English. A couple of fire-ships were sufficient to throw it into disorder; a season of storms set in, and the greater number of its galleons were swept to destruction.

The greatest Power in the world of that day had broken down in its attempt to crush the growing might of England, and the whole nation revelled in the exultant sense of victory.

VI

SHAKESPEARE AS ACTOR AND RETOUCHER OF OLD PLAYS—GREENE'S ATTACK

BETWEEN 1586 and 1592 we lose all trace of Shakespeare. We know only that he must have been an active member of a company of players. It is not proved that he ever belonged to any other company than the Earl of Leicester's, which owned the Blackfriars, and afterwards the Globe, theatre. It is proved by several passages in contemporary writings that, partly as actor, partly as adapter of older plays for the use of the theatre, he had, at the age of twenty-eight, made a certain name for himself, and had therefore become the object of envy and hatred.

A passage in Spenser's *Colin Clouts Come Home Again*, referring to a poet whose Muse " doth like himself heroically sound," may with some probability, though not with certainty, be applied to Shakespeare. The theory is supported by the fact that the word " gentle " is here, as so often in after-life, attached to his personality. Against it we must place the circumstance that the poem, although not published till 1594, seems to have been composed as early as 1591, when Shakespeare's muse was as yet scarcely heroic, and that Drayton, who had written under the pseudonym of Rowland, may have been the poet alluded to.

The first indubitable allusion to Shakespeare is of a quite different nature. It occurs in a pamphlet written on his deathbed by the dramatist Robert Greene, entitled *A Groat's Worth of Wit bought with a Million of Repentance* (August 1592). In it the utterly degraded and penniless poet calls upon his friends, Marlowe, Lodge or Nash, and Peele (without mentioning their names), to give up their vicious life, their blasphemy, and their " getting many enemies by bitter words," holding himself up as a deterrent example ; for he died, after a reckless life, of an illness said to have been induced by immoderate eating, and in such misery that he had to borrow money of his landlord, a poor shoemaker, while his landlord's wife was the sole attendant of his dying hours. He was so poor that his clothes had to be sold to procure him food. He sent his wife these lines:—

"Doll, I charge thee, by the loue of our youth and by my soules rest, that thou wilte see this man paide; for if hee and his wife had not succoured me, I had died in the streetes.
"ROBERT GREENE."

The passage in which he warns his friends and fellow-poets against the ingratitude of the players runs as follows:—

"Yes, trust them not: for there is an upstart crow, beautified with our feathers, that with his *Tygers heart wrapt in a Players hide*, supposes he is as well able to bumbast out a blanke verse as the best of you: and being an absolute *Johannes fac totum*, is in his owne conceit the only Shake-scene in a countrie."

The allusion to Shakespeare's name is unequivocal, and the words about the tiger's heart point to the outburst, "Oh Tyger's hart wrapt in a serpents hide!" which is found in two places: first in the play called *The True Tragedie of Richard Duke of Yorke, and the Death of the good King Henrie the Sixt*, and then (with "womans" substituted for "serpents"), in the third part of *King Henry VI.*, founded on the *True Tragedie*, and attributed to Shakespeare. It is preposterous to interpret this passage as an attack upon Shakespeare in his quality as an actor; Greene's words, beyond all doubt, convey an accusation of literary dishonesty. Everything points to the belief that Greene and Marlowe had collaborated in the older play, and that the former saw with disgust the success achieved by Shakespeare's adaptation of their text.

But that Shakespeare was already highly respected, and that the attack aroused general indignation, is proved by the apology put forth in December 1592 by Henry Chettle, who had published Greene's pamphlet. In the preface to his *Kind-hart's Dreame* he expressly deplores his indiscretion with regard to Shakespeare:—

"I am as sory as if the originall fault had beene my fault, because my selfe haue seene his demeanor no lesse ciuill than he exelent in the qualitie he professes. Besides, diuers of worship haue reported his vprightnes of dealing, which argues his honesty, and his facetious grace in writing, that aprooues his Art."

We see, then, that the company to which Shakespeare had attached himself, and in which he had already attracted notice as a promising poet, employed him to revise and furbish up the older pieces of their repertory. The theatrical announcements of the period would show us, even if we had no other evidence, that it was a constant practice to recast old plays, in order to heighten their powers of attraction. It is announced, for instance, that such-and-such a play will be acted as it was last presented before her Majesty, or before this or that nobleman. Poets sold their works outright to the theatre for such sums as five or ten pounds, or for a share in the receipts. As the interests of the theatre demanded that plays should not be printed, in order that rival companies might not obtain possession of them, they remained in manuscript (unless pirated), and the players could accordingly do what they pleased with the text.

None the less, of course, was the older poet apt to resent the re-touches made by the younger, as we see from this outburst of Greene's, and probably, too, from Ben Jonson's epigram, *On Poet-Ape*, even though this cannot, with any show of reason, be applied to Shakespeare.

In the view of the time, theatrical productions as a whole were not classed as literature. It was regarded as dishonourable for a man to sell his work first to a theatre and then to a bookseller, and Thomas Heywood declares, as late as 1630 (in the preface to his *Lucretia*), that he has never been guilty of this misdemeanour. We know, too, how much ridicule Ben Jonson incurred when, first among English poets, he in 1616 published his plays in a folio volume.

On the other hand, we see that not only Shakespeare's genius, but his personal amiability, the loftiness and charm of his nature, disarmed even those who, for one reason or another, had spoken disparagingly of his activity. As Chettle, after printing Greene's attack, hastened to make public apology, so also Ben Jonson, to whose ill-will and cutting allusions Shakespeare made no retort,[1] became, in spite of an unconquerable jealousy, his true friend and admirer, and after his death spoke of him warmly in prose, and with enthusiasm in verse, in the noble eulogy prefixed to the First Folio. His prose remarks upon

---

[1] He is said to have procured the production of Jonson's first play.

Shakespeare's character are introduced by a critical observation:—

"I remember the players have often mentioned it as an honour to Shakespeare, that in his writing (whatsoever he penned) he never blotted out a line. My answer hath been, Would he had blotted a thousand. Which they thought a malevolent speech. I had not told posterity this but for their ignorance, who chose that circumstance to commend their friend by, wherein he most faulted; and to justify mine own candour: for I loved the man, and do honour his memory, on this side idolatry, as much as any. He was (indeed) honest, and of an open and full nature; had an excellent phantasy, brave notions, and gentle expressions; wherein he flowed with that facility, that sometimes it was necessary he should be stopped: *Sufflaminandus erat*, as Augustus said of Haterius."

VII

THE "HENRY VI." TRILOGY

ONE might expect that it would be with the early plays in which Shakespeare only collaborated as with those Italian pictures of the best period of the Renaissance, in which the connoisseur identifies (for example) an angel's head by Leonardo in a Crucifixion of Andrea del Verrocchio's. The work of the pupil stands out sharp and clear, with pure contours, a picture within the picture, quite at odds with its style and spirit, but impressing us as a promise for the future. As a matter of fact, however, there is no analogy between the two cases.

A mystery hangs over the *Henry VI.* trilogy which neither Greene's venomous attack nor Chettle's apology enables us to clear up.

Of all the works attributed to Shakespeare, this is certainly the one whose origin affords most food for speculation. The inclusion of the three plays in the First Folio shows clearly that his comrades, who had full knowledge of the facts, regarded them as his literary property. That the two earlier plays which are preserved, the *First Part of the Contention* and the *True Tragedie* (answering to the second and third parts of *Henry VI.*), cannot be entirely Shakespeare's work is evidenced both by the imprint of the anonymous quartos and by the company which is stated to have produced them; for none of Shakespeare's genuine plays was published by this publisher or played by this company. It is proved quite clearly, too, by internal evidence, by the free and unrhymed versification of these plays. At the period from which they date, Shakespeare was still extremely addicted to the use of rhyme in his dramatic writing.

Nevertheless, the great majority of German Shakespeare students, and some English as well, are of opinion that the older plays are entirely Shakespeare's, either his first drafts or, as is more commonly maintained, stolen texts carelessly noted down.

Some English scholars, such as Malone and Dyce, go to the opposite extreme, and regard the second and third parts of *Henry VI.* as the work of another poet. The majority of English students look upon these plays as the result of Shakespeare's retouching of another man's, or rather other men's, work.

The affair is so complicated that none of these hypotheses is quite satisfactory.

Though there are doubtless in the older plays portions unworthy of Shakespeare, and more like the handiwork of Greene, while others strongly suggest Marlowe, both in matter, style, and versification, there are also passages in them which cannot be by any one else than Shakespeare. And while most of the alterations and additions which are found in the second and third parts of *Henry VI.* bear the mark of unmistakable superiority, and are Shakespearian in spirit no less than in style and versification, there are at the same time others which are decidedly un-Shakespearian and can almost certainly be attributed to Marlowe. He must, then, have collaborated with Shakespeare in the adaptation, unless we suppose that his original text was carelessly printed in the earlier quartos, and that it here reappears, in the Shakespearian *Henry VI.*, corrected and completed in accordance with his manuscript.

I agree with Miss Lee, the writer of the leading treatise[1] on these plays, and with the commentator in the Irving Edition, in holding that Shakespeare was not responsible for all the alterations in the definitive text. There are several which I cannot possibly believe to be his.

In the old quartos there appears not a line in any foreign language. But in the Shakespearian plays we find lines and exclamations in Latin scattered here and there, along with one in French.[2] If the early quartos are founded on a text taken down by ear, we can readily understand that the foreign expressions, not being understood, should be omitted. Such foreign sentences are extremely frequent in Marlowe, as in Kyd and the other older dramatists; they appear in season and out of season, but

---

[1] *New Shakspere Society's Transactions*, 1875-76, pp. 219-303.

[2] "Tantœne animis cœlestibus iræ !—Medice, te ipsum !—Gelidus timor occupat artus—La fin couronne les œuvres—Di faciant ! laudis summa sit ista tuæ."

always in irreconcilable conflict with the sounder taste of our time. Marlowe would even suffer a dying man to break out in a French or Latin phrase as he gave up the ghost, and this occurs here in two places (at Clifford's death and Rutland's). Shakespeare, who never bedizens his work with un-English phrases, would certainly not place them in the mouths of dying men, and least of all foist them upon an earlier purely English text.

Other additions also seem only to have restored the older form of the plays—those, to wit, which really add nothing new, but only elaborate, sometimes more copiously than is necessary or tasteful, a thought already clearly indicated. The original omission in such instances appears almost certainly to have been dictated by considerations of convenience in acting. One example is Queen Margaret's long speech in Part II., Act iii. 2, which is new with the exception of the first fourteen lines.

But there is another class of additions and alterations which surprises us by being unmistakably in Marlowe's style. If these additions are really by Shakespeare, he must have been under the influence of Marlowe to a quite extraordinary degree. Swinburne has pointed out how entirely the verses which open the fourth act of the Second Part are Marlowesque in rhythm, imagination, and choice of words; but characteristic as are these lines—

> "And now loud howling wolves arouse the jades
> That drag the tragic melancholy night,"

they are by no means the only additions which seem to point to Marlowe. We feel his presence particularly in the additions to Iden's speeches at the end of the fourth act, in such lines as—

> "Set limb to limb, and thou art far the lesser;
> Thy hand is but a finger to my fist;
> Thy leg a stick, compared with this truncheon;"

and especially in the concluding speech:—

> "Die, damned wretch, the curse of her that bare thee!
> And as I thrust thy body in with my sword,
> So wish I, I might thrust thy soul to hell.
> Hence will I drag thee headlong by the heels
> Unto a dunghill, which shall be thy grave,
> And there cut off thy most ungracious head."

There is Marlowesque emphasis in this wildness and ferocity, which reappears, in conjunction with Marlowesque learning, in Young Clifford's lines in the last act:—

> "Meet I an infant of the house of York,
> Into as many gobbets will I cut it,
> As wild Medea young Absyrtus did:
> In cruelty will I seek out my fame"—

and in those which, in Part III., Act iv. 2, are placed in the mouth of Warwick:—

> "Our scouts have found the adventure very easy:
> That as Ulysses, and stout Diomede,
> With sleight and manhood stole to Rhesus' tents,
> And brought from thence the Thracian fatal steeds;
> So we, well cover'd with the night's black mantle,
> At unawares may beat down Edward's guard,
> And seize himself."

And as in the additions there are passages the whole style of which belongs to Marlowe, or bears the strongest traces of his influence, so also there are passages in the earlier text which in every respect recall the manner of Shakespeare. For example, in Part II., Act iii. 2, Warwick's speech:—

> "Who finds the heifer dead, and bleeding fresh,
> And sees fast by a butcher with an axe,
> But will suspect 'twas he that made the slaughter?"

or Suffolk's to Margaret:—

> "If I depart from thee, I cannot live;
> And in thy sight to die, what were it else,
> But like a pleasant slumber in thy lap?
> Here could I breathe my soul into the air,
> As mild and gentle as the cradle-babe,
> Dying with mother's dug between its lips."

Most Shakespearian, too, is the manner in which, in Part III., Act ii. 1, York's two sons are made to draw their characters, each in a single line, when they receive the tidings of their father's death:—

> "*Edward.* O, speak no more! for I have heard too much.
> *Richard.* Say, how he died, for I will hear it all."

Again, we seem to hear the voice of Shakespeare when Margaret, after they have murdered her son before her eyes, bursts forth (Part III., Act v. 5):—

"You have no children, butchers! if you had
The thought of them would have stirred up remorse."

This passage anticipates, as it were, a celebrated speech in *Macbeth*. Most remarkable of all, however, are the Cade scenes in the Second Part. I cannot persuade myself that these were not from the very first the work of Shakespeare. It is evident that they cannot proceed from the pen of Marlowe. An attempt has been made to attribute them to Greene, on the ground that there are other folk-scenes in his works which display a similar strain of humour. But the difference is enormous. It is true that the text here follows the chronicle with extraordinary fidelity; but it was precisely in this ingenious adaptation of material that Shakespeare always showed his strength. And these scenes answer so completely to all the other folk-scenes in Shakespeare, and are so obviously the outcome of the habit of political thought which runs through his whole life, becoming ever more and more pronounced, that we cannot possibly accept them as showing only the trivial alterations and retouches which elsewhere distinguish his text from the older version.

These admissions made, however, there is on the whole no difficulty in distinguishing the work of other hands in the old texts. We can enjoy, point by point, not only Shakespeare's superiority, but his peculiar style, as we here find it in the very process of development; and we can study his whole method of work in the text which he ultimately produces.

We have here an almost unique opportunity of observing him in the character of a critical artist. We see what improvements he makes by a trivial retouch, or a mere rearrangement of words. Thus, when Gloucester says of his wife (Part. II., Act ii. 4)—

"Uneath may she endure the flinty streets,
To tread them with her tender-feeling feet,"

all his sympathy speaks in these words. In the old text it is she who says this of herself. In York's great soliloquy in the first act, beginning "Anjou and Maine are given to the French," the first twenty-four lines are Shakespeare's; the rest belong to the old text. From the second "Anjou and Maine" onwards, the verse is conventional and monotonous; the meaning ends with the end of each line, and a pause, as it were, ensues; whereas the verse of the opening passage is full of dramatic movement, life, and fire.

Again, if we turn to York's soliloquy in the third act (sc. 1)—

"Now, York, or never, steel thy fearful thoughts,"

and compare it in the two texts, we find their metrical differences so marked that, as Miss Lee has happily put it, the critic can no more doubt that the first version belongs to an earlier stage in the development of dramatic poetry, than the geologist can doubt that a stratum which contains simpler organisms indicates an earlier stage of the earth's development than one containing higher forms of organic life. There are portions of the Second Part which no one can believe that Shakespeare wrote, such as the old-fashioned fooling with Simpcox, which is quite in the manner of Greene. There are others which, without being unworthy of Shakespeare, not only indicate Marlowe in their general style, but are now and then mere variations of verses known to be his. Such, for example, is Margaret's line in Part III., Act i. :—

"Stern Faulconbridge commands the narrow seas,"

which clearly echoes the line in Marlowe's *Edward II.* :—

"The haughty Dane commands the narrow street."

What interests us most, perhaps, is the relation between Shakespeare and his predecessor with respect to the character of Gloucester. It cannot be denied or doubted that this character, the Richard III. of after-days, is completely outlined in the earlier text; so that in reality Shakespeare's own tragedy of *Richard III.*, written so much later, is still quite Marlowesque in the fundamental conception of its protagonist. Gloucester's two great soliloquies in the third part of *Henry VI.* are especially instructive to study. In the first (iii. 2) the keynote of the passion is indeed struck by Marlowe, but all the finest passages are Shakespeare's. Take, for example, the following :—

"Why then, I do but dream on sovereignty;
Like one that stands upon a promontory,

THE "HENRY VI." TRILOGY

> And spies a far-off shore where he would tread,
> Wishing his foot were equal with his eye;
> And chides the sea that sunders him from thence,
> Saying—he'll lade it dry to have his way:
> So do I wish the crown, being so far off,
> And so I chide the means that keep me from it;
> And so I say—I'll cut the causes off,
> Flattering me with impossibilities."

The last soliloquy (v. 6), on the other hand, belongs entirely to the old play. A thoroughly Marlowesque turn of phrase meets us at the very beginning:—

> "See, how my sword weeps for the poor king's death."

Shakespeare has here left the powerful and admirable text untouched, except for the deletion of a single superfluous and weakening verse, "I had no father, I am like no father," which is followed by the profoundest and most remarkable lines in the play:—

> "I have no brother, I am like no brother;
> And this word love, which greybeards call divine,
> Be resident in men like one another,
> And not in me: I am myself alone."

VIII

CHRISTOPHER MARLOWE AND HIS LIFE-WORK— TITUS ANDRONICUS

THE man who was to be Shakespeare's first master in the drama —a master whose genius he did not at the outset fully understand—was born two months before him. Christopher (Kit) Marlowe, the son of a shoemaker at Canterbury, was a foundation scholar at the King's School of his native town; matriculated at Cambridge in 1580; took the degree of B.A. in 1583, and of M.A. at the age of twenty-three, after he had left the University; appeared in London (so we gather from an old ballad) as an actor at the Curtain Theatre; had the misfortune to break his leg upon the stage; was no doubt on that account compelled to give up acting; and seems to have written his first dramatic work, *Tamburlaine the Great*, at latest in 1587. His development was much quicker than Shakespeare's, he attained to comparative maturity much earlier, and his culture was more systematic. Not for nothing had he gone through the classical curriculum; the influence of Seneca, the poet and rhetorician through whom English tragedy comes into relation with the antique, is clearly recognisable in him, no less than in his predecessors, the authors of *Gorboduc* and *Tancred and Gismunda* (the former composed by two, the latter by five poets in collaboration); only that the construction of these plays, with their monologues and their chorus, is directly imitated from Seneca, while the more independent Marlowe is influenced only in his diction and choice of material.

In him the two streams begin to unite which have their sources in the Biblical dramas of the Middle Ages and the later allegorical folk-plays on the one hand, and, on the other hand, in the Latin plays of antiquity. But he entirely lacks the comic vein which we find in the first English imitations of Plautus and

Terence—in *Ralph Roister Doister* and in *Gammer Gurton's Needle*, acted, respectively, in the middle of the century and in the middle of the sixties, by Eton schoolboys and Cambridge students.

Kit Marlowe is the creator of English tragedy. He it was who established on the public stage the use of the unrhymed iambic pentameter as the medium of English drama. He did not invent English blank verse—the Earl of Surrey (who died in 1547) had used it in his translation of the *Æneid*, and it had been employed in the old play of *Gorboduc* and others which had been performed at court. But Marlowe was the first to address the great public in this measure, and he did so, as appears from the prologue to *Tamburlaine*, in express contempt for "the jigging veins of rhyming mother-wits" and ."such conceits as clownage keeps in pay," seeking deliberately for tragic emphasis and "high astounding terms" in which to express the rage of Tamburlaine.

Before his day, rhymed couplets of long-drawn fourteen-syllable verse had been common in drama, and the monotony of these rhymes naturally hampered the dramatic life of the plays. Shakespeare does not seem at first to have appreciated Marlowe's reform, or quite to have understood the importance of this rejection of rhyme in dramatic writing. Little by little he came fully to realise it. In one of his first plays, *Love's Labour's Lost*, there are nearly twice as many rhymed as unrhymed verses, more than a thousand in all; in his latest works rhyme has disappeared. There are only two rhymes in *The Tempest*, and in *A Winter's Tale* none at all.

Similarly, in his first plays (like Victor Hugo in his first Odes), Shakespeare feels himself bound to make the sense end with the end of the verse; as time goes on, he gradually learns an ever freer movement. In *Love's Labour's Lost* there are eighteen end-stopped verses (in which the meaning ends with the line) for every one in which the sense runs on; in *Cymbeline* and *A Winter's Tale* they are only about two to one. This gradual development affords one method of determining the date of production of otherwise undated plays.

Marlowe seems to have led a wild life in London, and to have been entirely lacking in the commonplace virtues. He is said to have indulged in a perpetual round of dissipations, to have been dressed to-day in silk, to-morrow in rags, and to have lived in audacious defiance of society and the Church. Certain it is that he was killed in a brawl when only twenty-nine years old. He is said to have found a rival in company with his mistress, and to have drawn his dagger to stab him; but the other, a certain Francis Archer, wrested the dagger from his grasp, and thrust it through his eye into his brain. It is further related of him that he was an ardent and aggressive atheist, who called Moses a juggler and said that Christ deserved death more than Barabbas. These reports are probable enough. On the other hand, the assertion that he wrote books against the Trinity and uttered blasphemies with his latest breath, is evidently inspired by Puritan hatred for the theatre and everything concerned with it. The sole authority for these fables is Beard's *Theatre of God's Judgments* (1597), the work of a clergyman, a fanatical Puritan, which appeared six years after Marlowe's death.

There is no doubt that Marlowe led an extremely irregular life, but the legend of his debaucheries must be much exaggerated, if only from the fact that, though he was cut off before his thirtieth year, he has yet left behind him so large and puissant a body of work. The legend that he passed his last hours in blaspheming God is rendered doubly improbable by Chapman's express statement that it was in compliance with Marlowe's dying request that he continued his friend's paraphrase of *Hero and Leander*. The passionate, defiant youth, surcharged with genius, was fair game for the bigots and Pharisees, who found it only too easy to besmirch his memory.

It is evident that Marlowe's gorgeous and violent style, especially as it bursts forth in his earlier plays, made a profound impression upon the youthful Shakespeare. After Marlowe's death, Shakespeare made a kindly and mournful allusion to him in *As You Like It* (iii. 5), where Phebe quotes a line from his *Hero and Leander*:—

> " Dead shepherd ! now I find thy saw of might :
> ' Who ever lov'd, that lov'd not at first sight ? ' "

Marlowe's influence is unmistakable not only in the style and versification but in the sanguinary action of *Titus Andronicus*, clearly the oldest of the tragedies attributed to Shakespeare. The evidence for the Shakespearian authorship of this drama of horrors, though mainly external, is weighty and, it would seem, decisive. Meres, in 1598, names it among the poet's works, and his friends included it in the First Folio. We know from a gibe in Ben Jonson's Induction to his *Bartholomew Fair* that it was exceedingly popular. It is one of the plays most frequently alluded to in contemporary writings, being mentioned twice as often as *Twelfth Night*, and four or five times as often as *Measure for Measure* or *Timon*. It depicts savage deeds, executed with the suddenness with which people of the sixteenth century were wont to obey their impulses, cruelties as heartless and systematic as those which characterised the age of Machiavelli. In short, it abounds in such callous atrocities as could not fail to make a deep impression on iron nerves and hardened natures.

These horrors are not, for the most part, of Shakespeare's invention.

An entry in Henslowe's diary of April 11, 1592, mentions for the first time a play named *Titus and Vespasian* ("tittus and vespacia"), which was played very frequently between that date and January 1593, and was evidently a prime favourite. In its English form this play is lost; no Vespasian appears in our *Titus Andronicus*. But about 1600 a play was performed in Germany, by English actors, which has been preserved under the title, *Eine sehr klägliche Tragoedia von Tito Andronico und der hoffertigen Kayserin, darinnen denckwürdige actiones zubefinden*, and in this play a Vespasian duly appears, as well as the Moor Aaron, under the name of Morian; so that, clearly enough, we have here a translation, or rather a free adaptation, of the old play which formed the basis of Shakespeare's.

We see, then, that Shakespeare himself invented only a few of the horrors which form the substance of the play. The action, as he presents it, is briefly this:—

Titus Andronicus, returning to Rome after a victory over the Goths, is hailed as Emperor by the populace, but magnanimously hands over the crown to the rightful heir, Saturninus. Titus even wants to give him his daughter Lavinia in marriage, although she is already betrothed to the Emperor's younger brother Bassianus, whom she loves. When one of Titus's sons opposes this scheme, his father kills him on the spot.

In the meantime, Tamora, the captive Queen of the Goths, is

brought before the young Emperor. In spite of her prayers, Titus has ordered the execution of her eldest son, as a sacrifice to the manes of his own sons who have fallen in the war; but as Tamora is more attractive to the Emperor than his destined bride, the young Lavinia, Titus makes no attempt to enforce the promise he has just made, and actually imagines that Tamora is sincere when she pretends to have forgotten all the injuries he has done her. Tamora, moreover, has been and is the mistress of the cruel and crafty monster Aaron, the Moor.

At the Moor's instigation, she induces her two sons to take advantage of a hunting party to murder Bassianus; whereupon they ravish Lavinia, and tear out her tongue and cut off her hands, so that she cannot denounce them either in speech or writing. They remain undetected, until at last Lavinia unmasks them by writing in the sand with a stick which she holds in her mouth. Two of Titus's sons are thrown into prison, falsely accused of the murder of their brother-in-law; and Aaron gives Titus to understand that their death is certain unless he ransoms them by cutting off his own right hand and sending it to the Emperor. Titus cuts off his hand, only to be informed by Aaron, with mocking laughter, that his sons are already beheaded—he can have their heads, but not themselves.

He now devotes himself entirely to revenge. Pretending madness, after the manner of Brutus, he lures Tamora's sons to his house, ties their hands behind their backs, and stabs them like pigs, while Lavinia, with the stumps of her arms, holds a basin to catch their blood. He bakes their heads in a pie, and serves it up to Tamora at a feast given in her honour, at which he appears disguised as a cook.

In the slaughter which now sets in, Tamora, Titus, and the Emperor are killed. Ultimately Aaron, who has tried to save the bastard Tamora has secretly borne him, is condemned to be buried alive up to the waist, and thus to starve to death. Titus's son Lucius is proclaimed Emperor.

It will be seen that not only are we here wading ankle-deep in blood, but that we are quite outside all historical reality. Among the many changes which Shakespeare has made in the old play is the dissociation of this motley tissue of horrors from the name of the Emperor Vespasian. The part which he plays in the older drama is here shared between Titus's brother Marcus and his son Lucius, who succeeds to the throne. The woman who answers to Tamora is of similar character in the old play, but is Queen of Ethiopia. Among the horrors which Shakespeare found ready made are the rape and mutilation of Lavinia and the way in which the criminals are discovered, the hewing off of Titus's hand, and the scenes in which he takes his revenge in the dual character of butcher and cook.

The old English poet evidently knew his Ovid and his Seneca. The mutilation of Lavinia comes from the *Metamorphoses* (the story of Procne), and the cannibal banquet from the same source, as well as from Seneca's *Thyestis*. The German version of the tragedy, however, is written in a wretchedly flat and antiquated prose, while Shakespeare's is couched in Marlowesque pentameters.

The example set by Marlowe in *Tamburlaine* was no doubt in some measure to blame for the lavish effusion of blood in the play adapted by Shakespeare, which may in this respect be bracketed with two other contemporary dramas conceived under the influence of *Tamburlaine*, Robert Greene's *Alphonsus King of Arragon* and George Peele's *Battle of Alcazar*. Peele's tragedy has also its barbarous Moor, Mulcy Hamet, who, like Aaron, is probably the offspring of Marlowe's malignant Jew of Malta and his henchman, the sensual Ithamore.

Among the horrors added by Shakespeare, there are two which deserve a moment's notice. The first is Titus's sudden and unpremeditated murder of his son, who ventures to oppose his will. Shocking as it seems to us to-day, such an incident did not surprise the sixteenth century public, but rather appealed to them as a touch of nature. Such lives as Benvenuto Cellini's show that even in highly cultivated natures, anger, passion, and revenge were apt to take instantaneous effect in sanguinary deeds. Men of action were in those days as ungovernable as they were barbarously cruel when a sudden fury possessed them.

The other added trait is the murder of Tamora's son. We are reminded of the scene in *Henry VI.*, in which the young Prince Edward is murdered in the presence of Queen Margaret; and Tamora's entreaties for her son are among those verses in the play which possess the true Shakespearian ring.

Certain peculiar turns of phrase in *Titus Andronicus* remind us of Peele and Marlowe.[1] But whole lines occur which Shakespeare repeats almost word for word. Thus the verses—

"She is a woman, therefore may be woo'd;
She is a woman, therefore may be won,"

reappear very slightly altered in *Henry VI.*, Part I.:—

"She's beautiful, and therefore to be woo'd;
She is a woman, and therefore to be won;"

while a similar turn of phrase is found in Sonnet XLI.:—

"Gentle thou art, and therefore to be won;
Beauteous thou art, therefore to be assailed;"

and, finally, a closely related distich occurs in Richard the Third's famous soliloquy:

"Was ever woman in this humour woo'd?
Was ever woman in this humour won?"

It is true that the phrase "She is a woman, therefore may be won," occurs several times in Greene's romances, of earlier date than *Titus Andronicus*, and this seems to have been a sort of catchword of the period.

Although, on the whole, one may certainly say that this rough-hewn drama, with its piling-up of external effects, has very little in common with the tone or spirit of Shakespeare's mature tragedies, yet we find scattered through it lines in which the most diverse critics have professed to recognise Shakespeare's revising touch, and to catch the ring of his voice.

Few will question that such a line as this, in the first scene of the play—

",Romans—friends, followers, favourers of my right!"

comes from the pen which afterwards wrote *Julius Cæsar*. I may mention, for my own part, that lines which, as I read the play through before acquainting myself in detail with English criticism, had struck me as patently Shakespearian, proved to be precisely the lines which the best English critics attribute to Shakespeare.

---

[1] "Gallops the zodiac" (ii. 1, line 7) occurs twice in Peele. The phrase "A thousand deaths" (same scene, line 79) appears in Marlowe's *Tamburlaine*.

To one's own mind such coincidences of feeling naturally carry conviction. I may cite as an example Tamora's speech (iv. 4):—

> "King, be thy thoughts imperious, like thy name.
> Is the sun dimm'd, that gnats do fly in it?
> The eagle suffers little birds to sing,
> And is not careful what they mean thereby;
> Knowing that with the shadow of his wings
> He can at pleasure stint their melody.
> Even so may'st thou the giddy men of Rome."

Unmistakably Shakespearian, too, are Titus's moving lament (iii. 1) when he learns of Lavinia's mutilation, and his half-distraught outbursts in the following scene foreshadow even in detail a situation belonging to the poet's culminating period, the scene between Lear and Cordelia when they are both prisoners. Titus says to his hapless daughter:

> "Lavinia, go with me:
> I'll to thy closet; and go read with thee
> Sad stories chanced in the times of old."

In just the same spirit Lear exclaims:

> "Come, let's away to prison . . .
> . . . . so we'll live,
> And pray, and sing, and tell old tales."

It is quite unnecessary for any opponent of blind or exaggerated Shakespeare-worship to demonstrate to us the impossibility of bringing *Titus Andronicus* into harmony with any other than a barbarous conception of tragic poetry. But although the play is simply omitted without apology from the Danish translation of Shakespeare's works, it must by no means be overlooked by the student, whose chief interest lies in observing the genesis and development of the poet's genius. The lower its point of departure, the more marvellous its soaring flight.

IX

SHAKESPEARE'S CONCEPTION OF THE RELATIONS OF THE SEXES—HIS MARRIAGE VIEWED IN THIS LIGHT—LOVE'S LABOUR'S LOST—ITS MATTER AND STYLE—JOHN LYLY AND EUPHUISM—THE PERSONAL ELEMENT

DURING these early years in London, Shakespeare must have been conscious of spiritual growth with every day that passed. With his inordinate appetite for learning, he must every day have gathered new impressions in his many-sided activity as a hard-working actor, a furbisher-up of old plays in accordance with the taste of the day for scenic effects, and finally as a budding poet, in whose heart every mood thrilled into melody, and every conception clothed itself in dramatic form. He must have felt his spirit light and free, not least, perhaps, because he had escaped from his home in Stratford.

Ordinary knowledge of the world is sufficient to suggest that his association with a village girl eight years older than himself could not satisfy him or fill his life. The study of his works confirms this conjecture. It would, of course, be unreasonable to attribute conscious and deliberate autobiographical import to speeches torn from their context in different plays; but there are none the less several passages in his dramas which may fairly be taken as indicating that he regarded his marriage in the light of a youthful folly. Take, for example, this passage in *Twelfth Night* (ii. 4):—

"*Duke.* What kind of woman is't?
Vio. Of your complexion.
Duke. She is not worth thee then. What years, i' faith?
Vio. About your years, my lord.
Duke. Too old, by Heaven. Let still the woman take
An elder than herself; so wears she to him,

So sways she level in her husband's heart:
For, boy, however we do praise ourselves,
Our fancies are more giddy and unfirm,
More longing, wavering, sooner lost and worn,
Than women's are.
    Vio.   I think it well, my lord.
    Duke. Then, let thy love be younger than thyself,
Or thy affection cannot hold the bent;
For women are as roses, whose fair flower,
Being once display'd, doth fall that very hour."

And this is in the introduction to the Fool's exquisite song about the power of love, that song which "The spinsters and the knitters in the sun And the free maids, that weave their thread with bones, Do use to chant"—Shakespeare's loveliest lyric.

There are passages in other plays which seem to show traces of personal regret at the memory of this early marriage and the circumstances under which it came about. In the *Tempest*, for instance, we have Prospero's warning to Ferdinand (iv. 1):—

"If thou dost break her virgin-knot before
All sanctimonious ceremonies may,
With full and holy rite, be minister'd,
No sweet aspersion shall the heavens let fall
To make this contract grow, but barren hate,
Sour-ey'd disdain, and discord, shall bestrew
The union of your bed with weeds so loathly,
That you shall hate it both."

Two of the comedies of Shakespeare's first period are, as we might expect, imitations, and even in part adaptations, of older plays. By comparing them, where it is possible, with these earlier works, we can discover, among other things, the thoughts to which Shakespeare, in these first years in London, was most intent on giving utterance. It thus appears that he held strong views as to the necessary subordination of the female to the male, and as to the trouble caused by headstrong, foolish, or jealous women.

His *Comedy of Errors* is modelled upon the *Menæchmi* of Plautus, or rather on an English play of the same title dating from 1580, which was not itself taken direct from Plautus, but from Italian adaptations of the old Latin farce. Following the example of Plautus in the *Amphitruo*, Shakespeare has supplemented the confusion between the two Antipholuses by a parallel and wildly improbable confusion between their serving-men, who both go by the same name and are likewise twins. But it is in the contrast between the two female figures, the married sister Adriana and the unmarried Luciana, that we catch the personal note in the play. On account of the confusion of persons, Adriana rages against her husband, and is at last on the point of plunging him into lifelong misery. To her complaint that he has not come home at the appointed time, Luciana answers:—

> "A man is master of his liberty:
> Time is their master; and, when they see time,
> They'll go, or come: if so, be patient, sister.
> *Adriana.* Why should their liberty than ours be more?
> *Luciana.* Because their business still lies out o' door.
> *Adr.* Look, when I serve him so, he takes it ill.
> *Luc.* O! know he is the bridle of your will.
> *Adr.* There's none but asses will be bridled so.
> *Luc.* Why, headstrong liberty is lash'd with woe.
> There's nothing situate under heaven's eye
> But hath his bound, in earth, in sea, in sky:
> The beasts, the fishes, and the winged fowls,
> Are their males' subjects, and at their controls.
> Men, more divine, the masters of all these,
> Lords of the wide world, and wild wat'ry seas,
> .   .   .   .   .   .
> Are masters to their females, and their lords:
> Then, let your will attend on their accords."

In the last act of the comedy, Adriana, speaking to the Abbess, accuses her husband of running after other women:—

> "*Abbess.* You should for that have reprehended him.
> *Adriana.* Why, so I did.
> *Abb.*   Ay, but not rough enough.
> *Adr.* As roughly as my modesty would let me.
> *Abb.* Haply, in private.
> *Adr.*   And in assemblies too.
> *Abb.* Ay, but not enough.
> *Adr.* It was the copy of our conference.
> In bed, he slept not for my urging it:
> At board, he fed not for my urging it;
> Alone, it was the subject of my theme;

SHAKESPEARE'S CONCEPTION OF LOVE

> In company, I often glanced it:
> Still did I tell him it was vile and bad.
> *Abb.* And therefore came it that the man was mad:
> The venom clamours of a jealous woman
> Poison more deadly than a mad dog's tooth.
> It seems, his sleeps were hinder'd by thy railing,
> And thereof comes it that his head is light.
> Thou say'st, his meat was sauc'd with thy upbraidings:
> Unquiet meals make ill digestions;
> Thereof the raging fire of fever bred:
> And what's a fever but a fit of madness?"

At least as striking is the culminating point of Shakespeare's adaptation of the old play called *The Taming of a Shrew*. He took very lightly this piece of task-work, executed, it would seem, to the order of his fellow-players. In point of diction and metre it is much less highly finished than others of his youthful comedies; but if we compare the Shakespearian play (in whose title the Shrew receives the definite instead of the indefinite article) point by point with the original, we obtain an invaluable glimpse into Shakespeare's comic, as formerly into his tragic, workshop. Few examples are so instructive as this.

Many readers have no doubt wondered what was Shakespeare's design in presenting this piece, of all others, in the framework which we Danes know in Holberg's [1] *Jeppe paa Bjerget*. The answer is, that he had no particular design in the matter. He took the framework ready-made from the earlier play, which, however, he throughout remodelled and improved, not to say re-created. It is not only far ruder and coarser than Shakespeare's, but does not redeem its crude puerility by any raciness or power.

Nowhere does the difference appear more decisively than in the great speech in which Katharine, cured of her own shrewishness, closes the play by bringing the other rebellious women to reason. In the old play she begins with a whole cosmogony: "The first world was a form without a form," until God, the King of kings, "in six days did frame his heavenly work":—

> " Then to his image he did make a man,
> Olde Adam, and from his side asleepe

---

[1] Ludvig Holberg (1684-1754), the great comedy-writer of Denmark, and founder of the Danish stage.—(TRANS.)

> A rib was taken, of which the Lord did make
> The woe of man, so termd by Adam then,
> Woman for that by her came sinne to vs,
> And for her sin was Adam doomd to die.
> As Sara to her husband, so should we
> Obey them, loue them, keepe and nourish them
> If they by any meanes doo want our helpes,
> Laying our handes vnder theire feete to tread,
> If that by that we might procure there ease."

And she herself sets the example by placing her hand under her husband's foot.

Shakespeare omits all this theology and skips the Scriptural authorities, but only to arrive at the self-same result:—

> "Fie, fie! unknit that threatening unkind brow,
> And dart not scornful glances from those eyes,
> To wound thy lord, thy king, thy governor.
> . . . . . .
> A woman mov'd is like a fountain troubled,
> Muddy, ill-seeming, thick, bereft of beauty;
> And, while it is so, none so dry or thirsty
> Will deign to sip, or touch one drop of it.
> Thy husband is thy lord, thy life, thy keeper,
> Thy head, thy sovereign; one that cares for thee,
> And for thy maintenance; commits his body
> To painful labour, both by sea and land,
> To watch the night in storms, the day in cold,
> Whilst thou liest warm at home, secure and safe;
> And craves no other tribute at thy hands,
> But love, fair looks, and true obedience,
> Too little payment for so great a debt.
> Such duty as the subject owes the prince,
> Even such a woman oweth to her husband;
> And when she's froward, peevish, sullen, sour,
> And not obedient to his honest will,
> What is she but a foul contending rebel,
> And graceless traitor to her loving lord?"

In these adapted plays, then, partly from the nature of their subjects and partly because his thoughts ran in that direction, we find Shakespeare chiefly occupied with the relation between man and woman, and specially between husband and wife. They are not, however, his first works. At the age of five-and-twenty or thereabouts Shakespeare began his independent dramatic production, and, following the natural bent of youth and youthful vivacity, he began it with a light and joyous comedy.

We have several reasons, partly metrical (the frequency of rhymes), partly technical (the dramatic weakness of the play), for supposing *Love's Labour's Lost* to be his earliest comedy. Many allusions point to 1589 as the date of this play in its original form. For instance, the dancing horse mentioned in i. 2 was first exhibited in 1589; the names of the characters, Biron, Longaville, Dumain (Duc du Maine), suggest those of men who were prominent in French politics between 1581 and 1590; and, finally, when we remember that the King of Navarre, as the Princess's betrothed, becomes heir to the throne of France, we cannot but conjecture a reference to Henry of Navarre, who mounted that throne precisely in 1589. The play has not, however, reached us in its earliest form; for the title-page of the quarto edition shows that it was revised and enlarged on the occasion of its performance before Elizabeth at Christmas 1597. There are not a few places in which we can trace the revision, the original form having been inadvertently retained along with the revised text. This is apparent in Biron's long speech in the fourth act, sc. 3:—

> " For when would you, my lord, or you, or you,
> Have found the ground of study's excellence,
> Without the beauty of a woman's face?
> From women's eyes this doctrine I derive :
> They are the ground, the books, the academes,
> From whence doth spring the true Promethean fire."

This belongs to the older text. Farther on in the speech, where we find the same ideas repeated in another and better form, we have evidently the revised version before us :—

> " For when would you, my liege, or you, or you,
> In leaden contemplation have found out
> Such fiery numbers, as the prompting eyes
> Of beauty's tutors have enrich'd you with?
>   .   .   .   .   .   .
> From women's eyes this doctrine I derive :
> They sparkle still the right Promethean fire ;
> They are the books, the arts, the academes,
> That show, contain, and nourish all the world ;
> Else none at all in aught proves excellent."

The last two acts, which far surpass the earlier ones, have evidently been revised with special care, and some details, especially in the parts assigned to the Princess and Biron, now and then reveal Shakespeare's maturer style and tone of feeling.

No original source has been found for this first attempt of the young Stratfordian in the direction of comedy. For the first, and perhaps for the last time, he seems to have sought for no external stimulus, but set himself to evolve everything from within. The result is that, dramatically, the play is the slightest he ever wrote. It has scarcely ever been performed even in England, and may, indeed, be described as unactable.

It is a play of two motives. The first, of course, is love—what else should be the theme of a youthful poet's first comedy?—but love without a trace of passion, almost without deep personal feeling, a love which is half make-believe, tricked out in word-plays. For the second theme of the comedy is language itself, poetic expression for its own sake—a subject round which all the meditations of the young poet must necessarily have centred, as, in the midst of a cross-fire of new impressions, he set about the formation of a vocabulary and a style.

The moment the reader opens this first play of Shakespeare's, he cannot fail to observe that in several of his characters the poet is ridiculing absurdities and artificialities in the manner of speech of the day, and, moreover, that his personages, as a whole, display a certain half-sportive luxuriance in their rhetoric as well as in their wit and banter. They seem to be speaking, not in order to inform, persuade, or convince, but simply to relieve the pressure of their imagination, to play with words, to worry at them, split them up and recombine them, arrange them in alliterative sequences, or group them in almost identical antithetic clauses; at the same time making sport no less fantastical with the ideas the words represent, and illustrating them by new and far-fetched comparisons; until the dialogue appears not so much a part of the action or an introduction to it, as a tournament of words, clashing and swaying to and fro, while the rhythmic music of the verse and prose in turns expresses exhilaration, tenderness, affection, the joy of life, gaiety or scorn. Although there is a certain superficiality about it all, we can recognise in it that exuberance of all the vital spirits which characterises the Renaissance. To the appeal—

"White-handed mistress, one sweet word with thee,"

comes the answer—

"Honey, and milk, and sugar: there are three."

And well may Boyet say (v. 2):—

"The tongues of mocking wenches are as keen
As is the razor's edge invisible,
Cutting a smaller hair than may be seen;
Above the sense of sense, so sensible
Seemeth their conference; their conceits have wings
Fleeter than arrows, bullets, wind, thought, swifter things."

Boyet's words, however, refer merely to the youthful gaiety and quickness of wit which may be found in all periods. We have here something more than that: the diction of the leading characters, and the various extravagances of expression cultivated by the subordinate personages, bring us face to face with a linguistic phenomenon which can be understood only in the light of history.

The word Euphuism is employed as a common designation for these eccentricities of style—a word which owes its origin to John Lyly's romance, *Euphues, the Anatomy of Wit*, published in 1578. Lyly was also the author of nine plays, all written before 1589, and there is no doubt that he exercised a very important influence upon Shakespeare's dramatic style.

But it is a very narrow view of the matter which finds in him the sole originator of the wave of mannerism which swept over the English poetry of the Renaissance.

The movement was general throughout Europe. It took its rise in the new-born enthusiasm for the antique literatures, in comparison with whose dignity of utterance the vernacular seemed low and vulgar. In order to approximate to the Latin models, men devised an exaggerated and dilated phraseology, heavy with images, and even sought to attain amplitude of style by placing side by side the vernacular word and the more exquisite foreign expression for the same object. Thus arose the *alto estilo*, the *estilo culto*. In Italy, the disciples of Petrarch, with their *concetti*, were dominant in poetry; in Shakespeare's own time, Marini came to the front with his antitheses and word-plays. In France, Ronsard and his school obeyed the general tendency. In Spain, the new style was represented by Guevara, who directly influenced Lyly.

John Lyly was about ten years older than Shakespeare. He was born in Kent in 1553 or 1554, of humble parentage. Nevertheless he obtained a full share of the literary culture of his time, studied at Oxford, probably by the assistance of Lord Burleigh, took his Master's degree in 1575, afterwards went to Cambridge, and eventually, no doubt on account of the success of his *Euphues*, found a position at the court of Elizabeth. For a period of ten years he was Court Poet, what in our days would be called Poet Laureate. But his position was without emolument. He was always hoping in vain for the post of Master of the Revels, and two touching letters to Elizabeth, the one dated 1590, the other 1593, in which he petitions for this appointment, show that after ten years' labour at court he felt himself a shipwrecked man, and after thirteen years gave himself up to despair. All the duties and responsibilities of the office he coveted were heaped upon him, but he was denied the appointment itself. Like Greene and Marlowe, he lived a miserable life, and died in 1606, poor and indebted, leaving his family in destitution.

His book, *Euphues*, is written for the court of Elizabeth. The Queen herself studied and translated the ancient authors, and it was the fashion of her court to deal incessantly in mythological comparisons and allusions to antiquity. Lyly shows this tendency in all his writings. He quotes Cicero, imitates Plautus, cites numberless verses from Virgil and Ovid, reproduces almost word for word in his *Euphues* Plutarch's *Treatise on Education*, and borrows from Ovid's *Metamorphoses* the themes of several of his plays. In *A Midsummer Night's Dream*, when Bottom appears with an ass's head and exclaims, "I have a reasonable good ear for music; let's have the tongs and the bones," we may doubtless trace the incident back to the metamorphosis of Midas in Ovid, but through the medium of Lyly's *Mydas*.

It was not merely the relation of the age to antiquity that produced the fashionable style. The new intercourse between country and country had quite as much to do with it. Before the invention of printing, each country had been spiritually isolated; but the international exchange of ideas had by this time become very much easier. Every European nation begins in the sixteenth century to provide itself with a library of translations. Foreign manners and fashions, in language as well as in costume, came into vogue, and helped to produce a heterogeneous and motley style.

EUPHUISM 51

In England, moreover, we have to note the very important fact that, precisely at the time when the Renaissance began to bear literary fruit, the throne was occupied by a woman, and one who, without possessing any delicate literary sense or refined artistic taste, was interested in the intellectual movement. Vain, and inclined to secret gallantries, she demanded, and received, incessant homage, for the most part in extravagant mythological terms, from the ablest of her subjects—from Sidney, from Spenser, from Raleigh—and was determined, in short, that the whole literature of the time should turn towards her as its central point. Shakespeare was the only great poet of the period who absolutely declined to comply with this demand.

It followed from the relation in which literature stood to Elizabeth that it addressed itself as a whole to women, and especially to ladies of position. *Euphues* is a ladies' book. The new style may be described, not inaptly, as the development of a more refined method of address to the fair sex.

Sir Philip Sidney, in a masque, had done homage to Elizabeth, then forty-five years old, as "the Lady of the May." A letter which Sir Walter Raleigh, after his disgrace, addressed from his prison to Sir Robert Cecil on the subject of Elizabeth, affords a particularly striking example of the Euphuistic style, admirably fitted as it certainly was to express the passion affected by a soldier of forty for the maiden of sixty who held his fate in her hands:—

"While she was yet nigher at hand, that I might hear of her once in two or three days, my sorrows were the less; but even now my heart is cast into the depth of all misery. I that was wont to behold her riding like Alexander, hunting like Diana, walking like Venus, the gentle wind blowing her fair hair about her pure cheeks like a nymph; sometime sitting in the shade like a goddess; sometime singing like an angel; sometime playing like Orpheus. Behold the sorrow of this world! Once amiss, hath bereaved me of all."[1]

The German scholar Landmann, who has devoted special study to Euphuism,[2] has justly pointed out that the greatest extravagances of style, and the worst sins against taste, of that period are always to be found in books written for ladies, cele-

---

[1] *Raleigh*, by Edmund Gosse (English Worthies Series), p. 57.
[2] *New Shakspere Society's Transactions*, 1880-86, Pt. ii. p. 241.

brating the charms of the fair sex, and seeking to please by means of highly elaborated wit.

This may have been the point of departure of the new style; but it soon ceased to address itself specially to feminine readers, and became a means of gratifying the propensity of the men of the Renaissance to mirror their whole nature in their speech, making it peculiar to the point of affectation, and affected to the point of the most daring mannerism. Euphuism ministered to their passion for throwing all they said into high and highly coloured relief, for polishing it till it shone and sparkled like real or paste diamonds in the sunshine, for making it ring, and sing, and chime, and rhyme, without caring whether reason took any share in the sport.

As a slight but characteristic illustration of this tendency, note the reply of the page, Moth, to Armado (iii. 1):—

"*Moth.* Master, will you win your love with a French brawl?

"*Arm.* How meanest thou? brawling in French?

"*Moth.* No, my complete master; but to jig off a tune at the tongue's end, canary to it with your feet, humour it with turning up your eyelids, sigh a note, and sing a note; sometime through the throat, as if you swallowed love with singing love; sometime through the nose, as if you snuffed up love by smelling love; with your hat, penthouse-like, o'er the shop of your eyes; with your arms crossed on your thin belly-doublet, like a rabbit on a spit; or your hands in your pocket, like a man after the old painting; and keep not too long in one tune, but a snip and away. These are complements, these are humours, these betray nice wenches, that would be betrayed without these, and make them men of note (do you note me?), that most are affected to these."

Landmann has conclusively proved that John Lyly's *Euphues* is only an imitation, and at many points a very close imitation, of the Spaniard Guevara's book, an imaginary biography of Marcus Aurelius, which, in the fifty years since its publication, had been six times translated into English. It was so popular that one of these translations passed through no fewer than twelve editions. Both in style and matter *Euphues* follows Guevara's book, which, in Sir Thomas North's adaptation, bears the title of *The Dial of Princes*.

The chief characteristics of Euphuism were parallel and assonant antitheses, long strings of comparisons with real or imaginary natural phenomena (borrowed for the most part from Pliny's

Natural History), a partiality for images from antique history and mythology, and a love of alliteration.

Not till a later date did Shakespeare ridicule Euphuism properly so called—to wit, in that well-known passage in *Henry IV.*, Part I., where Falstaff plays the king. In his speech beginning "Peace, good pint-pot! peace, good tickle-brain!" Shakespeare deliberately parodies Lyly's similes from natural history. Falstaff says:—

"Harry, I do not only marvel where thou spendest thy time, but also how thou art accompanied: for though the camomile, the more it is trodden on, the faster it grows, yet youth, the more it is wasted, the sooner it wears."

Compare with this the following passage from Lyly (cited by Landmann):—

"Too much studie doth intoxicate their braines, for (say they) although yron, the more it is used, the brighter it is, yet silver with much wearing doth wast to nothing . . . though the Camomill, the more it is troden and pressed downe, the more it spreadeth, yet the Violet, the oftner it is handeled and touched, the sooner it withereth and decayeth."

Falstaff continues in the same exquisite strain:—

"There is a thing, Harry, which thou hast often heard of, and it is known to many in our land by the name of pitch: this pitch, as ancient writers do report, doth defile; so doth the company thou keepest."

This citation of "ancient writers" in proof of so recondite a phenomenon as the stickiness of pitch is again pure Lyly. Yet again, the adjuration, "Now I do not speak to thee in drink, but in tears; not in pleasure, but in passion; not in words only, but in woes also," is an obvious travesty of the Euphuistic style.

Strictly speaking, it is not against Euphuism itself that Shakespeare's youthful satire is directed in *Love's Labour's Lost*. It is certain collateral forms of artificiality in style and utterance that are aimed at. In the first place, bombast, represented by the ridiculous Spaniard, Armado (the suggestion of the Invincible Armada in the name cannot be unintentional); in the next place, pedantry, embodied in the schoolmaster Holofernes, for whom tradition states that Florio, the teacher of languages and translator of Montaigne, served as a model—a supposition, however, which seems scarcely probable when we remember Florio's close connection with Shakespeare's patron, Southampton. Further, we find throughout the play the over-luxuriant and far-fetched method of expression, universally characteristic of the age, which Shakespeare himself had as yet by no means succeeded in shaking off. Only towards the close does he rise above it and satirise it. That is the intent of Biron's famous speech (v. 2):—

> "Taffata phrases, silken terms precise,
> Three-pil'd hyperboles, spruce affectation,
> Figures pedantical: these summer-flies
> Have blown me full of maggot ostentation.
> I do forswear them; and I here protest,
> By this white glove, (how white the hand, God knows)
> Henceforth my wooing mind shall be express'd
> In russet yeas, and honest kersey noes."

In the very first scene of the play, the King describes Armado, in too indulgent terms, as—

> "A refined traveller of Spain;
> A man in all the world's new fashion planted,
> That hath a mint of phrases in his brain;
> One, whom the music of his own vain tongue
> Doth ravish like enchanting harmony."

Holofernes the pedant, nearly a century and a half before Holberg's Else Skolemesters,[1] expresses himself very much as she does:—

"*Holofernes.* The posterior of the day, most generous sir, is liable, congruent, and measurable for the afternoon: the word is well cull'd, chose; sweet and apt, I do assure you, sir; I do assure."

Armado's bombast may probably be accepted as a not too extravagant caricature of the bombast of the period. Certain it is that the schoolmaster Rombus, in Sir Philip Sidney's *Lady of the May*, addresses the Queen in a strain no whit less ridiculous than that of Holofernes. But what avails the justice of a parody if, in spite of the art and care lavished upon it, it remains as tedious as the mannerism it ridicules! And this is unfortunately the case in the present instance. Shakespeare had not yet

---

[1] The schoolmaster's wife in Ludvig Holberg's inimitable comedy, *Barselstuen*. —(TRANS.)

attained the maturity and detachment of mind which could enable him to rise high above the follies he attacks, and to sweep them aside with full authority. He buries himself in them, circumstantially demonstrates their absurdities, and is still too inexperienced to realise how he thereby inflicts upon the spectator and the reader the full burden of their tediousness. It is very characteristic of Elizabeth's taste that, even in 1598, she could still take pleasure in the play. All this fencing with words appealed to her quick intelligence; while, with the unabashed sensuousness characteristic of the daughter of Henry VIII. and Anne Boleyn, she found entertainment in the playwright's freedom of speech, even, no doubt, in the equivocal badinage between Boyet and Maria (iv. 1).

As was to be expected, Shakespeare is here more dependent on models than in his later works. From Lyly, the most popular comedy-writer of the day, he probably borrowed the idea of his Armado, who answers pretty closely to Sir Tophas in Lyly's *Endymion*, copied, in his turn, from Pyrgopolinices, the boastful soldier of the old Latin comedy. It is to be noted, also, that the braggart and pedant, the two comic figures of this play, are permanent types on the Italian stage, which in so many ways influenced the development of English comedy.

The personal element in this first sportive production is, however, not difficult to recognise: it is the young poet's mirthful protest against a life immured within the hard-and-fast rules of an artificial asceticism, such as the King of Navarre wishes to impose upon his little court, with its perpetual study, its vigils, its fasts, and its exclusion of womankind. Against this life of unnatural constraint the comedy pleads with the voice of Nature, especially through the mouth of Biron, in whose speeches, as Dowden has rightly remarked, we can not infrequently catch the accent of Shakespeare himself. In Biron and his Rosaline we have the first hesitating sketch of the masterly Benedick and Beatrice of *Much Ado About Nothing*. The best of Biron's speeches, those which are in unrhymed verse, we evidently owe to the revision of 1598; but they are conceived in the spirit of the original play, and merely express Shakespeare's design in stronger and clearer terms than he was at first able to compass. Even at the end of the third act Biron is still combating as well as he can the power of love:—

> "What! I love! I sue! I seek a wife!
> A woman, that is like a German clock,
> Still a repairing, ever out of frame,
> And never going aright, being a watch,
> But being watch'd that it may still go right!"

But his great and splendid speech in the fourth act is like a hymn to that God of Battles who is named in the title of the play, and whose outpost skirmishes form its matter:—

> "Other slow arts entirely keep the brain,
> And therefore, finding barren practisers,
> Scarce show a harvest of their heavy toil;
> But love, first learned in a lady's eyes,
> Lives not alone immured in the brain,
> But, with the motion of all elements,
> Courses as swift as thought in every power,
> And gives to every power a double power,
> Above their functions and their offices.
> It adds a precious seeing to the eye;
> A lover's eyes will gaze an eagle blind;
> A lover's ear will hear the lowest sound,
> When the suspicious head of theft is stopp'd:
> Love's feeling is more soft, and sensible,
> Than are the tender horns of cockled snails.
> . . . . . .
> Never durst poet touch a pen to write,
> Until his ink were temper'd with Love's sighs;
> O! then his lines would ravish savage ears,
> And plant in tyrants mild humility."

We must take Biron-Shakespeare at his word, and believe that in these vivid and tender emotions he found, during his early years in London, the stimulus which taught him to open his lips in song.

X

LOVE'S LABOUR'S WON: THE FIRST SKETCH OF ALL'S WELL THAT ENDS WELL—THE COMEDY OF ERRORS—THE TWO GENTLEMEN OF VERONA

As a counterpart to the comedy of *Love's Labour's Lost*, Shakespeare soon after composed another, entitled *Love's Labour's Won*. This we learn from the celebrated passage in Francis Meres' *Palladis Tamia*, where he enumerates the plays which Shakespeare had written up to that date, 1598. We know, however, that no play of that name is now included among the poet's works. Since it is scarcely conceivable that a play of Shakespeare's, once acted, should have been entirely lost, the only question is, which of the extant comedies originally bore that title. But in reality there is no question at all: the play is *All's Well that Ends Well*—not, of course, as we now possess it, in a form and style belonging to a quite mature period of the poet's life, but as it stood before the searching revision, of which it shows evident traces.

We cannot, indeed, restore the play as it originally issued from Shakespeare's youthful imagination. But there are passages in it which evidently belong to the older version, rhymed conversations, or at any rate fragments of dialogue, rhymed letters in sonnet form, and numerous details which entirely correspond with the style of *Love's Labour's Lost*.

The piece is a dramatisation of Boccaccio's story of Gillette of Narbonne. Only the comic parts are of Shakespeare's invention; he has added the characters of Parolles, Lafeu, the Clown, and the Countess. Even in the original sketch he no doubt gave new depth and vitality to the leading characters, who are mere outlines in the story. The comedy, as we know, has for its heroine a young woman who loves the haughty Bertram with an unrequited and despised passion, cures the King of France of a dangerous sickness, claims as her reward the right to choose a husband from among the courtiers, chooses Bertram, is repudiated by him, and, after a nocturnal meeting at which she takes the place of another woman whom he believes himself to have seduced, at last overcomes his resistance and is acknowledged as his wife.

Shakespeare has here not only shown the unquestioning acceptance of his original, which was usual even in his riper years, but has transferred to his play all its peculiarities and improbabilities. Even the psychological crudities he has swallowed as they stand—such, for instance, as the fact of a delicate woman forcing herself under cover of night upon the man who has left his home and country for the express purpose of escaping from her.

Shakespeare has drawn in Helena a patient Griselda, that type of loving and cruelly maltreated womanhood which reappears in German poetry in Kleist's *Käthchen von Heilbronn*—the woman who suffers everything in inexhaustible tenderness and humility, and never falters in her love until in the end she wins the rebellious heart.

The pity is that the unaccommodating theme compelled Shakespeare to make this pearl among women in the end enforce her rights, after the man she adores has not only treated her with contemptuous brutality, but has, moreover, shown himself a liar and hound in his attempt to blacken the character of the Italian girl whose lover he believes himself to have been.

It is very characteristic of the English renaissance, and of the public which Shakespeare had in view in his early plays, that he should make this noble heroine take part with Parolles in the long and jocular conversation (i. 1) on the nature of virginity, which is one of the most indecorous passages in his works. This dialogue must certainly belong to the original version of the play.

We must remember that Helena, in that version, was in all probability very different from the high-souled woman she became in the process of revision. She no doubt expressed herself freely, according to Shakespeare's youthful manner, in rhyming reveries on love and fate, such as the following (i. 1):—

> " Our remedies oft in ourselves do lie
> Which we ascribe to Heaven : the fated sky
> Gives us free scope ; only, doth backward pull
> Our slow designs, when we ourselves are dull.

> What power is it which mounts my love so high;
> That makes me see, and cannot feed mine eye?
> The mightiest space in fortune Nature brings
> To join like likes, and kiss like native things.
> Impossible be strange attempts to those
> That weigh their pains in sense, and do suppose,
> What hath been cannot be. Who ever strove
> To show her merit, that did miss her love?"

Or else he made her pour forth multitudinous swarms of images, each treading on the other's heels, like those in which she forecasts Bertram's love-adventures at the court of France (i. 1):—

> "There shall your master have a thousand loves,
> A mother, and a mistress, and a friend,
> A phœnix, captain, and an enemy,
> A guide, a goddess, and a sovereign,
> A counsellor, a traitress, and a dear;
> His humble ambition, proud humility,
> His jarring concord, and his discord dulcet,
> His faith, his sweet disaster; with a world
> Of pretty, fond, adoptious christendoms,
> That blinking Cupid gossips."

Love's Labour's Won was probably conceived throughout in this lighter tone.

There can be little doubt that the figure of Parolles was also sketched in the earlier play. It forms an excellent counterpart to Armado in *Love's Labour's Lost*. And in it we have undoubtedly the first faint outline of the figure which, seven or eight years later, becomes the immortal Falstaff. Parolles is a humorous liar, braggart, and "misleader of youth," like Prince Henry's fat friend. He is put to shame, just like Falstaff, in an ambuscade devised by his own comrades; and being, as he thinks, taken prisoner, he deserts and betrays his master. Falstaff hacks the edge of his sword in order to appear valiant; and Parolles says (iv. 1), "I would the cutting of my garments would serve the turn, or the breaking of my Spanish sword."

In comparison with Falstaff the character is, of course, meagre and faint. But if we compare it with such a figure as Armado in *Love's Labour's Lost*, we find it sparkling with gaiety. It was, in all probability, touched up and endowed with new wit during the revision.

On the other hand, there is a good deal of quite youthful whimsicality in the speeches of the Clown, especially in the first act, which there is no difficulty in attributing to Shakespeare's twenty-fifth year. The song which the Fool sings at this point (i. 3) seems to belong to the earlier form, and with it the speeches to which it gives rise:—

"*Countess.* What! one good in ten? you corrupt the song, sirrah.
"*Clown.* One good woman in ten, madam, which is a purifying o' the song. Would God would serve the world so all the year! we'd find no fault with the tithe-woman, if I were the parson. One in ten, quoth 'a! an we might have a good woman born but for every blazing star, or at an earthquake, 't would mend the lottery well."

In treating of *Love's Labour's Won*, we must necessarily fall back upon more or less plausible conjecture. But we possess other comedies dating from this early period of Shakespeare's career in which the improvement of his technique and his steady advance towards artistic maturity can be clearly traced.

First and foremost we have his *Comedy of Errors*, which must belong to this earliest period, even if it comes after the two Love's Labour comedies. It is written in a highly polished, poetical style; it contains fewer lines of prose than any other of Shakespeare's comedies; but its diction is full of dramatic movement, the rhymes do not impede the lively flow of the dialogue, and it has three times as many unrhymed as rhymed verses.

Yet it must follow pretty close upon the plays we have just reviewed. Certain phrases in the burlesque portrait of the fat cook drawn by Dromio of Syracuse (iii. 2) help to put us on the track of its date. His remark, that Spain sent whole "armadoes of caracks" to ballast themselves with the rubies and carbuncles on her nose, indicates a time not far remote from the Armada troubles. A more exact indication may be found in the answer which the servant gives to his master's question as to where France is situated upon the globe suggested by the cook's spherical figure. "Where France?" asks Antipholus; and Dromio replies, "In her forehead; arm'd and reverted, making war against her heir." Now, in 1589, Henry of Navarre really ceased to be the heir to the French throne, although his struggle for the possession of it lasted until his acceptance of Catholicism in 1593. Thus we may place the date of the play somewhere between the years 1589 and 1591.

This comedy on the frontier-line of farce shows with what giant strides Shakespeare progresses in the technique of his art. It has the blood of the theatre in its veins; we can already discern the experienced actor in the dexterity with which the threads of the intrigue are involved, and woven into an ever more intricate tangle, until the simple solution is arrived at. While *Love's Labour's Lost* still dragged itself laboriously over the boards, here we have an impetus and a *brio* in all the dramatic passages which reveal an artist and foretell a master. Only the rough outlines of the play are taken from Plautus; and the motive, the possibility of incessant confusion between two masters and two servants, is manipulated with a skill and certainty which astound us in a beginner, and sometimes with quite irresistible whimsicality. No doubt the merry play is founded upon an extreme improbability. So exact is the mutual resemblance of each pair of twins, no less in clothing than in feature, that not a single person for a moment doubts their identity. Astonishing resemblances between twins do, however, occur in real life; and when once we have accepted the premises, the consequences develop naturally, or at any rate plausibly. We may even say that in the art of intrigue-spinning, which was afterwards somewhat foreign and unattractive to him, the poet here shows himself scarcely inferior to the Spaniards of his own or of a later day, remarkable as was their dexterity.

Now and then the movement is suspended for the sake of an exchange of word-plays between master and servant; but it is generally short and entertaining. Now and then the action pauses to let Dromio of Syracuse work off one of his extravagant witticisms, as for example (iii. 2) :—

"*Dromio S.* And yet she is a wondrous fat marriage.

"*Antipholus S.* How dost thou mean a fat marriage?

"*Dro. S.* Marry, sir, she's the kitchen-wench, and all grease; and I know not what use to put her to, but to make a lamp of her, and run from her by her own light. I warrant, her rags, and the tallow in them, will burn a Poland winter: if she lives till doomsday, she'll burn a week longer than the whole world."

As a rule, however, the interest is so evenly sustained that the spectator is held in constant curiosity and suspense as to the upshot of the adventure.

At one single point the style rises to a beauty and intensity which show that, though Shakespeare here abandons himself to the light play of intrigue, it is a diversion to which he only condescends for the moment. The passage is that between Luciana and Antipholus of Syracuse (iii. 2), with its tender erotic cadences. Listen to such verses as these:—

> "*Ant. S.* Sweet mistress (what your name is else, I know not,
> Nor by what wonder you do hit of mine),
> Less in your knowledge, and your grace, you show not,
> Than our earth's wonder; more than earth divine.
> Teach me, dear creature, how to think and speak:
> Lay open to my earthy-gross conceit,
> Smother'd in errors, feeble, shallow, weak,
> The folded meaning of your words' deceit.
> Against my soul's pure truth, why labour you
> To make it wander in an unknown field?
> Are you a god? would you create me new?
> Transform me then, and to your power I'll yield."

Since the play was first published in the Folio of 1623, it is, of course, not impossible that Shakespeare may have worked over this lovely passage at a later period. But the whole structure of the verses, with their interwoven rhymes, points in the opposite direction. We here catch the first notes of that music which is soon to fill *Romeo and Juliet* with its harmonies.

The play which in all probability stands next on the chronological list of Shakespeare's works, *The Two Gentlemen of Verona*, is also one in which we catch several anticipatory glimpses of later productions, and is in itself a promising piece of work. It surpasses the earlier comedies in two respects: first, in the beauty and clearness with which the two young women are outlined, and then in the careless gaiety which makes its first triumphant appearance in the parts of the servants. Only now and then, in one or two detached scenes, do Speed and Launce bore us with euphuistic word-torturings; as a rule they are quite entertaining fellows, who seem to announce, as with a flourish of trumpets, that, unlike either Lyly or Marlowe, Shakespeare possesses the inborn gaiety, the keen sense of humour, the sparkling playfulness, which are to enable him, without any strain on his invention, to kindle the laughter of his audiences, and send it flashing round the theatre from the groundlings to the gods. He does not as yet display any particular talent for individualising his clowns. Nevertheless we notice that, while Speed impresses us chiefly by his astonishing volubility, the true English humour makes its entrance upon the Shakespearian stage when Launce appears, dragging his dog by a string.

Note the torrent of eloquence in this speech of Speed's, enumerating the symptoms from which he concludes that his master is in love :—

"First, you have learn'd, like Sir Proteus, to wreath your arms, like a malcontent; to relish a love-song, like a robin-redbreast; to walk alone, like one that had the pestilence; to sigh, like a school-boy that had lost his A B C; to weep, like a young wench that had buried her grandam; to fast, like one that takes diet; to watch, like one that fears robbing; to speak puling, like a beggar at Hallowmas. You were wont, when you laugh'd, to crow like a cock; when you walk'd, to walk like one of the lions; when you fasted, it was presently after dinner; when you look'd sadly, it was for want of money; and now you are metamorphosed with a mistress, that, when I look on you, I can hardly think you my master."

All these similes of Speed's are apt and accurate; it is only the way in which he piles them up that makes us laugh. But when Launce opens his mouth, unbridled whimsicality at once takes the upper hand. He comes upon the scene with his dog :—

"Nay, 'twill be this hour ere I have done weeping; all the kind of the Launces have this very fault. . . . I think Crab, my dog, be the sourest-natured dog that lives: my mother weeping, my father wailing, my sister crying, our maid howling, our cat wringing her hands, and all our house in a great perplexity, yet did not this cruel-hearted cur shed one tear. He is a stone, a very pebble-stone, and has no more pity in him than a dog; a Jew would have wept to have seen our parting: why, my grandam, having no eyes, look you, wept herself blind at my parting. Nay, I'll show you the manner of it. This shoe is my father: —no, this left shoe is my father;—no, no, this left shoe is my mother;— nay, that cannot be so, neither:—yes, it is so, it is so; it hath the worser sole. This shoe, with the hole in it, is my mother, and this my father. A vengeance on 't! there 't is: now, sir, this staff is my sister; for, look you, she is as white as a lily, and as small as a wand: this hat is Nan, our maid: I am the dog;—no, the dog is himself, and I am the dog, —O! the dog is me, and I am myself: ay, so, so."

Here we have nothing but joyous nonsense, and yet nonsense of a highly dramatic nature. That is to say, here reigns that youthful exuberance of spirit which laughs with a childlike grace, even where it condescends to the petty and low; exuberance as of one who glories in the very fact of existence, and rejoices to feel life pulsing and seething in his veins; exuberance such as belongs of right, in some degree, to every well-constituted man in the light-hearted days of his youth—how much more, then, to one who possesses the double youth of years and genius among a people which is itself young, and more than young: liberated, emancipated, enfranchised, like a colt which has broken its tether and scampers at large through the luxuriant pastures.

The Two Gentlemen of Verona—which, by the way, is Shakespeare's first declaration of love to Italy—is a graceful, entertaining, weakly constructed comedy, dealing with faithful and faithless love, with the treachery of man and the devotion of woman. Its hero, a noble and wrongfully-banished youth, comes to live the life of a robber captain, like Schiller's Karl von Moor two centuries later, but without a spark of his spirit of rebellion. The solution of the imbroglio, by means of the instant and unconditional forgiveness of the villain, is so naïve, so senselessly conciliatory, that we feel it to be the outcome of a joyous, untried, and unwounded spirit.

Shakespeare has borrowed part of his matter from a novel entitled *Diana*, by the Portuguese Montemayor (1520–1562). The translation, by Bartholomew Yong, was not printed until 1598, but the preface states that it had then been completed for fully sixteen years, and manuscript copies of it had no doubt passed from hand to hand, according to the fashion of the time. On comparing the essential portion of the romance[1] with *The Two Gentlemen of Verona*, we find that Proteus's infidelity and Julia's idea of following her lover in male attire, with all that comes of it, belong to Montemayor. Moreover, in the novel, Julia, disguised as a page, is present when Proteus serenades Sylvia (Celia in the original). She also goes to Sylvia at Proteus's orders to plead his cause with her; but in the novel the fair lady falls in love with the messenger in male attire—an incident which Shakespeare reserved for *Twelfth Night*. We even find in *Diana* a

[1] *The Shepherdess Felismena* in Hazlitt's *Shakespeare's Library*, Pt. I. vol. i. ed. 1875.

sketch of the second scene of the first act, between Julia and Lucetta, in which the mistress, for appearance' sake, repudiates the letter which she is burning to read.

One or two points in the play remind us of *Love's Labour's Won*, which Shakespeare had just completed in its original form; for example, the journey in male attire in pursuit of the scornful loved one. Many things, on the other hand, point forward to Shakespeare's later work. The inconstancy of the two men in *A Midsummer Night's Dream* is a variation and parody of Proteus's fickleness in this play. The beginning of the second scene of the first act, where Julia makes Lucetta pass judgment on her different suitors, is the first faint outline of the masterly scene to the same effect between Portia and Nerissa in *The Merchant of Venice*. The conversation between Sylvia and Julia, which brings the fourth act to a close, answers exactly to that between Olivia and Viola in the first act of *Twelfth Night*. Finally, the fact that Valentine, after learning the full extent of his false friend's treachery, offers to resign to him his beautiful betrothed, Sylvia, in order to prove by this sacrifice the strength of his friendship, however foolish and meaningless it may appear in the play, is yet an anticipation of the humble renunciation of the beloved for the sake of the friend and of friendship, which impresses us so painfully in Shakespeare's Sonnets.

In almost every utterance of the young women in this comedy we see nobility of soul, and in the lyric passages a certain pre-Raphaelite grace. Take, for example, what Julia says of her love in the last scene of the second act :—

> "The current, that with gentle murmur glides,
> Thou know'st, being stopp'd, impatiently doth rage;
> But, when his fair course is not hindered,
> He makes sweet music with the enamell'd stones,
> Giving a gentle kiss to every sedge
> He overtaketh in his pilgrimage.
> .   .   .   .   .   .
> I'll be as patient as a gentle stream,
> And make a pastime of each weary step,
> Till the last step have brought me to my love;
> And there I'll rest, as, after much turmoil,
> A blessed soul doth in Elysium."

And although the men are here of inferior interest to the

women, we yet find in the mouth of Valentine outbursts of great lyric beauty. For example (iii. 1):—

> "Except I be by Silvia in the night,
> There is no music in the nightingale;
> Unless I look on Silvia in the day,
> There is no day for me to look upon.
> She is my essence; and I leave to be,
> If I be not by her fair influence
> Foster'd, illumin'd, cherish'd, kept alive."

Besides the strains of passion and of gaiety in this light acting play, a third note is clearly struck, the note of nature. There is fresh air in it, a first breath of those fragrant midland memories which prove that this child of the country must many a time have said to himself with Valentine (v. 4):—

> "How use doth breed a habit in a man!
> This shadowy desert, unfrequented woods,
> I better brook than flourishing peopled towns."

In many passages of this play we are conscious for the first time of that keen love of nature which never afterwards deserts Shakespeare, and which gives to some of the most mannered of his early efforts, as, for example, to his short narrative poems, their chief interest and value.

XI

VENUS AND ADONIS: DESCRIPTIONS OF NATURE — THE RAPE OF LUCRECE: RELATION TO PAINTING

ALTHOUGH Shakespeare did not publish *Venus and Adonis* until the spring of 1593, when he was twenty-nine years old, the poem must certainly have been conceived, and probably written, several years earlier. In dedicating it to the Earl of Southampton, then a youth of twenty, he calls it "the first heire of my invention;" but it by no means follows that it is literally the first thing he ever wrote. The expression may merely imply that his work for the theatre was not regarded as an independent exercise of his poetic talent. But the over-luxuriant style betrays the youthful hand, and we place it, therefore, among Shakespeare's writings of about 1590–91.

He had at this period, as we have seen, won a firm footing as an actor, and had made himself not only useful but popular as an adapter of old plays and an independent dramatist. But the drama of that time was not reckoned as literature. There was all the difference in the world between a "playwright" and a real poet. When Sir Thomas Bodley, about the year 1600, extended and remodelled the old University Library, and gave it his name, he decreed that no such "riffe-raffes" as playbooks should ever find admittance to it.

Without being actually ambitious, Shakespeare felt the highly natural wish to make a name for himself in literature. He wanted to take his place among the poets, and to win the approval of the young noblemen whose acquaintance he had made in the theatre. He also wanted to show that he was familiar with the spirit of antiquity.

Spenser (born 1553) had just attracted general attention by publishing the first books of his great narrative poem. What more natural than that Shakespeare should be tempted to measure his strength against Spenser, as he already had against Marlowe, his first master in the drama?

The little poem of *Venus and Adonis*, and its companion-piece, *The Rape of Lucrece*, which appeared in the following year, have this great value for us, that here, and here only, are we certain of possessing a text exactly as Shakespeare wrote it, since he himself superintended its publication.

Italy was at this time the centre of all culture. The lyric and minor epic poetry of England were entirely under the influence of the Italian style and taste. Shakespeare, in *Venus and Adonis*, aims at the insinuating sensuousness of the Italians. He tries to strike the tender and languorous notes of his Southern forerunners. Among the poets of antiquity, Ovid is naturally his model. He takes two lines from Ovid's *Amores* as the motto of his poem, which is, indeed, nothing but an expanded version of a scene in the *Metamorphoses*.

The name of Shakespeare, like the names of Æschylus, Michael Angelo, and Beethoven, is apt to ring tragically in our ears. We have almost forgotten that he had a Mozartean vein in his nature, and that his contemporaries not only praised his personal gentleness and "honesty," but also the "sweetness" of his singing.

In *Venus and Adonis* glows the whole fresh sensuousness of the Renaissance and of Shakespeare's youth. It is an entirely erotic poem, and contemporaries aver that it lay on the table of every light woman in London.

The conduct of the poem presents a series of opportunities and pretexts for voluptuous situations and descriptions. The ineffectual blandishments lavished by Venus on the chaste and frigid youth, who, in his sheer boyishness, is as irresponsive as a bashful woman—her kisses, caresses, and embraces, are depicted in detail. It is as though a Titian or Rubens had painted a model in a whole series of tender situations, now in one attitude, now in another. Then comes the suggestive scene in which Adonis's horse breaks away in order to meet the challenge of a mare which happens to wander by, together with the goddess's comments thereupon. Then new advances and solicitations, almost inadmissibly daring, according to the taste of our day.

An element of feeling is introduced in the portrayal of Venus's anguish when Adonis expresses his intention of hunting the boar. But it is to sheer description that the poet chiefly devotes himself —description of the charging boar, description of the fair young body bathed in blood, and so forth. There is a fire and rapture of colour in it all, as in a picture by some Italian master of a hundred years before.

Quite unmistakable is the insinuating, luscious, almost saccharine quality of the writing, which accounts for the fact that, when his immediate contemporaries speak of Shakespeare's diction, honey is the similitude that first suggests itself to them. John Weever, in 1595, calls him "honey-tongued," and in 1598 Francis Meres uses the same term, with the addition of "mellifluous."

There is, indeed, an extraordinary sweetness in these strophes. Tenderness, every here and there, finds really entrancing utterance. When Adonis has for the first time harshly repulsed Venus, in a speech of some length:—

> "'What! canst thou talk?' quoth she, 'hast thou a tongue?
> O, would thou hadst not, or I had no hearing!
> Thy mermaid's voice hath done me double wrong;
> I had my load before, now press'd with bearing:
> Melodious discord, heavenly tune harsh-sounding,
> Ear's deep-sweet music, and heart's deep-sore wounding.'"

But the style also exhibits numberless instances of tasteless Italian artificiality. Breathing the "heavenly moisture" of Adonis's breath, she

> "Wishes her cheeks were gardens full of flowers,
> So they were dew'd with such distilling showers."

Of Adonis's dimples it is said:—

> "These lovely caves, these round enchanting pits,
> Open'd their mouths to swallow Venus' liking."

"My love to love," says Adonis, "is love but to disgrace it." Venus enumerates the delights he would afford to each of her senses separately, supposing her deprived of all the rest, and concludes thus:—

> "'But, O, what banquet wert thou to the taste,
> Being nurse and feeder of the other four

> Would they not wish the feast might ever last,
> And bid Suspicion double-lock the door,
>   Lest Jealousy, that sour unwelcome guest,
>   Should, by his stealing in, disturb the feast?' "

Such lapses of taste are not infrequent in Shakespeare's early comedies as well. They answer, in their way, to the riot of horrors in *Titus Andronicus*—analogous mannerisms of an as yet undeveloped art.

At the same time, the puissant sensuousness of this poem is as a prelude to the large utterance of passion in *Romeo and Juliet*, and towards its close Shakespeare soars, so to speak, symbolically, from a delineation of the mere fever of the senses to a forecast of that love in which it is only one element, when he makes Adonis say:—

> " ' Love comforteth like sunshine after rain,
>   But Lust's effect is tempest after sun;
>   Love's gentle spring doth always fresh remain,
>   Lust's winter comes ere summer half be done:
>   Love surfeits not, Lust like a glutton dies;
>   Love is all truth, Lust full of forged lies.' "

It would, of course, be absurd to lay too much stress on these edifying antitheses in this unedifying poem. It is more important to note that the descriptions of animal life—for example, that of the hare's flight—are unrivalled for truth and delicacy of observation, and to mark how, even in this early work, Shakespeare's style now and then rises to positive greatness.

This is especially the case in the descriptions of the boar and of the horse. The boar—his back "set with a battle of bristly pikes," his eyes like glow-worms, his snout "digging sepulchres where'er he goes," his neck short and thick, and his onset so fierce that

> "The thorny brambles and embracing bushes,
>   As fearful of him, part; through which he rushes"

—this boar seems to have been painted by Snyders in a hunting-piece, in which the human figures came from the brush of Rubens.

Shakespeare himself seems to have realised with what mastery he had depicted the stallion; for he says:—

> " Look, when a painter would surpass the life,
>   In limning out a well-proportion'd steed,

His art with nature's workmanship at strife,
As if the dead the living should exceed;
So did this horse excel a common one,
In shape, in courage, colour, pace, and bone."

We can feel Shakespeare's love of nature in such a stanza as this:—

"Round-hoof'd, short-jointed, fetlocks shag and long,
Broad breast, full eye, small head, and nostril wide,
High crest, short ears, straight legs, and passing strong,
Thin mane, thick tail, broad buttock, tender hide:
Look, what a horse should have, he did not lack,
Save a proud rider on so proud a back."

How consummate, too, is the description of all his movements:—

"Sometime he scuds far off, and there he stares;
Anon he starts at stirring of a feather."

We hear "the high wind singing through his mane and tail." We are almost reminded of the magnificent picture of the horse at the end of the Book of Job: "He swalloweth the ground with fierceness and rage. . . . He smelleth the battle afar off, the thunder of the captains, and the shouting." So great is the compass of style in this little poem of Shakespeare's youth: from Ovid to the Old Testament, from modish artificiality to grandiose simplicity.

Lucrece, which appeared in the following year, was, like *Venus and Adonis*, dedicated to the Earl of Southampton, in distinctly more familiar, though still deferential terms. The poem is designed as a counterpart to its predecessor. The one treats of male, the other of female, chastity. The one portrays ungovernable passion in a woman; the other, criminal passion in a man. But in *Lucrece* the theme is seriously and morally handled. It is almost a didactic poem, dealing with the havoc wrought by unbridled and brutish desire.

It was not so popular in its own day as its predecessor, and it does not afford the modern reader any very lively satisfaction. It shows an advance in metrical accomplishment. To the six-line stanza of *Venus and Adonis* a seventh line is added, which heightens its beauty and its dignity. The strength of *Lucrece* lies in its graphic and gorgeous descriptions, and in its sometimes microscopic psychological analysis. For the rest, its pathos consists of elaborate and far-fetched rhetoric.

The lament of the heroine after the crime has been committed is pure declamation, extremely eloquent no doubt, but copious and artificial as an oration of Cicero's, rich in apostrophes and antitheses. The sorrow of "Collatine and his consorted lords" is portrayed in laboured and quibbling speeches. Shakespeare's knowledge and mastery are most clearly seen in the reflections scattered through the narrative—such, for instance, as the following profound and exquisitely written stanza on the softness of the feminine nature:—

> "For men have marble, women waxen minds,
> And therefore are they form'd as marble will;
> The weak oppress'd, the impression of strange kinds
> Is form'd in them by force, by fraud, or skill:
> Then call them not the authors of their ill,
>   No more than wax shall be accounted evil,
>   Wherein is stamp'd the semblance of a devil."

In point of mere technique the most remarkable passage in the poem is the long series of stanzas (lines 1366 to 1568) describing a painting of the destruction of Troy, which Lucrece contemplates in her despair. The description is marked by such force, freshness, and naïveté as might suggest that the writer had never seen a picture before:—

> "Here one man's hand leaned on another's head,
> His nose being shadowed by his neighbour's ear."

So dense is the throng of figures in the picture, so deceptive the presentation,

> "That for Achilles' image stood his spear,
> Grip'd in an armed hand: himself behind
> Was left unseen, save to the eye of mind.
>   A hand, a foot, a face, a leg, a head,
>   Stood for the whole to be imagined."

Here, as in all other places in which Shakespeare mentions pictorial or plastic art, it is realism carried to the point of illusion that he admires and praises. The paintings in the Guild Chapel at Stratford were, doubtless, as before mentioned, the first he ever saw. He may also, during his Stratford period, have seen works of art at Kenilworth Castle or at St. Mary's Church in Coventry. In London, in the Hall belonging to the Merchants of the Steel-Yard, he had no doubt seen two greatly admired pictures by Holbein which hung there. Moreover, there were in London at that time not only numerous portraits by Dutch masters, but also a few Italian pictures. It appears, for example, from a list of "Pictures and other Works of Art" drawn up in 1613 by John Ernest, Duke of Saxe-Weimar, that there hung at Whitehall a painting of Julius Cæsar, and another of Lucretia, said to have been "very artistically executed." This picture may possibly have suggested to Shakespeare the theme of his poem. Larger compositions were no doubt familiar to him in the tapestries of the period (the hangings at Theobald's presented scenes from Roman history); and he may very likely have seen the excellent Dutch and Italian pictures at Nonsuch Palace, then in the height of its glory.

His reflections upon art led him, as aforesaid, to the conclusion that it was the artist's business to keep a close watch upon nature, to master or transcend her. Again and again he ranks truth to nature as the highest quality in art. He evidently cared nothing for allegorical or religious painting; he never so much as mentions it. Nor, with all his love for "the concord of sweet sounds," does he ever allude to church music.

The description of the great painting of the fall of Troy is no mere irrelevant decoration to the poem; for the fall of Troy symbolises the fall of the royal house of Tarquin as a consequence of Sextus's crime. Shakespeare did not look at the event from the point of view of individual morality alone; he makes us feel that the honour of a royal family, and even its dynastic existence, are hazarded by criminal aggression upon a noble house. All the conceptions of honour belonging to mediæval chivalry are transferred to ancient Rome. "Knights, by their oaths, should right poor ladies' harms," says Lucrece, in calling upon her kinsmen to avenge her.

In his picture of the sack of Troy, Shakespeare has followed the second book of Virgil's *Æneid*; for the groundwork of his poem as a whole he has gone to the short but graceful and sympathetic rendering of the story of Lucretia in Ovid's *Fasti* (ii. 685-852).

A comparison between Ovid's style and that of Shakespeare

certainly does not redound to the advantage of the modern poet. In opposition to this semi-barbarian, Ovid seems the embodiment of classic severity. Shakespeare's antithetical conceits and other lapses of taste are painfully obtrusive. Every here and there we come upon such stumbling-blocks as these:—

> "Some of her blood still pure and red remain'd,
> And some look'd black, and that false Tarquin stain'd;"

or,

> "If children pre-decease progenitors,
> We are their offspring, and they none of ours."

This lack of nature and of taste is not only characteristic of the age in general, but is bound up with the great excellences and rare capacities which Shakespeare was now developing with such amazing rapidity. His momentary leaning towards this style was due, in part at least, to the influence of his fellow-poets, his friends, his rivals in public favour—the influence, in short, of that artistic microcosm in whose atmosphere his genius shot up to sudden maturity.

We talk of "schools" in literature, and it is no exaggeration to say that every period of rich productivity presupposes a school or schools. But the word "school," beautiful in its original Greek signification, has been narrowed and specialised by modern usage. We ought to say "forcing-house" instead of "school"—to talk of the classic and the romantic forcing-house, the Renaissance forcing-house,[1] and so forth. In very small communities, where there is none of that emulation which alone can call forth all an artist's energies, absolute mastery is as a rule unattainable. Under such conditions, a man will often make a certain mark early in life, and find his success his ruin. Others seek a forcing-house outside their native land—Holberg in Holland, England, and France; Thorvaldsen in Rome; Heine in Paris. The moment he set foot in London, Shakespeare was in such a forcing-house. Hence the luxuriant burgeoning of his genius.

He lived in constant intercourse and rivalry with vivid and daringly productive spirits. The diamond was polished in diamond dust.

The competitive instinct (as Rümelin has rightly pointed out)

---

[1] The author's idea is, I think, best rendered by this literal translation; but the Danish word *Drivhus* is much less cumbrous than its English equivalent.—TRANS.

was strong in the English poets of that period. Shakespeare could not but strive from the first to outdo his fellows in strength and skill. At last he comes to think, like Hamlet: however deep they dig—

"it shall go hard
But I will delve one yard below their mines"

—one of the most characteristic utterances of Hamlet and of Shakespeare.

This sense of rivalry contributed to the formation of Shakespeare's early manner, both in his narrative poems and in his plays. Hence arose that straining after subtleties, that absorption in quibbles, that wantoning in word-plays, that bandying to and fro of shuttlecocks of speech. Hence, too, that state of overheated passion and over-stimulated fancy, in which image begets image with a headlong fecundity, like that of the low organisms which pullulate by mere scission.

This man of all the talents had the talent for word-plays and thought-quibbles among the rest; he was too richly endowed to be behind-hand even here. But there was in all this something foreign to his true self. When he reaches the point at which his inmost personality begins to reveal itself in his writings, we are at once conscious of a far deeper and more emotional nature than that which finds expression in the teeming conceits of the narrative poems and the incessant scintillations of the early comedies.

XII

A MIDSUMMER NIGHT'S DREAM—ITS HISTORICAL CIRCUMSTANCES—ITS ARISTOCRATIC, POPULAR, COMIC, AND SUPERNATURAL ELEMENTS

IN spite of the fame and popularity which *Venus and Adonis* and *Lucrece* won for Shakespeare, he quickly understood, with his instinctive self-knowledge, that it was not narrative but dramatic poetry which offered the fullest scope for his powers.

And now it is that we find him for the first time rising to the full height of his genius. This he does in a work of dramatic form; but, significantly enough, it is not as yet in its dramatic elements that we recognise the master-hand, but rather in the rich and incomparable lyric poetry with which he embroiders a thin dramatic canvas.

His first masterpiece is a masterpiece of grace, both lyrical and comic. *A Midsummer Night's Dream* was no doubt written as a festival-play or masque, before the masque became an established art-form, to celebrate the marriage of a noble patron; probably for the May festival after the private marriage of Essex with the widow of Sir Philip Sidney in the year 1590. In Oberon's great speech to Puck (ii. 2) there is a significant passage about a throned vestal, invulnerable to Cupid's darts, which is obviously a flattering reference to Elizabeth in relation to Leicester; while the lines about a little flower wounded by the fiery shaft of love mournfully allude, in the like allegorical fashion, to Essex's mother and her marriage with Leicester, after his courtship had been rejected by the Queen. Other details also point to Essex as the bridegroom typified in the person of Theseus.

How is one to speak adequately of *A Midsummer Night's Dream*? It is idle to dwell upon the slightness of the character-drawing, for the poet's effort is not after characterisation; and, whatever its weak points, the poem as a whole is one of the tenderest, most original, and most perfect Shakespeare ever produced.

It is Spenser's fairy-poetry developed and condensed; it is Shelley's spirit-poetry anticipated by more than two centuries. And the airy dream is shot with whimsical parody. The frontiers of Elf-land and Clown-land meet and mingle.

We have here an element of aristocratic distinction in the princely couple, Theseus and Hippolyta, and their court. We have here an element of sprightly burlesque in the artisans' performance of Pyramus and Thisbe, treated with genial irony and divinely felicitous humour. And here, finally, we have the element of supernatural poetry, which soon after flashes forth again in *Romeo and Juliet*, where Mercutio describes the doings of Queen Mab. Puck and Pease-blossom, Cobweb and Mustard-seed—pigmies who hunt the worms in a rosebud, tease bats, chase spiders, and lord it over nightingales—are the leading actors in an elfin play, a fairy carnival of inimitable mirth and melody, steeped in a midsummer atmosphere of mist-wreaths and flower-scents, under the afterglow that lingers through the sultry night. This miracle of happy inspiration contains the germs of innumerable romantic achievements in England, Germany, and Denmark, more than two centuries later.

There is in French literature a graceful mythological play of somewhat later date—Molière's *Psyché*—in which the exquisite love-verses which stream from the heroine's lips were written by the sexagenarian Corneille. It is, in its way, an admirable piece of work. But read it and compare it with the nature-poetry of *A Midsummer Night's Dream*, and you will feel how far the great Englishman surpasses the greatest Frenchmen in pure unrhetorical lyrism and irrepressibly playful, absolutely poetical poetry, with its scent of clover, its taste of wild honey, and its airy and shifting dream-pageantry.

We have here no pathos. The hurricane of passion does not as yet sweep through Shakespeare's work. No; it is only the romantic and imaginative side of love that is here displayed, the magic whereby longing transmutes and idealises its object, the element of folly, infatuation, and illusion in desire, with its consequent variability and transitoriness. Man is by nature a being with no inward compass, led astray by his instincts and dreams, and for ever deceived either by himself or by others. This Shakespeare realises, but does not, as yet, take the matter very tragically. Thus the characters whom he here presents, even, or rather especially, in their love-affairs, appear as anything but reasonable beings. The lovers seek and avoid each other by turns, they love and are not loved again; the couples attract each other at cross-purposes; the youth runs after the maiden who shrinks from him, the maiden flees from the man who adores her; and the poet's delicate irony makes the confusion reach its height and find its symbolic expression when the Queen of the Fairies, in the intoxication of a love-dream, recognises her ideal in a journeyman weaver with an ass's head.

It is the love begotten of imagination that here bears sway. Hence these words of Theseus (v. 1):—

> " Lovers and madmen have such seething brains,
> Such shaping fantasies, that apprehend
> More than cool reason ever comprehends.
> The lunatic, the lover, and the poet,
> Are of imagination all compact."

And then follows Shakespeare's first deliberate utterance as to the nature and art of the poet. He is not, as a rule, greatly concerned with the dignity of the poet as such. Quite foreign to him is the self-idolatry of the later romantic poets, posing as the spiritual pastors and masters of the world. Where he introduces poets in his plays (as in *Julius Cæsar* and *Timon*), it is generally to assign them a pitiful part. But here he places in the mouth of Theseus the famous and exquisite words:—

> " The poet's eye, in a fine frenzy rolling,
> Doth glance from heaven to earth, from earth to heaven;
> And, as imagination bodies forth
> The forms of things unknown, the poet's pen
> Turns them to shapes, and gives to airy nothing
> A local habitation and a name.
> Such tricks hath strong imagination."

When he wrote this he felt that his wings had grown.

As *A Midsummer Night's Dream* was not published until 1600, it is impossible to assign an exact date to the text we possess. In all probability the piece was altered and amplified before it was printed.

Attention was long ago drawn to the following lines in Theseus's speech at the beginning of the fifth act:—

" *The thrice three Muses mourning for the death
Of Learning, late deceas'd in beggary.*
This is some satire, keen and critical."

Several commentators have seen in these lines an allusion to the death of Spenser, which, however, did not occur until 1599, so late that it can scarcely be the event alluded to. Others have conjectured a reference to the death of Robert Greene in 1592. The probability is that the words refer to Spenser's poem, *The Tears of the Muses*, published in 1591, which was a complaint of the indifference of the nobility towards the fine arts. If the play, as we have so many reasons for supposing, was written for the marriage of Essex, these lines must have been inserted later, as they might easily be in a passage like this, where a whole series of different subjects for masques is enumerated.

The important passage (ii. 2) where Oberon recounts his vision has already been mentioned. It follows Oberon's description of the mermaid seated on a dolphin's back—

"Uttering such dulcet and harmonious breath
That certain stars shot madly from their spheres,"

—an allusion, not, as some have supposed, to Mary Stuart, who was married to the Dauphin of France, but to the festivities and firework displays which celebrated Elizabeth's visit to Kenilworth in 1575. The passage is interesting, among other reasons, because we have here one of the few allegories to be found in Shakespeare —an allegory which has taken that form because the matters to which it alludes could not be directly handled. Shakespeare is here referring back, as English criticism has long ago pointed out,[1] to the allegory in Lyly's mythological play, *Endymion*. There can be no doubt that Cynthia (the moon-goddess) in Lyly's play stands for Queen Elizabeth, while Leicester figures as Endymion, who is represented as hopelessly enamoured of Cynthia. Tellus and Floscula, of whom the one loves Endymion's "person," the other his "virtues," represent the Countesses of Sheffield and Essex, who stood in amatory relations to Leicester. The play is one

[1] N. J. Halpin: *Oberon's Vision in the Midsummer Night's Dream, illustrated by a Comparison with Lylie's Endymion*, 1842.

tissue of adulation for Elizabeth, but is so constructed as at the same time to flatter and defend Leicester. In defiance of the actual fact, it exhibits the Queen as entirely inaccessible to her adorer's homage, and Leicester's intrigue with the Countess of Sheffield as a mere mask for his passion for the Queen; in other words, it represents these relations as the Queen would wish to have them understood by the people, and Leicester by the Queen. The Countess of Essex, who was afterwards to play so large a part in Leicester's life, plays a very small part in the drama. Her love finds expression only in one or two unobtrusive phrases, such as her cry of joy on seeing Endymion, after the forty years' sleep in which he has grown an old man, rejuvenated by a single kiss from Cynthia's lips.

The relation between Leicester and Lettice, Countess of Essex, must certainly have made a deep impression upon Shakespeare. By Leicester's contrivance, her husband had been for a long time banished to Ireland, first as commander of the troops in Ulster, and afterwards as Earl-Marshal; and when he died, in 1576—commonly thought, though without proof, to have been poisoned—his widow, after a lapse of only a few days, went through a secret marriage with his supposed murderer. When Leicester, twelve years later, met with a sudden death, also, according to popular belief, by poison, the event was regarded as a judgment on a great criminal. In all probability, Shakespeare found in these events one of the motives of his *Hamlet*. Whether the Countess Lettice was actually Leicester's mistress during her husband's lifetime is, of course, uncertain; in any case, the Countess's relation to Robert, Earl of Essex, her son by her first marriage, was always of the best. She was, however, punished by the Queen's displeasure, which was so vehement that she was forbidden to show herself at court.

Shakespeare has retained Lyly's names, merely translating them into English. Cynthia has become the moon, Tellus the earth, Floscula the little flower; and with this commentary, we are in a position to admire the delicate and poetical way in which he has touched upon the family circumstances of the supposed bridegroom, the Earl of Essex:—

> "*Oberon.* That very time I saw (but thou couldst not),
> Flying between the cold moon and the earth,

> Cupid all arm'd : a certain aim he took
> At a fair vestal throned by the west,
> And loos'd his love-shaft smartly from his bow,
> As it should pierce a hundred thousand hearts.
> But I might see young Cupid's fiery shaft
> Quench'd in the chaste beams of the wat'ry moon,
> And the imperial votaress passed on,
> In maiden meditation, fancy-free.
> Yet mark'd I where the bolt of Cupid fell:
> It fell upon a little western flower,
> Before milk-white, now purple with love's wound,
> And maidens call it Love-in-idleness."

It is with the juice of this flower that Oberon makes every one upon whose eyes it falls dote upon the first living creature they happen to see.

The poet's design in the flattery addressed to Elizabeth—one of the very few instances of the kind in his works—was no doubt to dispose her favourably towards his patron's marriage, or, in other words, to deprecate the anger with which she was in the habit of regarding any attempt on the part of her favourites, or even of ordinary courtiers, to marry according to their own inclinations. Essex in particular had stood very close to her, since, in 1587, he had supplanted Sir Walter Raleigh in her favour; and although the Queen, now in her fifty-seventh year, was fully thirty-four years older than her late adorer, Shakespeare did not succeed in averting her anger from the young couple. The bride was commanded "to live very retired in her mother's house."

A Midsummer Night's Dream is the first consummate and immortal masterpiece which Shakespeare produced.

The fact that the pairs of lovers are very slightly individualised, and do not in themselves awaken any particular sympathy, is a fault that we easily overlook, amid the countless beauties of the play. The fact that the changes in the lovers' feelings are entirely unmotived is no fault at all, for Oberon's magic is simply a great symbol, typifying the sorcery of the erotic imagination. There is deep significance as well as drollery in the presentation of Titania as desperately enamoured of Bottom with his ass's head. Nay, more; in the lovers' ever-changing attractions and repulsions we may find a whole sportive love-philosophy.

The rustic and popular element in Shakespeare's genius here

appears more prominently than ever before. The country-bred youth's whole feeling for and knowledge of nature comes to the surface, permeated with the spirit of poetry. The play swarms with allusions to plants and insects, and all that is said of them is closely observed and intimately felt. In none of Shakespeare's plays are so many species of flowers, fruits, and trees mentioned and characterised. H. N. Ellacombe, in his essay on *The Seasons of Shakspere's Plays*,[1] reckons no fewer than forty-two species. Images borrowed from nature meet us on every hand. For example, in Helena's beautiful description of her school friendship with Hermia (iii. 2), she says :—

> " So we grew together,
> Like to a double cherry, seeming parted,
> But yet an union in partition ;
> Two lovely berries moulded on one stem."

When Titania exhorts her elves to minister to every desire of her asinine idol, she says (iii. 1):—

> "Be kind and courteous to this gentleman :
> Hop in his walks, and gambol in his eyes ;
> Feed him with apricocks, and dewberries,
> With purple grapes, green figs, and mulberries.
> The honey-bags steal from the humble-bees,
> And for night-tapers crop their waxen thighs,
> And light them at the fiery glow-worm's eyes,
> To have my love to bed, and to arise ;
> And pluck the wings from painted butterflies,
> To fan the moonbeams from his sleeping eyes.
> Nod to him, elves, and do him courtesies."

The popular element in Shakespeare is closely interwoven with his love of nature. He has here plunged deep into folk-lore, seized upon the figments of peasant superstition as they survive in the old ballads, and mingled brownies and pixies with the delicate creations of artificial poetry, with Oberon, who is of French descent ("Auberon," from *l'aube du jour*), and Titania, a name which Ovid gives in his *Metamorphoses* (iii. 173) to Diana as the sister of the Titan Sol. *The Maydes Metamorphosis*, a play attributed to Lyly, although not printed till 1600, may be

[1] *New Shakspere Society's Transactions*, 1880–86, p. 67.

older than *A Midsummer Night's Dream*. In that case Shakespeare may have found the germ of some of his fairy dialogue in the pretty fairy song which occurs in it. There is a marked similarity even in details of dialogue. For example, this conversation between Bottom and the fairies (iii. 1) reminds us of Lyly [1]:—

"*Bot.* I cry your worship's mercy, heartily.—I beseech your worship's name.

"*Cob.* Cobweb.

"*Bot.* I shall desire you of more acquaintance, good Master Cobweb. If I cut my finger, I shall make bold with you. Your name, honest gentleman?

"*Peas.* Pease-blossom.

"*Bot.* I pray you, commend me to Mistress Squash, your mother, and to Master Peascod, your father. Good Master Pease-blossom, I shall desire you of more acquaintance too.—Your name, I beseech you, sir.

"*Mus.* Mustard-seed.

"*Bot.* Good Master Mustard-seed, I know your patience well: that same cowardly, giant-like oxbeef hath devoured many a gentleman of your house. I promise you, your kindred hath made my eyes water ere now. I desire you of more acquaintance, good Master Mustard-seed."

The contrast between the rude artisans' prose and the poetry of the fairy world is exquisitely humorous, and has been frequently imitated in the nineteenth century: in Germany by Tieck; in Denmark by J. L. Heiberg, who has written no fewer than three imitations of *A Midsummer Night's Dream*—*The Elves*, *The Day of the Seven Sleepers*, and *The Nutcrackers*.

The fairy element introduced into the comedy brings in its train not only the many love-illusions, but other and external forms of thaumaturgy as well. People are beguiled by wandering voices, led astray in the midnight wood, and victimised in many innocent ways. The fairies retain from first to last their grace

---

[1] The passage in *The Maydes Metamorphosis* runs as follows:—

"*Mopso.* I pray you, what might I call you?
1st Fairy. My name is Penny.
Mopso. I am sorry I cannot purse you.
Frisco. I pray you, sir, what might I call you?
2nd Fairy. My name is Cricket.
Frisco. I would I were a chimney for your sake."

and sportiveness, but the individual physiognomies, in this stage of Shakespeare's development, are as yet somewhat lacking in expression. Puck, for instance, is a mere shadow in comparison with a creation of twenty years later, the immortal Ariel of *The Tempest.*

Brilliant as is the picture of the fairy world in *A Midsummer Night's Dream*, the mastery to which Shakespeare had attained is most clearly displayed in the burlesque scenes, dealing with the little band of worthy artisans who are moved to represent the history of Pyramus and Thisbe at the marriage of Theseus and Hippolyta. Never before has Shakespeare risen to the sparkling and genial humour with which these excellent simpletons are portrayed. He doubtless drew upon childish memories of the plays he had seen performed in the market-place at Coventry and elsewhere. He also introduced some whimsical strokes of satire upon the older English drama. For instance, when Quince says (i. 2), "Marry, our play is—The most lamentable comedy, and most cruel death of Pyramus and Thisby," there is an obvious reference to the long and quaint title of the old play of *Cambyses:* "A lamentable tragedy mixed full of pleasant mirth,"[1] &c.

Shakespeare's elevation of mind, however, is most clearly apparent in the playful irony with which he treats his own art, the art of acting, and the theatre of the day, with its scanty and imperfect appliances for the production of illusion. The artisan who plays Wall, his fellow who enacts Moonshine, and the excellent amateur who represents the Lion are deliciously whimsical types.

It was at all times a favourite device with Shakespeare, as with his imitators, the German romanticists of two centuries later, to introduce a play within a play. The device is not of his own invention. We find it already in Kyd's *Spanish Tragedie* (perhaps as early as 1584), a play whose fustian Shakespeare often ridicules, but in which he nevertheless found the germ of his own *Hamlet.* But from the very first the idea of giving an air of greater solidity to the principal play by introducing into it a company of actors had a great attraction for him. We may compare with the Pyramus and Thisbe scenes in this play the

---

[1] The passion for alliteration in his contemporaries is satirised in these lines of he prologue to *Pyramus and Thisbe:*—

"Whereat with blade, with bloody blameful blade,
He bravely broach'd his boiling bloody breast."

appearance of Costard and his comrades as Pompey, Hector, Alexander, Hercules, and Judas Maccabæus in the fifth act of *Love's Labour's Lost*. Even there the Princess speaks with a kindly tolerance of the poor amateur actors:—

> "That sport best pleases, that doth least know how:
> Where zeal strives to content, and the contents
> Die in the zeal of them which it presents,
> Their form confounded makes most form in mirth;
> When great things labouring perish in their birth."

Nevertheless, there is here a certain youthful cruelty in the courtiers' ridicule of the actors, whereas in *A Midsummer Night's Dream* everything passes off in the purest, airiest humour. What can be more perfect, for example, than the Lion's reassuring address to the ladies?—

> " 'You, ladies, you, whose gentle hearts do fear
> The smallest monstrous mouse that creeps on floor,
> May now, perchance, both quake and tremble here,
> When lion rough in wildest rage doth roar.
> Then know, that I, one Snug the joiner, am
> No lion fell, nor else no lion's dam:
> For, if I should as lion come in strife
> Into this place, 't were pity on my life.' "

And how pleasant, when he at last comes in with his roar, is Demetrius' comment, of proverbial fame, "Well roared, lion!"

It is true that *A Midsummer Night's Dream* is rather to be described as a dramatic lyric than a drama in the strict sense of the word. It is a lightly-flowing, sportive, lyrical fantasy, dealing with love as a dream, a fever, an illusion, an infatuation, and making merry, in especial, with the irrational nature of the instinct. That is why Lysander, turning, under the influence of the magic flower, from Hermia, whom he loves, to Helena, who is nothing to him, but whom he now imagines that he adores, is made to exclaim (ii. 3):—

> "The will of man is by his reason sway'd,
> And reason says you are the worthier maid."

Here, more than anywhere else, he is the mouthpiece of the poet's irony. Shakespeare is far from regarding love as an expression of human reason; throughout his works, indeed, it is only by way of exception that he makes reason the determining factor in human conduct. He early felt and divined how much wider is the domain of the unconscious than of the conscious life, and saw that our moods and passions have their root in the unconscious. The germs of a whole philosophy of life are latent in the wayward love-scenes of *A Midsummer Night's Dream*.

And it is now that Shakespeare, on the farther limit of early youth, and immediately after writing *A Midsummer Night's Dream*, for the second time takes the most potent of youthful emotions as his theme, and treats it no longer as a thing of fantasy, but as a matter of the deadliest moment, as a glowing, entrancing, and annihilating passion, the source of bliss and agony, of life and death. It is now that he writes his first independent tragedy, *Romeo and Juliet*, that unique, imperishable love-poem, which remains to this day one of the loftiest summits of the world's literature. As *A Midsummer Night's Dream* is the triumph of grace, so *Romeo and Juliet* is the apotheosis of pure passion.

XIII

ROMEO AND JULIET—THE TWO QUARTOS—ITS ROMANESQUE STRUCTURE—THE USE OF OLD MOTIVES—THE CONCEPTION OF LOVE

Romeo and Juliet, in its original form, must be presumed to date from 1591, or, in other words, from Shakespeare's twenty-seventh year.

The matter was old; it is to be found in a novel by Masuccio of Salerno, published in 1476, which was probably made use of by Luigi da Porta when, in 1530, he wrote his *Hystoria novellamente ritrovata di dui nobili Amanti*. After him came Bandello, with his tale, *La sfortunata morte di due infelicissimi amanti;* and upon it an English writer founded a play of *Romeo and Juliet*, which seems to have been popular in its day (before 1562), but is now lost.

An English poet, Arthur Brooke, found in Bandello's *Novella* the matter for a poem: *The tragicall Historye of Romeus and Juliet, written first in Italian by Bandell and now in Englishe by Ar. Br.* This poem is composed in rhymed iambic verses of twelve and fourteen syllables alternately, whose rhythm indeed jogs somewhat heavily along, but is not unpleasant and not too monotonous. The method of narration is very artless, loquacious, and diffuse; it resembles the narrative style of a clever child, who describes with minute exactitude and circumstantiality, going into every detail, and placing them all upon the same plane.[1]

Shakespeare founded his play upon this poem, in which the

[1] Here is a specimen. Romeo says to Juliet—

" Since, lady, that you like to honor me so much
As to accept me for your spouse, I yeld my selfe for such.
In true witness whereof, because I must depart,
Till that my deed do prove my woord, I leave in pawne my hart.
Tomorrow eke bestimes, before the sunne arise,
To Fryer Lawrence will I wende, to learne his sage advise."

two leading characters, Friar Laurence, Mercutio, Tybalt, the Nurse, and the Apothecary, were ready to his hand, in faint outlines. Romeo's fancy for another woman immediately before he meets Juliet is also here, set forth at length; and the action as a whole follows the same course as in the tragedy.

The First Quarto of *Romeo and Juliet* was published in 1597, with the following title: *An excellent conceited Tragedie of Romeo and Juliet. As it hath been often (with great applause) plaid publiquely, by the right Honourable the L. of Hunsdon his Seruants.* Lord Hunsdon died in July 1596, during his tenure of office as Lord Chamberlain; his successor in the title was appointed to the office in April 1597; in the interim his company of actors was not called the Lord Chamberlain's, but only Lord Hunsdon's servants, and it must, therefore, have been at this time that the play was first acted.

Many things, however, suggest a much earlier origin for it, and the Nurse's allusion to the earthquake (i. 3) is of especial importance in determining its date. She says—

" 'Tis since the earthquake now eleven years;"

and a little later—

" And since that time it is eleven years."

There had been an earthquake in England in the year 1580. But we must not, of course, take too literally the babble of a garrulous old servant.

But even if Shakespeare began to work upon the theme in 1591, there is no doubt that, according to his frequent practice, he went through the play again, revised and remoulded it, somewhere between that date and 1599, when it appeared in the Second Quarto almost in the form in which we now possess it. This Second Quarto has on its title-page the words, "newly corrected, augmented and amended." Not until the fourth edition does the author's name appear.

No one can doubt that Tycho Mommsen and that excellent Shakespeare scholar Halliwell-Phillips are right in declaring the 1597 Quarto to be a pirated edition. But it by no means follows that the complete text of 1599 already existed in 1597, and was merely carelessly abridged. In view of those passages (such as the seventh scene of the second act) where a whole long sequence of dialogue is omitted as superfluous, and where the old text is replaced by one totally new and very much better, this impression will not hold ground.

We have here, then, as elsewhere—but seldom so indubitably and obviously as here—a play of Shakespeare's at two different stages of its development.

In the first place, all that is merely sketched in the earlier edition is elaborated in the later. Descriptive scenes and speeches, which afford a background and foil to the action, are added. The street skirmish in the beginning is much developed; the scene between the servants and the scene with the musicians are added. The Nurse, too, has become more loquacious and much more comic; Mercutio's wit has been enriched by some of its most characteristic touches; old Capulet has acquired a more lifelike physiognomy; the part of Friar Laurence, in particular, has grown to almost twice its original dimensions; and we feel in these amplifications that care on Shakespeare's part, which appears in other places as well, to prepare, in the course of revision, for what is to come, to lay its foundations and foreshadow it. The Friar's reply, for example, to Romeo's vehement outburst of joy (ii. 6) is an added touch:—

"These violent delights have violent ends,
And in their triumphs die: like fire and powder,
Which, as they kiss, consume."

New, too, is his reflection on Juliet's lightness of foot:—

"A lover may bestride the gossamer
That idles in the wanton summer air,
And yet not fall; so light is vanity."

With the exception of the first dozen lines, the Friar's splendidly eloquent speech to Romeo (iii. 3) when, in his despair, he has drawn his sword to kill himself, is almost entirely new. The added passage begins thus:—

"Why rail'st thou on thy birth, the heaven, and earth?
Since birth, and heaven, and earth, all three do meet
In thee at once, which thou at once wouldst lose.
Fie, fie! thou sham'st thy shape, thy love, thy wit;
Which, like an usurer, abound'st in all,

And usest none in that true use indeed
Which should bedeck thy shape, thy love, thy wit."

New, too, is the Friar's minute description to Juliet (iv. 1) of the action of the sleeping-draught, and his account of how she will be borne to the tomb, which paves the way for the masterly passage (iv. 3), also added, where Juliet, with the potion in her hand, conquers her terror of awakening in the grisly underground vault.

But the essential change lies in the additional earnestness, and consequent beauty, with which the characters of the two lovers have been endowed in the course of the revision. For example, Juliet's speech to Romeo (ii. 2) is inserted:—

"And yet I wish but for the thing I have.
My bounty is as boundless as the sea,
My love as deep; the more I give to thee,
The more I have, for both are infinite."

In the passage (ii. 5) where Juliet is awaiting the return of the Nurse with a message from Romeo, almost the whole expression of her impatience is new; for example, the lines:—

"Had she affections, and warm youthful blood,
She'd be as swift in motion as a ball;
My words would bandy her to my sweet love,
And his to me:
But old folks, many feign as they were dead;
Unwieldy, slow, heavy and pale as lead."

In Juliet's celebrated soliloquy (iii. 2), where, with that mixture of innocence and passion which forms the groundwork of her character, she awaits Romeo's first evening visit, only the four opening lines, with their mythological imagery, are found in the earlier text:—

"*Jul.* Gallop apace, you fiery-footed steeds,
Towards Phœbus' lodging: such a waggoner
As Phaethon would whip you to the west,
And bring in cloudy night immediately."

Not till he put his final touches to the work did Shakespeare find for the young girl's love-longing that marvellous utterance which we all know:—

> "Spread thy close curtain, love-performing night!
> That runaways' eyes may wink, and Romeo
> Leap to these arms, untalk'd-of, and unseen!
>
> . . . . . .
>
> Hood my unmann'd blood, bating in my cheeks,
> With thy black mantle; till strange love, grown bold,
> Think true love acted simple modesty.
> Come, night! come, Romeo! come, thou day in night!"

Almost the whole of the following scene between the Nurse and Juliet, in which she learns of Tybalt's death and Romeo's banishment, is likewise new. Here occur some of the most daring and passionate expressions which Shakespeare has placed in Juliet's mouth:—

> "Some word there was, worser than Tybalt's death,
> That murder'd me. I would forget it fain.
>
> . . . . . .
>
> That 'banished,' that one word 'banished,'
> Hath slain ten thousand Tybalts. Tybalt's death
> Was woe enough, if it had ended there:
> Or,—if sour woe delights in fellowship,
> And needly will be rank'd with other griefs,—
> Why follow'd not, when she said—Tybalt's dead,
> Thy father, or thy mother, nay, or both,
> Which modern lamentation might have mov'd?
> But, with a rearward following Tybalt's death,
> 'Romeo is banished!'—to speak that word,
> Is father, mother, Tybalt, Romeo, Juliet,
> All slain, all dead."

To the original version, on the other hand, belong not only the highly indecorous witticisms and allusions with which Mercutio garnishes the first scene of the second act, but also the majority of the speeches in which the conceit-virus rages. The uncertainty of Shakespeare's taste, even at the date of the revision, is apparent in the fact that he has not only let all these speeches stand, but has interpolated not a few of equal extravagance.

So little did it jar upon him that Romeo, in the original text, should thus apostrophise love (i. 1):—

> "O heavy lightness! serious vanity!
> Misshapen chaos of well-seeming forms!

> Feather of lead, bright smoke, cold fire, sick health!
> Still-waking sleep, that is not what it is!"

that in the course of revision he must needs place in Juliet's mouth these quite analogous ejaculations (iii. 2):—

> "Beautiful tyrant! fiend angelical!
> Dove-feather'd raven! wolvish-ravening lamb!
> Despised substance of divinest show!"

Romeo in the old text indulges in this deplorably affected outburst (i. 2):—

> "When the devout religion of mine eye
> Maintains such falsehood, then turn tears to fires;
> And these, who, often drown'd, could never die,
> Transparent heretics, be burnt for liars."

In the old text, too, we find the barbarously tasteless speech in which Romeo, in his despair, envies the fly which is free to kiss Juliet's hand (iii. 2):—

> "More validity,
> More honourable state, more courtship lives
> In carrion flies, than Romeo: they may seize
> On the white wonder of dear Juliet's hand,
> And steal immortal blessing from her lips;
> Who, even in pure and vestal modesty,
> Still blush, as thinking their own kisses sin;
> But Romeo may not; he is banished.
> Flies may do this, but I from this must fly:
> They are free men, but I am banished."

It is astonishing to come upon these lapses of taste, which are not surpassed by any of the absurdities in which the French *Précieuses Ridicules* of the next century delighted, side by side with outbursts of the most exquisite lyric poetry, the most brilliant wit, and the purest pathos to be found in the literature of any country or of any age.

Romeo and Juliet is perhaps not such a flawless work of art as *A Midsummer Night's Dream*. It is not so delicately, so absolutely harmonious. But it is an achievement of much greater significance and moment; it is the great and typical love-tragedy of the world.

It soars immeasurably above all later attempts to approach it.

The Danish critic who should mention such a tragedy as *Axel and Valborg* in the same breath with this play would show more patriotism than artistic sense. Beautiful as Oehlenschläger's drama is, the very nature of its theme forbids us to compare it with Shakespeare's. It celebrates constancy rather than love; it is a poem of tender emotions, of womanly magnanimity and chivalrous virtue, at war with passion and malignity. It is not, like *Romeo and Juliet*, at once the pæan and the dirge of passion.

Romeo and Juliet is the drama of youthful and impulsive love-at-first-sight, so passionate that it bursts every barrier in its path, so determined that it knows no middle way between happiness and death, so strong that it throws the lovers into each other's arms with scarcely a moment's pause, and, lastly, so ill-fated that death follows straightway upon the ecstasy of union.

Here, more than anywhere else, has Shakespeare shown in all its intensity the dual action of an absorbing love in filling the soul with gladness to the point of intoxication, and, at the same time, with despair at the very idea of parting.

While in *A Midsummer Night's Dream* he dealt with the imaginative side of love, its fantastic and illusive phases, he here regards it in its more passionate aspect, as the source of rapture and of doom.

His material enabled Shakespeare to place his love-story in the setting best fitted to throw into relief the beauty of the emotion, using as his background a vendetta between two noble families, which has grown from generation to generation through one sanguinary reprisal after another, until it has gradually infected the whole town around them. According to the traditions of their race, the lovers ought to hate each other. The fact that, on the contrary, they are so passionately drawn together in mutual ecstasy, bears witness from the outset to the strength of an emotion which not only neutralises prejudice in their own minds, but continues to assert itself in opposition to the prejudices of their surroundings. This is no peaceful tenderness. It flashes forth like lightning at their first meeting, and its violence, under the hapless circumstances, hurries these young souls straight to their tragic end.

Between the lovers and the haters Shakespeare has placed Friar Laurence, one of his most delightful embodiments of reason.

Such figures are rare in his plays, as they are in life, but ought not to be overlooked, as they have been, for example, by Taine in his somewhat one-sided estimate of Shakespeare's greatness. Shakespeare knows and understands passionlessness; but he always places it on the second plane. It comes in very naturally here, in the person of one who is obliged by his age and his calling to act as an onlooker in the drama of life. Friar Laurence is full of goodness and natural piety, a monk such as Spinoza or Goethe would have loved, an undogmatic sage, with the astuteness and benevolent Jesuitism of an old confessor—brought up on the milk and bread of philosophy, not on the fiery liquors of religious fanaticism.

It is very characteristic of the freedom of spirit which Shakespeare early acquired, in the sphere in which freedom was then hardest of attainment, that this monk is drawn with so delicate a touch, without the smallest ill-will towards conquered Catholicism, yet without the smallest leaning towards Catholic doctrine —the emancipated creation of an emancipated poet. The poet here rises immeasurably above his original, Arthur Brooke, who, in his naïvely moralising "Address to the Reader," makes the Catholic religion mainly responsible for the impatient passion of Romeo and Juliet and the disasters which result from it.[1]

It would be to misunderstand the whole spirit of the play if we were to reproach Friar Laurence with the not only romantic but preposterous nature of the means he adopts to help the lovers —the sleeping-potion administered to Juliet. This Shakespeare simply accepted from his original, with his usual indifference to external detail.

The poet has placed in the mouth of Friar Laurence a tranquil life-philosophy, which he first expresses in general terms, and then applies to the case of the lovers. He enters his cell with a basket full of herbs from the garden. Some of them have curative properties, others contain death-dealing juices; a plant which has a sweet and salutary smell may be poisonous to the taste; for good and evil are but two sides to the same thing (ii. 3):—

---

[1] "A coople of vnfortunate louers, thralling themselues to vnhonest desire, neglecting the authoritie and aduise of parents and frendes, conferring their principall counsels with dronken gossyppes and superstitious friers (the naturally fitte instrumentes of unchastitie), attemptyng all aduentures of peryll for thattaynyng of their wished lust, vsyng auriculer confession (the key of whoredom and treason). . . ."

"Virtue itself turns vice, being misapplied,
And vice sometimes 's by action dignified.
Within the infant rind of this sweet flower
Poison hath residence, and medicine power:
For this, being smelt, with that part cheers each part;
Being tasted, slays all senses with the heart.
Two such opposed kings encamp them still
In man as well as herbs,—grace, and rude will;
And where the worser is predominant,
Full soon the canker death eats up that plant."

When Romeo, immediately before the marriage, defies sorrow and death in the speech beginning (ii. 6)—

"Amen, Amen! but come what sorrow can,
It cannot countervail the exchange of joy
That one short minute gives me in her sight,"

Laurence seizes the opportunity to apply his view of life. He fears this overflowing flood-tide of happiness, and expounds his philosophy of the golden mean—that wisdom of old age which is summed up in the cautious maxim, "Love me little, love me long." Here it is that he utters the above-quoted words as to the violent ends ensuing on violent delights, like the mutual destruction wrought by the kiss of fire and gunpowder. It is remarkable how the idea of gunpowder and of explosions seems to have haunted Shakespeare's mind while he was busied with the fate of Romeo and Juliet. In the original sketch of Juliet's soliloquy in the fifth scene of the second act we read:—

"Loue's heralds should be thoughts,
And runne more swift, than hastie powder fierd,
Doth hurrie from the fearfull cannons mouth."

When Romeo draws his sword to kill himself, the Friar says (iii. 3):—

"Thy wit, that ornament to shape and love,
Misshapen in the conduct of them both,
Like powder in a skilless soldier's flask,
Is set a-fire by thine own ignorance,
And thou dismember'd with thine own defence."

Romeo himself, finally, in his despair over the false news of Juliet's death, demands of the apothecary a poison so strong that

"the trunk may be discharg'd of breath
As violently, as the hasty powder fir'd,
Doth hurry from the fatal cannon's womb."

In other words, these young creatures have gunpowder in their veins, undamped as yet by the mists of life, and love is the fire which kindles it. / Their catastrophe is inevitable, and it was Shakespeare's deliberate purpose so to represent it; but it is not deserved, in the moral sense of the word: it is not a punishment for guilt.' The tragedy does not afford the smallest warranty for the pedantically moralising interpretation devised for it by Gervinus and others.

Romeo and Juliet, as a drama, still represents in many ways the Italianising tendency in Shakespeare's art. Not only the rhymed couplets and stanzas and the abounding *concetti* betray Italian influence: the whole structure of the tragedy is very Romanesque. All Romanesque, like all Greek art, produces its effect by dint of order, which sometimes goes the length of actual symmetry. Purely English art has more of the freedom of life itself; it breaks up symmetry in order to attain a more delicate and unobtrusive harmony, much as an excellent prose style shuns the symmetrical regularity of verse, and aims at a subtler music of its own.

The Romanesque type is apparent in all Shakespeare's earlier plays. He sometimes even goes beyond his Romanesque models. In *Love's Labour's Lost* the King with his three courtiers is opposed to the Princess and her three ladies. In *The Two Gentlemen of Verona* the faithful Valentine has his counterpart in the faithless Proteus, and each of them has his comic servant. In the *Menæchmi* of Plautus there is only one slave; in *The Comedy of Errors* the twin masters have twin servants. In *A Midsummer Night's Dream* the heroic couple (Theseus and Hippolyta) have as a counterpart the fairy couple (Oberon and Titania); and, further, there is a complex symmetry in the fortunes of the Athenian lovers, Hermia being at first wooed by two men, while Helena stands alone and deserted, whereas afterwards it is Hermia who is left without a lover, while the two men centre their suit upon Helena. Finally, there is a fifth couple in Pyramus and Thisbe, represented by the artisans, who in burlesque and sportive fashion complete the symmetrical design.

The French critics who have seen in Shakespeare the antithesis to the Romanesque principle in art have overlooked these his beginnings. Voltaire, after more careful study, need not have expressed himself horrified; and if Taine, in his able essay, had gone somewhat less summarily to work, he would not have found everywhere in Shakespeare a fantasy and a technique entirely foreign to the genius of the Latin races.

The composition of *Romeo and Juliet* is quite as symmetrical as that of the comedies, indeed almost architectural in its equipoise. First, two of Capulet's servants enter, then two of Montague's; then Benvolio, of the Montague party; then Tybalt, of the Capulets; then citizens of both parties; then old Capulet and his wife; then old Montague and his; and finally, as the "keystone of the arch," the Prince, the central figure around whom all the characters range themselves, and by whom the fate of the lovers is to be determined.[1]

But it is not as a drama that *Romeo and Juliet* has won all hearts. Although, from a dramatic point of view, it stands high above *A Midsummer Night's Dream*, yet it is in virtue of its exquisite lyrism that this erotic masterpiece of Shakespeare's youth, like its fantastic predecessor, has bewitched the world. It is from the lyrical portions of the tragedy that the magic of romance proceeds, which sheds its glamour and its glory over the whole.

The finest lyrical passages are these: Romeo's declaration of love at the ball, Juliet's soliloquy before their bridal night, and their parting at the dawn.

Gervinus, a conscientious and learned student, in spite of his tendency to see in Shakespeare the moralist specially demanded by the Germany of his own day, has followed Halpin in pointing out that in all these three passages Shakespeare has adopted age-old lyric forms. In the first he almost reproduces the Italian sonnet; in the second he approaches, both in matter and form, to the bridal song, the Epithalamium; in the third he takes as his model the mediæval Dawn-Song, the *Tagelied*. But we may be sure that Shakespeare did not, as the commentators think, deliberately choose these forms in order to give perspective to the situation, but instinctively gave it a deep and distant background in his effort to find the truest and largest utterance for the emotion he was portraying.

[1] See Dowden: *Shakspere: his Mind and Art*, p. 60.

The first colloquy between Romeo and Juliet (i. 5), being merely the artistic idealisation of an ordinary passage of ballroom gallantry, turns upon the prayer for a kiss, which the English fashion of the day authorised each cavalier to demand of his lady, and is cast in a sonnet form more or less directly derived from Petrarch. But whereas Petrarch's style is simple and pure, here we have far-fetched turns of speech, quibbling appeals, and expressions of admiration suggested by the intellect rather than the feelings. The passage opens with a quatrain of unspeakable tenderness:—

> "*Romeo.* If I profane with my unworthiest hand
> This holy shrine, the gentle fine is this;
> My lips, two blushing pilgrims, ready stand
> To smooth that rough touch with a tender kiss."

And though the scene proceeds in the somewhat artificial style of the later Italians—

> "*Romeo.* Thus from my lips, by thine, my sin is purg'd.
> [*Kissing her.*]
> *Juliet.* Then have my lips the sin that they have took.
> *Rom.* Sin from my lips? O trespass sweetly urg'd!
> Give me my sin again.
> *Jul.*   You kiss by the book"

—yet so much soul is breathed into the Italian love-fencing that under its somewhat affected grace we can distinguish the pulse-throbs of awakening desire.

Juliet's soliloquy before the bridal night (iii. 2) lacks only rhyme to be, in good set form, an epithalamium of the period. These compositions spoke of Hymen and Cupid, and told how Hymen at first appears alone, while Cupid lurks concealed, until, at the door of the bridal chamber, the elder brother gives place to the younger.

It is noteworthy that the mythological opening lines, which belong to the earlier form of the play, contain a clear reminiscence of a passage in Marlowe's *King Edward II.* Marlowe's

> "Gallop apace, bright Phœbus, through the sky!"

reappears in Shakespeare in the form of

> "Gallop apace, you fiery-footed steeds,
> Towards Phœbus' lodging!"

The rest of the soliloquy, as we have seen above, ranks among the loveliest things Shakespeare ever wrote. One of its most delicately daring expressions is imitated in Milton's *Comus;* and the difference between the original and the imitation is curiously typical of the difference between the poet of the Renaissance and the poet of Puritanism. Juliet implores love-performing night to spread its close curtain, that Romeo may leap unseen to her arms; for—

> "Lovers can see to do their amorous rites
> By their own beauties ; or, if love be blind,
> It best agrees with night."

Milton annexes the thought and the turn of phrase; but the part played by beauty in Shakespeare, Milton assigns to virtue :—

> " Virtue could see to do what virtue would
> By her own radiant light."

There is in Juliet's utterance of passion a healthful delicacy that ennobles it; and it need not be said that the presence of this very passion in Juliet's monologue renders it infinitely more chaste than the old epithalamiums.

The exquisite dialogue in Juliet's chamber at daybreak (iii. 5) is a variation on the motive of all the old Dawn-Songs. They always turn upon the struggle in the breasts of two lovers who have secretly passed the night together, between their reluctance to part and their dread of discovery—a struggle which sets them debating whether the light they see comes from the sun or the moon, and whether it is the nightingale or the lark whose song they hear.

How gracefully is this motive here employed, and what added depth is given to the situation by our knowledge that the banished Romeo's life is forfeit if he lingers until day!—

> "*Juliet.* Wilt thou be gone? it is not yet near day:
> It was the nightingale, and not the lark,
> That pierc'd the fearful hollow of thine ear;
> Nightly she sings on yon pomegranate-tree :
> Believe me, love, it was the nightingale.
>   *Romeo.* It was the lark, the herald of the morn,
> No nightingale : look, love, what envious streaks
> Do lace the severing clouds in yonder east."

Romeo is a well-born youth, richly endowed by nature, enthusiastic and reserved. At the beginning of the play we find him indifferent as to the family feud, and absorbed in his hopeless fancy for a lady of the hostile house, Capulet's fair niece, Rosaline, whom Mercutio describes as a pale wench with black eyes. The Rosaline of *Love's Labour's Lost* is also described by Biron, at the end of the third act, as

"A whitely wanton with a velvet brow,
With two pitch-balls stuck in her face for eyes,"

so that the two namesakes may not improbably have had a common model.

Shakespeare has retained this first passing fancy of Romeo's, which he found in his sources, because he knew that the heart is never more disposed to yield to a new love than when it is bleeding from an old wound, and because this early feeling already shows Romeo as inclined to idolatry and self-absorption. The young Italian, even before he has seen the woman who is to be his fate, is reticent and melancholy, full of tender longings and forebodings of evil. Then he is seized as though with an overwhelming ecstasy at the first glimpse of Rosaline's girl-kinswoman.

Romeo's character is less resolute than Juliet's; passion ravages it more fiercely; he, as a youth, has less control over himself than she as a maiden. But none the less is his whole nature elevated and beautified by his relation to her. He finds expressions for his love for Juliet quite different from those he had used in the case of Rosaline. There occur, indeed, in the balcony scene, one or two outbursts of the extravagance so natural to the rhetoric of young love. The envious moon is sick and pale with grief because Juliet is so much more fair than she; two of the fairest stars, having some business, do entreat her eyes to twinkle in their spheres till they return. But side by side with these conceits we find immortal lines, the most exquisite words of love that ever were penned:—

"With love's light wings did I o'erperch these walls;
For stony limits cannot hold love out . . ."

or—

"It is my soul that calls upon my name:
How silver-sweet sound lovers' tongues by night,
Like softest music to attending ears!"

His every word is steeped in a sensuous-spiritual ecstasy.

Juliet has grown up in an unquiet and not too agreeable home. Her testy, unreasonable father, though not devoid of kindliness, is yet so brutal that he threatens to beat her and turn her out of doors if she does not comply with his wishes; and her mother is a cold-hearted woman, whose first thought, in her rage against Romeo, is to have him put out of the way by means of poison. She has thus been left for the most part to the care of the humorous and plain-spoken Nurse, one of Shakespeare's most masterly figures (foretelling the Falstaff of a few years later), whose babble has tended to prepare her mind for love in its frankest manifestations.

Although a child in years, Juliet has the young Italian's mastery in dissimulation. When her mother proposes to have Romeo poisoned, she agrees without moving a muscle, and thus secures the promise that no one but she shall be allowed to mix the potion. Her beauty must be conceived as dazzling. I saw her one day in the streets of Rome, in all the freshness of her fourteen years. My companion and I looked at each other, and exclaimed with one consent, "Juliet!" Romeo's exclamation on first beholding her—

"Beauty too rich for use, for earth too dear,"

conveys an instant impression of nobility, high mental gifts, and unsullied purity, combined with the utmost ardour of temperament. In a few days the child ripens into a heroine.

We make acquaintance with her at the ball in the palace of the Capulets, and in the moonlit garden where the nightingale sings in the pomegranate-tree—surroundings which harmonise as completely with the whole spirit and tone of the play as the biting wintry air on the terrace at Kronborg, filled with echoes of the King's carouse, harmonises with the spirit and tone of *Hamlet*. But Juliet is no mere creature of moonshine. She is practical. While Romeo wanders off into high-strung raptures of vague enthusiasm, she, on the contrary, promptly suggests a secret marriage, and promises on the instant to send the Nurse to him to make a more definite arrangement. After the killing of her kinsman, it is Romeo who despairs and she who takes up the battle, daring all to escape the marriage with Paris. With a firm hand and a steadfast heart she drains the sleeping-potion, and arms herself with her dagger, so that, if all else fails, she may still be mistress of her own person.

How shall we describe the love that indues her with all this strength?

Modern critics in Germany and Sweden are agreed in regarding it as a purely sensual passion, by no means admirable—nay, essentially reprehensible. They insist that there is a total absence of maidenly modesty in Juliet's manner of feeling, thinking, speaking, and acting. She does not really know Romeo, they say; is there anything more, then, in this unbashful love than the attraction of mere bodily beauty?[1]

As if it were possible thus to analyse and discriminate! As if, in such a case, body and soul were twain! As if a love which, from the first moment, both lovers feel to be, for them, the arbiter of life and death, were to be decried in favour of an affection founded on mutual esteem—the variety which, it appears, "our age demands."

Ah no! these virtuous philosophers and worthy professors have no feeling for the spirit of the Renaissance: they are altogether too remote from it. The Renaissance means, among many other things, a new birth of warm-blooded humanity and pagan innocence of imagination.

It is no love of the head that Juliet feels for Romeo, no admiring affection that she reasons herself into; nor is it a sentimental love, a riot of idealism apart from nature. But still less is it a mere ferment of the senses. It is based upon instinct, the infallible instinct of the child of nature, and it is in her, as in him, a vibration of the whole being in longing and desire, a quivering

---

[1] Edward von Hartmann, from the lofty standpoint of German morality, has launched a diatribe against Juliet. He asserts her immeasurable moral inferiority to the typical German maiden, both of poetry and of real life. Schiller's Thekla has undeniably less warm blood in her veins.

A Swedish professor, Henrik Schück, in an able work on Shakespeare, says of Juliet: "On examining into the nature of the love to which she owes all this strength, the unprejudiced reader cannot but recognise in it a purely sensual passion. . . . A few words from the lips of this well-favoured youth are sufficient to awaken in its fullest strength the slumbering desire in her breast. But this love possesses no psychical basis; it is not founded on any harmony of souls. They scarcely know each other. . . . Can their love, then, be anything more than the merely sensual passion aroused by the contemplation of a beautiful body? . . . So much I say with confidence, that the woman who, inaccessible to the spiritual element in love, lets herself be carried away on this first meeting by the joy of the senses . that woman is ignorant of the love which our age demands."

of all its chords, from the highest to the lowest, so intense that neither he nor she can tell where body ends and soul begins.

Romeo and Juliet dominate the whole tragedy; but the two minor creations of Mercutio and the Nurse are in no way inferior to them in artistic value. In this play Shakespeare manifests for the first time not only the full majesty but the many-sidedness of his genius, the suppleness of style which is equal at once to the wit of Mercutio and to the racy garrulity of the Nurse. *Titus Andronicus* was as monotonously sombre as a tragedy of Marlowe's. *Romeo and Juliet* is a perfect orb, embracing the twin hemispheres of the tragic and the comic. It is a symphony so rich that the strain from fairyland in the Queen Mab speech harmonises with the note of high comedy in Mercutio's sparkling, cynical, and audacious sallies, with the wanton flutings of farce in the Nurse's anecdotes, with the most rapturous descants of passion in the antiphonies of Romeo and Juliet, and with the deep organ-tones in the soliloquies and speeches of Friar Laurence.

How intense is the life of Romeo and Juliet in their environment! Hark to the gay and yet warlike hubbub around them, the sport and merriment, the high words and the ring of steel in the streets of Verona! Hark to the Nurse's strident laughter, old Capulet's jesting and chiding, the low tones of the Friar, and the irrepressible rattle of Mercutio's wit! Feel the magic of the whole atmosphere in which they are plunged, these embodiments of tumultuous youth, living and dying in love, in magnanimity, in passion, in despair, under a glowing Southern sky, softening into moonlight nights of sultry fragrance—and realise that Shakespeare had at this point completed the first stage of his triumphal progress!

XIV

LATTER-DAY ATTACKS UPON SHAKESPEARE—THE BACONIAN THEORY — SHAKESPEARE'S KNOWLEDGE, PHYSICAL AND PHILOSOPHICAL

IN one of his sonnets Robert Browning says that Shakespeare's name, like the Hebrew name of God, ought never to be taken in vain. A timely monition to an age which has seen this great name besmirched by American and European imbecility!

It is well known that in recent days a troop of less than half-educated people have put forth the doctrine that Shakespeare lent his name to a body of poetry with which he had really nothing to do — which he could not have understood, much less have written. Literary criticism is an instrument which, like all delicate tools, must be handled carefully, and only by those who have a vocation for it. Here it has fallen into the hands of raw Americans and fanatical women. Feminine criticism on the one hand, with its lack of artistic nerve, and Americanism on the other hand, with its lack of spiritual delicacy, have declared war to the knife against Shakespeare's personality, and have within the last few years found a considerable number of adherents. We have here another proof, if any were needed, that the judgment of the multitude, in questions of art, is a negligible quantity.[1]

Before the middle of this century, it had occurred to no human being to doubt that—trifling exceptions apart—the works attributed to Shakespeare were actually written by him. It has been

---

[1] According to W. H. Wyman's *Bibliography of the Bacon-Shakespeare Controversy* (Cincinnati, 1884), there had been published up to that date 255 books, pamphlets, and essays as to the authorship of Shakespeare's plays. In America 161 treatises of considerable bulk had been devoted to the question, and in England 69. Of these, 73 were decidedly opposed to Shakespeare's authorship, while 65 left the question undetermined. In other words, out of 161 books, only 23 were in favour of Shakespeare. And since then the proportion has no doubt remained much the same.

ATTACKS UPON SHAKESPEARE 105

reserved for the last forty years to see an ever-increasing stream of obloquy and contempt directed against what had hitherto been the most honoured name in modern literature.

At first the attack upon Shakespeare's memory was not so dogmatic as it has since become. In 1848 an American, Hart by name, gave utterance to some general doubts as to the origin of the plays. Then, in August 1852, there appeared in *Chambers's Edinburgh Journal* an anonymous article, the author of which declared his conviction that William Shakespeare, uneducated as he was, must have hired a poet, some penniless famished Chatterton, who was willing to sell him his genius, and let him take to himself the credit for its creations. We see, he says, that his plays steadily improve as the series proceeds, until suddenly Shakespeare leaves London with a fortune, and the series comes to an abrupt end. In the case of so strenuously progressive a genius, can we account for this otherwise than by supposing that the poet had died, while his employer survived him?

This is the first definite expression of the fancy that Shakespeare was only a man of straw who had arrogated to himself the renown of an unknown immortal.

In 1856 a Mr. William Smith issued a privately-printed letter to Lord Ellesmere, in which he puts forth the opinion that William Shakespeare was, by reason of his birth, his upbringing, and his lack of culture, incapable of writing the plays attributed to him. They must have been the work of a man educated to the highest point by study, travel, knowledge of books and men—a man like Francis Bacon, the greatest Englishman of his time. Bacon had kept his authorship secret, because to have avowed it would have been to sacrifice his position both in his profession and in Parliament; but he saw in these plays a means of strengthening his economic position, and he used the actor Shakespeare as a man of straw. Smith maintains that it was Bacon who, after having fallen into disgrace in 1621, published the First Folio edition of the plays in 1623.

If there were no other objection to this far-fetched theory, we cannot but remark that Bacon was scrupulously careful as to the form in which his works appeared, rewrote them over and over again, and corrected them so carefully that scarcely a single error of the press is to be found in his books. Can he have been responsible for the publication of these thirty-six plays, which swarm with misreadings and contain about twenty thousand errors of the press!

The delusion did not take serious shape until, in the same year, a Miss Delia Bacon put forward the same theory in American magazines: her namesake Bacon, and not Shakespeare, was the author of the renowned dramas. In the following year she published a quite unreadable book on the subject, of nearly 600 pages. And close upon her heels followed her disciple, Judge Nathaniel Holmes, also an American, with a book of no fewer than 696 pages, full of denunciations of the ignorant vagabond William Shakespeare, who, though he could scarcely write his own name and knew no other ambition than that of money-grubbing, had appropriated half the renown of the great Bacon.

The assumption is always the same: Shakespeare, born in a provincial town, of illiterate parents, his father being, among other things, a butcher, was an ignorant boor, a low fellow, a "butcher-boy," as his assailants currently call him. In Holmes, as in later writers, the main method of proving Bacon's authorship of the Shakespearian plays is to bring together passages of somewhat similar import in Bacon and Shakespeare, in total disregard of context, form, or spirit.

Miss Delia Bacon literally dedicated her life to her attack upon Shakespeare. She saw in his works, not poetry, but a great philosophico-political system, and maintained that the proof of her doctrine would be found deposited in Shakespeare's grave. She had discovered in Bacon's letters the key to a cipher which would clear up everything; but unfortunately she became insane before she had imparted this key to the world.[1] She went to Stratford, obtained permission to have the grave opened, hovered about it day and night, but at last left it undisturbed, as it did not appear to her large enough to contain the posthumous papers of the Elizabeth Club. She did not, however, expect to find in the

---

[1] One of her many followers, an American lawyer, Ignatius Donnelly, formerly Member of Congress and Senator from Minnesota, claims to have found the key. His crazy book is called *The Great Cryptogram: Francis Bacon's Cipher in the so-called Shakespeare Plays*. It sets forth how Bacon embodied in the First Folio a cipher-confession of his authorship. Apart from the general madness of such a proceeding, Bacon must thus have made the editors, Heminge and Condell, his accomplices in his meaningless deception, and must even have induced Ben Jonson to confirm it by his enthusiastic introductory poem.

grave the original manuscripts of Shakespeare's plays. No! she exclaims in her article on "William Shakespeare and his Plays" (*Putnam's Magazine*, January 1856), Lord Leicester's groom, of course, cared nothing for them, but only for the profit to be made out of them. What was to prevent him from lighting the fire with them? "He had those manuscripts! . . . He had the original *Hamlet* with its last finish; he had the original *Lear* with his own final readings; he had them all, as they came from the gods. . . . And he left us to wear out our youth and squander our lifetime in poring over and setting right the old garbled copies of the playhouse! . . . Traitor and miscreant! what did you do with them? You have skulked this question long enough. You will have to account for them. . . . The awakening ages will put you on the stand, and you will not leave it until you answer the question, 'What did you do with them?'"

It is hard to be the greatest dramatic genius in the world's history, and then, two centuries and a half after your death, to be called to account in such a tone as this for the fact that your manuscripts have disappeared. As regards purely external evidence, it is worth mentioning that the greatest student of Bacon's works, his editor and biographer, James Spedding, being challenged by Holmes to give his opinion, made a statement which begins thus:—"I have read your book on the authorship of Shakespeare faithfully to the end, and . . . I must declare myself not only unconvinced but undisturbed. To ask me to believe that 'Bacon was the author of these dramas' is like asking me to believe that Lord Brougham was the author not only of Dickens' novels, but of Thackeray's also, and of Tennyson's poems besides. I deny," he concludes, "that a *primâ facie* case is made out for questioning Shakespeare's title. But if there were any reason for supposing that somebody else was the real author, I think I am in a condition to say that, whoever it was, it was not Bacon" (*Reviews and Discussions*, 1879, pp. 369–374).

What most amazes a critical reader of the Baconian impertinences is the fact that all the different arguments for the impossibility of attributing these plays to Shakespeare are founded upon the universality of knowledge and insight displayed in them, which must have been unattainable, it is urged, to a man of Shakespeare's imperfect scholastic training. Thus all that these detractors bring forward to Shakespeare's dishonour serves, rightly considered, to show in a clearer light the wealth of his genius.

On the other hand, the arguments adduced in support of Bacon's authorship are so ridiculous as almost to elude criticism. Opponents of the doctrine have dwelt upon such details as the philistinism of Bacon's essays "Of Love," "Of Marriage and Single Life," contrasted with the depth and the wit of Shakesperian utterances on these subjects; or they have cited certain lines from the miserable translations of seven Hebrew psalms which Bacon produced in the last years of his life, contrasting them with passages from *Richard III.* and *Hamlet,* in which Shakespeare has dealt with exactly similar ideas — the harvest that follows from a seed-time of tears, and the leaping to light of secret crimes. But it is a waste of time to go into details. Any one who has read even a few of Bacon's essays or a stanza or two of his verse translations, and who can discover in them any trace of Shakespeare's style in prose or verse, is no more fitted to have a voice on such questions than an inland bumpkin is fitted to lay down the law upon navigation.

Even putting aside the conjecture with regard to Bacon, and looking merely at the theory that Shakespeare did not write the plays, we cannot but find it unrivalled in its ineptitude. How can we conceive that not only contemporaries in general, but those with whom Shakespeare was in daily intercourse — the players to whom he gave these dramas for production, who received his instructions about them, who saw his manuscripts and have described them to us (in the foreword to the First Folio); the dramatists who were constantly with him, his rivals and afterwards his comrades, like Drayton and Ben Jonson; the people who discussed his works with him in the theatre, or, over the evening glass, debated with him concerning his art; and, finally, the young noblemen whom his genius attracted and who became his patrons and afterwards his friends—how can we conceive that none of these, no single one, should ever have observed that he was not the man he pretended to be, and that he did not even understand the works he fraudulently declared to be his! How can we conceive that none of all this intelligent and critical circle should ever have discovered the yawning gulf which separated his ordinary thought and speech from the thought and style of his alleged works!

In sum, then, the only evidence against Shakespeare lies in the fact that his works give proof of a too many-sided knowledge and insight!

The knowledge of English law which Shakespeare displays is so surprising as to have led to the belief that he must for some time in his youth have been a clerk in an attorney's office—a theory which was thought to be supported by the belief, now discredited, that an attack by the satirist Thomas Nash upon lawyers who had deserted the law for poetry was directed against him.[1]

Shakespeare shows a quite unusual fondness for the use of legal expressions. He knows to a nicety the technicalities of the bar, the formulas of the bench. While most English writers of his period are guilty of frequent blunders as to the laws of marriage and inheritance, lawyers of a later date have not succeeded in finding in Shakespeare's references to the law a single error or deficiency. Lord Campbell, an eminent lawyer, has written a book on *Shakespeare's Legal Acquirements*. And it was not through the lawsuits of Shakespeare's riper years that he attained this knowledge. It is to be found even in his earliest works. It appears, quaintly enough, in the mouth of the goddess in *Venus and Adonis* (verse 86, &c.), and it obtrudes itself in Sonnet xlvi., with its somewhat tasteless and wire-drawn description of a formal lawsuit between the eye and the heart. It is characteristic that his knowledge does not extend to the laws of foreign countries; otherwise we should scarcely find *Measure for Measure* founded upon such an impossible state of the law as that which is described as obtaining in Vienna. Shakespeare's accurate knowledge begins and ends with what comes within the sphere of his personal observation.

He seems equally at home in all departments of human life. If we might conclude from his knowledge of law that he had been

---

[1] The passage runs thus: "It is a common practice now a days among a sort of shifting companions that run through every art and thrive by none, to leave the trade of *noverint*, whereto they were born, and busy themselves with the endeavours of art, that could scarcely latinize their neck-verse if they should have need; yet English Seneca, read by candlelight, yields many good sentences, as *Blood is a beggar*, and so forth; and if you entreat him fair in a frosty morning, he will afford you whole *Hamlets*, I should say handfuls, of tragical speeches." Although this passage seems at first sight an evident gibe at Shakespeare, it has in reality no reference to him, since *An Epistle to the Gentlemen Students of both Universities*, by Thomas Nash, although not printed till 1589, can be proved to have been written as early as 1587, many years before Shakespeare so much as thought of *Hamlet*.

a lawyer, we might no less confidently infer from his knowledge of typography that he had been a printer's devil. An English printer named Blades has written an instructive book, *Shakespeare and Typography*, to show that if the poet had passed his whole life in a printing-office he could not have been more familiar with the many peculiarities of nomenclature belonging to the handicraft. Bishop Charles Wordsworth has written a highly esteemed, very pious, but, I regret to say, quite unreadable work, *Shakespeare's Knowledge and Use of the Bible*, in which he makes out that the poet was impregnated with the Biblical spirit, and possessed a unique acquaintance with Biblical forms of expression.

Shakespeare's knowledge of nature is not simply such as can be acquired by any one who passes his childhood and youth in the open air and in the country. But even of this sort of knowledge he has an astonishing store. Whole books have been written as to his familiarity with insect life alone (R. Patterson: *The Natural History of the Insects mentioned by Shakespeare;* London, 1841), and his knowledge of the characteristics of the larger animals and birds seems to be inexhaustible. Appleton Morgan, one of the champions of the Baconian theory, adduces in *The Shakespearean Myth* a whole series of examples.

In *Much Ado* (v. 2) Benedick says to Margaret—

"Thy wit is as quick as the greyhound's mouth; it catches."

The greyhound alone among dogs can seize its prey while in full career.

In *As You Like It* (i. 2) Celia says—

"Here comes Monsieur Le Beau.
  Rosalind. With his mouth full of news.
  Celia. Which he will put on us as pigeons feed their young."

Pigeons have a way, peculiar to themselves, of passing food down the throats of their young.

In *Twelfth Night* (iii. 1) the Clown says to Viola—

"Fools are as like husbands, as pilchards are to herrings,—the husband's the bigger."

The pilchard is a fish of the herring family, which is caught in the Channel; it is longer and has larger scales.

In the same play (ii. 5) Maria says of Malvolio—

"Here comes the trout that must be caught with tickling."

When a trout is tickled on the sides or the belly it becomes so stupefied that it lets itself be caught in the hand.

In *Much Ado* (iii. 1) Hero says—

"For look where Beatrice, like a lapwing, runs
Close by the ground, to hear our conference."

The lapwing, which runs very swiftly, bends its neck towards the ground in running, in order to escape observation.

In *King Lear* (i. 4) the Fool says—

"The hedge-sparrow fed the cuckoo so long,
That it had its head bit off by its young."

In England, it is in the hedge-sparrow's nest that the cuckoo lays its eggs.

In *All's Well that Ends Well* (ii. 5) Lafeu says—

"I took this lark for a bunting."

The English bunting is a bird of the same colour and appearance as the lark, but it does not sing so well.

It would be easy to show that Shakespeare was as familiar with the characteristics of plants as with those of animals. Strangely enough, people have thought this knowledge of nature so improbable in a great poet, that in order to explain it they have jumped at the conclusion that the author must have been a man of science as well.

More comprehensible is the astonishment which has been awakened by Shakespeare's insight in other domains of nature not lying so open to immediate observation. His medical knowledge early attracted attention. In 1860 a Doctor Bucknill devoted a whole book to the subject, in which he goes so far as to attribute to the poet the most advanced knowledge of our own time, or, at any rate, of the 'sixties, in this department. Shakespeare's representations of madness surpass all those of other poets. Alienists are full of admiration for the accuracy of the symptoms in Lear and Ophelia. Nay, more, Shakespeare appears to have divined the more intelligent modern treatment of the insane, as opposed to the cruelty prevalent in his own time and long after.

He even had some notions of what we in our days call medical jurisprudence; he was familiar with the symptoms of violent death in contradistinction to death from natural causes. Warwick says in the second part of *Henry VI.* (iii. 2):—

> "See, how the blood is settled in his face.
> Oft have I seen a timely-parted ghost,
> Of ashy semblance, meagre, pale, and bloodless,
> Being all descended to the labouring heart."

These lines occur in the oldest text. In the later text, undoubtedly the result of Shakespeare's revision, we read:—

> "But see, his face is black, and full of blood;
> His eye-balls further out than when he liv'd,
> Staring full ghastly like a strangled man:
> His hair uprear'd, his nostrils stretch'd with struggling;
> His hands abroad display'd, as one that grasp'd
> And tugg'd for life, and was by strength subdued.
> Look, on the sheets, his hair, you see, is sticking;
> His well-proportion'd beard made rough and rugged,
> Like to the summer's corn by tempest lodg'd.
> It cannot be but he was murder'd here;
> The least of all these signs were probable."

Shakespeare seems, in certain instances, to be not only abreast of the natural science of his time, but in advance of it. People have had recourse to the Baconian theory in order to explain the surprising fact that although Harvey, who is commonly represented as the discoverer of the circulation of the blood, did not announce his discovery until 1619, and published his book upon it so late as 1628, yet Shakespeare, who, as we know, died in 1616, in many passages of his plays alludes to the blood as circulating through the body. Thus, for example, in *Julius Cæsar* (ii. 1), Brutus says to Portia—

> "You are my true and honourable wife;
> As dear to me as are the ruddy drops
> That visit my sad heart."

Again, in *Coriolanus* (i. 1) Menenius makes the belly say of its food—

> "I send it through the rivers of your blood,
> Even to the court, the heart, to the seat o' the brain;

And, through the cranks and offices of man,
The strongest nerves, and small inferior veins,
From me receive that natural competency
Whereby they live."

But apart from the fact that the highly gifted and unhappy Servetus, whom Calvin burned, had, between 1530 and 1540, made the discovery and lectured upon it, all men of culture in England knew very well before Harvey's time that the blood flowed, even that it circulated, and, more particularly, that it was driven from the heart to the different limbs and organs ; only, it was generally conceived that the blood passed from the heart through the veins, and not, as is actually the case, through the arteries. And there is nothing in the seventy-odd places in Shakespeare where the circulation of the blood is mentioned to show that he possessed this ultimate insight, although his general understanding of these questions bears witness to his high culture.

Another point which some people have held inexplicable, except by the Baconian theory, may be stated thus: Although the law of gravitation was first discovered by Newton, who was born in 1642, or fully twenty-six years after Shakespeare's death, and although the general conception of gravitation towards the centre of the earth had been unknown before Kepler, who discovered his third law of the mechanism of the heavenly bodies two years after Shakespeare's death, nevertheless in *Troilus and Cressida* (iv. 2) the heroine thus expresses herself :—

"Time, force, and death,
Do to this body what extremes you can,
But the strong base and building of my love
Is as the very centre of the earth,
Drawing all things to it."

So carelessly does Shakespeare throw out such an extraordinary divination. His achievement in thus, as it were, rivalling Newton may seem in a certain sense even more extraordinary than Goethe's botanical and osteological discoveries ; for Goethe had enjoyed a very different education from his, and had, moreover, all desirable leisure for scientific research. But Newton cannot rightly be said to have discovered the law of gravitation ; he only applied it to the movements of the heavenly bodies. Even Aristotle had defined weight as "the striving of heavy bodies towards the centre of the earth." Among men of classical culture in England in Shakespeare's time, the knowledge that the centre point of the earth attracts everything to it was quite common. The passage cited only affords an additional proof that several of the men whose society Shakespeare frequented were among the most highly-developed intellects of the period. That his astronomical knowledge was not, on the whole, in advance of his time is proved by the expression, "the glorious planet Sol" in *Troilus and Cressida* (i. 3). He never got beyond the Ptolemaic system.

Another confirmation of the theory that Bacon must have written Shakespeare's plays has been found in the fact that the poet clearly had some conception of geology; whereas geology, as a science, owes its origin to Niels Steno, who was born in 1638, twenty-two years after Shakespeare's death. In the second part of *Henry IV*. (iii. 1), King Henry says:—

> "O God! that one might read the book of fate,
> And see the revolution of the times
> Make mountains level, and the continent,
> Weary of solid firmness, melt itself
> Into the sea! and, other times, to see
> The beachy girdle of the ocean
> Too wide for Neptune's hips; how chances mock,
> And changes fill the cup of alteration
> With divers liquors!"

The purport of this passage is simply to show that in nature, as in human life, the law of transformation reigns; but no doubt it is implied that the history of the earth can be read in the earth itself, and that changes occur through upheavals and depressions. It looks like a forecast of the doctrine of Neptunism.

Here, again, people have gone to extremities in order artificially to enhance the impression made by the poet's brilliant divination. It was Steno who first systematised geological conceptions; but he was by no means the first to hold that the earth had been formed little by little, and that it was therefore possible to trace in the record of the rocks the course of the earth's development. His chief service lay in directing attention to stratification, as affording the best evidence of the processes which have fashioned the crust of the globe.

It is, no doubt, a sign of Shakespeare's many-sided genius that here, too, he anticipates the scientific vision of later times; but there is nothing in these lines that presupposes any special or technical knowledge. Here is an analogous case: In Michael Angelo's picture of the creation of Adam, where God wakens the first man to life by touching the figure's outstretched finger-tip with his own, we seem to see a clear divination of the electric spark. Yet the induction of electricity was not known until the eighteenth century, and Michael Angelo could not possibly have any scientific understanding of its nature.

Shakespeare's knowledge was not of a scientific cast. He learned from men and from books with the rapidity of genius. Not, we may be sure, without energetic effort, for nothing can be had for nothing; but the effort of acquisition must have come easy to him, and must have escaped the observation of all around him. There was no time in his life for patient research; he had to devote the best part of his days to the theatre, to uneducated and unconsidered players, to entertainments, to the tavern. We may fancy that he must have had himself in mind when, in the introductory scene to *Henry V.*, he makes the Archbishop of Canterbury thus describe his hero, the young king:—

> "Hear him but reason in divinity,
> And, all-admiring, with an inward wish
> You would desire the king were made a prelate:
> Hear him debate of commonwealth affairs,
> You would say, it hath been all-in-all his study:
> List his discourse of war, and you shall hear
> A fearful battle render'd you in music:
> Turn him to any cause of policy,
> The Gordian knot of it he will unloose,
> Familiar as his garter; that, when he speaks,
> The air, a charter'd libertine, is still,
> And the mute wonder lurketh in men's ears,
> To steal his sweet and honey'd sentences;
> So that the art and practic part of life
> Must be the mistress to this theoric:
> Which is a wonder, how his grace should glean it,
> Since his addiction was to courses vain;
> His companies unletter'd, rude, and shallow;
> His hours fill'd up with riots, banquets, sports;
> And never noted in him any study,

Any retirement, any sequestration
From open haunts and popularity."

To this the Bishop of Ely answers very sagely, "The strawberry grows underneath the nettle." We cannot but conceive, however, that, by a beneficent provision of destiny, Shakespeare's genius found in the highest culture of his day precisely the nourishment it required.

XV

*THE THEATRES—THEIR SITUATION AND ARRANGEMENTS—
THE PLAYERS—THE POETS—POPULAR AUDIENCES—THE
ARISTOCRATIC PUBLIC—SHAKESPEARE'S ARISTOCRATIC
PRINCIPLES*

ON swampy ground beside the Thames lay the theatres, of which the largest were wooden sheds, only half thatched with rushes, with a trench around them and a flagstaff on the roof. After the middle of the fifteen-seventies, when the first was built, they shot up rapidly, and in the early years of the new century theatre-building took such a start that, as we learn from Prynne's *Histriomastix*, there were in 1633 no fewer than nineteen permanent theatres in London, a number which no modern town of 300,000 inhabitants can equal. These figures show how keen and how widespread was the interest in the drama.

More than a hundred years before the first theatre was built there had been professional actors in England. Their calling had developed from that of the travelling jugglers, who varied their acrobatic performances with "plays." The earliest scenic representations had been given by the Church, and the Guilds had inherited the tradition. Priests and choir-boys were the first actors of the Middle Ages, and after them came the mummers of the Guilds. But none of these performers acted except at periodical festivals; none of them were professional actors. From the days of Henry the Sixth onwards, however, members of the nobility began to entertain companies of actors, and Henry VII. and Henry VIII. had their own private comedians. A "Master of the Revels" was appointed to superintend the musical and dramatic entertainments at court. About the middle of the sixteenth century, Parliament begins to keep an eye upon theatrical representations. It forbids the performance of anything conflicting with the doctrines of the Church, and prohibits miracle-plays, but does not object to songs or plays designed to attack vice and represent virtue. In other words, dramatic art escapes condemnation when it is emphatically moral, and thrives best when it keeps to purely secular matters.

Under Mary, religious plays once more came into honour. Elizabeth began by strictly prohibiting all dramatic representations, but sanctioned them again in 1560, subjecting them, however, to a censorship. This measure was dictated at least as much by political as by religious motives. The censorship must, however, have been exercised somewhat loosely, since a statute of 1572 declared that all actors who were not attached to the service of a nobleman should be treated as "rogues and vagabonds," or, in other words, might be whipped out of any town in which they appeared. This decree, of course, compelled all actors to enter the service of one or other great man, and we see that the aristocracy felt bound to protect their art. A large number of the first men in the kingdom, during Elizabeth's reign, had each his company of actors. The player received from the nobleman whose "servant" he was a cloak bearing the arms of the family. On the other hand, he received no salary, but was simply paid for each performance given before his patron. We must thus conceive Shakespeare as bearing on his cloak the arms of Leicester, and afterwards of the Lord Chamberlain, until about his fortieth year. From 1604 onwards, when the company was promoted by James I. to be "His Majesty's Servants," it was the Royal arms that he wore. One is tempted to say that he exchanged a livery for a uniform.

In 1574 Elizabeth had given permission to Lord Leicester's Servants to give scenic representations of all sorts for the delectation of herself and her lieges, both in London and anywhere else in England. But neither in London nor in other towns did the local authorities recognise this patent, and the hostile attitude of the Corporation of London forced the players to erect their theatres outside its jurisdiction. For if they played in the City itself, as had been the custom, either in the great halls of the Guilds or in the open inn-yards, they had to obtain the Lord Mayor's sanction for each individual performance, and to hand over half their receipts to the City treasury.

It was with anything but satisfaction that the peaceable burgesses of London saw a playhouse rise in the neighbourhood of their homes. The theatre brought in its train a loose, frivolous, and rowdy population. Around the playhouses, at the hours of performance, the narrow streets of that period became so crowded that business suffered in the shops, processions and funerals were obstructed, and perpetual causes of complaint arose. Houses of ill-fame, moreover, always clustered round a theatre; and, although the performances took place by day, there was always the danger of fire inseparable from theatres, and especially from wooden erections with thatched roofs.

But the chief opposition to the theatres did not come from the mere Philistinism of the industrious middle-class, but from the fanatical Puritanism which was now rearing its head. It is the Puritans who have killed the old Merry England, abolishing its May-games, its popular dances, its numerous rustic sports. They could not look on with equanimity, and see the drama, which had once been a spiritual institution, become a platform for mere worldliness.

Their chief accusation against the dramatic poets was that they lied. For intelligences of this order, there was no difference between a fiction and a falsehood. The players they attacked on the ground that when they played female parts they appeared in women's attire, which was expressly forbidden in the Bible (Deut. xxii. 5) as an abomination to the Lord. They saw in this masquerading in the guise of the other sex a symptom of unnatural and degrading vices. They not only despised the actors as jugglers and loathed them as persons living beyond the pale of respectability, but they further accused them of cultivating in private all the vices which they were in the habit of portraying on the stage.

There can be no doubt that from a very early period the influence of Puritanism made itself felt in the attitude of the City authorities.

It can easily be understood, then, that the leaders of the new theatrical industry tried to escape from their jurisdiction; and this they did by choosing sites outside the City, and yet as near its boundaries as possible. To the south of the Thames lay a stretch of land not belonging to the City but to the Bishop of Winchester, a spiritual magnate who tried to make his territory as profitable as he could without inquiring too closely as to the uses to which it was put. Here lay the Bear Garden; here were numerous houses of ill-fame; and here arose the different theatres, the "Hope," the "Swan," the "Rose," &c. When James Burbage's successors, in the year 1598, found themselves compelled, after a lawsuit, to pull down the building known as the Theatre (in Bishopsgate Street), they employed the material to erect on this artistic no-man's-land the celebrated Globe Theatre, which was opened in 1599.

The theatres were of two classes, one known as private, the other as public, a distinction which was at one time rather obscure, since the difference was clearly not that admission to the private theatres took place by invitation, and to the public ones by payment. A nobleman could hire any theatre, whether private or public, and engage the company to give a performance for him and his invited guests. The real distinction was, that the private theatres were designed on the model of the Guildhalls or Town Halls, in which, before the period of special buildings, representations had been given; while the public theatres were constructed on the lines of the inn-yard. The private theatres, then, were fully roofed, and, being the more fashionable, had seats in every part of the house, including the parterre, here known as the pit. Being roofed, they could be used not only in the daytime, but by artificial light. In the public theatres, on the other hand, as in ancient Greece and to this day in the Tyrol, only the stage was roofed, the auditorium being open to the sky, so that performances could be given only by daylight. But in Greece the air is pure, the climate mild; in the Tyrol performances take place only on a few summer days. Here plays were acted while rain and snow fell upon the spectators, fogs enwrapped them, and the wind plucked at their garments. As the prototype of these theatres was the old inn-yard, in which some of the spectators stood, while others were seated in the open galleries running all round it, the parterre, which retained the name of *yard*, was here devoted to the poorest and roughest of the public, who stood throughout the performance, while the galleries (*scaffolds*), running along the walls in two or three tiers, offered seats to wealthier playgoers of both sexes.

The days of performance at these theatres were announced by the hoisting of a flag on the roof. The time of beginning was three o'clock punctually, and the performance went straight on, uninterrupted by entr'actes. It lasted, as a rule, for only two hours or two hours and a half.

Close to the Globe Theatre lay the Bear Garden, the rank smell from which greeted the nostrils, even before it came in sight. The famous bear Sackerson, who is mentioned in *The Merry Wives of Windsor*, now and then broke his chain and put female theatre-goers shrieking to flight.

Tickets there were none. A penny was the price of admission to standing-room in the yard; and those who wanted better places put their money in a box held out to them for that purpose, the amount varying from a penny to half-a-crown, in accordance with the places required. When we remember that one shilling of Queen Elizabeth's was equivalent to five of Queen Victoria's, the price of the dearer places seems very considerable in comparison with those current to-day. The wealthiest spectators gave more than twelve shillings (in modern money) for their places in the proscenium-boxes on each side of the stage. At the Globe Theatre the orchestra was placed in the upper proscenium-box on the right; it was the largest in London, consisting of ten performers, all distinguished in their several lines, playing lutes, oboes, trumpets, and drums.

The most fashionable seats were on the stage itself, approached, not by the ordinary entrances, but through the players' tiring-room. There sat the amateurs, the noble patrons of the theatre, Essex, Southampton, Pembroke, Rutland; there snobs, upstarts, and fops took their places on chairs or stools; if there were not seats enough, they spread their cloaks upon the pine-sprigs that strewed the boards, and (like Bracchiano in Webster's *Vittoria Corombona*) lay upon them. There, too, sat the author's rivals, the dramatic poets, who had free admissions; and there, lastly, sat the shorthand writers, commissioned by piratical booksellers, who, under pretence of making critical notes, secretly took down the dialogue —men who were a nuisance to the players and, as a rule, a thorn in the side to the poets, but to whom posterity no doubt owes the preservation of many plays which would otherwise have been lost.

All these notabilities on the stage carry on half-audible conversations, and make the servitors of the theatre bring them drinks and light their pipes, while the actors can with difficulty thread their way among them—arrangements which cannot have heightened the illusion, but perhaps did less to mar it than we might imagine.

For the audience is not easily disturbed, and does not demand any of the illusion which is supplied by modern mechanism. Movable scenery was unknown before 1660. The walls of the stage were either hung with loose tapestries or quite uncovered, so that the wooden doors which led to the players' tiring-rooms at the back were clearly visible. In battle-scenes, whole armies entered triumphant, or were driven off in confusion and defeat, through a single door. When a tragedy was acted the stage was usually hung with black; for a comedy the hangings were blue.

As in the theatre of antiquity, rude machines were employed to raise or lower actors through the stage; trap-doors were certainly in use, and probably "bridges," or small platforms, which could be elevated into the upper regions. In somewhat earlier times still ruder appliances had been in vogue. For example, in the religious and allegorical plays, Hell-mouth was represented by a huge face of painted canvas with shining eyes, a large red nose, and movable jaws set with tusks. When the jaws opened, they seemed to shoot out flames, torches being no doubt waved behind them. The theatrical property-room of that time was incomplete without a "rybbe colleryd red" for the mystery of the Creation. But in Shakespeare's day scarcely anything of this sort was required. It was Inigo Jones who first introduced movable scenery and decorations at the court entertainments. They were certainly not in use at the popular playhouses at any time during Shakespeare's connection with the stage.

Audiences felt no need for such aids to illusion; their imagination instantly supplied the want. They saw whatever the poet required them to see—as a child sees whatever is suggested to its fancy, as little girls see real-life dramas in their games with their dolls. For the spectators were children alike in the freshness and in the force of their imagination. If only a placard were hung on one of the doors of the stage bearing in large letters the name of Paris or of Venice, the spectators were at once transported to France or Italy. Sometimes the Prologue informed them where the scene was placed. Men of classical culture, who insisted on unity of place in the drama, were offended by the continual changes of scene and the pitiful appliances by which they were indicated. Sir Philip Sidney, in his *Defense of Poesy*, published in 1583, ridicules the plays in which "You shall have Asia of the one side, and Afric of the other, and so many other under-kingdoms, that the player, when he cometh in, must ever begin with telling where he is, or else the tale will not be conceived."

This alacrity of imagination on the part of popular audiences was unquestionably an advantage to the English stage in its youth. If an actor made a movement as though he were plucking a flower, the scene was at once understood to be a garden; as in *Henry VI.*, where the adoption of the red rose and white rose as party badges is represented. If an actor spoke as though he were standing on a ship's deck in a heavy sea, the convention was at once accepted; as in the famous scene in *Pericles* (iii. 2). Shakespeare, though he did not hesitate to take advantage of this accommodating humour on the part of his public, and made no attempt at illusive decoration, nevertheless ridiculed, as we have seen, in *A Midsummer Night's Dream*, the meagre scenic apparatus of his time (especially, we may suppose, on the provincial stage); while in the Prologue to his *Henry V.* he deplores and apologises for the narrowness of his stage and the poverty of his resources :—

> "Pardon, gentles all,
> The flat unraised spirits that have dar'd
> On this unworthy scaffold to bring forth
> So great an object : can this cockpit hold
> The vasty fields of France? or may we cram
> Within this wooden O the very casques,
> That did affright the air at Agincourt?
> O, pardon! since a crooked figure may
> Attest in little place a million ;
> And let us, ciphers to this great accompt,
> On your imaginary forces work.
> Suppose, within the girdle of these walls
> Are now confin'd two mighty monarchies."

These monarchies, then, were mounted in a frame formed of young noblemen, critics and stage-struck gallants, who bantered the boy-heroines, fingered the embroideries on the costumes, smoked their clay pipes, and otherwise made themselves entirely at their ease.

A curtain, which did not rise, but parted in the middle, separated the stage from the auditorium.

The only extant drawing of the interior of an Elizabethan

theatre was recently discovered by Karl Gaedertz in the University Library at Utrecht. It is a sketch of the Swan Theatre, executed in 1596 by the Dutch scholar, Jan de Witt. The stage, resting upon strong posts, has no other furniture than a single bench, on which one of the performers is seated. The background is formed by the tiring-house, into which two doors lead. Over it is a roofed balcony, which could be used, no doubt, both by the players and by the audience. Above the roof of the tiring-house rises a second story, crowned by a sort of hutch, over which waves a flag bearing the image of a swan. At an open door of the hutch is seen a trumpeter giving a signal of some sort. The theatre is oval in shape, and has three tiers of seats, while the pit is left open for the standing " groundlings."

The balcony over the tiring-house answers in this case to the inner stage of other and better-equipped theatres.

This smaller raised platform at the back of the principal stage was exceedingly useful, and, in a certain measure, supplied the place of the scenic apparatus of later times. Tieck, who probably went further than any other critic in his dislike for modern mechanism and his enthusiasm for the primitive arrangements of Shakespeare's day, has elaborately reconstructed it in his novel, *Der junge Tischlermeister.*

In the middle of the deep stage, according to him, rose two wooden pillars, eight or ten feet high, which supported a sort of balcony. Three broad steps led from the front stage to the inner alcove under the balcony, which was sometimes open, sometimes curtained off. It represented, according to circumstances, a cave, a room, a summer-house, a family vault, and so forth. It was here that, in *Macbeth,* the ghost of Banquo appeared seated at the table. Here stood the bed on which Desdemona was smothered. Here, in *Hamlet,* the play within a play was acted. Here Gloucester's eyes were put out. On the balcony above, Juliet waited for her Romeo, and Sly took his place to see *The Taming of the Shrew.* When the siege of a town had to be represented, the defenders of the walls stood and parleyed on this balcony, while the assailants were grouped in the foreground.

It is probable that at each side a pretty broad flight of steps led up to this balcony. Here sat senates, councils, and princes with their courts. It needed but few figures to fill the inner stage, so narrow were its dimensions. Macbeth mounted these stairs, and so did Falstaff in the *Merry Wives*. Melancholy or contemplative personages leaned against the pillars. The structure offered a certain facility for effective groupings, somewhat like that in Raffaelle's " School of Athens." Figures in front did not obstruct the view of those behind, and groups gathered to the right and left of the main stage could, without an overstrain of make-believe, be supposed not to see each other.

The only department of decoration which involved any considerable expense was the costumes of the actors. On these such large sums were lavished that the Puritans made this extravagance one of their chief points of attack upon theatres. In Henslowe's Diary we find such entries as £4, 14s. for a pair of breeches, and £16 for a velvet cloak. It is even on record that a famous actor once gave £20, 10s. for a mantle. In an inventory of the property belonging to the Lord Admiral's Company in the year 1598, we find many splendid dresses enumerated: for example, " 1 payr of carnatyon satten Venesyons [breeches] layd with gold lace," and " 1 orenge taney [tawny] satten dublet, layd thycke with gowld lace."[1] The sums paid for these costumes are glaringly out of keeping with the paltry fees allotted to the author. Up to the year 1600 the ordinary price of a play was from five to six pounds—scarcely more than the cost of a pair of breeches to be worn by the actor who played the Prince or King.

In the boxes ("rooms") sat the better sort of spectators, officers, City merchants, sometimes with their wives; but ladies always wore a mask of silk or velvet, partly for protection against sun and air, partly in order to blush (or not to blush) unseen, at the frivolous and often licentious things that were said upon the stage. The mask was then as common an article of female attire as is the veil in our days. But the front rows of what we should now call the first tier were occupied by beauties who had no desire whatever to conceal their countenances, though they might use the mask (as in later times the fan) for purposes of coquetry. These were the kept mistresses of men of quality, and other gorgeously decked ladies, who resorted to the playhouse in order to make acquaintances. Behind them sat the respectable citizens. But in the gallery above a rougher public assembled—sailors, artisans, soldiers, and loose women of the lowest class.

No women ever appeared upon the stage.

[1] See Appendix to *Diary of Philip Henslowe* (Shakspere Society's Publications).

The frequenters of the pit, with their coarse boisterousness, were the terror of the actors. They all had to stand—coal-heavers and bricklayers, dock-labourers, serving-men, and idlers. Refreshment-sellers moved about among them, supplying them with sausages and ale, with apples and nuts. They ate and drank, drew corks, smoked tobacco, fought with each other, and often, when they were out of humour, threw fragments of food, and even stones, at the actors. Now and then they would come to loggerheads with the fine gentlemen on the stage, so that the performance had to be interrupted and the theatre closed. The sanitary arrangements were of the most primitive description, and the groundlings resisted all attempts at reform on the part of the management. When the evil smells became intolerable, juniper-berries were burnt by way of freshening the atmosphere.

The theatrical public made and executed its own laws. There was no police in the theatre. Now and then a pickpocket would be caught in the act, and tied to a post at the corner of the stage beside the railing which divided it from the auditorium.

The beginning of the performance was announced by three trumpet-blasts. The actor who spoke the Prologue appeared in a long cloak, with a laurel-wreath on his head, probably because this duty was originally performed by the poet himself. After the play, the Clown danced a jig, at the same time singing some comic jingle and accompanying himself on a small drum and flute. The Epilogue consisted of, or ended in, a prayer for the Queen, in which all the actors took part, kneeling.

Elizabeth herself and her court did not visit these theatres. There was no Royal box, and the public was too mixed. On the other hand, the Queen could, without derogating from her state, summon the players to court, and the Lord Chamberlain's Company, to which Shakespeare belonged, was very often commanded to perform before her, especially upon festivals such as Christmas Day, Twelfth Night, and so forth. Thus Shakespeare is known to have acted before the Queen in two comedies presented at Greenwich Palace at Christmas 1594. He is mentioned along with the leading actors, Burbage and Kemp.

Elizabeth paid for such performances a fee of twenty nobles, and a further gratuity of ten nobles—in all, £10.

As the Queen, however, was not content with thus witnessing plays at rare intervals, she formed companies of her own, the so-called Children's Companies, recruited from the choir-boys of the Chapels-Royal, whose music-schools thus developed, as it were, into nurseries for the stage. These half-grown boys, who were, of course, specially fitted to represent female characters, won no small favour, both at court and with the public; and we see that one such troupe, consisting of the choir-boys of St. Paul's, for some time competed, at the Blackfriars Theatre, with Shakespeare's company. We may gather from the bitter complaint in *Hamlet* (ii. 2) how serious was this competition:—

"*Hamlet.* Do they [the players] hold the same estimation they did when I was in the city? Are they so followed?

"*Rosencrantz.* No, indeed, they are not.

"*Ham.* How comes it? Do they grow rusty?

"*Ros.* Nay, their endeavour keeps in the wonted pace: but there is, sir, an aery of children, little eyases, that cry out on the top of question, and are most tyrannically clapped for 't: these are now the fashion; and so berattle the common stages (so they call them), that many wearing rapiers are afraid of goose-quills, and dare scarce come thither.

. . . .

"*Ham.* Do the boys carry it away?

"*Ros.* Ay, that they do, my lord; Hercules and his load too." [1]

The number of players in a company was not great—not more, as a rule, than eight or ten; never, probably, above twelve. The players were of different grades. The lowest were the so-called hirelings, who received wages from the others and were in some sense their servants. They appeared as supernumeraries or in small speaking parts, and had nothing to do with the management of the theatre. The actors, properly so called, differed in standing according as they shared in the receipts only as actors, or were entitled to a further share as part-proprietors of the theatre. There was no manager. The actors themselves decided what plays should be performed, distributed the parts, and divided the receipts according to an established scale. The most advantageous position, of course, was that of a shareholder in the theatre; for half of the gross receipts went to the shareholders, who provided the costumes and paid the wages of the hirelings.

Shakespeare's comparatively early rise to affluence can be

[1] A figure of Hercules with the globe on his shoulders served as sign to the Globe Theatre.

accounted for only by assuming that, in his dual capacity as poet and player, he must quickly have become a shareholder in the theatre.

As an actor he does not seem to have attained the highest eminence—fortunately, for if he had, he would probably have found very little time for writing. The parts he played appear to have been dignified characters of the second order; for there is no evidence that he was anything of a comedian. We know that he played the Ghost in *Hamlet*—a part of no great length, it is true, but of the first importance. It is probable, too, that he played old Adam in *As You Like It*, and pretty certain that he played old Knowell in Ben Jonson's *Every Man in His Humour*. It may possibly be in the costume of Knowell that he is represented in the well-known Droeshout portrait at the beginning of the First Folio. Tradition relates that he once played his own Henry IV. at court, and that the Queen, in passing over the stage, dropped her glove as a token of her favour, whereupon Shakespeare handed it back to her with the words:—

> "And though now bent on this high embassy,
> Yet stoop we to take up our cousin's glove."

In all lists of the players belonging to his company he is named among the first and most important.

Not least among the marvels connected with his genius is the fact that, with all his other occupations, he found time to write so much. His mornings would be given to rehearsals, his afternoons to the performances; he would have to read, revise, accept or reject a great number of plays; and he often passed his evenings either at the Mermaid Club or at some tavern; yet for eighteen years on end he managed to write, on an average, two plays a year—and such plays!

In order to understand this we have to recollect that although between 1557 and 1616 there were forty noteworthy and two hundred and thirty-three inferior English poets, who issued works in epic or lyric form, yet the characteristic of the period was the immense rush of productivity in the direction of dramatic art. Every Englishman of talent in Elizabeth's time could write a tolerable play, just as every second Greek in the age of Pericles could model a tolerable statue, or as every European of to-day can write a passable newspaper article. The Englishmen of that time were born dramatists, as the Greeks were born sculptors, and as we hapless moderns are born journalists. The Greek, with an inborn sense of form, had constant opportunities for observing the nude human body and admiring its beauty. If he saw a man ploughing a field, he received a hundred impressions and ideas as to the play of the muscles in the naked leg. The modern European possesses a certain command of language, is practised in argument, has a knack of putting thoughts and events into words, and is, finally, a confirmed newspaper-reader—all characteristics which make for the multiplication of newspaper articles. The Englishman of that day was keenly observant of human destinies, and of the passions which, after the fall of Catholicism and before the triumph of Puritanism, revelled in the brief freedom of the Renaissance. He was accustomed to see men following their instincts to the last extremity—which was not infrequently the block. The high culture of the age did not exclude violence, and this violence led to dramatic vicissitudes of fortune. It was but a short way from the palace to the scaffold —witness the fate of Henry VIII.'s wives, of Mary Stuart, of Elizabeth's great lovers, Essex and Raleigh. The Englishman of that age had always before his eyes pictures of extreme prosperity followed by sudden ruin and violent death. Life itself was dramatic, as in Greece it was plastic, as in our days it is journalistic, photographic—that is to say, striving in vain to give permanence to formless and everyday events and thoughts.

A dramatic poet in those days, no less than a journalist in ours, had to study his public closely. All the intellectual conflicts of the period were for sixty years fought out in the theatre, as they are nowadays in the press. Passionate controversies between one poet and another were cast in dramatic form. Rosencrantz says to Hamlet, "There was, for a while, no money bid for argument, unless the poet and the player went to cuffs in the question." The efflorescence of the drama on British soil was of short duration—as short as that of painting in Holland. But while it lasted the drama was the dominant art-form and medium of intellectual expression, and it was consequently supported by a large public.

Shakespeare never wrote a play "for the study," nor could he have imagined himself doing anything of the sort. As playwright and player in one, he had the stage always in his eye, and what he wrote had never long to wait for performance, but took scenic shape forthwith. Although, like all productive spirits, he thought first of satisfying himself in what he wrote, yet he must necessarily have borne in mind the public to whom the play appealed. He could by no means avoid considering the tastes of the average playgoer. The average playgoer, indeed, made no bad audience, but an audience which had to be amused, and which could not, for too long at a stretch, endure unrelieved seriousness or lofty flights of thought. For the sake of the common people, then, scenes of grandeur and refinement were interspersed with passages of burlesque. To please the many-headed, the Clown was brought on at every pause in the action, much as he is in the circus of to-day. The points of rest which are now marked by the fall of the curtain between the acts were then indicated by conversations such as that between Peter and the musicians in *Romeo and Juliet* (iv. 5); it merely implies that the act is over.

For the rest, Shakespeare did not write for the average spectator. He did not value his judgment. Hamlet says to the First Player (ii. 2):—

"I heard thee speak me a speech once,—but it was never acted; or, if it was, not above once; for the play, I remember, pleased not the million; 'twas caviare to the general: but it was (as I received it, and others, whose judgments in such matters cried in the top of mine) an excellent play."

All Shakespeare lies in the words, "It pleased not the million."

The English drama as it took shape under Shakespeare's hand addressed itself primarily to the best elements in the public. But "the best" were the noble young patrons of the theatre, to whom he personally owed a great deal of his culture, almost all his repute, and, moreover, the insight he had attained into the aristocratic habit of mind.

A young English nobleman of that period must have been one of the finest products of humanity, a combination of the Belvedere Apollo with a prize racehorse; he must have felt himself at once a man of action and an artist.

We have seen how early Shakespeare must have made the acquaintance of Essex, before his fall the mightiest of the mighty. He wrote *A Midsummer Night's Dream* for his marriage, and

SHAKESPEARE'S ARISTOCRATIC PRINCIPLES 131

he introduced a compliment to him into the Prologue to the fifth act of *Henry V*. England received her victorious King, he says—

> "As, by a lower but loving likelihood,
> Were now the general of our gracious empress
> (As, in good time, he may) from Ireland coming,
> Bringing rebellion broached on his sword,
> How many would the peaceful city quit,
> To welcome him!"

We have seen, moreover, how early and how intimate was his connection with the young Earl of Southampton, to whom he dedicated the only two books which he himself gave to the press.

It must have been from young aristocrats such as these that Shakespeare acquired his aristocratic method of regarding the course of history. How else could he regard it? A large part of the middle class was hostile to him, despised his calling, and treated him as one outside the pale; the clergy condemned and persecuted him; the common people were in his eyes devoid of judgment. The ordinary life of his day did not, on the whole, appeal to him. We find him totally opposed to the realistic dramatisation of everyday scenes and characters, to which many contemporary poets devoted themselves. This sort of truth to nature was foreign to him, so foreign that he suffered for lack of it. Towards the close of his artistic career he was outstripped in popularity by the realists of the day.

His heroes are princes and noblemen, the kings and barons of England. It is always they, in his eyes, who make history, of which he shows throughout a naïvely heroic conception. In the wars which he presents, it is always an individual leader and hero on whom everything depends. It is Henry V. who wins the day at Agincourt, just as in Homer it is Achilles who conquers before Troy. Yet the whole issue of these wars depended upon the foot-soldiers. It was the English archers, 14,000 in number, who at Agincourt defeated the French army of 50,000 men, with a loss of only 1600, as against 10,000 on the other side. Shakespeare certainly did not divine that it was the rise of the middle classes and their spirit of enterprise that constituted the strength of England under Elizabeth. He regarded his age from the point of view of the man who was accustomed to see in richly endowed and princely young noblemen the very crown of humanity, the patrons of all lofty effort, and the originators of all great achievements. And, with his necessarily scanty historic culture, he saw bygone periods, of Roman as well as of English history, in the same light as his own times.

This tendency appears already in the second part of *Henry VI*. Note the picture of Jack Cade's rebellion (iv. 2), which contains some inimitable touches:—

"*Cade.* Be brave then; for your captain is brave, and vows reformation. There shall be in England seven halfpenny loaves sold for a penny; the three-hooped pot shall have ten hoops; and I will make it felony to drink small beer. All the realm shall be in common, and in Cheapside shall my palfrey go to grass. And, when I am king (as king I will be),—

"*All.* God save your majesty!

"*Cade.* I thank you, good people:—there shall be no money; all shall eat and drink on my score; and I will apparel them all in one livery, that they may agree like brothers, and worship me their lord.

"*Dick.* The first thing we do, let's kill all the lawyers.

"*Cade.* Nay, that I mean to do. Is not this a lamentable thing, that of the skin of an innocent lamb should be made parchment? that parchment, being scribbled o'er, should undo a man?

. . . . .

"*Enter some, bringing in the Clerk of Chatham.*

"*Smith.* The clerk of Chatham: he can write and read, and cast accompt.

"*Cade.* O monstrous!

"*Smith.* We took him setting of boys' copies.

"*Cade.* Here's a villain!

"*Smith.* Has a book in his pocket, with red letters in 't.

. . . .

"*Cade.* Let me alone.—Dost thou use to write thy name, or hast thou a mark to thyself, like an honest plain-dealing man?

"*Clerk.* Sir, I thank God, I have been so well brought up, that I can write my name.

"*All.* He hath confessed: away with him! he's a villain and a traitor.

"*Cade.* Away with him, I say: hang him with his pen and ink-horn about his neck."

What is so remarkable and instructive in these brilliant scenes is that Shakespeare here, quite against his custom, departs from his authority. In Holinshed, Jack Cade and his followers do not

SHAKESPEARE'S ARISTOCRATIC PRINCIPLES

appear at all as the crazy Calibans whom Shakespeare depicts. The chief of their grievances, in fact, was that the King alienated the crown revenues and lived on the taxes; and, moreover, they complained of abuses of all sorts in the execution of the laws and the raising of revenue. The third article of their memorial stands in striking contrast to their action in the play; for it points out that nobles of royal blood (probably meaning York) are excluded from the King's "dailie presence," while he gives advancement to "other meane persons of lower nature," who close the King's ears to the complaints of the country, and distribute favours, not according to law, but for gifts and bribes. Moreover, they complain of interferences with freedom of election, and, in short, express themselves quite temperately and constitutionally. Finally, in more than one passage of the complaint, they give utterance to a thoroughly English and patriotic resentment of the loss of Normandy, Gascony, Aquitaine, Anjou, and Maine.

But it did not at all suit Shakespeare to show a Jack Cade at the head of a popular movement of this sort. He took no interest in anything constitutional or parliamentary. In order to find the colours he wanted for the rebellion, he hunts up in Stow's *Summarie of the Chronicles of England* the picture of Wat Tyler's and Jack Straw's risings under Richard II., two outbursts of wild communistic enthusiasm, reinforced by religious fanaticism. From this source he borrows, almost word for word, some of the rebels' speeches. In these risings, as a matter of fact, all "men of law, justices, and jurors" who fell into the hands of the leaders were beheaded, and all records and muniments burnt, so that owners of property might not in future have the means of establishing their rights.

This contempt for the judgment of the masses, this antidemocratic conviction, having early taken possession of Shakespeare's mind, he keeps on instinctively seeking out new evidences in its favour, new testimonies to its truth; and therefore he transforms facts, where they do not suit his view, on the model of other facts which do.

XVI

*THE THEATRES CLOSED ON ACCOUNT OF THE PLAGUE—
DID SHAKESPEARE VISIT ITALY?—PASSAGES WHICH
FAVOUR THIS CONJECTURE*

FROM the autumn of 1592 until the summer of 1593 all the London theatres were closed. That frightful scourge, the plague, from which England had so long been free, was raging in the capital. Even the sittings of the Law Courts had to be suspended. At Christmas 1592 the Queen refrained from ordering any plays at court, and the Privy Council had at an earlier date issued a proclamation forbidding all public theatrical performances, on the reasonable ground that convalescents, weary of their long confinement, made haste to resort to such entertainments before they were properly out of quarantine, and thus spread the contagion.

The matter has a particular bearing upon the biography of Shakespeare, since, if he ever travelled on the continent of Europe, it was probably at this period, while the theatres were closed.

That it must have been now, if ever, there can be no great doubt. But it remains exceedingly difficult to determine whether Shakespeare ever crossed the Channel.

We have noticed what an attraction Italy possessed for him, even from the beginning of his career. To this *The Two Gentlemen of Verona* and *Romeo and Juliet* bear witness. But in these plays we as yet find nothing which points definitely to the conclusion that the poet had seen with his own eyes the country in which his action is placed. It is different with the dramas of Italian scene which Shakespeare produces about the year 1596— the adaptation of the old *Taming of a Shrew* and *The Merchant of Venice;* it is different, too, with *Othello*, which comes much later. Here we find definite local colour, with such an abundance of details pointing to actual vision that it is hard to account for them otherwise than by assuming a visit on the poet's part to such cities as Verona, Venice, and Pisa.

It is on the face of it highly probable that Shakespeare should wish to see Italy as soon as he could find an opportunity. To the Englishman of that day Italy was the goal of every longing. It was the great home of culture. Men studied its literature and imitated its poetry. It was the beautiful land where dwelt the joy of life. Venice in especial exercised a fascination stronger than that of Paris. It needed no great wealth to make a pilgrimage to Italy. One could travel inexpensively, perhaps on foot, like that Coryat who discovered the use of the fork; one could pass the night at cheap hostelries. Many of the distinguished men of the time are known to have visited Italy—men of science, like Bacon, and afterwards Harvey; authors and poets like Lyly, Munday, Nash, Greene, and Daniel, the form of whose sonnets determined that of Shakespeare's. Among the artists of Shakespeare's time, the widely-travelled Inigo Jones had made a stay in Italy. Most of these men have themselves given us some account of their travels; but as Shakespeare has left us no biographical records whatever, the absence of any direct mention of such a journey on his part is of little moment, if other significant facts can be adduced in its favour.

And such facts are not wanting.

There were in Shakespeare's time no guide-books for the use of travellers. What he knows, then, of foreign lands and their customs he cannot have gathered from such sources. Of Venice, which Shakespeare has so livingly depicted, no description was published in England until after he had written his *Merchant of Venice*. Lewkenor's description of the city (itself a mere compilation at second hand) dates from 1598, Coryat's from 1611, Moryson's from 1617.

In Shakespeare's *Taming of the Shrew*, we notice with surprise not only the correctness of the Italian names, but the remarkable way in which, at the very beginning of the play, several Italian cities and districts are characterised in a single phrase. Lombardy is "the pleasant garden of great Italy;" Pisa is "renowned for grave citizens;" and here the epithet "grave" is especially noteworthy, since many testimonies concur to show that it was particularly characteristic of the inhabitants of Pisa. C. A. Brown, in *Shakespeare's Autobiographical Poems*, has pointed out the remarkable form of the betrothal of Petruchio and Katherine (namely, that her father joins their hands in the presence of two witnesses), and observes that this form was not English, but peculiarly Italian. It is not to be found in the older play, the scene of which, however, is laid in Athens.

Special attention was long ago directed to the following speech at the end of the second act, where Gremio reckons up all the goods and gear with which his house is stocked:—

> "First, as you know, my house within the city
> Is richly furnished with plate and gold:
> Basins, and ewers, to lave her dainty hands;
> My hangings all of Tyrian tapestry;
> In ivory coffers I have stuff'd my crowns;
> In cypress chests my arras, counterpoints,
> Costly apparel, tents, and canopies,
> Fine linen, Turkey cushions boss'd with pearl,
> Valance of Venice gold in needlework,
> Pewter and brass, and all things that belong
> To house, or housekeeping."

Lady Morgan long ago remarked that she had seen literally all of these articles of luxury in the palaces of Venice, Genoa, and Florence. Miss Martineau, in ignorance alike of Brown's theory and Lady Morgan's observation, expressed to Shakespeare's biographer, Charles Knight, her feeling that the local colour of *The Taming of the Shrew* and *The Merchant of Venice* displays such an intimate acquaintance, not only with the manners and customs of Italy, but with the minutest details of domestic life, that it cannot possibly have been gleaned from books or from mere conversations with this man or that who happened to have floated in a gondola.

On such a question as this, the decided impressions of feminine readers are not without a certain weight.

Brown has pointed out as specifically Italian such small traits as Iago's scoffing at the Florentine Cassio as "a great arithmetician," "a counter-caster," the Florentines being noted as masters of arithmetic and bookkeeping. Another such trait is the present of a dish of pigeons which Gobbo, in *The Merchant of Venice*, brings to his son's master.

Karl Elze, who has strongly insisted upon the probability of Shakespeare's having travelled Italy in the year 1593, dwells particularly upon his apparent familiarity with Venice. The name of Gobbo is a genuine Venetian name, and suggests, moreover, the kneeling stone figure, "Il Gobbo di Rialto," that forms the base of the granite pillar to which, in former days, the decrees of the Republic were affixed. Shakespeare knew that the Exchange was held on the Rialto island. An especially weighty argument lies in the fact that the study of the Jewish nature, to which his Shylock bears witness, would have been impossible in England, where no Jews were permitted by law to reside since their expulsion, begun in the time of Richard Cœur-de-Lion, and completed in 1290. Not until Cromwell's time was the embargo removed in a few cases. On the other hand, there were in Venice more than eleven hundred Jews (according to Coryat, as many as from five to six thousand).[1]

One of the most striking details as regards *The Merchant of Venice* is this: Portia sends her servant Balthasar with an important message to Padua, and orders him to ride quickly and meet her at "the common ferry which trades to Venice." Now Portia's palace at Belmont may be conceived as one of the summer residences, rich in art treasures, which the merchant princes of Venice at that time possessed on the banks of the Brenta. From Dolo, on the Brenta, it is twenty miles to Venice —just the distance which Portia says that she must "measure" in order to reach the city. If we conceive Belmont as situated at Dolo, it would be just possible for the servant to ride rapidly to Padua, and on the way back to overtake Portia, who would travel more slowly, at the ferry, which was then at Fusina, at the mouth of the Brenta. How exactly Shakespeare knew this, and how uncommon the knowledge was in his day, is shown in the expressions he uses, and in the misunderstanding of these expressions on the part of his printers and editors. The lines in the fourth scene of the third act, as they appear in all the Quartos and Folios, are these:—

> "Bring them, I pray thee, with imagined speed
> Unto the tranect, to the common ferry,
> Which trades to Venice."

---

[1] A very few Jews were, indeed, tolerated in England in spite of the prohibition, but it is not probable that Shakespeare knew any of them.

"Tranect," which means nothing, is, of course, a misprint for "traject," an uncommon expression which the printers clearly did not understand. This, as Elze has pointed out, is simply the Venetian word *traghetto* (Italian *tragitto*). How should Shakespeare have known either of the word or the thing if he had not been on the spot?

Other details in the second of these plays, written immediately after his conjectured return, strengthen this impression. In the Induction to *The Taming of the Shrew*, where the nobleman proposes to show Sly his pictures, there occur the lines:—

> "We'll show thee Io as she was a maid,
> And how she was beguiled and surpris'd,
> As lively painted as the deed was done."

These lines, as Elze has justly urged, convey the impression that Shakespeare had seen Correggio's famous picture of Jupiter and Io. This is quite possible if he travelled in North Italy at the time suggested, for from 1585 to 1600 the picture was in the palace of the sculptor Leoni at Milan, and was constantly visited by travellers. If we add that Shakespeare's numerous references to sea-voyages, storms at sea, the agonies of sea-sickness, &c., together with his illustrations and metaphors borrowed from provisions and dress at sea,[1] point to his having made a sea-passage of some length,[2] we cannot but regard it as highly probable that he possessed a closer knowledge of Italy than could be gained from oral descriptions and from books.

It is impossible, however, to arrive at any certainty on the point. His pictures of Italy are sometimes notably lacking in traits which could scarcely have been overlooked by one who knew the places. And the reader cannot but feel a certain scepticism when he observes how scholars have converted every seeming piece of ignorance on Shakespeare's part into a proof of his miraculous knowledge.

In virtue of this determination to make every apparent blot in Shakespeare redound to his advantage, it could be shown

---

[1] See *Pericles, The Tempest, Cymbeline* (i. 7), *As You Like It* (ii. 7), *Hamlet* (v. 2).

[2] It must be remembered that the sea route to Italy was practically closed by Spanish cruisers.

DID SHAKESPEARE VISIT ITALY   139

that he had been in Italy before he began to write plays at
all. In *The Two Gentlemen of Verona* it is said that Valentine
takes ship at Verona to go to Milan. This seems to betray a
gross ignorance of the geography of Italy. Karl Elze, however,
has discovered that in the sixteenth century Verona and Milan
were actually connected by a canal. In *Romeo and Juliet* the
heroine says to Friar Laurence, "Shall I come again at evening
mass?" This sounds strange, as the Catholic Church knows
nothing of evening masses; but R. Simpson has discovered that
they were actually in use at that time, and especially in Verona.
Shakespeare probably knew no more of these details than he did
of the fact that, about 1270, Bohemia possessed provinces on the
Adriatic, so that he could with an easy conscience accept from
Greene the voyage to the coast of Bohemia in *The Winter's
Tale*.

On the whole, scholars have been far too eager to find confirmation of every trivial detail in Shakespeare's allusions to
Italian localities. Knight, for instance, declared that "the Sagit-
tary," mentioned in *Othello*, "was the residence at the arsenal of
the commanding officers of the navy and army of the Republic,"
and that Shakespeare had "probably looked upon" the figure of
an archer over the gates; whereas it now appears that the commanding officer never had any residence in the arsenal, and that
no figure of an archer ever existed there. Elze, again, has gone
into most uncritical raptures over Shakespeare's marvellously
exact characterisation of Giulio Romano (*The Winter's Tale*, v. 2)
as that "rare Italian master who, had he himself eternity, and
could put breath into his works, would beguile Nature of her
custom, so perfectly he is her ape." As a matter of fact, Shakespeare has simply attributed to an artist whose fame had reached
his ears that characteristic which, as we have seen above, he
regarded as the highest in pictorial art. Giulio Romano, with
his crude superficiality, could not possibly have aroused his
admiration had he known his work. That he did not know
it is sufficiently evident from the fact that he has made him
a sculptor, and praised him in that capacity, and not as a
painter.

Elze, confronted with this fact, takes refuge in a Latin epitaph
on Romano, quoted by Vasari, which speaks of "Corpora sculpta
pictaque" by him, and here again finds a testimony to Shake-

speare's omniscience, since he knew of works of sculpture by Romano which no one else has seen or heard of. We can only see in this a new proof of the fact that critical idolatry of departed greatness can now and then lead the student as far astray as uncritical prejudice.

XVII

*SHAKESPEARE TURNS TO HISTORIC DRAMA—HIS RICHARD
II. AND MARLOWE'S EDWARD II.—LACK OF HUMOUR AND
OF CONSISTENCY OF STYLE—ENGLISH NATIONAL PRIDE*

ABOUT the age of thirty, even men of an introspective disposition are apt to turn their gaze outwards. When Shakespeare approaches his thirtieth year, he begins to occupy himself in earnest with history, to read the chronicles, to project and work out a whole series of historical plays. Several years had now passed since he had revised and furbished up the old dramas on the subject of Henry VI. This task had whetted his appetite, and had cultivated his sense for historic character and historic nemesis. Having now given expression to the high spirits, the lyrism, and the passion of youth, in lyrical and dramatic productions of scintillant diversity, he once more turned his attention to the history of England. In so doing he obeyed a dual vocation, both as a poet and as a patriot.

Shakespeare's plays founded on English history number ten in all, four dealing with the House of Lancaster (*Richard II.*, the two parts of *Henry IV.* and *Henry V.*), four devoted to the House of York (the three parts of *Henry VI.* and *Richard III.*), and two which stand apart from the main series, *King John*, of an earlier historic period, and *Henry VIII.*, of a later.

The order of production of these plays is, however, totally unconnected with their historical order, which does not, therefore, concern us. At the same time it is worthy of remark that all these plays (with the single exception of *Henry VIII.*) were produced in the course of one decade, the decade in which England's national sentiment burst into flower and her pride was at its highest. These English "histories" are, however, of very unequal value, and can by no means be treated as standing on one plane.

Henry VI. was a first attempt and a mere adaptation. Now, in the year 1594, Shakespeare attacks the theme of *Richard II.;* and in this, his first independent historical drama, we see his originality still struggling with the tendency to imitation.

There were older plays on the subject of *Richard II.*, but Shakespeare does not seem to have made any use of them. The model he had in his mind's eye was Marlowe's finest tragedy, his *Edward II.* Shakespeare's play is, however, much more than a clever imitation of Marlowe's; it is not only better composed, with a more concentrated action, but has also a great advantage in the full-blooded vitality of its style. Marlowe's style is here monotonously dry and sombre. Swinburne, moreover, has done Shakespeare an injustice in preferring Marlowe's character-drawing to that of *Richard II.*

The first half of Marlowe's drama is entirely taken up with the King's morbid and unnatural passion for his favourite Gaveston; Edward's every speech either expresses his grief at Gaveston's banishment and his longing for his return, or consists of glowing outbursts of joy on seeing him again. This passion makes Edward dislike his Queen and loathe the Barons, who, in their aristocratic pride, contemn the low-born favourite. He will risk everything rather than part from one who is so dear to himself and so obnoxious to his surroundings. The half-erotic fervour of his partiality renders the King's character distasteful, and deprives him of the sympathy which the poet demands for him at the end of the play.

For in the fourth and fifth acts, weak and unstable though he be, Edward has all Marlowe's sympathies. There is, indeed, something moving in his loneliness, his grief, and his brooding self-reproach. "The griefs," he says,

> "of private men are soon allay'd;
> But not of kings. The forest deer, being struck,
> Runs to an herb that closeth up the wounds:
> But when the imperial lion's flesh is gor'd,
> He rends and tears it with his wrathful paw."

The simile is not true to nature, like Shakespeare's, but it forcibly expresses the meaning of Marlowe's personage. Now and then he reminds us of Henry VI. The Queen's relation to Mortimer recalls that of Margaret to Suffolk. The abdication-

SHAKESPEARE AND MARLOWE

scene, in which the King first vehemently refuses to lay down the crown, and is then forced to consent, gave Shakespeare the model for Richard the Second's abdication. In the murder-scene, on the other hand, Marlowe displays a reckless naturalism in the description and representation of the torture inflicted on the King, an unabashed effect-hunting in the contrast between the King's magnanimity, dread, and gratitude on the one side, and the murderers' hypocritical cruelty on the other, which Shakespeare, with his gentler nature and his almost modern tact, has rejected. It is true that we find in Shakespeare several cases in which the severed head of a person whom we have seen alive a moment before is brought upon the stage. But he would never place before the eyes of the public such a murder-scene as this, in which the King is thrown down upon a feather-bed, a table is overturned upon him, and the murderers trample upon it until he is crushed.

Marlowe's more callous nature betrays itself in such details, while something of his own wild and passionate temperament has passed into the minor characters of the play—the violent Barons, with the younger Mortimer at their head—who are drawn with a firm hand. The time had scarcely passed when a murder was reckoned an absolute necessity in a drama. In 1581, Wilson, one of Lord Leicester's men, received an order for a play which should not only be original and entertaining, but should also include "all sorts of murders, immorality, and robberies."

Richard II. is one of those plays of Shakespeare's which have never taken firm hold of the stage. Its exclusively political action and its lack of female characters are mainly to blame for this. But it is exceedingly interesting as his first attempt at independent treatment of a historical theme, and it rises far above the play which served as its model.

The action follows pretty faithfully the course of history as the poet found it in Holinshed's Chronicle. The character of the Queen, however, is quite unhistorical, being evidently invented by Shakespeare for the sake of having a woman in his play. He wanted to gain sympathy for Richard through his wife's devotion to him, and saw an opportunity for pathos in her parting from him when he is thrown into prison. In 1398, when the play opens, Isabella of France was not yet ten years old, though she had nominally been married to Richard in 1396.

Finally, the King's end, fighting bravely, sword in hand, is not historical: he was starved to death in prison, in order that his body might be exhibited without any wound.

Shakespeare has vouchsafed no indication to facilitate the spectators' understanding of the characters in this play. Their action often takes us by surprise. But Swinburne has done Shakespeare a great wrong in making this a reason for praising Marlowe at his expense, and exalting the subordinate characters in *Edward II.* as consistent pieces of character-drawing, while he represents as inconsistent and obscure such a personage as Shakespeare's York. We may admit that in the opening scene Norfolk's figure is not quite clear, but here all obscurity ends. York is self-contradictory, unprincipled, vacillating, composite, and incoherent, but in no sense obscure. He in the first place upbraids the King with his faults, then accepts at his hands an office of the highest confidence, then betrays the King's trust, while he at the same time overwhelms the rebel Bolingbroke with reproaches, then admires the King's greatness in his fall, then hastens his dethronement, and finally, in virtuous indignation over Aumerle's plots against the new King, rushes to him to assure him of his fidelity and to clamour for the blood of his own son. There lies at the root of this conception a profound political bitterness and an early-acquired experience. Shakespeare must have studied attentively that portion of English history which lay nearest to him, the shufflings and vacillations that went on under Mary and Elizabeth, in order to have received so deep an impression of the pitifulness of political instability.

The character of old John of Gaunt, loyal to his King, but still more to his country, gives Shakespeare his first opportunity for expressing his exultation over England's greatness and his pride in being an Englishman. He places in the mouth of the dying Gaunt a superbly lyrical outburst of patriotism, deploring Richard's reckless and tyrannical policy. All comparison with Marlowe is here at an end. Shakespeare's own voice makes itself clearly heard in the rhetoric of this speech, which, with its self-controlled vehemence, its equipoise in unrest, soars high above Marlowe's wild magniloquence. In the thunderous tones of old Gaunt's invective against the King who has mortgaged his English realm, we can hear all the patriotic enthusiasm of young England in the days of Elizabeth :—

" This royal throne of kings, this sceptr'd isle,
This earth of majesty, this seat of Mars,
This other Eden, demi-paradise,
This fortress, built by Nature for herself,
Against infection, and the hand of war;
This happy breed of men, this little world,
This precious stone set in the silver sea,
Which serves it in the office of a wall,
Or as a moat defensive to a house,
Against the envy of less happier lands;
This blessed plot, this earth, this realm, this England,
This nurse, this teeming womb of royal kings,
Fear'd by their breed, and famous by their birth,

. . . .

This land of such dear souls, this dear, dear land,
Dear for her reputation through the world,
Is now leas'd out, I die pronouncing it,
Like to a tenement, or pelting farm.
England, bound in with the triumphant sea,
Whose rocky shore beats back the envious siege
Of watery Neptune, is now bound in with shame,
With inky blots, and rotten parchment bonds:
That England, that was wont to conquer others,
Hath made a shameful conquest of itself.
Ah! would the scandal vanish with my life,
How happy then were my ensuing death!" (ii. 1).

Here we have indeed the roar of the young lion, the vibration of Shakespeare's own voice.

But it is upon the leading character of the play that the poet has centred all his strength; and he has succeeded in giving a vivid and many-sided picture of the Black Prince's degenerate but interesting son. As the protagonist of a tragedy, however, Richard has exactly the same defects as Marlowe's Edward. In the first half of the play he so repels the spectator that nothing he can do in the second half suffices to obliterate the unfavourable impression. Not only has he, before the opening of the piece, committed such thoughtless and politically indefensible acts as have proved him unworthy of the great position he holds, but he behaves with such insolence to the dying Gaunt, and, after his uncle's death, displays such a low and despicable rapacity, that he can no longer appeal, as he does, to his personal right. It is true that the right of which he holds himself an embodiment is very different from the common earthly rights which he has overridden. He is religiously, dogmatically convinced of his inviolability as a king by the grace of God. But since this conviction, in his days of prosperity, has brought with it no sense of correlative duties to the crown he wears, it cannot touch the reader's sympathies as it ought to for the sake of the general effect.

We see the hand of the beginner in the way in which the poet here leaves characters and events to speak for themselves without any attempt to range them in a general scheme of perspective. He conceals himself too entirely behind his work. As there is no gleam of humour in the play, so, too, there is no guiding and harmonising sense of style.

It is from the moment that the tide begins to turn against Richard that he becomes interesting as a psychological study. After the manner of weak characters, he is alternately downcast and overweening. Very characteristically, he at one place answers Bolingbroke's question whether he is content to resign the crown: "Ay, no;—no, ay." In these syllables we see the whole man. But his temperament was highly poetical, and misfortune reveals in him a vein of reverie. He is sometimes profound to the point of paradox, sometimes fantastically overwrought to the verge of superstitious insanity (see, for instance, Act iii. 3). His brooding melancholy sometimes reminds us of Hamlet's—

> "Of comfort no man speak:
> Let's talk of graves, of worms, and epitaphs;
> Make dust our paper, and with rainy eyes
> Write sorrow on the bosom of the earth.
> Let's choose executors, and talk of wills:
> . . . . . .
> For God's sake, let us sit upon the ground,
> And tell sad stories of the death of kings:—
> How some have been depos'd, some slain in war,
> Some haunted by the ghosts they have depos'd.
> Some poison'd by their wives, some sleeping kill'd,
> All murder'd:—for within the hollow crown,
> That rounds the mortal temples of a king,
> Keeps Death his court, and there the antick sits,
> Scoffing his state, and grinning at his pomp;
> Allowing him a breath, a little scene,
> To monarchise, be fear'd, and kill with looks" (iii. 2).

In these moods of depression, in which Richard gives his wit and intellect free play, he knows very well that a king is only a human being like any one else :—

> "For you have but mistook me all this while :
> I live with bread like you, feel want, taste grief,
> Need friends. Subjected thus,
> How can you say to me, I am a king?" (iii. 2).

But at other times, when his sense of majesty and his monarchical fanaticism master him, he speaks in a quite different tone :—

> "Not all the water in the rough rude sea
> Can wash the balm from an anointed king;
> The breath of worldly men cannot depose
> The deputy elected by the Lord.
> For every man that Bolingbroke hath press'd,
> To lift shrewd steel against our golden crown,
> God for his Richard hath in heavenly pay
> A glorious angel" (iii. 2).

Thus, too, at their first meeting (iii. 3) he addresses the victorious Henry of Hereford, to whom he immediately after "debases himself ":—

> "My master, God omnipotent,
> Is mustering in his clouds on our behalf
> Armies of pestilence; and they shall strike
> Your children yet unborn, and unbegot,
> That lift your vassal hands against my head,
> And threat the glory of my precious crown."

Many centuries after Richard, King Frederick William IV. of Prussia displayed just the same mingling of intellectuality, superstition, despondency, monarchical arrogance, and fondness for declamation.

In the fourth and fifth acts, the character of Richard and the poet's art rise to their highest point. The scene in which the groom, who alone has remained faithful to the fallen King, visits him in his dungeon, is one of penetrating beauty. What can be more touching than his description of how the "roan Barbary," which had been Richard's favourite horse, carried Henry of Lancaster on his entry into London, "so proudly as if he had disdained the ground." The Arab steed here symbolises with fine simplicity the attitude of all those who had sunned themselves in the prosperity of the now fallen King.

The scene of the abdication (iv. 1) is admirable by reason of the delicacy of feeling and imagination which Richard displays. His speech when he and Henry have each one hand upon the crown is one of the most beautiful Shakespeare has ever written:—

> "Now is this golden crown like a deep well,
> That owes two buckets filling one another;
> The emptier ever dancing in the air,
> The other down, unseen, and full of water:
> That bucket down, and full of tears, am I,
> Drinking my griefs, whilst you mount up on high."

This scene is, however, a downright imitation of the abdication-scene in Marlowe. When Northumberland in Shakespeare addresses the dethroned King with the word "lord," the King answers, "No lord of thine." In Marlowe the speech is almost identical: "Call me not lord!"

The Shakespearian scene, it should be mentioned, has its history. The censorship under Elizabeth would not suffer it to be printed, and it first appears in the Fourth Quarto, of 1608.[1] The reason of this veto was that Elizabeth, strange as it may appear, was often compared with Richard II. The action of the censorship renders it probable that it was Shakespeare's *Richard II.* (and not one of the earlier plays on the same theme) which, as appears in the trial of Essex, was acted by the Lord Chamberlain's Company before the conspirators, at their leaders' command, on the evening before the outbreak of the rebellion (February 7, 1601). There is nothing inconsistent with this theory in the fact that the players then called it an old play, which was already "out of use;" for the interval between 1593–94 and 1601 was sufficient, according to the ideas of that time, to render a play antiquated. Nor does it conflict with this view that in the last scenes of the play the King is sympathetically treated. On the very points on which he was comparable with Elizabeth there could be no doubt that he was in the wrong; while Henry of Hereford figures in

---

[1] Its title runs, "The Tragedie of King Richard the Second: with new additions of the Parliament Sceane, and the deposing of King Richard, As it hath been lately acted by the Kinges Maiesties Seruantes, at the Globe. By William Shake-speare. At London. Printed by W. W. For Mathew Law, and are to be sold at his shop in Paules Church-yard, at the Signe of the Foxe. 1608."

the end as the bearer of England's future, and, for the not over-sensitive nerves of the period, that was sufficient. He, who was soon to play a leading part in two other Shakespearian dramas, is here endowed with all the qualities of the successful usurper and ruler: cunning and insight, power of dissimulation, ingratiating manners, and promptitude in action.

In a single speech (v. 3) the new-made Henry IV. sketches the character of his "unthrifty son," Shakespeare's hero: he passes his time in the taverns of London with riotous boon-companions, who now and then even rob travellers on the highway; but, being no less daring than dissolute, he gives certain "sparks of hope" for a nobler future.

XVIII

RICHARD III. PSYCHOLOGY AND MONOLOGUES — SHAKE-SPEARE'S POWER OF SELF-TRANSFORMATION — CONTEMPT FOR WOMEN — THE PRINCIPAL SCENES — THE CLASSIC TENDENCY OF THE TRAGEDY

IN the year 1594-95 Shakespeare returns to the material which passed through his hands during his revision of the Second and Third Parts of *Henry VI*. He once more takes up the character of Richard of York, there so firmly outlined; and, as in *Richard II*. he had followed in Marlowe's footsteps, so he now sets to work with all his might upon a Marlowesque figure, but only to execute it with his own vigour, and around it to construct his first historic tragedy with well-knit dramatic action. The earlier "histories" were still half epical; this is a true drama. It quickly became one of the most effective and popular pieces on the stage, and has imprinted itself on the memory of all the world in virtue of the monumental character of its protagonist.

The immediate occasion of Shakespeare's taking up this theme was probably the fact that in the year 1594 an old and worthless play on the subject was published under the title of *The True Tragedy of Richard III*. The publication of this play may have been due to the renewed interest in its hero awakened by the performances of *Henry VI*.

It is impossible to assign a precise date to Shakespeare's play. The first Quarto of *Richard II*. was entered in the Stationers' Register on the 29th August 1597, and the first edition of *Richard III*. was entered on the 20th October of the same year. But there is no doubt that its earliest form is of much older date. The diversities in its style indicate that Shakespeare worked over the text even before it was first printed; and the difference between the text of the first Quarto and that of the first Folio bears witness to a radical revision having taken place in the interval between the two editions. It is certainly to this play that

John Weever alludes when, in his poem, *Ad Gulielmum Shake-speare*, written as early as 1595, he mentions Richard among the poet's creations.

From the old play of *Richard III.* Shakespeare took nothing at all, or, to be precise, possibly one or two lines in the first scene of the second act. He throughout followed Holinshed, whose Chronicle is here copied word for word from Hall, who, in his turn, merely translated Sir Thomas More's history of Richard III. We can even tell what edition of Holinshed Shakespeare used, for he has copied a slip of the pen or error of the press which appears in that edition alone. In Act v. scene 3, line 324, he writes:—

"Long kept in Bretagne at our *mother's* cost,"

instead of *brother's*.

The text of *Richard III.* presents no slight difficulties to the editors of Shakespeare. Neither the first Quarto nor the greatly amended Folio is free from gross and baffling errors. The editors of the Cambridge Edition have attempted to show that both the texts are taken from bad copies of the original manuscripts. It would not surprise us, indeed, that the poet's own manuscript, being perpetually handled by the prompter and stage-manager, should quickly become so ragged that now one page and now another would have to be replaced by a copy. But the Cambridge editors have certainly undervalued the augmented and amended text of the First Folio. James Spedding has shown in an excellent essay (*The New Shakspere Society's Transactions*, 1875-76, pp. 1-119) that the changes which some have thought accidental and arbitrary, and therefore not the work of the poet himself, are due to his desire, sometimes to improve the form of the verse, sometimes to avoid the repetition of a word, sometimes to get rid of antiquated words and turns of phrase.

Every one who has been nurtured upon Shakespeare has from his youth dwelt wonderingly upon the figure of Richard, that fiend in human shape, striding, with savage impetuosity, from murder to murder, wading through falsehood and hypocrisy to ever-new atrocities, becoming in turn regicide, fratricide, tyrant, murderer of his wife and of his comrades, until, besmirched with treachery and slaughter, he faces his foes with invincible greatness.

When J. L. Heiberg refused to produce *Richard III.* at the Royal Theatre in Copenhagen, he expressed a doubt whether "we could ever accustom ourselves to seeing Melpomene's dagger converted into a butcher's knife." Like many other critics before and after him, he took exception to the line in Richard's opening soliloquy, "I am determined to prove a villain." He doubted, justly enough, the psychological possibility of this phrase; but the monologue, as a whole, is a non-realistic unfolding of secret thoughts in words, and, with a very slight change in the form of expression, the idea is by no means indefensible. Richard does not mean that he is determined to be what he himself regards as criminal, but merely declares with bitter irony that, since he cannot "prove a lover To entertain these fair well-spoken days," he will play the part of a villain, and give the rein to his hatred for the "idle pleasures" of the time.

There is in the whole utterance a straightforwardness, as of a programme, that takes us aback. Richard comes forward naïvely in the character of Prologue, and foreshadows the matter of the tragedy. It seems almost as though Shakespeare had determined to guard himself at the outset against the accusation of obscurity which had possibly been brought against his *Richard II.* But we must remember that ambitious men in his day were less composite than in our times, and, moreover, that he was not here depicting even one of his own contemporaries, but a character which appeared to his imagination in the light of a historical monster, from whom his own age was separated by more than a century. His Richard is like an old portrait, dating from the time when the physiognomy of dangerous, no less than of noble, characters was simpler, and when even intellectual eminence was still accompanied by a bull-necked vigour of physique such as in later times we find only in the savage chieftains of distant corners of the world.

It is against such figures as this of Richard that the critics who contest Shakespeare's rank as a psychologist are fondest of directing their attacks. But Shakespeare was no miniature-painter. Minutely detailed psychological painting, such as in our days Dostoyevsky has given us, was not his affair; though, as he proved in *Hamlet*, he could on occasion grapple with complex characters. Even here, however, he gets his effect of complexity, not by unravelling a tangle of motives, but by producing the impression of an inward infinity in the character. It is clear that, in his age, he had not often the chance of observing how circumstances, experience, and changing conditions cut and polish a personality into shimmering facets. With the exception of Hamlet, who in some respects stands alone, his characters have sides indeed, but not facets.

Take, for instance, this Richard. Shakespeare builds him up from a few simple characteristics: deformity, the potent consciousness of intellectual superiority, and the lust for power. His whole personality can be traced back to these simple elements.

He is courageous out of self-esteem; he plays the lover out of ambition; he is cunning and false, a comedian and a bloodhound, as cruel as he is hypocritical—and all in order to attain to that despotism on which he has set his heart.

Shakespeare found in Holinshed's Chronicle certain fundamental traits: Richard was born with teeth, and could bite before he could smile; he was ugly; he had one shoulder higher than another; he was malicious and witty; he was a daring and openhanded general; he loved secrecy; he was false and hypocritical out of ambition, cruel out of policy.

All this Shakespeare simplifies and exaggerates, as every artist must. Delacroix has finely said, "*L'art, c'est l'exagération à propos.*"

The Richard of the tragedy is deformed; he is undersized and crooked, has a hump on his back and a withered arm.

He is not, like so many other hunchbacks, under any illusion as to his appearance. He does not think himself handsome, nor is he loved by the daughters of Eve, in whom deformity is so apt to awaken that instinct of pity which is akin to love.

No, Richard feels himself maltreated by Nature; from his birth upwards he has suffered wrong at her hands, and in spite of his high and strenuous spirit, he has grown up an outcast. He has from the first had to do without his mother's love, and to listen to the gibes of his enemies. Men have pointed at his shadow and laughed. The dogs have barked at him as he halted by. But in this luckless frame dwells an ambitious soul. Other people's paths to happiness and enjoyment are closed to him. But he will rule; for that he was born. Power is everything to him, his fixed idea. Power alone can give him his revenge upon the people around him, whom he hates, or despises, or both. The glory of the diadem shall rest upon the head that crowns this misshapen body. He sees its golden splendour afar off. Many lives stand between him and his goal; but he will shrink from no falsehood, no treachery, no bloodshed, if only he can reach it.

Into this character Shakespeare transforms himself in imagination. It is the mark of the dramatic poet to be always able to get out of his own skin and into another's. But in later times some of the greatest dramatists have shrunk shuddering from the out-and-out criminal, as being too remote from them. For example, Goethe. His wrong-doers are only weaklings, like Weislingen or Clavigo; even his Mephistopheles is not really evil. Shakespeare, on the other hand, made the effort to feel like Richard. How did he set about it? Exactly as we do when we strive to understand another personality; for example, Shakespeare himself. He imagines himself into him; that is to say, he projects his mind into the other's body and lives in it for the time being. The question the poet has to answer is always this: How should I feel and act if I were a prince, a woman, a conqueror, an outcast, and so forth?

Shakespeare takes, as his point of departure, the ignominy inflicted by Nature; Richard is one of Nature's victims. How can Shakespeare feel with him here—Shakespeare, to whom deformity of body was unknown, and who had been immoderately favoured by Nature? But he, too, had long endured humiliation, and had lived under mean conditions which afforded no scope either to his will or to his talents. Poverty is itself a deformity; and the condition of an actor was a blemish like a hump on his back. Thus he is in a position to enter with ease into the feelings of one of Nature's victims. He has simply to give free course to all the moods in his own mind which have been evoked by personal humiliation, and to let them ferment and run riot.

Next comes the consciousness of superiority in Richard, and the lust of power which springs from it. Shakespeare cannot have lacked the consciousness of his personal superiority, and, like every man of genius, he must have had the lust of power in his soul, at least as a rudimentary organ. Ambitious he must assuredly have been, though not after the fashion of the actors and dramatists of our day. Their mere jugglery passes for art, while his art was regarded by the great majority as mere jugglery. His artistic self-esteem received a check in its growth; but none the less there was ambition behind the tenacity of purpose which in a few years raised him from a servitor in the theatre to a shareholder and director, and which led him to develop the greatest productive talent of his country, till he outshone all rivals in his calling, and won the appreciation of the leaders of fashion and taste. He now transposed into another sphere of life, that of temporal rule, a habit of mind which was his own. The instinct of his soul, which never suffered him to stop or pause, but forced him from one great intellectual achievement to another, restlessly onward from masterpiece to masterpiece—the fierce instinct, with its inevitable egoism, which led him in his youth to desert his family, in his maturity to amass property without any tenderness for his debtors, and (*per fas et nefas*) to attain his modest patent of gentility—this instinct enables him to understand and feel that passion for power which defies and tramples upon every scruple. And all the other characteristics (for example, the hypocrisy, which in the Chronicle holds the foremost place) he uses as mere instruments in the service of ambition.

Note how he has succeeded in individualising this passion. It is hereditary. In the Second Part of *Henry VI.* (iii. 1) Richard's father, the Duke of York, says—

" Let pale-fac'd fear keep with the mean-born man,
And find no harbour in a royal heart.
Faster than spring-time showers comes thought on thought,
And not a thought but thinks on dignity.

. . . . .

Well, nobles, well ; 't is politicly done,
To send me packing with an host of men :
I fear me, you but warm the starved snake,
Who, cherish'd in your breasts, will sting your hearts."

In the Third Part of *Henry VI.*, Richard shows himself the true son of his father. His brother runs after the smiles of women ; he dreams only of might and sovereignty. If there was no crown to be attained, the world would have no joy to offer him. He says himself (iii. 2)—

" Why, love forswore me in my mother's womb :
And, for I should not deal in her soft laws,
She did corrupt frail nature with some bribe,

To shrink mine arm up like a wither'd shrub;
To make an envious mountain on my back.

. . . . . .

To disproportion me in every part;
Like to a chaos, or an unlick'd bear-whelp,
That carries no impression like the dam.
And am I then a man to be belov'd?
O monstrous fault, to harbour such a thought!
Then, since this earth affords no joy to me
But to command, to check, to o'erbear such
As are of better person than myself,
I'll make my heaven to dream upon the crown."

The lust of power is an inward agony to him. He compares himself to a man "lost in a thorny wood, That rends the thorns and is rent by the thorns;" and he sees no way of deliverance except to "hew his way out with a bloody axe." Thus is he tormented by his desire for the crown of England; and to achieve it he will "drown more sailors than the mermaid shall; . . . Deceive more slyly than Ulysses could; . . . add colours to the chameleon; . . . And send the murd'rous Machiavel to school." (The last touch is an anachronism, for Richard died fifty years before *The Prince* was published.)

If this is to be a villain. then a villain he is. And for the sake of the artistic effect, Shakespeare has piled upon Richard's head far more crimes than the real Richard can be historically proved to have committed. This he did, because he had no doubt of the existence of such characters as rose before his imagination while he read in Holinshed of Richard's misdeeds. He believed in the existence of villains—a belief largely undermined in our days by a scepticism which greatly facilitates the villains' operations. He has drawn more villains than one: Edmund in *Lear*, who is influenced by his illegitimacy as Richard is by his deformity, and the grand master of all evil, Iago in *Othello*.

But let us get rid of the empty by-word villain, which Richard applies to himself. Shakespeare no doubt believed theoretically in the free-will which can choose any course it pleases, and villainy among the rest; but none the less does he in practice assign a cause to every effect.

On three scenes in this play Shakespeare evidently expended

particular care—the three which imprint themselves on the memory after even a single attentive reading.

The first of these scenes is that in which Richard wins over the Lady Anne, widow of one of his victims, Prince Edward, and daughter-in-law of another, Henry VI. Shakespeare has here carried the situation to its utmost extremity. It is while Anne is accompanying the bier of the murdered Henry VI. that the murderer confronts her, stops the funeral procession with drawn sword, calmly endures all the outbursts of hatred, loathing, and contempt with which Anne overwhelms him, and, having shaken off her invectives like water from a duck's back, advances his suit, plays his comedy of love, and there and then so turns the current of her will that she allows him to hope, and even accepts his ring.

The scene is historically impossible, since Queen Margaret took Anne with her in her flight after the battle of Tewkesbury, and Clarence kept her in concealment until two years after the death of Henry VI., when Richard discovered her in London. It has, moreover, something astonishing, or rather bewildering, about it at the first reading, appearing as though written for a wager or to outdo some predecessor. Nevertheless it is by no means unnatural. What may with justice be objected to it is that it is unprepared. The mistake is, that we are first introduced to Anne in the scene itself, and can consequently form no judgment as to whether her action does or does not accord with her character. The art of dramatic writing consists almost entirely in preparing for what is to come, and then, in spite of, nay, in virtue of the preparation, taking the audience by surprise. Surprise without preparation loses half its effect.

But this is only a technical flaw which so great a master would in riper years have remedied with ease. The essential feature of the scene is its tremendous daring and strength, or, psychologically speaking, the depth of early-developed contempt for womankind into which it affords us a glimpse. For the very reason that the poet has not given any individual characteristics to this woman, it seems as though he would say: Such is feminine human nature. It is quite evident that in his younger years he was not so much alive to the beauties of the womanly character as he became at a later period of his life. He is fond of drawing unamiable women like Adriana in *The Comedy of Errors*, violent and corrupt women like Tamora in *Titus Andronicus*, and Margaret in *Henry VI.*, or scolding women like Katherine in *The Taming of the Shrew*. Here he gives us a picture of peculiarly feminine weakness, and personifies in Richard his own contempt for it.

Exasperate a woman against you (he seems to say), do her all the evil you can think of, kill her husband, deprive her thereby of the succession to a crown, fill her to overflowing with hatred and execration—then if you can only cajole her into believing that in all you have done, crimes and everything, you have been actuated simply and solely by burning passion for her, by the hope of approaching her and winning her hand—why, then the game is yours, and sooner or later she will give in. Her vanity cannot hold out. If it is proof against ten measures of flattery, it will succumb to a hundred; and if even that is not enough, then pile on more. Every woman has a price at which her vanity is for sale; you have only to dare greatly and bid high enough. So Shakespeare makes this crookbacked assassin accept Anne's insults without winking and retort upon them his declaration of love—he at once seems less hideous in her eyes from the fact that his crimes were committed for her sake. Shakespeare makes him hand her his drawn sword, to pierce him to the heart if she will; he is sure enough that she will do nothing of the sort. She cannot withstand the intense volition in his glance; he hypnotises her hatred; the exaltation with which his lust of power inspires him bewilders and overpowers her, and he becomes almost beautiful in her eyes when he bares his breast to her revenge. She yields to him under the influence of an attraction in which are mingled dizziness, terror, and perverted sensuality. His very hideousness becomes a stimulus the more. There is a sort of fearful billing-and-cooing in the stichomythy in the style of the antique tragedy, which begins:—

> "*Anne.* I would I knew thy heart.
> *Gloucester.* 'Tis figured in my tongue.
> *Anne.* I fear me both are false.
> *Gloucester.* Then never man was true."

But triumph seethes in his veins—

> "Was ever woman in this humour wooed?
> Was ever woman in this humour won?"

—triumph that he, the hunchback, the monster, has needed but to show himself and use his polished tongue in order to stay the curses on her lips, dry the tears in her eyes, and awaken desire in her soul. This courtship has procured him the intoxicating sensation of irresistibility.

The fact of the marriage Shakespeare found in the Chronicle; and he led up to it in this brilliant fashion because his poetic instinct told him to make Richard great, and thereby possible as a tragic hero. In reality, he was by no means so dæmonic. His motive for paying court to Anne was sheer cupidity. Both Clarence and Gloucester had schemed to possess themselves of the vast fortune left by the Earl of Warwick, although the Countess was still alive and legally entitled to the greater part of it. Clarence, who had married the elder daughter, was certain of his part in the inheritance, but Richard thought that by marrying the younger daughter, Prince Edward's widow, he would secure the right to go halves. By aid of an Act of Parliament, the matter was arranged so that each of the brothers received his share in the booty. For this low rapacity in Richard, Shakespeare has substituted the hunchback's personal exultation on finding himself a successful wooer.

Nevertheless, it was not his intention to represent Richard as superior to all feminine wiles. This opening scene has its counterpart in the passage (iv. 4) where the King, after having rid himself by poison of the wife he has thus won, proposes to Elizabeth, the widow of Edward IV., for the hand of her daughter.

The scene has the air of a repetition. Richard has made away with Edward's two sons in order to clear his path to the throne. Here again, then, the murderer woos the nearest kinswoman of his victims, and, in this case, through the intermediary of their mother. Shakespeare has lavished his whole art on this passage. Elizabeth, too, expresses the deepest loathing for him. Richard answers that, if he has deprived her sons of the throne, he will now make amends by raising her daughter to it. Here also the dialogue takes the form of a stichomythy, which clearly enough indicates that these passages belong to the earliest form of the play:—

"*King Richard.* Infer fair England's peace by this alliance.
Queen Elizabeth. Which she shall purchase with still lasting war.
K. Rich. Tell her, the king, that may command, entreats.
Q. Eliz. That at her hands, which the kings' King forbids."

Richard not only asserts the purity and strength of his feelings, but insists that by this marriage alone can he be prevented from bringing misery and destruction upon thousands in the kingdom. Elizabeth pretends to yield, and Richard bursts forth, just as in the first act—

"Relenting fool, and shallow changing woman!"

But it is he himself who is overreached. Elizabeth has only made a show of acquiescence in order immediately after to offer her daughter to his mortal foe.

The second unforgetable passage is the Baynard's Castle scene in the third act. Richard has cleared away all obstacles on his path to the throne. His elder brother Clarence is murdered —drowned in a butt of wine. Edward's young sons are presently to be strangled in prison. Hastings has just been hurried to the scaffold without trial or form of law. The thing is now to avoid all appearance of complicity in these crimes, and to seem austerely disinterested with regard to the crown. To this end he makes his rascally henchman, Buckingham, persuade the simple-minded and panic-stricken Lord Mayor of London, with other citizens of repute, to implore him, in spite of his seeming reluctance, to mount the throne. Buckingham prepares Richard for their approach (iii. 7):—

"Intend some fear;
Be not you spoke with but by mighty suit:
And look you get a prayer-book in your hand,
And stand between two churchmen, good my lord:
For on that ground I'll make a holy descant:
And be not easily won to our requests;
Play the maid's part, still answer nay, and take it."

Then come the citizens. Catesby bids them return another time. His grace is closeted with two right reverend fathers; he is "divinely bent to meditation," and must not be disturbed in his devotions by any "worldly suits." They renew their entreaties to his messenger, and implore the favour of an audience with his grace "in matter of great moment."

Not till then does Gloucester show himself upon the balcony between two bishops.

When, at the election of 1868, which turned upon the Irish Church question, Disraeli, a very different man from Richard, was relying on the co-operation of both English and Irish prelates, *Punch* depicted him in fifteenth-century attire, standing on a balcony, prayer-book in hand, with an indescribable expression of sly humility, while two bishops, representing the English and the Irish Church, supported him on either hand. The legend ran, in the words of the Lord Mayor: "See where his grace stands 'tween two clergymen!"—whereupon Buckingham remarks—

> "Two props of virtue for a Christian prince,
> To stay him from the fall of vanity;
> And, see, a book of prayer in his hand,
> True ornament to know a holy man."

The deputation is sternly repulsed, until Richard at last lets mercy stand for justice, and recalling the envoys of the City, yields to their insistence.

The third master-scene is that in Richard's tent on Bosworth Field (v. 3). It seems as though his hitherto immovable self-confidence had been shaken; he feels himself weak; he will not sup. "Is my beaver easier than it was? . . . Fill me a bowl of wine. . . . Look that my staves be sound and not too heavy." Again: "Give me a bowl of wine."

> "I have not that alacrity of spirit,
> Nor cheer of mind, that I was wont to have."

Then, in a vision, as he lies sleeping on his couch, with his armour on and his sword-hilt grasped in his hand, he sees, one by one, the spectres of all those he has done to death. He wakens in terror. His conscience has a thousand tongues, and every tongue condemns him as a perjurer and assassin:—

> "I shall despair.—There is no creature loves me;
> And if I die no soul shall pity me."

These are such pangs of conscience as would sometimes beset even the strongest and most resolute in those days when faith and superstition were still powerful, and when even one who scoffed at religion and made a tool of it had no assurance in his heart of hearts. There is in these words, too, a purely human sense of loneliness and of craving for affection, which is valid for all time.

Most admirable is the way in which Richard summons up his

manhood and restores the courage of those around him. These are the accents of one who will give despair no footing in his soul:—

> "Conscience is but a word that cowards use,
> Devis'd at first to keep the strong in awe;"

and there is in his harangue to the soldiers an irresistible roll of fierce and spirit-stirring martial music; it is constructed like strophes of the *Marseillaise*:—

> "Remember whom you are to cope withal;—
> A sort of vagabonds, rascals, runaways.
> (*Que veut cette horde d'esclaves?*)
> You having lands, and bless'd with beauteous wives,
> They would restrain the one, distain the other.
> (*Égorger vos fils, vos compagnes.*)
> Let's whip these stragglers o'er the seas again."

But there is a ferocity, a scorn, a popular eloquence in Richard's words, in comparison with which the rhetoric of the *Marseillaise* seems declamatory, even academic. His last speeches are nothing less than superb:—

> "Shall these enjoy our lands? lie with our wives?
> Ravish our daughters?—[*Drum afar off.*] Hark; I hear their drum.
> Fight, gentlemen of England! fight, bold yeomen!
> Draw, archers, draw your arrows to the head!
> Spur your proud horses hard, and ride in blood:
> Amaze the welkin with your broken staves!
>
> *Enter a Messenger.*
>
> What says Lord Stanley? will he bring his power?
> *Mess.* My lord, he doth deny to come.
> *K. Rich.* Off with his son George's head!
> *Norfolk.* My lord, the enemy is pass'd the marsh:
> After the battle let George Stanley die.
> *K. Rich.* A thousand hearts are great within my bosom.
> Advance our standards! set upon our foes!
> Our ancient word of courage, fair Saint George,
> Inspire us with the spleen of fiery dragons!
> Upon them! Victory sits on our helms.
>
> . . . . .
>
> *K. Rich.* A horse! a horse! my kingdom for a horse!
> *Catesby.* Withdraw, my lord; I'll help you to a horse.

K. Rich. Slave! I have set my life upon a cast,
And I will stand the hazard of the die.
I think there be six Richmonds in the field;
Five have I slain to-day, instead of him.—
A horse! a horse! my kingdom for a horse!"

In no other play of Shakespeare's, we may surely say, is the leading character so absolutely predominant as here. He absorbs almost the whole of the interest, and it is a triumph of Shakespeare's art that he makes us, in spite of everything, follow him with sympathy. This is partly because several of his victims are so worthless that their fate seems well deserved. Anne's weakness deprives her of our sympathy, and Richard's crime loses something of its horror when we see how lightly it is forgiven by the one who ought to take it most to heart. In spite of all his iniquities, he has wit and courage on his side —a wit which sometimes rises to Mephistophelean humour, a courage which does not fail him even in the moment of disaster, but sheds a glory over his fall which is lacking to the triumph of his coldly correct opponent. However false and hypocritical he may be towards others, he is no hypocrite to himself. He is chemically free from self-delusion, even applying to himself the most derogatory terms; and this candour in the depths of his nature appeals to us. It must be said for him, too, that threats and curses recoil from him innocuous, that neither hatred nor violence nor superior force can dash his courage. Strength of character is such a rare quality that it arouses sympathy even in a criminal. If Richard's reign had lasted longer, he would perhaps have figured in history as a ruler of the type of Louis XI.: crafty, always wearing his religion on his sleeve, but far-seeing and resolute. As a matter of fact, in history as in the drama, his whole time was occupied in defending himself in the position to which he had fought his way, like a bloodthirsty beast of prey. His figure stands before us as his contemporaries have drawn it: small and wiry, the right shoulder higher than the left, wearing his rich brown hair long in order to conceal this malformation, biting his under-lip, always restless, always with his hand on his dagger-hilt, sliding it up and down in its sheath, without entirely drawing it. Shakespeare has succeeded in throwing a halo of poetry around this tiger in human shape.

The figures of the two boy princes, Edward's sons, stand in

the strongest contrast to Richard. The eldest child already shows greatness of soul, a kingly spirit, with a deep feeling for the import of historic achievement. The fact that Julius Cæsar built the Tower, he says, even were it not registered, ought to live from age to age. He is full of the thought that while Cæsar's "valour did enrich his wit," yet it was his wit "that made his valour live," and he exclaims with enthusiasm, "Death makes no conquest of this conqueror." The younger brother is childishly witty, imaginative, full of boyish mockery for his uncle's grimness, and eager to play with his dagger and sword. In a very few touches Shakespeare has endowed these young brothers with the most exquisite grace. The murderers "weep like to children in their death's sad story":—

"Their lips were four red roses on a stalk,
And, in their summer beauty, kiss'd each other."

Finally, the whole tragedy of Richard's life and death is enveloped, as it were, in the mourning of women, permeated with their lamentations. In its internal structure, it bears no slight resemblance to a Greek tragedy, being indeed the concluding portion of a tetralogy.

Nowhere else does Shakespeare approach so nearly to the classicism on the model of Seneca which had found some adherents in England.

The whole tragedy springs from the curse which York, in the Third Part of *Henry VI.* (i. 4), hurls at Margaret of Anjou. She has insulted her captive enemy, and given him in mockery a napkin soaked in the blood of his son, the young Rutland, stabbed to the heart by Clifford.

Therefore she loses her crown and her son, the Prince of Wales. Her lover, Suffolk, she has already lost. Nothing remains to attach her to life.

But now it is her turn to be revenged.

The poet has sought to incarnate in her the antique Nemesis, has given her supernatural proportions and set her free from the conditions of real life. Though exiled, she has returned unquestioned to England, haunts the palace of Edward IV., and gives free vent to her rage and hatred in his presence and that of his kinsfolk and his courtiers. So, too, she wanders around under Richard's rule, simply and solely to curse her enemies—

and even Richard himself is seized with a superstitious shudder at these anathemas.

Never again did Shakespeare so depart from the possible in order to attain a scenic effect. And yet it is doubtful whether the effect is really attained. In reading, it is true, these curses strike us with extraordinary force; but on the stage, where she only disturbs and retards the action, and takes no effective part in it, Margaret cannot but prove wearisome.

Yet, though she herself remains inactive, her curses are effectual enough. Death overtakes all those on whom they fall —the King and his children, Rivers and Dorset, Lord Hastings and the rest.

She encounters the Duchess of York, the mother of Edward IV., Queen Elizabeth, his widow, and finally Anne, Richard's daringly-won and quickly-repudiated wife. And all these women, like a Greek chorus, give utterance in rhymed verse to imprecations and lamentations of high lyric fervour. In two passages in particular (ii. 2 and iv. 1) they chant positive choral odes in dialogue form. Take as an example of the lyric tone of the diction these lines (iv. 1):—

> "*Duchess of York* [*To Dorset.*] Go thou to Richmond, and good fortune guide thee!—
> [*To Anne.*] Go thou to Richard, and good angels tend thee!—
> [*To Q. Elizabeth.*] Go thou to sanctuary, and good thoughts possess thee!—
> I to my grave, where peace and rest lie with me!
> Eighty odd years of sorrow have I seen,
> And each hour's joy wrack'd with a week of teen."

Such is this work of Shakespeare's youth, firm, massive, and masterful throughout, even though of very unequal merit. Everything is here worked out upon the surface; the characters themselves tell us what sort of people they are, and proclaim themselves evil or good, as the case may be. They are all transparent, all self-conscious to excess. They expound themselves in soliloquies, and each of them is judged in a sort of choral ode. The time is yet to come when Shakespeare no longer dreams of making his characters formally hand over to the spectators the key to their mystery—when, on the contrary, with his sense of the secrets and inward contradictions of the spiritual life, he sedulously hides that key in the depths of personality.

XIX

SHAKESPEARE LOSES HIS SON—TRACES OF HIS GRIEF IN KING JOHN—THE OLD PLAY OF THE SAME NAME—DISPLACEMENT OF ITS CENTRE OF GRAVITY—ELIMINATION OF RELIGIOUS POLEMICS—RETENTION OF THE NATIONAL BASIS—PATRIOTIC SPIRIT—SHAKESPEARE KNOWS NOTHING OF THE DISTINCTION BETWEEN NORMANS AND ANGLO-SAXONS, AND IGNORES THE MAGNA CHARTA

IN the Parish Register of Stratford-on-Avon for 1596, under the heading of burials, we find this entry, in a clear and elegant handwriting :—

"*August* 11, *Hamnet filius William Shakespeare.*"

Shakespeare's only son was born on the 2nd of February 1585 ; he was thus only eleven and a half when he died.

We cannot doubt that this loss was a grievous one to a man of Shakespeare's deep feeling; doubly grievous, it would seem, because it was his constant ambition to restore the fallen fortunes of his family, and he was now left without an heir to his name.

Traces of what his heart must have suffered appear in the work he now undertakes, *King John*, which seems to date from 1596-97.

One of the main themes of this play is the relation between John Lackland, who has usurped the English crown, and the rightful heir, Arthur, son of John's elder brother, in reality a boy of about fourteen at the date of the action, but whom Shakespeare, for the sake of poetic effect, and influenced, perhaps, by his private preoccupations of the moment, has made considerably younger, and consequently more childlike and touching.

The King has got Arthur into his power. The most famous scene in the play is that (iv. 1) in which Hubert de Burgh, the

King's chamberlain, who has received orders to sear out the eyes of the little captive, enters Arthur's prison with the irons, and accompanied by the two servants who are to bind the child to a chair and hold him fast while the atrocity is being committed. The little prince, who has no mistrust of Hubert, but only a general dread of his uncle's malice, as yet divines no danger, and is full of sympathy and childlike tenderness. The passage is one of extraordinery grace :—

"*Arthur.* You are sad.
Hubert. Indeed, I have been merrier.
Arth. Mercy on me!
Methinks, nobody should be sad but I:
.   .   .   .   .   .
I would to Heaven,
I were your son, so you would love me, Hubert.
Hub. [*Aside.*] If I talk to him, with his innocent prate
He will awake my mercy, which lies dead:
Therefore I will be sudden, and despatch.
Arth. Are you sick, Hubert? you look pale to-day.
In sooth, I would you were a little sick,
That I might sit all night, and watch with you:
I warrant, I love you more than you do me."

Hubert gives him the royal mandate to read :—

"*Hubert.* Can you not read it? is it not fair writ?
Arthur. Too fairly, Hubert, for so foul effect.
Must you with hot irons burn out both mine eyes?
Hub. Young boy, I must.
Arth. And will you?
Hub. And I will.
Arth. Have you the heart? When your head did but ache,
I knit my handkerchief about your brows,
(The best I had, a princess wrought it me,)
And I did never ask it you again;
And with my hand at midnight held your head."

Hubert summons the executioners, and the child promises to sit still and offer no resistance if only he will send these "bloody men" away. One of the servants as he goes out speaks a word of pity, and Arthur is in despair at having "chid away his friend." In heart-breaking accents he begs mercy of Hubert until the iron has grown cold, and Hubert has not the heart to heat it afresh.

Arthur's entreaties to the rugged Hubert to spare his eyes, must have represented in Shakespeare's thought the prayers of his little Hamnet to be suffered still to see the light of day, or rather Shakespeare's own appeal to Death to spare the child— prayers and appeals which were all in vain.

It is, however, in the lamentations of Arthur's mother, Constance, when the child is carried away to prison (iii. 4), that we most clearly recognise the accents of Shakespeare's sorrow:—

> "*Pandulph.* Lady, you utter madness, and not sorrow.
> *Constance.* I am not mad: this hair I tear is mine.
>
> . . . .
>
> If I were mad, I should forget my son,
> Or madly think, a babe of clouts were he.
> I am not mad: too well, too well I feel
> The different plague of each calamity."

She pours forth her anguish at the thought of his sufferings in prison:—

> "Now will canker sorrow eat my bud,
> And chase the native beauty from his cheek,
> And he will look as hollow as a ghost,
> As dim and meagre as an ague's fit,
> And so he'll die.
>
> . . . . .
>
> *Pandulph.* You hold too heinous a respect of grief.
> *Constance.* He talks to me, that never had a son.
> *K. Philip.* You are as fond of grief as of your child.
> *Const.* Grief fills the room up of my absent child,
> Lies in his bed, walks up and down with me,
> Puts on his pretty looks, repeats his words,
> Remembers me of all his gracious parts,
> Stuffs out his vacant garments with his form."

It seems as though Shakespeare's great heart had found an outlet for its own sorrows in transfusing them into the heart of Constance.

Shakespeare used as the basis of his *King John* an old play on the same subject published in 1591.[1] This play is quite

---

[1] The full title runs thus: "The Troublesome Raigne of *John*, King of *England*, with the discouerie of King Richard Cordelions Base sonne (vulgarly named The Bastard Fawconbridge): also the death of King John at Swinstead Abbey. As it was (sundry times) publikely acted by the Queenes Maiesties Players, in the honorable Citie of London."

artless and spiritless, but contains the whole action, outlines all the characters, and suggests almost all the principal scenes. The poet did not require to trouble himself with the invention of external traits. He could concentrate his whole effort upon vitalising, spiritualising, and deepening everything. Thus it happens that this play, though never one of his most popular (it seems to have been but seldom performed during his lifetime, and remained in manuscript until the appearance of the First Folio), nevertheless contains some of his finest character-studies and a multitude of pregnant, imaginative, and exquisitely worded speeches.

The old play was a mere Protestant tendency-drama directed against Catholic aggression, and full of the crude hatred and coarse ridicule of monks and nuns characteristic of the Reformation period. Shakespeare, with his usual tact, has suppressed the religious element, and retained only the national and political attack upon Roman Catholicism, so that the play had no slight actuality for the Elizabethan public. But he has also displaced the centre of gravity of the old play. Everything in Shakespeare turns upon John's defective right to the throne: therein lies the motive for the atrocity he plans, which leads (although it is not carried out as he intended) to the barons' desertion of his cause.

Despite its great dramatic advantages over *Richard II.*, the play suffers from the same radical weakness, and in an even greater degree: the figure of the King is too unsympathetic to serve as the centre-point of a drama. His despicable infirmity of purpose, which makes him kneel to receive his crown at the hands of the same Papal legate whom he has shortly before defied in blusterous terms; his infamous scheme to assassinate an innocent child, and his repentance when he sees that its supposed execution has alienated the chief supporters of his throne—all this hideous baseness, unredeemed by any higher characteristics, leads the spectator rather to attach his interest to the subordinate characters, and thus the action is frittered away before his eyes. It lacks unity, because the King is powerless to hold it together.

He himself is depicted for all time in the masterly scene (iii. 3) where he seeks, without putting his thought into plain words, to make Hubert understand that he would fain have Arthur murdered :—

> "Or if that thou couldst see me without eyes,
> Hear me without thine ears, and make reply
> Without a tongue, using conceit alone,
> Without eyes, ears, and harmful sound of words:
> Then, in despite of brooded-watchful day,—
> I would into thy bosom pour my thoughts.
> But, ah! I will not:—yet I love thee well."

Hubert protests his fidelity and devotion. Even if he were to die for the deed, he would execute it for the King's sake. Then John's manner becomes hearty, almost affectionate. "Good Hubert, Hubert!" he says caressingly. He points to Arthur, bidding Hubert "throw his eye on yon young boy;" and then follows this masterly dialogue:—

> "I'll tell thee what, my friend,
> He is a very serpent in my way;
> And wheresoe'er this foot of mine doth tread,
> He lies before me. Dost thou understand me?
> Thou art his keeper.
> *Hub.* And I'll keep him so,
> That he shall not offend your majesty.
> *K. John.* Death.
> *Hub.* My Lord.
> *K. John.* A grave.
> *Hub.* He shall not live.
> *K. John.* Enough.
> *I could be merry now.* Hubert, I love thee;
> Well, I'll not say what I intend for thee:
> Remember.—Madam, fare you well:
> I'll send those powers o'er to your majesty.
> *Elinor.* My blessing go with thee!"

The character that bears the weight of the piece, as an acting play, is the illegitimate son of Richard Cœur-de-Lion, Philip Faulconbridge. He is John Bull himself in the guise of a mediæval knight, equipped with great strength and a racy English humour, not the wit of a Mercutio, a gay Italianising cavalier, but the irrepressible ebullitions of rude health and blunt gaiety befitting an English Hercules. The scene in the first act, in which he appears along with his brother, who seeks to deprive him of his inheritance as a Faulconbridge on the ground of his alleged illegitimacy, and the subsequent scene with his mother, from whom he tries to wring the secret of his paternity, both appear in the old play; but in it everything that the Bastard says is in grim earnest—the embroidery of wit belongs to Shakespeare alone. It is he who has placed in Faulconbridge's mouth such sayings as this:—

> "Madam, I was not old Sir Robert's son:
> Sir Robert might have eat his part in me
> Upon Good Friday, and ne'er broke his fast."

And it is quite in Shakespeare's spirit when the son, after her confession, thus consoles his mother:—

> "Madam, I would not wish a better father.
> Some sins do bear their privilege on earth,
> And so doth yours."

In later years, at a time when his outlook upon life was darkened, Shakespeare accounted for the villainy of Edmund, in *King Lear*, and for his aloofness from anything like normal humanity, on the ground of his irregular birth; in the Bastard of this play, on the contrary, his aim was to present a picture of all that health, vigour, and full-blooded vitality which popular belief attributes to a "love-child."

The antithesis to this national hero is Limoges, Archduke of Austria, in whom Shakespeare, following the old play, has mixed up two entirely distinct personalities: Vidomar, Viscount of Limoges, at the siege of one of whose castles Richard Cœur-de-Lion was killed, in 1199, and Leopold V., Archduke of Austria, who had kept Cœur-de-Lion in prison. Though the latter, in fact, died five years before Richard, we here find him figuring as the dastardly murderer of the heroic monarch. In memory of this deed he wears a lion's skin on his shoulders, and thus brings down upon himself the indignant scorn of Constance and Faulconbridge's taunting insults:—

> "*Constance.* Thou wear a lion's hide! doff it for shame,
> And hang a calf's-skin on those recreant limbs.
> *Austria.* O, that a man should speak those words to me!
> *Bastard.* And hang a calf's-skin on those recreant limbs.
> *Aust.* Thou dar'st not say so, villain, for thy life.
> *Bast.* And hang a calf's-skin on those recreant limbs."

Every time the Archduke tries to get in a word of warning or counsel, Faulconbridge silences him with this coarse sarcasm.

Faulconbridge is at first full of youthful insolence, the true mediæval nobleman, who despises the burgess class simply as such. When the inhabitants of Angiers refuse to open their gates either to King John or to King Philip of France, who has espoused the cause of Arthur, the Bastard is so indignant at this peace-loving circumspection that he urges the kings to join their forces against the unlucky town, and cry truce to their feud until the ramparts are levelled to the earth. But in the course of the action he ripens more and more, and displays ever greater and more estimable qualities—humanity, right-mindedness, and a fidelity to the King which does not interfere with generous freedom of speech towards him.

His method of expression is always highly imaginative, more so than that of the other male characters in the play. Even the most abstract ideas he personifies. Thus he talks (iii. 1) of—

"Old Time, the clock-setter, that bald sexton Time."

In the old play whole scenes are devoted to his execution of the task here allotted him of visiting the monasteries of England and lightening the abbots' bursting money-bags. Shakespeare has suppressed these ebullitions of an anti-Catholic fervour, which he did not share. On the other hand, he has endowed Faulconbridge with genuine moral superiority. At first he is only a cheery, fresh-natured, robust personality, who tramples upon all social conventions, phrases, and affectations; and indeed he preserves to the last something of that contempt for "cockered silken wantons" which Shakespeare afterwards elaborates so magnificently in Henry Percy. But there is real greatness in his attitude when, at the close of the play, he addresses the vacillating John in this manly strain (v. 1) :—

> "Let not the world see fear, and sad distrust,
> Govern the motion of a kingly eye :
> Be stirring as the time ; be fire with fire ;
> Threaten the threatener, and outface the brow
> Of bragging horror : so shall inferior eyes,
> That borrow their behaviours from the great,
> Grow great by your example, and put on
> The dauntless spirit of resolution."

Faulconbridge is in this play the spokesman of the patriotic spirit. But we realise how strong was Shakespeare's determination to make this string sound at all hazards, when we find that the first eulogy of England is placed in the mouth of England's enemy, Limoges, the slayer of Cœur-de-Lion, who speaks (ii. 1) of—

> "That pale, that white-fac'd shore,
> Whose foot spurns back the ocean's roaring tides,
> And coops from other lands her islanders,
> . . . that England, hedg'd in with the main,
> That water-walled bulwark, still secure
> And confident from foreign purposes."

How slight is the difference between the eulogistic style of the two mortal enemies, when Faulconbridge, who has in the meantime killed Limoges, ends the play with a speech, which is, however, only slightly adapted from the older text:—

> "This England never did, nor never shall,
> Lie at the proud foot of a conqueror.
> .   .   .   .   .
> Come the three corners of the world in arms,
> And we shall shock them. Naught shall make us rue,
> If England to itself do rest but true."

Next to Faulconbridge, Constance is the character who bears the weight of the play; and its weakness arises in great part from the fact that Shakespeare has killed her at the end of the third act. So lightly is her death treated, that it is merely announced in passing by the mouth of a messenger. She does not appear at all after her son Arthur is put out of the way, possibly because Shakespeare feared to lengthen the list of sorrowing and vengeful mothers already presented in his earlier histories.

He has treated this figure with a marked predilection, such as he usually manifests for those characters which, in one way or another, forcibly oppose every compromise with lax worldliness and euphemistic conventionality. He has not only endowed her with the most passionate and enthusiastic motherly love, but with a wealth of feeling and of imagination which gives her words a certain poetic magnificence. She wishes that "her tongue were in the thunder's mouth, Then with a passion would she shake the world" (iii. 4). She is sublime in her grief for the loss of her son:—

> "I will instruct my sorrows to be proud,
> For grief is proud, and makes his owner stoop.

> To me, and to the state of my great grief,
> Let kings assemble;
>
> . . . . . .
> Here I and sorrows sit;
> Here is my throne, bid kings come bow to it.
> [*Seats herself on the ground.*"

Yet Shakespeare is already preparing us, in the overstrained violence of these expressions, for her madness and death.

The third figure which fascinates the reader of *King John* is that of Arthur. All the scenes in which the child appears are contained in the old play of the same name, and, among the rest, the first scene of the second act, which seems to dispose of Fleay's conjecture that the first two hundred lines of the act were hastily inserted after Shakespeare had lost his son. Nevertheless almost all that is gracious and touching in the figure is due to the great reviser. The old text is at its best in the scene where Arthur meets his death by jumping from the walls of the castle. Shakespeare has here confined himself for the most part to free curtailment; in the old *King John*, his fatal fall does not prevent Arthur from pouring forth copious lamentations to his absent mother and prayers to "sweete Iesu." Shakespeare gives him only two lines to speak after his fall.

In this play, as in almost all the works of Shakespeare's younger years, the reader is perpetually amazed to find the finest poetical and rhetorical passages side by side with the most intolerable euphuistic affectations. And we cannot allege the excuse that these are legacies from the older play. On the contrary, there is nothing of the kind to be found in it; they are added by Shakespeare, evidently with the express purpose of displaying delicacy and profundity of thought. In the scenes before the walls of Angiers, he has on the whole kept close to the old drama, and has even followed faithfully the sense of all the more important speeches. For example, it is a citizen on the ramparts, who, in the old play, suggests the marriage between Blanch and the Dauphin; Shakespeare merely re-writes his speech, introducing into it these beautiful lines (ii. 2):—

> " If lusty love should go in quest of beauty,
> Where should he find it fairer than in Blanch?
> If zealous love should go in search of virtue,
> Where should he find it purer than in Blanch?

> If love ambitious sought a match of birth,
> Whose veins bound richer blood than Lady Blanch?"

The surprising thing is that the same hand which has just written these verses should forthwith lose itself in a tasteless tangle of affectations like this:—

> "Such as she is, in beauty, virtue, birth,
> Is the young Dauphin every way complete:
> If not complete of, say, he is not she;
> And she again wants nothing, to name want,
> If want it be not, that she is not he:"

and this profound thought is further spun out with a profusion of images. Can we wonder that Voltaire and the French critics of the eighteenth century were offended by a style like this, even to the point of letting it blind them to the wealth of genius elsewhere manifested?

Even the touching scene between Arthur and Hubert is disfigured by false cleverness of this sort. The little boy, kneeling to the man who threatens to sear out his eyes, introduces, in the midst of the most moving appeals, such far-fetched and contorted phrases as this (iv. 1):—

> "The iron of itself, though heat red-hot,
> Approaching near these eyes, would drink my tears,
> And quench this fiery indignation
> Even in the matter of mine innocence;
> Nay, after that, consume away in rust,
> But for containing fire to harm mine eye."

And again, when Hubert proposes to reheat the iron:—

> "An if you do, you will but make it blush,
> And glow with shame of your proceedings, Hubert."

The taste of the age must indeed have pressed strongly upon Shakespeare's spirit to prevent him from feeling the impossibility of these quibbles upon the lips of a child imploring in deadly fear that his eyes may be spared to him.

As regards their ethical point of view, there is no essential difference between the old play and Shakespeare's. The King's defeat and painful death is in both a punishment for his wrongdoing. There has only been, as already mentioned, a certain displacement of the centre of gravity. In the old play, the dying

John stammers out an explicit confession that from the moment he surrendered to the Roman priest he has had no more happiness on earth; for the Pope's curse is a blessing, and his blessing a curse. In Shakespeare the emphasis is laid, not upon the King's weakness in the religio-political struggle, but upon the wrong to Arthur. Faulconbridge gives utterance to the fundamental idea of the play when he says (iv. 3):—

> "From forth this morsel of dead royalty,
> The life, the right, and truth of all this realm
> Is fled to heaven."

Shakespeare's political standpoint is precisely that of the earlier writer, and indeed, we may add, of his whole age.

The most important contrasts and events of the period he seeks to represent do not exist for him. He naïvely accepts the first kings of the House of Plantagenet, and the Norman princes in general, as English national heroes, and has evidently no suspicion of the deep gulf that separated the Normans from the Anglo-Saxons down to this very reign, when the two hostile races, equally oppressed by the King's tyranny, began to fuse into one people. What would Shakespeare have thought had he known that Richard Cœur-de-Lion's favourite formula of denial was "Do you take me for an Englishman?" while his pet oath, and that of his Norman followers, was "May I become an Englishman if——," &c.?

Nor does a single phrase, a single syllable, in the whole play, refer to the event which, for all after-times, is inseparably associated with the memory of King John—the signing of the Magna Charta. The reason of this is evidently, in the first place, that Shakespeare kept close to the earlier drama, and, in the second place, that he did not attribute to the event the importance it really possessed, did not understand that the Magna Charta laid the foundation of popular liberty, by calling into existence a middle class which supported even the House of Tudor in its struggle with an overweening oligarchy. But the chief reason why the Magna Charta is not mentioned was, no doubt, that Elizabeth did not care to be reminded of it. She was not fond of any limitations of her royal prerogative, and did not care to recall the defeats suffered by her predecessors in their struggles with warlike and independent vassals. And the nation was willing enough to humour her in this respect. People felt that they had to thank her government for a great national revival, and therefore showed no eagerness either to vindicate popular rights against her, or to see them vindicated in stage-history. It was not until long after, under the Stuarts, that the English people began to cultivate its constitution. The chronicle-writers of the period touch very lightly upon the barons' victory over King John in the struggle for the Great Charter; and Shakespeare thus followed at once his own personal bias with regard to history, and the current of his age.

XX

"THE TAMING OF THE SHREW" AND "THE MERCHANT OF VENICE" — SHAKESPEARE'S PREOCCUPATION WITH THOUGHTS OF PROPERTY AND GAIN—HIS GROWING PROSPERITY—HIS ADMISSION TO THE RANKS OF THE "GENTRY"—HIS PURCHASE OF HOUSES AND LAND—MONEY TRANSACTIONS AND LAWSUITS

THE first plays in which we seem to find traces of Italian travel are *The Taming of the Shrew* and *The Merchant of Venice*, the former written at latest in 1596, the latter almost certainly in that or the following year.

Enough has already been said of *The Taming of the Shrew*. It is only a free and spirited reconstruction of an old piece of scenic architecture, which Shakespeare demolished in order to erect from its materials a spacious and airy hall. The old play itself had been highly popular on the stage; it took new life under Shakespeare's hands. His play is not much more than a farce, but it possesses movement and fire, and the leading male character, the somewhat coarsely masculine Petruchio, stands in amusing and typical contrast to the spoilt, headstrong, and passionate little woman whom he masters.

The Merchant of Venice, Shakespeare's first important comedy, is a piece of work of a very different order, and is elaborated to a very different degree. There is far more of his own inmost nature in it than in the light and facile farce.

No doubt he found in Marlowe's *Jew of Malta* the first, purely literary, impulse towards *The Merchant of Venice*. In Marlowe's play the curtain rises upon the chief character, Barabas, sitting in his counting-house, with piles of gold before him, and revelling in the thought of the treasures which it takes a soliloquy of nearly fifty lines to enumerate—pearls like pebble-stones, opals, sapphires, amethysts, jacinths, topazes, grass-green emeralds, beauteous rubies and sparkling diamonds. At the beginning of the play, he is possessed of all the riches wherewith the Genie of the Lamp endowed Aladdin, which have at one time or another sparkled in the dreams of all poor poets.

Barabas is a Jew and usurer, like Shylock. Like Shylock, he has a daughter who is in love with a poor Christian; and, like him, he thirsts for revenge. But he is a monster, not a man. When he has been misused by the Christians, and robbed of his whole fortune, he becomes a criminal fit only for a fairy-tale or for a madhouse: he uses his own daughter as an instrument for his revenge, and then poisons her along with all the nuns in whose cloister she has taken refuge. Shakespeare was attracted by the idea of making a real man and a real Jew out of this intolerable demon in a Jew's skin.

But this slight impulse would scarcely have set Shakespeare's genius in motion had it found him engrossed in thoughts and images of an incongruous nature. It took effect upon his mind because it was at that moment preoccupied with the ideas of acquisition, property, money-making, wealth. He did not, like the Jew, who was in all countries legally incapable of acquiring real estate, dream of gold and jewels; but, like the genuine country-born Englishman he was, he longed for land and houses, meadows and gardens, money that yielded sound yearly interest, and, finally, a corresponding advancement in rank and position.

We have seen with what indifference he treated his plays, how little he thought of winning fame by their publication. All the editions of them which appeared in his lifetime were issued without his co-operation, and no doubt against his will, since the sale of the books did not bring him in a farthing, but, on the contrary, diminished his profits by diminishing the attendance at the theatre on which his livelihood depended. Furthermore, when we see in his Sonnets how discontented he was with his position as an actor, and how humiliated he felt at the contempt in which the stage was held, we cannot doubt that the calling into which he had drifted in his needy youth was in his eyes simply and solely a means of making money. It is true that actors like himself and Burbage were, in certain circles, welcomed and respected as men who rose above their calling; but they were admitted on sufferance, they had not full rights of citizenship, they were not "gentlemen." There is extant a copy of verses by John Davies of Hereford, beginning, "*Players*, I love yee, and your *Qualitie*," with a marginal note citing as examples "W. S., R. B." [William Shakespeare, Richard Burbage]; but they are clearly looked upon as exceptions:—

> "And though the *stage* doth staine pure gentle *bloud*,
> Yet generous yee are in *minde* and *moode*."

The calling of an actor, however, was a lucrative one. Most of the leading players became well-to-do, and it seems clear that this was one of the reasons why they were evilly regarded. In *The Return from Parnassus* (1606), Kemp assures two Cambridge students who apply to him and Burbage for instruction in acting, that there is no better calling in the world, from a financial point of view, than that of the player. In a pamphlet of the same year, *Ratsey's Ghost*, the executed thief, with a satirical allusion to Shakespeare, advises a strolling player to buy property in the country when he is tired of play-acting, and by that means attain honour and dignity. In an epigram entitled *Theatrum Licentia* (in *Laquei Ridiculosi*, 1616), we read of the actor's calling:—

> "For here's the spring (saith he) whence pleasures flow
> And brings them damnable excessive gains."

The primary object of Shakespeare's aspirations was neither renown as a poet nor popularity as an actor, but worldly prosperity, and prosperity regarded specially as a means of social advancement. He had taken greatly to heart his father's decline in property and civic esteem; from youth upwards he had been passionately bent on restoring the sunken name and fame of his family. He had now, at the age of only thirty-two, amassed a small capital, which he began to invest in the most advantageous way for the end he had in view—that of elevating himself above his calling.

His father had been afraid to cross the street lest he should be arrested for debt. He himself, as a youth, had been whipped and consigned to the lock-up at the command of the lord of the manor. The little town which had witnessed this disgrace should also witness the rehabilitation. The townspeople, who had heard of his equivocal fame as an actor and playwright, should see him in the character of a respected householder and landowner. At Stratford and elsewhere, those who had classed him with the proletariat should recognise in him a *gentleman*. According to a tradition which Rowe reports on the authority of Sir William Davenant, Lord Southampton is said to have laid the foundation of Shakespeare's prosperity by a gift of £1000. Though Bacon received more than this from Essex, the magnitude of the sum discredits the tradition—it is equivalent to something like £5000 in modern money. No doubt the young Earl gave the poet a present in acknowledgment of the dedication of his two poems; for the poets of that time did not live on royalties, but on their dedications. But as the ordinary acknowledgment of a dedication was only £5, a gift of even £50 would have been reckoned princely. What is practically certain is, that Shakespeare was early in a position to become a shareholder in the theatre; and he evidently had a special talent for putting the money he earned to profitable use. His firm determination to work his way up in the world, combined with the Englishman's inborn practicality, made him an excellent man of business; and he soon develops such a decided talent for finance as only two other great national writers, probably, have ever possessed—to wit, Holberg and Voltaire.

It is from the year 1596 onwards that we find evidences of his growing prosperity. In this year his father, no doubt prompted and supplied with means by Shakespeare himself, makes application to the Heralds' College for a coat-of-arms, the sketch of which is preserved, dated October 1596. The conferring of a coat-of-arms implied formal admittance into the ranks of "the gentry." It was necessary before either father or son could append the word "gentleman" (*armiger*) to his name, as we find Shakespeare doing in legal documents after this date, and in his will. But Shakespeare himself was not in a position to apply for a coat-of-arms. That was out of the question—a player was far too mean a person to come within the cognisance of heraldry. He therefore adopted the shrewd device of furnishing his father with means for making the application on his own behalf.

According to the ideas and regulations of the time, indeed, not even Shakespeare senior had any real right to a coat-of-arms. But the Garter-King-at-Arms for the time being, Sir William Dethick, was an exceedingly compliant personage, probably not inaccessible to pecuniary arguments. He was sharply criticised in his own day, and indeed at last superseded, on account of the facility with which he provided applicants with armorial bearings, and we possess his defence in this very matter of the Shakespeare coat-of-arms. All sorts of small falsehoods were alleged; for instance, that John Shakespeare had, twenty years before, had "his aunstient cote of arms assigned to him," and that he was then "Her Majestie's officer and baylefe," whereas his office had in fact been merely municipal. Nevertheless, there must have been some hitch in the negotiations, for in 1597 John Shakespeare is still described as *yeoman*, and not until 1599 did the definite assignment of the coat-of-arms take place, along with the permission (of which the son, however, did not avail himself) to impale the Shakespeare arms with those of the Arden family. The coat-of-arms is thus described:—"Gould on a bend sable a speare of the first, the poynt steeled, proper, and for creast or cognizance, a faulcon, his wings displayed, argent, standing on a wreathe of his coullors, supporting a speare gould steled as aforesaid." The motto runs (with a suspicion of irony), *Non sans droict*. Yet to what insignia had not *he* the right!

In the spring of 1597, William Shakespeare bought the mansion of New Place, the largest, and at one time the handsomest, house in Stratford, which had now fallen somewhat out of repair, and was therefore sold at the comparatively low price of £60. He thoroughly restored the house, attached two gardens to it, and soon extended his domain by new purchases of land, some of it arable; for we see that during the corn-famine of 1598 (February), he appears on the register as owner of ten quarters of corn and malt—that is to say, the third largest stock in the town. The house stood opposite the Guild Chapel, the sound of whose bells must have been among his earliest memories.

At the same time he gives his father money to revive the lawsuit against John Lambert concerning the property of Asbies, mortgaged nineteen years before—that lawsuit whose unfavourable issue young Shakespeare had taken so much to heart, as we have seen, that he introduced a gibe at the Lambert family into the Induction to *The Taming of the Shrew*, now just completed.

A letter of January 24, 1597–8, written by a certain Abraham Sturley in Stratford to his brother-in-law, Richard Quiney, whose son afterwards married Shakespeare's youngest daughter, shows that the poet already passed for a man of substance, since one of his fellow-townsmen sends him a message recommending him, instead of buying land at Shottery, to lease part of the Stratford tithes. This would be advantageous both to him and to the town, for the purchase of tithes was generally a good investment, and the character of the purchaser was of importance to the town, since a portion of the sum raised went into the municipal treasury.[1]

It appears, however, that the purchase-money required was still beyond Shakespeare's means, for not until seven years later, in 1605, does he buy, for the considerable sum of £440, a moiety of the lease of the tithes of Stratford, Old Stratford, Bishopton, and Welcombe. These tithes originally belonged to the Church, but passed to the town in 1554, and from 1580 onwards were farmed by private persons. As might have been expected, the purchase of them involved Shakespeare in several lawsuits.

In a letter of 1598 or 1599, Adrian Quiney, of Stratford, writes to his son Richard, who looked after the interests of his fellow-townsmen in the capital : " Yff yow bargen with Wm. Sha. or receve money therfor, brynge youre money homme that yow maye." This Richard Quiney is the writer of the only extant letter addressed to Shakespeare (probably never despatched), in which he begs his "loveinge contreyman," in moving and pious terms, for a loan of £30, promising security and interest. Another letter from Sturley, dated November 4, 1598, mentions the news "that our countriman Mr. Wm. Shak. would procure us monei, which I will like of as I shall heare when, and wheare, and howe."

All these documents render it sufficiently apparent that Shakespeare did not share the loathing of interest which it was the fashion of his day to affect, and which Antonio, in *The Merchant of Venice*, flaunts in the face of Shylock. The taking of interest was at that time regarded as forbidden to a Christian, but was usual nevertheless ; and Shakespeare seems to have charged the current rate, namely, ten per cent.

During the following years he continued to acquire still more

---

[1] Sturley writes :—" This is one speciall remembrance from ur fathers motion. Itt semeth bi him that our countriman, Mr. Shaksper, is willinge to disburse some monei upon some od yarde land or other att Shotterie or neare about us ; he thinketh it a veri fitt patterne to move him to deale in the matter of our tithes. Bi the instruccions u can geve him theareof, and bi the frendes he can make therefore, we thinke it a faire marke for him to shoote att, and not unpossible to hitt. It obtained would advance him in deede, and would do us muche good."

land. In 1602 he buys, at Stratford, arable land of the value of no less than £320, and pays £60 for a house and a piece of ground. In 1610 he adds twenty acres to his property. In 1612, in partnership with three others, he buys a house and garden in London for £140.

And Shakespeare was a strict man of business. We find him proceeding by attorney against a poor devil named Philip Rogers of Stratford, who in the years 1603-4 had bought small quantities of malt from him to the total value of £1, 19s. 10d., and who had besides borrowed two shillings of him. Six shillings he had repaid; and Shakespeare now sets the law in motion to recover the balance of £1, 15s. 10d. In 1608-9 he again brings an action against a Stratford debtor. This time he gets a verdict for £6, with £1, 4s. of costs; and as the debtor has absconded, Shakespeare proceeds against his security.

All these details show, in the first place, how closely Shakespeare kept up his connection with Stratford during his residence in London. By the year 1599 he has succeeded in restoring the credit of his family. He has made his poor, debt-burdened father a gentleman with a coat-of-arms, and has himself become one of the largest and richest landowners in his native place. He continues steadily to increase his capital and his property at Stratford; and it is obviously a mere corollary to this whole course of action that he should, while still in the full vigour of manhood, leave London, the theatre, and literature behind him, to return to Stratford and pass his last years as a prosperous landowner.

We next observe Shakespeare's eagerness to rise above his calling as a player. From 1599 onwards, he had the satisfaction of being able to write himself down: *Wm. Shakespeare of Stratford-upon-Avon in the County of Warwick, gentleman.* But it must not, of course, be understood that he was now in a position of equality with men of genuinely noble birth. So little was this the case, that even in the "Epistle Dedicatorie" to the Folio of 1623, the two actors, his comrades, who issue the book, describe him as the "servant" of the Earls of Pembroke and Montgomery, whose "dignity" they know to be "greater than to descend to the reading of these trifles." They nevertheless inscribe the "trifles" to the "incomparable paire of brethren" out of gratitude for the great "indulgence" and "favour" which they had "used" to the deceased poet.

The chief interest, however, of these old contracts and business letters lies in the insight they give us into a region of Shakespeare's soul, the existence of which, in their absence, we should never have divined. We see that he may very well have been thinking of himself when he makes Hamlet (v. 1) say beside Ophelia's open grave: "This fellow might be in's time a great buyer of land, with his statutes, his recognizances, his fines, his double vouchers, his recoveries: is this the fine of his fines, and the recovery of his recoveries, to have his fine pate full of fine dirt?"

And—to return to our point of departure—we see that when Shakespeare, in *The Merchant of Venice*, makes the whole play turn upon the different relations of different men to property, position, and wealth, the problem was one with which he was at the moment personally preoccupied.

XXI

THE MERCHANT OF VENICE—ITS SOURCES—ITS CHARACTERS, ANTONIO, PORTIA, SHYLOCK—MOONLIGHT AND MUSIC—SHAKESPEARE'S RELATION TO MUSIC

WE learn from Ben Jonson's *Volpone* (iv. 1) that the traveller who arrived in Venice first rented apartments, and then applied to a Jew dealer for the furniture. If the traveller happened to be a poet, he would thus have an opportunity, which he lacked in England, of studying the Jewish character and manner of expression. Shakespeare seems to have availed himself of it. The names of the Jews and Jewesses who appear in *The Merchant of Venice* he has taken from the Old Testament. We find in Genesis (x. 24) the name Salah (Hebrew Schelach; at that time appearing, as the name of a Maronite from Lebanon: Scialac) out of which Shakespeare has made Shylock; and in Genesis (xi. 29) there occurs the name Iscah (she who looks out, who spies), spelt "Jeska" in the English translations of 1549 and 1551, out of which he made his Jessica, the girl whom Shylock accuses of a fondness for "clambering up to casements" and "thrusting her head into the public street" to see the masquers pass.

Shakespeare's audiences were familiar with several versions of the story of the Jew who relentlessly demanded the pound of flesh pledged to him by his Christian debtor, and was at last sent empty and baffled away, and even forced to become a Christian. The story has been found in Buddhist legends (along with the adventure of the Three Caskets, here interwoven with it), and many believe that it came to Europe from India. It may, however, have migrated in just the opposite direction. Certain it is, as one of Shakespeare's authorities points out, that the right to take payment in the flesh of the insolvent debtor was admitted in the Twelve Tables of ancient Rome. As a matter of fact, this antique trait was quite international, and Shakespeare has only transferred it from old and semi-barbarous times to the Venice of his own day.

The story illustrates the transition from the unconditional enforcement of strict law to the more modern principle of equity. Thus it afforded an opening for Portia's eloquent contrast between justice and mercy, which the public understood as an assertion of the superiority of Christian ethics to the Jewish insistence on the letter of the law.

One of the sources on which Shakespeare drew for the figure of Shylock, and especially for his speeches in the trial scene, is *The Orator* of Alexander Silvayn. The 95th Declamation of this work bears the title: "Of a Jew who would for his debt have a pound of the flesh of a Christian." Since an English translation of Silvayn's book by Anthony Munday appeared in 1596, and *The Merchant of Venice* is mentioned by Meres in 1598 as one of Shakespeare's works, there can scarcely be any doubt that the play was produced between these dates.

In *The Orator* both the Merchant and the Jew make speeches, and the invective against the Jew is interesting in so far as it gives a lively impression of the current accusations of the period against the Israelitish race :—

"But it is no marvaile if this race be so obstinat and cruell against us, for they doe it of set purpose to offend our God whom they have crucified: and wherefore? Because he was holie, as he is yet so reputed of this worthy Turkish nation : but what shall I say? Their own bible is full of their rebellion against God, against their Priests, Judges, and leaders. What did not the verie Patriarks themselves, from whom they have their beginning? They sold their brother. . . ." &c.

Shakespeare's chief authority, however, for the whole play was obviously the story of Gianetto, which occurs in the collection entitled *Il Pecorone*, by Ser Giovanni Fiorentino, published in Milan in 1558.

A young merchant named Gianetto comes with a richly laden ship to a harbour near the castle of Belmonte, where dwells a lovely young widow. She has many suitors, and is, indeed, prepared to surrender her hand and her fortune, but only on one condition, which no one has hitherto succeeded in fulfilling, and which is stated with mediæval simplicity and directness. She challenges the aspirant, at nightfall, to share her bed and make her his own; but at the same time she gives him a sleeping-draught which plunges him in profound unconsciousness from the moment his head touches the pillow, so that at daybreak he has forfeited his ship and its cargo to the fair lady, and is sent on his way, despoiled and put to shame.

This misfortune happens to Gianetto; but he is so deeply in love that he returns to Venice and induces his kind foster-father, Ansaldo, to fit out another ship for him. But his second visit to Belmonte ends no less disastrously, and in order to enable him to make a third attempt his foster-father is forced to borrow 10,000 ducats from a Jew, upon the conditions which we know. By following the advice of a kindly-disposed waiting-woman, the young man this time escapes the danger, becomes a happy bride-groom, and in his rapture forgets Ansaldo's obligation to the Jew. He is not reminded of it until the very day when it falls due, and then his wife insists that he shall instantly start for Venice, taking with him a sum of 100,000 ducats. She herself presently follows, dressed as an advocate, and appears in Venice as a young lawyer of great reputation, from Bologna. The Jew rejects every proposition for the deliverance of Ansaldo, even the 100,000 ducats. Then the trial-scene proceeds, just as in Shakespeare; Gianetto's young wife delivers judgment, like Portia; the Jew receives not a stiver, and dares not shed a drop of Ansaldo's blood. When Gianetto, in his gratitude, offers the young advocate the whole 100,000 ducats, she, as in the play, demands nothing but the ring which Gianetto has received from his wife; and the tale ends with the same gay unravelling of the sportive complication, which gives Shakespeare the matter for his fifth act.

Being unable to make use of the condition imposed by the fair lady of Belmonte in *Il Pecorone*, Shakespeare cast about for another, and found it in the *Gesta Romanorum*, in the tale of the three caskets, of gold, silver, and lead. Here it is a young girl who makes the choice in order to win the Emperor's son. The inscription on the golden casket promises that whoever chooses that shall find what he deserves. The girl rejects this out of humility, and rightly, since it proves to contain dead men's bones. The inscription on the silver casket promises to whoever chooses it what his nature craves. The girl rejects that also; for, as she says naïvely, "My nature craves for fleshly delights." Finally, the leaden casket promises that whoever chooses it shall find what God has decreed for him; and it proves to be full of jewels.

In Shakespeare, Portia, in accordance with her father's will, makes her suitors choose between the three caskets (here furnished with other legends), of which the humblest contains her portrait.

It is not probable that Shakespeare made any use of an older play, now lost, of which Stephen Gosson, in his *School of Abuse* (1579), says that it represented "the greedinesse of worldly chusers, and the bloody mindes of usurers."

The great value of *The Merchant of Venice* lies in the depth and seriousness which Shakespeare has imparted to the vague outlines of character presented by the old stories, and in the ravishing moonlight melodies which bring the drama to a close.

In Antonio, the royal merchant, who, amid all his fortune and splendour, is a victim to melancholy and spleen induced by forebodings of coming disaster, Shakespeare has certainly expressed something of his own nature. Antonio's melancholy is closely related to that which, in the years immediately following, we shall find in Jaques in *As You Like It*, in the Duke in *Twelfth Night*, and in Hamlet. It forms a sort of mournful undercurrent to the joy of life which at this period is still dominant in Shakespeare's soul. It leads, after a certain time, to the substitution of dreaming and brooding heroes for those men of action and resolution who, in the poet's brighter youth, had played the leading parts in his dramas. For the rest, despite the princely elevation of his nature, Antonio is by no means faultless. He has insulted and baited Shylock in the most brutal fashion on account of his faith and his blood. We realise the ferocity and violence of the mediæval prejudice against the Jews when we find a man of Antonio's magnanimity so entirely a slave to it. And when, with a little more show of justice, he parades his loathing and contempt for Shylock's money-dealings, he strangely (as it seems to us) overlooks the fact that the Jews have been carefully excluded from all other means of livelihood, and have been systematically allowed to scrape together gold in order that their hoards may always be at hand when circumstances render it convenient to plunder them. Antonio's attitude towards Shylock cannot possibly be Shakespeare's own. Shylock cannot understand Antonio, and characterises him (iii. 3) in the words—

"This is the fool that lent out money gratis."

But Shakespeare himself did not belong to this class of fools. He has endowed Antonio with an ideality which he had neither the resolution nor the desire to emulate. Such a man's conduct towards Shylock explains the outcast's hatred and thirst for revenge.

Shakespeare has lavished peculiar and loving care upon the figure of Portia. Both in the circumstances in which she is placed at the outset, and in the conjuncture to which Shylock's bond gives rise, there is a touch of the fairy tale. In so far, the two sides of the action harmonise well with each other. Now-a-days, indeed, we are apt to find rather too much of the nursery story in the preposterous will by which Portia is bound to marry whoever divines the very simple answer to a riddle—to the effect that a showy outside is not always to be trusted. The fable of the three caskets pleased Shakespeare so much as a means of expressing and enforcing his hatred of all empty show that he ignored the grotesque improbability of the method of selecting a bridegroom.

His thought seems to have been: Portia is not only nobly born; she is thoroughly genuine, and can therefore be won only by a suitor who rejects the show for the substance. This is suggested in Bassanio's long speech before making his choice (iii. 2). If there is anything that Shakespeare hated with a hatred somewhat disproportionate to the triviality of the matter, a hatred which finds expression in every stage of his career, it is the use of rouge and false hair. Therefore he insists upon the fact that Portia's beauty owes nothing to art; with others the case is different:—

> "Look on beauty,
> And you shall see 'tis purchas'd by the weight;
> . . . . . .
> So are those crisped snaky golden locks,
> Which make such wanton gambols with the wind,
> Upon supposed fairness, often known
> To be the dowry of a second head,
> The skull that bred them, in the sepulchre."

And he deduces the moral:—

> "Thus ornament is but the guiled shore
> To a most dangerous sea."

"THE MERCHANT OF VENICE"

Before the choice, Portia dares not openly avow her feelings towards Bassanio, but does so nevertheless by means of a graceful and sportive slip of the tongue:—

> "Beshrew your eyes,
> They have o'erlook'd me, and divided me:
> One half of me is yours, the other half yours,—
> Mine own, I would say; but if mine, then yours,
> And so all yours!"

Bassanio answers by begging permission to make instant choice between the caskets, since he lives upon the rack until his fate is sealed; whereupon Portia makes some remarks as to confessions on the rack, which seem to allude to an occurrence of a few years earlier, the barbarous execution of Elizabeth's Spanish doctor, Don Roderigo Lopez, in 1594, after two ruffians had been racked into making confessions which, no doubt falsely, incriminated him. Portia says jestingly—

> "Ay, but I fear, you speak upon the rack,
> Where men, enforced, do speak anything;"

and Bassanio answers—

> "Promise me life, and I'll confess the truth."

When the choice has been made and has fallen as she hoped and desired, her attitude clearly expresses Shakespeare's ideal of womanhood at this period of his life. It is not Juliet's passionate self-abandonment, but the perfect surrender in tenderness of the wise and delicate woman. For her own sake she does not wish herself better than she is, but for him "she would be trebled twenty times herself." She knows that she—

> "Is an unlesson'd girl, unschool'd, unpractis'd:
> Happy in this, she is not yet so old
> But she may learn; happier than this,
> She is not bred so dull but she can learn;
> Happiest of all is, that her gentle spirit
> Commits itself to yours to be directed,
> As from her lord, her governor, her king."

In such humility does she love this weak spendthrift, whose sole motive in seeking her out was originally that of clearing off the debts in which his frivolity had involved him. It thus happens, quaintly enough, that what her father thought to prevent by his strange device, namely, that Portia should be won by a mercenary suitor, is the very thing that happens—though it is true that her personal charms throw his original motive into the background.

In spite of Portia's womanly self-surrender in love, there is something independent, almost masculine, in her character. She has the orphan heiress's habit and power of looking after herself, directing others, and acting on her own responsibility without seeking advice or taking account of convention. The poet has borrowed traits from the Italian novel in order to make her as prompt in counsel as she is magnanimous. How much money does Antonio owe? she asks. Three thousand ducats? Give the Jew six thousand, and tear up the bond.

Shakespeare has equipped her with the bright and victorious temperament with which he henceforth, for a certain time, endows nearly all the heroines of his comedies. To another of these ladies it is said, "Without question, you were born in a merry hour." She answers, "No, sure, my lord, my mother cried; but then there was a star danced, and under that I was born." All these young women were born under a star that danced. Even the most subdued of them overflows with the rapture of existence.

Portia's nature is health, its utterance joy. Radiant happiness is her element. She is descended from happiness, she has grown up in happiness, she is surrounded with all the means and conditions of happiness, and she distributes happiness with both hands. She is noble to the heart's core. She is no swan born in the duck-yard, but is in complete harmony with her surroundings and with herself.

Shylock's riches consist of gold and jewels, easy to conceal or to transport at a moment's notice, but also inviting to robbery and rapine. Antonio's riches consist in cargoes tossed on many seas, and exposed to danger from storms and from pirates. What Portia owns she owns in security: estates and palaces inherited from her fathers. There has needed, perhaps, as much as a century of direct preparation for the birth of such a creature. Her noble forefathers for generations back must have led free and stainless lives, favoured by destiny, prosperous and happy, in order to amass the riches which are her pedestal, to gain the respect which is her throne, to gather the household which forms her retinue, to decorate the palace in which she rules as a princess, and to endow her mind with the high faculty and culture befitting a reigning sovereign. She is healthy, though she is delicate; she is gay, although she is mentally a head taller than any of those around her; and she is young, although she is wise. She is of a fresher stock than the nervous women of to-day. She is borne aloft by an unfailing serenity of nature, which has never suffered any rude disturbance. It manifests itself in her gaiety under circumstances of painful uncertainty, in her self-control in overwhelming joy, and in her promptitude of action in an unforeseen and threatening conjuncture. She has inexhaustible resources in her soul, a profusion of ideas and inspirations, as great a superabundance of wit as of wealth. In contradistinction to her lover, she never makes a display of what is not her own to command. Hence her equilibrium and queenly repose. If we do not realise this radiant joy of life in the inmost chambers of her soul, we are apt, even from her first scene with Nerissa, to think her jesting forced and her wit far-fetched, and are almost ready to make the criticism that only a poor intelligence plays tricks with speech and fantasticates in words. But when we have looked into the depths of this well-spring of health, we understand how her thoughts gush forth, flashing and plashing, as freely and inevitably as the jets of a fountain rise into the air. She evokes and discards image after image, as one plucks and throws away flowers in a luxuriant garden. She delights to wreath and plait her words, as she wreaths and plaits her hair.

It harmonises with her whole nature when she says (i. 2): "The brain may devise laws for the blood; but a hot temper leaps o'er a cold decree: such a hare is madness, the youth, to skip o'er the meshes of good counsel, the cripple." Such phrases must be conceived as springing from a delight in laughter and sport for the sport's sake; otherwise they would be stiff and cumbrous. In the same way, such a sally as this (iv. 1)—

"Your wife would give you little thanks for that,
If she were by to hear you make the offer,"

must be taken as springing from a gleeful assurance of victory, else it might seem to show callous indifference to Antonio's apparently hopeless plight. There is an innate harmony in Portia's soul; but it is full-toned, complex, and woven of strongly contrasted elements, so that it requires some imagination to represent it to ourselves. There is something in the harmonious subtlety of her physiognomy which reminds us of Lionardo's female heads. Dignity and tenderness, the power to command and to obey, acuteness such as thrives in courts, and simple womanliness, an almost inflexible seriousness and an almost mischievous gaiety, are here cunningly commingled and combined.

How Shakespeare himself would have us regard her may be gathered from the enthusiasm with which he makes Jessica describe her to her lover (iii. 5). When one young woman so warmly eulogises another, we may safely assume that her merits are unimpeachable. "It is very meet," she says,

> "The Lord Bassanio live an upright life,
> For, having such a blessing in his lady,
> He finds the joys of heaven here on earth;
> And, if on earth he do not mean it, then
> In reason he should never come to heaven.
> Why, if two gods should play some heavenly match,
> And on the wager lay two earthly women,
> And Portia one, there must be something else
> Pawn'd with the other, for the poor rude world
> Hath not her fellow."

The central figure of the play, however, in the eyes of modern readers and spectators, is of course Shylock, though there can be no doubt that he appeared to Shakespeare's contemporaries a comic personage, and, since he makes his final exit before the last act, by no means the protagonist. In the humaner view of a later age, Shylock appears as a half-pathetic creation, a scapegoat, a victim; to the Elizabethan public, with his rapacity and his miserliness, his usury and his eagerness to dig for another the pit into which he himself falls, he seemed, not terrible, but ludicrous. They did not even take him seriously enough to feel any real uneasiness as to Antonio's fate, since they all knew beforehand the issue of the adventure. They laughed when he went to Bassanio's feast "in hate, to feed upon the prodigal Christian;" they laughed when, in the scene with Tubal, he suffered himself to be bandied about between exultation over Antonio's misfortunes and rage over the prodigality of his runaway daughter; and they found him odious when he exclaimed, "I would my daughter were dead at my foot and the jewels in her ear!" He was, simply as a Jew, a despised creature; he belonged to the race which had crucified God himself; and he was doubly despised as an extortionate usurer. For the rest, the English public—like the Norwegian public so lately as the first half of this century—had no acquaintance with Jews except in books and on the stage. From 1290 until the middle of the seventeenth century the Jews were entirely excluded from England. Every prejudice against them was free to flourish unchecked.

Did Shakespeare in a certain measure share these religious prejudices, as he seems to have shared the patriotic prejudices against the Maid of Orleans, if, indeed, he is responsible for the part she plays in *Henry VI.?* We may be sure that he was very slightly affected by them, if at all. Had he made a more undisguised effort to place himself at Shylock's standpoint, the censorship, on the one hand, would have intervened, while, on the other hand, the public would have been bewildered and alienated. It is quite in the spirit of the age that Shylock should suffer the punishment which befalls him. To pay him out for his stiff-necked vengefulness, he is mulcted not only of the sum he lent Antonio, but of half his fortune, and is finally, like Marlowe's *Jew of Malta,* compelled to change his religion. The latter detail gives something of a shock to the modern reader. But the respect for personal conviction, when it conflicted with orthodoxy, did not exist in Shakespeare's time. It was not very long since Jews had been forced to choose between kissing the crucifix and mounting the faggots; and in Strasburg, in 1349, nine hundred of them had in one day chosen the latter alternative. It is strange to reflect, too, that just at the time when, on the English stage, one Mediterranean Jew was poisoning his daughter, and another whetting his knife to cut his debtor's flesh, thousands of heroic and enthusiastic Hebrews in Spain and Portugal, who, after the expulsion of the 300,000 at the beginning of the century, had secretly remained faithful to Judaism, were suffering themselves to be tortured, flayed, and burnt alive by the Inquisition, rather than forswear the religion of their race.

It is the high-minded Antonio himself who proposes that Shylock shall be forced to become a Christian. This is done for his good; for baptism opens to him the possibility of salvation after death; and his Christian antagonists, who, by dint of the most childish sophisms, have despoiled him of his goods and forced him to forswear his God, can still pose as representing the Christian principle of mercy, in opposition to one who has taken his stand upon the Jewish basis of formal law.

That Shakespeare himself, however, in nowise shared the fanatical belief that a Jew was of necessity damned, or could be saved by compulsory conversion, is rendered clear enough for the modern reader in the scene between Launcelot and Jessica (iii. 5), where Launcelot jestingly avers that Jessica is damned. There is only one hope for her, and that is, that her father may not be her father :—

"*Jessica.* That were a kind of bastard hope, indeed: so the sins of my mother should be visited upon me.

"*Launcelot.* Truly then I fear you are damned both by father and mother: thus when I shun Scylla, your father, I fall into Charybdis, your mother. Well, you are gone both ways.

"*Jes.* I shall be saved by my husband; he hath made me a Christian.

"*Laun.* Truly, the more to blame he: we were Christians enow before; e'en as many as could well live one by another. This making of Christians will raise the price of hogs: if we grow all to be pork-eaters, we shall not shortly have a rasher on the coals for money."

And Jessica repeats Launcelot's saying to Lorenzo :—

"He tells me flatly, there is no mercy for me in heaven, because I am a Jew's daughter: and he says, you are no good member of the commonwealth, for, in converting Jews to Christians, you raise the price of pork."

No believer would ever speak in this jesting tone of matters that must seem to him so momentous.

It is none the less astounding how much right in wrong, how much humanity in inhumanity, Shakespeare has succeeded in imparting to Shylock. The spectator sees clearly that, with the treatment he has suffered, he could not but become what he is. Shakespeare has rejected the notion of the atheistically-minded Marlowe, that the Jew hates Christianity and despises Christians as fiercer money-grubbers than himself. With his calm humanity, Shakespeare makes Shylock's hardness and cruelty result at once from his passionate nature and his abnormal position ; so that, in spite of everything, he has come to appear in the eyes of later times as a sort of tragic symbol of the degradation and vengefulness of an oppressed race.

There is not in all Shakespeare a greater example of trenchant and incontrovertible eloquence than Shylock's famous speech (iii. 1):—

"I am a Jew. Hath not a Jew eyes? hath not a Jew hands, organs, dimensions, senses, affections, passions? fed with the same food, hurt with the same weapons, subject to the same diseases, healed by the same means, warmed and cooled by the same winter and summer, as a Christian is? If you prick us, do we not bleed? if you tickle us, do we not laugh? if you poison us, do we not die? and if you wrong us, shall we not revenge? If we are like you in the rest, we will resemble you in that. If a Jew wrong a Christian, what is his humility? revenge. If a Christian wrong a Jew, what should his sufferance be by Christian example? why, revenge. The villany you teach me, I will execute; and it shall go hard but I will better the instruction."

But what is most surprising, doubtless, is the instinct of genius with which Shakespeare has seized upon and reproduced racial characteristics, and emphasised what is peculiarly Jewish in Shylock's culture. While Marlowe, according to his custom, made his Barabas revel in mythological similes, Shakespeare indicates that Shylock's culture is founded entirely upon the Old Testament, and makes commerce his only point of contact with the civilisation of later times. All his parallels are drawn from the Patriarchs and the Prophets. With what unction he speaks when he justifies himself by the example of Jacob! His own race is always "our sacred nation," and he feels that "the curse has never fallen upon it" until his daughter fled with his treasures. Jewish, too, is Shylock's respect for, and obstinate insistence on, the letter of the law, his reliance upon statutory rights, which are, indeed, the only rights society allows him, and the partly instinctive, partly defiant restriction of his moral ideas to the principle of retribution. He is no wild animal; he is no heathen who simply gives the rein to his natural instincts; his hatred is not ungoverned; he restrains it within its legal rights, like a tiger in its cage. He is entirely lacking, indeed, in the freedom and serenity, the easy-going, light-hearted carelessness which characterises a ruling caste in its virtues and its vices, in its charities as in its prodigalities; but he has not a single twinge of conscience about anything that he does; his actions are in perfect harmony with his ideals.

Sundered from the regions, the social forms, the language, in which his spirit is at home, he has yet retained his Oriental character. Passion is the kernel of his nature. It is his passion that has enriched him; he is passionate in action, in calculation, in sensation, in hatred, in revenge, in everything. His vengefulness is many times greater than his rapacity. Avaricious though he be, money is nothing to him in comparison with revenge. It is not until he is exasperated by his daughter's robbery and flight that he takes such hard measures against Antonio, and refuses to accept three times the amount of the loan. His conception of honour may be unchivalrous enough, but, such as it is, his honour is not to be bought for money. His hatred of Antonio is far more intense than his love for his jewels; and it is this passionate hatred, not avarice, that makes him the monster he becomes.

From this Hebrew passionateness, which can be traced even in details of diction, arises, among other things, his loathing of sloth and idleness. To realise how essentially Jewish is this trait we need only refer to the so-called Proverbs of Solomon. Shylock dismisses Launcelot with the words, "Drones hive not with me." Oriental, rather than specially Jewish, are the images in which he gives his passion utterance, approaching, as they so often do, to the parable form. (See, for example, his appeal to Jacob's cunning, or the speech in vindication of his claim, which begins, "You have among you many a purchased slave.") Specially Jewish, on the other hand, is the way in which this ardent passion throughout employs its images and parables in the service of a curiously sober rationalism, so that a sharp and biting logic, which retorts every accusation with interest, is always the controlling force. This sober logic, moreover, never lacks dramatic impetus. Shylock's course of thought perpetually takes the form of question and answer, a subordinate but characteristic trait which appears in the style of the Old Testament, and reappears to this day in representations of primitive Jews. One can feel through his words that there is a chanting quality in his voice; his movements are rapid, his gestures large. Externally and internally, to the inmost fibre of his being, he is a type of his race in its degradation.

Shylock disappears with the end of the fourth act in order that no discord may mar the harmony of the concluding scenes. By means of his fifth act, Shakespeare dissipates any preponderance of pain and gloom in the general impression of the play.

MOONLIGHT AND MUSIC

This act is a moonlit landscape thrilled with music. It is altogether given over to music and moonshine. It is an image of Shakespeare's soul at that point of time. Everything is here reconciled, assuaged, silvered over, and borne aloft upon the wings of music.

The speeches melt into each other like voices in part-singing:—

"*Lorenzo.* The moon shines bright.—In such a night as this,
When the sweet wind did gently kiss the trees,
And they did make no noise, in such a night,
Troilus, methinks, mounted the Trojan walls,
And sigh'd his soul toward the Grecian tents,
Where Cressid lay that night.
   Jessica.   In such a night
Did Thisbe fearfully o'ertrip the dew;
.   .   .   .
   Lor.   In such a night
Stood Dido with a willow in her hand;"

and so on for four more speeches—the very poetry of moonlight arranged in antiphonies.

The conclusion of *The Merchant of Venice* brings us to the threshold of a term in Shakespeare's life instinct with highpitched gaiety and gladness. In this, his brightest period, he fervently celebrates strength and wisdom in man, intellect and wit in woman; and these most brilliant years of his life are also the most musical. His poetry, his whole existence, seem now to be given over to music, to harmony.

He had been early familiar with the art of music, and must have heard much music in his youth.[1] Even in his earliest plays, such as *The Two Gentlemen of Verona*, we find a considerable insight into musical technique, as in the conversation between Julia and Lucetta (i. 2). He must often have heard the Queen's choir, and the choirs maintained by noble lords and ladies, like that which Portia has in her palace. And he no doubt heard much music performed in private. The English were in his day, what they have never been since, a musical people. It was the Puritans who cast out music from the daily life of England. The spinet was the favourite instrument of the time. Spinets stood in the barbers' shops, for the use of customers waiting their turn.

[1] Förster: *Shakespeare und die Tonkunst, Shakespeare-Jahrbuch*, ii. 155; Karl Elze: *William Shakespeare*, p. 474; Henrik Schück: *William Shakespere*, p. 313.

Elizabeth herself played on the spinet and the lute. In his Sonnet cxxviii., addressed to the lady whom he caressingly calls " my music," Shakespeare has described himself as standing beside his mistress's spinet and envying the keys which could kiss her fingers. In all probability he was personally acquainted with John Dowland, the chief English musician of the time, although the poem in which he is named, published as Shakespeare's in *The Passionate Pilgrim*, is not by him, but by Richard Barnfield.

In *The Taming of the Shrew* (iii. 1), written just before *The Merchant of Venice*, he had utilised his knowledge of singing and lute-playing in a scene of gay comedy. " The cause why music was ordained," says Lucentio—

" Was it not to refresh the mind of man,
After his studies, or his usual pain ? "

Its influence upon mental disease was also known to Shakespeare, and noted both in *King Lear* and in *The Tempest*. But here, in *The Merchant of Venice*, where music is wedded to moonlight, his praise of it takes a higher flight :—

" How sweet the moonlight sleeps upon this bank !
Here we will sit, and let the sounds of music
Creep in our ears : soft stillness, and the night,
Become the touches of sweet harmony."

And Shakespeare, who never mentions church music, which seems to have had no message for his soul, here makes the usually unimpassioned Lorenzo launch out into genuine Renaissance rhapsodies upon the music of the spheres :—

" Sit, Jessica : look, how the floor of heaven
Is thick inlaid with patines of bright gold.
There's not the smallest orb, which thou behold'st,
But in his motion like an angel sings,
Still quiring to the young-ey'd cherubins ;
Such harmony is in immortal souls ;
But, whilst this muddy vesture of decay
Doth grossly close it in, we cannot hear it."

Sphere-harmony and soul-harmony, not bell-ringing or psalm-singing, are for him the highest music.

Shakespeare's love of music, so incomparably expressed in

the last scenes of *The Merchant of Venice*, appears at other points in the play.. Thus Portia says, when Bassanio is about to make his choice between the caskets (iii. 2) :—

> "Let music sound, while he doth make his choice;
> Then, if he lose, he makes a swan-like end,
> Fading in music.
> . . . . .
>   He may win;
> And what is music then? then music is
> Even as the flourish when true subjects bow
> To a new-crowned monarch."

It seems as though Shakespeare, in this play, had set himself to reveal for the first time how deeply his whole nature was penetrated with musical feeling. He places in the mouth of the frivolous Jessica these profound words, " I am never merry when I hear sweet music." And he makes Lorenzo answer, "The reason is, your spirits are attentive." The note of the trumpet, he says, will calm a wanton herd of " unhandled colts;" and Orpheus, as poets feign, drew trees and stones and floods to follow him :—

> "Since nought so stockish, hard, and full of rage,
> But music for the time doth change his nature.
> The man that hath no music in himself,
> Nor is not mov'd with concord of sweet sounds,
> Is fit for treasons, stratagems, and spoils;
> The motions of his spirit are dull as night,
> And his affections dark as Erebus.
> Let no such man be trusted.—Mark the music."

This must not, of course, be taken too literally. But note the characters whom Shakespeare makes specially unmusical: in this play, Shylock, who loathes "the vile squeaking of the wry-necked fife;" then Hotspur, the hero-barbarian; Benedick, the would-be woman-hater; Cassius, the fanatic politician; Othello, the half-civilised African; and finally creatures like Caliban, who are nevertheless enthralled by music as though by a wizard's spell.

On the other hand, all his more delicate creations are musical. In the First Part of *Henry IV.* (iii. 1) we have Mortimer and his Welsh wife, who do not understand each other's speech :—

"But I will never be a truant, love,
. Till I have learn'd thy language; for thy tongue
Makes Welsh as sweet as ditties highly penn'd,
Sung by a fair queen in a summer's bower,
With ravishing division, to her lute."

Musical, too, are the pathetic heroines, such as Ophelia and Desdemona, and characters like Jaques in *As You Like It*, and the Duke and Viola in *Twelfth Night*. The last-named comedy, indeed, is entirely interpenetrated with music. The keynote of musical passion is struck in the opening speech:—

"If music be the food of love, play on;
Give me excess of it, that, surfeiting,
The appetite may sicken, and so die.—
That strain again! it had a dying fall:
O! it came o'er my ear like the sweet south
That breathes upon a bank of violets,
Stealing and giving odour."

Here, too, Shakespeare's love of the folk-song finds expression, when he makes the Duke say (ii. 4):—

"Now, good Cesario, but that piece of song,
That old and antique song, we heard last night;
Methought, it did relieve my passion much,
More than light airs, and recollected terms,
Of these most brisk and giddy-paced times:
Come; but one verse."

No less sensitive and devoted to music than the Duke in *Twelfth Night* or Lorenzo in *The Merchant of Venice* must their creator himself have been in the short and happy interval in which, as yet unmastered by the melancholy latent in his as in all deep natures, he felt his talents strengthening and unfolding, his life every day growing fuller and more significant, his inmost soul quickening with creative impulse and instinct with harmony. The rich concords which bring *The Merchant of Venice* to a close symbolise, as it were, the feeling of inward wealth and equipoise to which he had now attained.

XXII

*"EDWARD III." AND "ARDEN OF FEVERSHAM"—SHAKE-
SPEARE'S DICTION—THE FIRST PART OF "HENRY IV."
—FIRST INTRODUCTION OF HIS OWN EXPERIENCES OF
LIFE IN THE HISTORIC DRAMA—WHY THE SUBJECT
APPEALED TO HIM—TAVERN LIFE—SHAKESPEARE'S
CIRCLE—SIR JOHN FALSTAFF—FALSTAFF AND THE
GRACIOSO OF THE SPANISH DRAMA—RABELAIS AND
SHAKESPEARE—PANURGE AND FALSTAFF*

THERE is extant a historical play, dating from 1596, entitled *The Raigne of King Edward third. As it hath bin sundrie times plaied about the Citie of London*, which several English students and critics, among them Halliwell-Phillips, have attributed in part to Shakespeare, arguing that the better scenes, at least, must have been carefully retouched by him. Although the drama, as a whole, is not much more Shakespearean in style than many other Elizabethan plays, and although Swinburne, the highest of all English authorities, has declared the piece to be the work of an imitator of Marlowe, yet there is a good deal to be said in favour of the hypothesis that Shakespeare had some hand in *Edward III*. His touch may be recognised in several passages; and especially noteworthy are the following lines from a speech of Warwick's:—

> "A spacious field of reasons could I urge
> Between his glory, daughter, and thy shame:
> That poison shows worst in a golden cup;
> Dark night seems darker by the lightning flash;
> *Lilies that fester smell far worse than weeds,*
> And every glory that inclines to sin,
> The shame is treble by the opposite."

The italicised verse reappears as the last line of Shakespeare's Sonnet xciv.; and as this Sonnet seems to refer (as we shall afterwards see) to circumstances in Shakespeare's life which did not arise until 1600, we cannot suppose that it was one of those written at an earlier date and circulated in manuscript. The probability is that Shakespeare simply reclaimed this line from a speech contributed by him to another man's play.

It is natural that a foreign student should shrink from opposing his judgment to that of English critics, where English diction and style are in question. Nevertheless he is sometimes driven into dissent with regard to the many Elizabethan plays which now one critic, and now another, has attributed wholly or in part to Shakespeare. Take, for instance, *Arden of Feversham*, certainly one of the most admirable plays of that rich period, whose merit impresses one even when one reads it for the first time in uncritical youth. Swinburne writes of it (*Study of Shakespeare*, p. 141):—

" I cannot but finally take heart to say, even in the absence of all external or traditional testimony, that it seems to me not pardonable merely nor permissible, but simply logical and reasonable, to set down this poem, a young man's work on the face of it, as the possible work of no man's youthful hand but Shakespeare's."

However small my authority in comparison with Swinburne's upon such a question as this, I find it impossible to share his view. Highly as I esteem *Arden of Feversham*, I cannot believe that Shakespeare wrote a single line of it. It was not like him to choose such a subject, and still less to treat it in such a fashion. The play is a domestic tragedy, in which a wife, after repeated attempts, murders her kind and forbearing husband, in order freely to indulge her passion for a worthless paramour. It is a dramatisation of an actual case, the facts of which are closely followed, but at the same time animated with great psychological insight. That Shakespeare had a distaste for such subjects is proved by his consistent avoidance of them, except in this problematical instance; whereas if he had once succeeded so well with such a theme, he would surely have repeated the experiment. The chief point is, however, that only in a few places, in the soliloquies, do we find the peculiar note of Shakespeare's style— that wealth of imagination, that luxuriant lyrism, which plays like sunlight over his speeches. In *Arden of Feversham* the style is a uniform drab.

SHAKESPEARE'S DICTION

Shakespeare's great characteristic is precisely the resilience which he gives to every word and to every speech. We take one step on earth, and at the next we are soaring in air. His verse always tends towards a rich and stately melody, is never flat or commonplace. In the English historical plays, his diction sometimes verges upon the style of the ballad or romance. There is a continual undercurrent of emotion, of enthusiasm, or of pure fantasy, which carries us away with it. We are always far remote from the humdrum monotony of everyday speech. For everyday speech is devoid of fantasy, and all Shakespeare's characters, with the exception of those whose humour lies in their stupidity, have a highly-coloured imagination.

We could find no better proof of this than the diction of the great work which he undertakes immediately after *The Merchant of Venice*—the First Part of *Henry IV*.

Harry Percy in this play is placed in opposition to the magniloquent, visionary, thaumaturgic Glendower, as the man of sober intelligence, who keeps to the common earth, and believes only in what his senses aver and his reason accepts. But there is nevertheless a spring within him which need only be touched in order to send him soaring into almost dithyrambic poetry. The King (i. 3) has called Mortimer a traitor; whereupon Percy protests that it was no sham warfare that Mortimer waged against Glendower :—

"To prove that true,
Needs no more but one tongue for all those wounds,
Those mouthed wounds, which valiantly he took,
When on the gentle Severn's sedgy bank,
In single opposition, hand to hand,
He did confound the best part of an hour
In changing hardiment with great Glendower.
Three times they breath'd, and three times did they drink,
Upon agreement, of swift Severn's flood,
Who then, affrighted with their bloody looks,
Ran fearfully among the trembling reeds,
And hid his crisp head in the hollow bank
Blood-stained with these valiant combatants."

Thus Homer sings of the Scamander.

Worcester broaches to Percy an enterprise

"As full of peril and adventurous spirit,

> As to o'er-walk a current, roaring loud,
> On the unsteadfast footing of a spear;"

whereon Percy bursts forth:—

> "Send danger from the east unto the west,
> So honour cross it from the north to south,
> And let them grapple ⊦—O! the blood more stirs
> To rouse a lion than to start a hare."

Northumberland then says of him that "Imagination of some great exploit Drives him beyond the bounds of patience," and Percy answers:—

> "By Heaven, methinks, it were an easy leap
> To pluck bright honour from the pale-fac'd moon,
> Or dive into the bottom of the deep,
> Where fathom-line could never touch the ground,
> And pluck up drowned honour by the locks."

What a profusion of imagery is placed in the mouth of this despiser of rhetoric and music! From the comparatively weak metaphor of the speaking wounds up to actual myth-making! The river, affrighted by the bloody looks of the combatants, hides its crisp head in the reeds—a naiad fantasy in classic style. Danger, rushing from east to west, hurtles against Honour, crossing it from north to south—two northern Valkyries in full career. The wreath of honour is hung on the crescent moon—a metaphor from the tilting-yard, expressed in terms of fairy romance. Drowned Honour is to be plucked up by the locks from the bottom of the deep—having now become, by a daring personification, a damsel who has fallen into the sea and must be rescued. And all this in three short speeches!

Where this irrepressible vivacity of fancy is lacking, as in *Arden of Feversham*, Shakespeare's sign-manual is lacking along with it. Even when his style appears sober and measured, it is saturated with what may be called latent fantasy (as we speak of latent electricity), which at the smallest opportunity bursts its bounds, explodes, flashes forth before our eyes like the figures in a pyrotechnic set-piece, and fills our ears as with the music of a rushing, leaping waterfall.[1]

---

[1] It was this characteristic of Shakespeare's style, at the period we are now considering, that so deeply influenced Goethe and the contemporaries of his youth, Lenz and Klinger (and, in Denmark, Hauch and Bredahl), determining the diction of their tragic dramas. Björnson shows traces of the same influence in his *Maria Stuart* and *Sigurd Slembe*.

In 1598 appeared a Quarto with the following title: *The History of Henrie the Fourth; With the battell at Shrewsburie, betweene the King and Lord Henry Percy, surnamed Henrie Hotspur of the North. With the humorous conceits of Sir John Falstaffe. At London. Printed by P. S. for Andrew Wise, dwelling in Paules Churchyard, at the signe of the Angell.* 1598. This was the First Part of Shakespeare's *Henry IV.*, which must have been written in 1597 the play in which Shakespeare first attains his great and overwhelming individuality. At the age of thirty-three, he stands for the first time at the summit of his artistic greatness. In wealth of character, of wit, of genius, this play has never been surpassed. Its dramatic structure is somewhat loose, though closer knit and technically stronger than that of the Second Part. But, as a poetical creation, it is one of the great masterpieces of the world's literature, at once heroic and burlesque, thrilling and side-splitting. And these contrasted elements are not, as in Victor Hugo's dramas, brought into hard-and-fast rhetorical antithesis, but move and mingle with all the freedom of life.

When it was written, the sixteenth century, that great period in the history of the human spirit, was drawing to its close; but no one had then conceived the cowardly idea of making the end of a century a sort of symbol of decadence in energy and vitality. Never had the waves of healthy self-confidence and productive power run higher in the English people or in Shakespeare's own mind. *Henry IV.*, and its sequel *Henry V.*, are written throughout in a major key which we have not hitherto heard in Shakespeare, and which we shall not hear again.

Shakespeare finds the matter for these plays in Holinshed's Chronicle, and in an old, quite puerile play, *The Famous Victories of Henry the fifth, conteining the Honorable Battell of Agin-court*, in which the young Prince is represented as frequenting the company of roisterers and highway robbers. It was this, no doubt, that suggested to him the novel and daring idea of transferring direct to the stage, in historical guise, a series of scenes from the everyday life of the streets and taverns around him, and blending them with the dramatised chronicle of the Prince whom he regarded as the national hero of England. To this blending we owe the matchless freshness of the whole picture.

For the rest, Shakespeare found scarcely anything in the

foolish old play, acted between 1580 and 1588, which could in any way serve his purpose. He took from it only the anecdote of the box on the ear given by the Prince of Wales to the Lord Chief-Justice, and a few names—the tavern in Eastcheap, Gadshill, Ned, and the name, not the character, of Sir John Oldcastle, as Falstaff was originally called.

Shakespeare felt himself attracted to the hero, the young Prince, by some of the most deep-rooted sympathies of his nature. We have seen how vividly and persistently the contrast between appearance and reality preoccupied him; we saw it last in *The Merchant of Venice*. In proportion as he was irritated and repelled by people who try to pass for more than they are, by creatures of affectation and show, even by women who resort to artificial colours and false hair in quest of a beauty not their own, so his heart beat warmly for any one who had appearances against him, and concealed great qualities behind an unassuming and misinterpreted exterior. His whole life, indeed, was just such a paradox—his soul was replete with the greatest treasures, with rich humanity and inexhaustible genius, while externally he was little better than a light-minded mountebank, touting, with quips and quiddities, for the ha'pence of the mob. Now and then, as his Sonnets show, the pressure of this outward prejudice so weighed upon him that he came near to being ashamed of his position in life, and of the tinsel world in which his days were passed; and then he felt with double force the inward need to assure himself how great may be the gulf between the apparent and the real worth of human character.

Moreover, this view of his material gave him an occasion, before tuning the heroic string of his lyre, to put in a word for the right of high-spirited youth to have its fling, and indirectly to protest against the hasty judgments of narrow-minded moralists and Puritans. He would here show that great ambitions and heroic energy could pass unscathed through the dangers even of exceedingly questionable diversions. This Prince of Wales was "merry England" and "martial England" in one and the same person.

For the young noblemen among the audience, again, nothing could be more attractive than to see this great King, in his youth, haunting such resorts as they themselves frequented, and yet, as the best of them also tried to do, preserving the consciousness of his high dignity, the hope of a great future, and the determination to achieve renown, even while associating with Falstaff and Bardolph, Dame Quickly and Doll Tearsheet.

These young English aristocrats, who in Shakespeare appear under the names of Mercutio and Benedick, Gratiano and Lorenzo, made pleasure their pursuit through the whole of the London day. Dressed in silk or ash-coloured velvet, and with gold lace on his cloak, the young man of fashion began by riding to St. Paul's and promenading half-a-dozen times up and down its middle aisle. He then " repaired to the Exchange, and talked pretty Euphuisms to the citizens' daughters," or looked in at the bookseller's to inspect the latest play-book or pamphlet against tobacco. Next he rode to the ordinary where he had appointed to meet his friends and dine. At dinner he discussed Drake's expedition to Portugal, or Essex's exploits at Cadiz, or told how he had yesterday broken a lance with Raleigh himself at the Tilt-yard. He would mingle snatches of Italian and Spanish with his talk, and let himself be persuaded, after dinner, to recite a sonnet of his own composition. At three he betook himself to the theatre, saw Burbage as Richard III., and applauded Kemp in his new jig; after which he would spend an hour at the bear-garden. Then to the barber's, to have his hair and beard trimmed, in preparation for the carouse of the evening at whichever tavern he and his friends had selected— the " Mitre," the " Falcon," the " Apollo," the " Boar's Head," the " Devil," or (most famous of all) the " Mermaid," where the literary club, the Syren, founded by none other than Sir Walter Raleigh himself, held its meetings.[1] In these places the young aristocrat rubbed shoulders with the leading players, such as Burbage and Kemp, and with the best-known men of letters, such as John Lyly, George Chapman, John Florio, Michael Drayton, Samuel Daniel, John Marston, Thomas Nash, Ben Jonson, William Shakespeare.

Thornbury has aptly remarked that the characteristic of the Elizabethan age was its sociability. People were always meeting at St. Paul's, the theatre, or the tavern. Family intercourse, on the other hand, was almost unknown; women, as in ancient Greece, played no prominent part in society. The men gathered at the tavern club to drink, talk, and enjoy themselves. The festive bowl circulated freely, even more so than in Denmark, which nevertheless passed for the toper's paradise. (Compare

[1] Thornbury: *Shakspere's England*, i. 104, *et seq.*

the utterances on this subject in *Hamlet*, i. 4, and *Othello*, ii. 3.) The taverns were, moreover, favourite places for the rendezvous of court gallants with citizens' wives; fast young men would bring their mistresses with them, and here, after supper, gambling went on merrily.

At the taverns, writers and poets met in good fellowship, and carried on wordy wars, battles of wit, sparkling with mirth and fantasy. They were like tennis-rallies of words, in which the great thing was to tire out your adversary; they were skirmishes in which the combatants poured into each other whole volleys of conceits. Beaumont has celebrated them in some verses to Ben Jonson, who, both as a great drinker and as an entertaining *magister bibendi*, was much admired and fêted:—

> "What things have we seen
> Done at the Mermaid! heard words that have been
> So nimble, and so full of subtile flame,
> As if that every one from whence they came
> Had meant to put his whole wit in a jest
> And had resolv'd to live a fool the rest
> Of his dull life."

In his comedy *Every Man out of His Humour* (v. 4), Ben Jonson has introduced either himself or Marston, under the name of Carlo Buffone, waiting alone for his friends at the "Mitre," and has placed these words in Carlo's mouth when the waiter, George, has brought him the wine he had ordered:—

"*Carlo (drinks)*. Ay, marry, sir, here's purity; O George—I could bite off his nose for this now, sweet rogue, he has drawn nectar, the very soul of the grape! I'll wash my temples with some on't presently, and drink some half a score draughts; 'twill heat the brain, kindle my imagination, I shall talk nothing but crackers and fireworks to-night. So, sir! please you to be here, sir, and I here: so. (*Sets the two cups asunder, drinks with the one, and pledges with the other, speaking for each of the cups, and drinking alternately.*)"

Well known and often quoted is the passage in Fuller's *Worthies* as to the many wit-combats between Shakespeare and the learned Ben:—

"Which two I behold like a *Spanish great Gallion* and an *English man of War:* Master *Johnson* (like the former) was built far higher in

Learning; *Solid*, but *Slow* in his performances. *Shake-spear*, with the *English man of War*, lesser in *bulk*, but lighter in *sailing*, could turn with all tides, tack about, and take advantage of all winds, by the quickness of his Wit and Invention."

Although Fuller was not himself present at these symposia, yet his account of them bears the stamp of complete authenticity.

Among the members of the circle which Shakespeare in his youth frequented, there must, of course, have been types of every kind, from the genius down to the grotesque; and there were some, no doubt, in whom the genius and the grotesque, the wit and the butt, must have quaintly intermingled. As every great household had at that time its *jester*, so every convivial circle had its clown or buffoon. The jester was the terror of the kitchen—for he would steal a pudding the moment the cook's back was turned—and the delight of the dinner-table, where he would mimic voices, crack jokes, play pranks, and dissipate the spleen of the noble company. The comic man of the tavern circle was both witty himself and the cause of wit in others. He was always the butt of the others' merriment, yet he always held his own in the contest, and ended by getting the best of his tormentors.

To Shakespeare's circle Chettle must doubtless have belonged, that Chettle who in bygone days had published Greene's *Groatsworth of Wit*, and afterwards made amends to Shakespeare for Greene's coarse attack upon him. In Dekker's tract, *A Knights Conjuring*, dating from 1607, he figures among the poets in Elysium, where he is introduced in the following terms:—" In comes Chettle sweating and blowing, by reason of his fatnes; to welcome whom, because hee was of olde acquaintance, all rose vp, and fell presentlie on their knees, to drinck a health to all the louers of Hellicon." Elze has conjectured, possibly with justice, that in this puffing and sweating old tun of flesh, who is so whimsically greeted with mock reverence by the whole gay company, we have the very model from whom Shakespeare drew his demigod, the immortal Sir John Falstaff, beyond comparison the gayest, most concrete, and most entertaining figure in European comedy.

In his close-woven and unflagging mirthfulness, in the inexhaustible wealth of drollery concentrated in his person, Falstaff surpasses all that antiquity and the Middle Ages have produced in the way of comic character, and all that the stage of later times can show.

There is in him something of the old Greek Silenus, swag-bellied and infinitely jovial, and something of the *Vidushakas* of the old Indian drama, half court-fool, half friend and comrade to the hero. He unites in himself the two comic types of the old Roman comedy, Artotrogus and Pyrgopolinices, the parasite and the boastful soldier. Like the Roman *scurra*, he leaves his patron to pay the reckoning, and in return entertains him with his jests, and, like the *Miles Gloriosus*, he is a braggart above all braggarts, a liar above all liars. Yet he is in his single person richer and more entertaining than all the ancient Silenuses and court-fools and braggarts and parasites put together.

In the century after he came into existence, Spain and France each developed its own theatre. In France there is only one quaint and amusing person, Moron in Molière's *La Princesse d'Élide*, who bears some faint resemblance to Falstaff. In Spain, where the great and delightful character of Sancho Panza affords the starting-point for the whole series of comic figures in the works of Calderon, the *Gracioso* stands in perpetual contrast to the hero, and here and there reminds us for a moment of Falstaff, but always only as an abstraction of one side or another of his nature, or because of some external similarity of situation. In *La Dama Duende* he is a drunkard and coward; in *La Gran Cenobia* he boasts fantastically, and, like Falstaff, becomes entangled in his lies. In *La Puente de Mantible* he actually becomes (as it appears from the scenes with the Chief Justice and Colevile that Falstaff also was) renowned and dreaded for his military valour; yet he is, like Falstaff, extremely ill at ease when there is any fighting to be done, often creeping into cover, hiding himself behind a bush, or climbing a tree. In *La Hija del Ayre* and *El Principe Constante* he uses precisely the device adopted by Falstaff and certain lower animals, of lying down and shamming death. Hernando in *Los Empeños de un Acaso* (like Molière's Moron) expresses sentiments very similar to those of Falstaff in his celebrated discourse upon honour. Falstaff's airs of protection, his bland fatherliness, we find in Fabio in *El Secreto a Voces*. Thus single characteristics, detached sides of Falstaff's character, have to do duty as complete personages. Calderon as a rule looks with fatherly benevolence upon his Gracioso. Yet he sometimes loses patience, as it were, with his buffoon's epicurean, unchristian, and unchivalrous view of life. In *La Vida es Sueño*, for instance, a cannon-ball kills poor Clarin, who has crept behind a bush during the battle; the moral being that the coward does not escape danger any more than the brave man. Calderon bestows on him a very solemn funeral speech, almost as moral as King Henry's parting words to Falstaff.

It is certain, of course, that neither Calderon nor Molière knew anything of Shakespeare or of Falstaff; and Shakespeare, for his part, was equally uninfluenced by any of his predecessors on the comic stage, when he conceived his fat knight.

Nevertheless there is among Shakespeare's predecessors a great writer, one of the greatest, with whom we cannot but compare him; to wit, Rabelais, the master spirit of the early Renaissance in France. He is, moreover, one of the few great writers with whom Shakespeare is known to have been acquainted. He alludes to him in *As You Like It* (iii. 2), where Celia says, when Rosalind asks her a dozen questions and bids her answer in one word: "You must borrow me Gargantua's mouth first: 'tis a word too great for any mouth of this age's size."

If we compare Falstaff with Panurge, we see that Rabelais stands to Shakespeare in the relation of a Titan to an Olympian god. Rabelais is gigantic, disproportioned, potent, but formless. Shakespeare is smaller and less excessive, poorer in ideas, though richer in fancies, and moulded with the utmost firmness of outline.

Rabelais died at the age of seventy, ten years before Shakespeare was born; there is between them all the difference between the morning and the noon of the Renaissance. Rabelais is a poet, philosopher, polemist, reformer, "even to the very fire exclusively," but always threatened with the stake. Shakespeare's coarseness compared with Rabelais's is as a manure-bed compared with the *Cloaca Maxima*. Burlesque uncleanness pours in floods from the Frenchman's pen.

His Panurge is larger than Falstaff, as Utgard-Loki is larger than Asa-Loki. Panurge, like Falstaff, is loquacious, witty, crafty, and utterly unscrupulous, a humorist who stops the mouths of all around him by unblushing effrontery. In war, Panurge is no more of a hero than Falstaff, but, like Falstaff, he stabs the foemen who have already fallen. He is superstitious, yet his buffoonery holds nothing sacred, and he steals from the church-plate. He is thoroughly selfish, sensual, and slothful, shameless, revengeful, and light-fingered, and as time goes on becomes ever a greater poltroon and braggart.

Pantagruel is the noble knight, a king's son, like Prince Henry. Like the Prince, he has one foible: he cannot resist the attractions of low company. When Panurge is witty, Pantagruel cannot deny himself the pleasure of laughing at his side-splitting drolleries.

But Panurge, unlike Falstaff, is a satire on the largest scale. In representing him as a notable economist or master of finance, who calls borrowing credit-creating, and has 63 methods of raising money and 214 methods of spending it, Rabelais made him an abstract and brief chronicle of the French court of his day. In giving him a yearly revenue from his barony of "6,789,106,789 royaulx en deniers certain," to say nothing of the fluctuating revenue of the locusts and periwinkles, "montant bon an mal an de 2,435,768 à 2,435,769 moutons à la grande laine," Rabelais was aiming his satire direct at the unblushing extortion which was at that time the glory and delight of the French feudal nobility.

Shakespeare does not venture so far in the direction of satire. He is only a poet, and as a poet stands simply on the defensive. The only power he can be said to attack is Puritanism (*Twelfth Night, Measure for Measure*, &c.), and that only in self-defence. His attacks, too, are exceedingly mild in comparison with those of the cavalier poets before the victory of Puritanism and after the reopening of the theatres. But Shakespeare was what Rabelais was not, an artist; and as an artist he was a very Prometheus in his power of creating human beings.

As an artist he has also the exuberant fertility which we find in Rabelais, even surpassing him in some respects. Max Müller has long ago remarked upon the wealth of his vocabulary. In this he seems to surpass all other writers. An Italian opera-libretto seldom contains more than 600 or 700 words. A well-educated modern Englishman, in social intercourse, will rarely use more than 3000 or 4000. It has been calculated that acute thinkers and great orators in England are masters of as many as 10,000 words. The Old Testament contains only 5642 words. Shakespeare has employed more than 15,000 words in his poems and plays; and in few of the latter do we find such overflowing fulness of expression as in *Henry IV.*

SIR JOHN FALSTAFF

In the original form of the play, Falstaff's name, as already mentioned, was Sir John Oldcastle. A trace of this remains in the second scene of the first act (Part I.), where the Prince calls the fat knight "my old lad of the castle." In the second scene of the second act the line, "Away, good Ned, Falstaff sweats to death," is short of a syllable, because the dissyllable Falstaff has been substituted for the trisyllable Oldcastle. In the earliest Quarto of the Second Part, the contraction *Old.* has been left before one of Falstaff's speeches; and in Act ii. Sc. 2 of the same play, it is said of Falstaff that he was page to Thomas Mowbray, Duke of Norfolk, a position which the historic Oldcastle actually held. Oldcastle, however, was so far from being the boon companion depicted by Shakespeare that he was, at the instance of Henry V. himself, handed over to the Ecclesiastical Courts as an adherent of Wicklif's heresies, and roasted over a slow fire outside the walls of London on Christmas morning 1417. His descendants having protested against the degradation to which the name of their ancestor was subjected in the play, the fat knight was rechristened. Therefore, too, it is stated in the Epilogue to the Second Part that the author intends to produce a further continuation of the story, "where, for anything I know, Falstaff shall die of a sweat . . . *for Oldcastle died a martyr, and this is not the man.*"

Under the name of Falstaff he became, after the lapse of half a century, the most popular of Shakespeare's creations. Between 1642 and 1694 he is more frequently mentioned than any other of Shakespeare's characters. But it is noteworthy that in his own time, although popular enough, he was not alluded to nearly so often as Hamlet, who, up to 1642, is mentioned forty-five times to Falstaff's twenty; even *Venus and Adonis* and *Romeo and Juliet* are mentioned oftener than he, and *Lucrece* quite as often.[1] The element of low comedy in his figure made it, according to the notions of the day, obviously less distinguished, and people stood too near to Falstaff to appreciate him fully.

He was, as it were, the wine-god of merry England at the meeting of the centuries. Never before or since has England enjoyed so many sorts of beverages. There was ale, and all other kinds of strong and small beer, and apple-drink, and honey-drink, and strawberry-drink, and three sorts of mead (meath, metheglin,

---
[1] *Fresh Allusions to Shakespeare*, p. 372.

hydromel), and every drink was fragrant of flowers and spiced with herbs. In white meath alone there was infused rosemary and thyme, sweet-briar, pennyroyal, bays, water-cresses, agrimony, marsh-mallow, liverwort, maiden-hair, betony, eye-bright, scabious, ash-leaves, eringo roots, wild angelica, rib-wort, sennicle, Roman wormwood, tamarisk, mother thyme, saxifrage, philipendula; and strawberries and violet-leaves were often added. Cherry-wine and sack were mixed with gillyflower syrup.[1]

There were fifty-six varieties of French wine in use, and thirty-six of Spanish and Italian, to say nothing of the many home-made kinds. But among the foreign wines none was so famous as Falstaff's favourite sherris-sack. It took its name from Xeres in Spain, but differed from the modern sherry in being a sweet wine. It was the best of its kind, possessing a much finer bouquet than sack from Malaga or the Canary Islands (Jeppe paa Bjergets, "Canari-Sæk"),[2] although these were stronger and sweeter. Sweet as it was too, people were in the habit of putting sugar into it. The English taste has never been very delicate. Falstaff always put sugar into his wine. Hence his words when he is playing the Prince while the Prince impersonates the king (Pt. First, ii. 4):—"If sack and sugar be a fault, God help the wicked." He puts not only sugar but toast in his wine: "Go fetch me a quart of sack, put a toast in it" (*Merry Wives*, iii. 5). On the other hand, he does not like (as others did) to have it mulled with eggs: "Brew me a pottle of sack . . . simple of itself; I'll no pullet-sperm in my brewage" (*Merry Wives*, iii. 5). And no less did he resent its sophistication with lime, an ingredient which the vintners used to increase its strength and make it keep: "You rogue, here's lime in this sack, too. . . . A coward is worse than a cup of sack with lime in it" (I. *Henry IV.*, ii. 4). Falstaff is as great a wine-knower and wine-lover as Silenus himself. But he is infinitely more than that.

He is one of the brightest and wittiest spirits England has ever produced. He is one of the most glorious creations that ever sprang from a poet's brain. There is much rascality and much genius in him, but there is no trace of mediocrity. He is

---

[1] Thornbury: *Shakspere's England*, i. 227; Nathan Drake, *Shakespeare and His Times*, ii. 131.

[2] Jeppe paa Bjerget, a Danish Abou Hassan or Christopher Sly, is the hero of one of Holberg's most admirable comedies.

always superior to his surroundings, always resourceful, always witty, always at his ease, often put to shame, but, thanks to his inventive effrontery, never put out of countenance. He has fallen below his social position; he lives in the worst (though also in the best) society; he has neither soul, nor honour, nor moral sense; but he sins, robs, lies, and boasts, with such splendid exuberance, and is so far above any serious attempt at hypocrisy, that he seems unfailingly amiable whatever he may choose to do. Therefore he charms every one, although he is a butt for the wit of all. He perpetually surprises us by the wealth of his nature. He is old and youthful, corrupt and harmless, cowardly and daring, "a knave without malice, a liar without deceit; and a knight, a gentleman, and a soldier, without either dignity, decency, or honour."[1] The young Prince shows good taste in always and in spite of everything seeking out his company.

How witty he is in the brilliant scene where Shakespeare is daring enough to let him parody in advance the meeting between Prince Henry and his offended father! And with what sly humour does Shakespeare, through his mouth, poke fun at Lyly and Greene and the old play of King Cambyses! How delightful is Falstaff's unabashed self-mockery when he thus apostrophises the hapless merchants whom he is plundering:—

"Ah! whoreson caterpillars! bacon-fed knaves! they hate us youth: down with them; fleece them. . . . Hang ye, gorbellied knaves. Are ye undone? No, ye fat chuffs; I would your store were here! On, bacons, on! What! ye knaves, young men must live."

And what humour there is in his habit of self-pitying regret that his youth and inexperience should have been led astray:—

"I'll be damned for never a king's son in Christendom. . . . I have forsworn his company hourly any time this two-and-twenty years, and yet I am bewitched with the rogue's company. . . . Company, villainous company, hath been the spoil of me."

But if he has not been led astray, neither is he the "abominable misleader of youth" whom Prince Henry, impersonating the King, makes him out to be. For to this character there belongs

[1] Maurice Morgann: *An Essay on the Dramatic Character of Sir John Falstaff*, p. 150.

malicious intent, of which Falstaff is innocent enough. It is unmistakable, however, that while in the First Part of *Henry IV.* Shakespeare keeps Falstaff a purely comic figure, and dissipates in the ether of laughter whatever is base and unclean in his nature, the longer he works upon the character, and the more he feels the necessity of contrasting the moral strength of the Prince's nature with the worthlessness of his early surroundings, the more is he tempted to let Falstaff deteriorate. In the Second Part his wit becomes coarser, his conduct more indefensible, his cynicism less genial; while his relation to the hostess, whom he cozens and plunders, is wholly base. In the First Part of the play he takes a whole-hearted delight in himself, in his jollifications, his drolleries, his exploits on the highway, and his almost purposeless mendacity; in the Second Part he falls more and more under the suspicion of making capital out of the Prince, while he is found in ever worse and worse company. The scheme of the whole, indeed, demands that there shall come a moment when the Prince, who has succeeded to the throne and its attendant responsibilities, shall put on a serious countenance and brandish the thunderbolts of retribution.

But here, in the First Part, Falstaff is still a demi-god, supreme alike in intellect and in wit. With this figure the popular drama which Shakespeare represented won its first decisive battle over the literary drama which followed in the footsteps of Seneca. We can actually hear the laughter of the "yard" and the gallery surging around his speeches like waves around a boat at sea. It was the old sketch of Parolles in *Love's Labour's Won* (see above, p. 59), which had here taken on a new amplitude of flesh and blood. There was much to delight the groundlings—Falstaff is so fat and yet so mercurial, so old and yet so youthful in all his tastes and vices. But there was far more to delight the spectators of higher culture, in his marvellous quickness of fence, which can parry every thrust, and in the readiness which never leaves him tongue-tied, or allows him to confess himself beaten. Yes, there was something for every class of spectators in this mountain of flesh, exuding wit at every pore, in this hero without shame or conscience, in this robber, poltroon, and liar, whose mendacity is quite poetic, Münchausenesque, in this cynic with the brazen forehead and a tongue as supple as a Toledo blade. His talk is like Bellman's after him :—

SIR JOHN FALSTAFF

"A dance of all the gods upon Olympus,
With fauns and graces and the muses twined."[1]

The men of the Renaissance revelled in his wit, much as the men of the Middle Ages had enjoyed the popular legends of Reinecke Fuchs and his rogueries.

Falstaff reaches his highest point of wit and drollery in that typical soliloquy on honour, in which he indulges on the battlefield of Shrewsbury (1. *Henry IV.*, v. 1), a soliloquy which almost categorically sums him up, in contradistinction to the other leading personages. For all the characters here stand in a certain relation to the idea of honour—the King, to whom honour means dignity; Hotspur, to whom it means the halo of renown; the Prince, who loves it as the opposite of outward show; and Falstaff, who, in his passionate appetite for the material good things of life, rises entirely superior to it and shows its nothingness:—

"Honour pricks me on. Yea, but how if honour prick me off when I come on? how then? Can honour set to a leg? No. Or an arm? No. Or take away the grief of a wound? No. Honour hath no skill in surgery then? No. What is honour? A word. What is that word honour? Air. A trim reckoning!—Who hath it? He that died o' Wednesday. Doth he feel it? No. Doth he hear it? No. Is it insensible then? Yea, to the dead. But will it not live with the living? No. Why? Detraction will not suffer it.—Therefore, I'll none of it: honour is a mere scutcheon; and so ends my catechism."

Falstaff will be no slave to honour; he will rather do without it altogether. He demonstrates in practice how a man can live without it, and we do not miss it in him, so perfect is he in his way.

[1] From a poem by Tegnér on Bellman, the Swedish convivial lyrist.

XXIII

HENRY PERCY—THE MASTERY OF THE CHARACTER-DRAWING—HOTSPUR AND ACHILLES

IN contrast to Falstaff, Shakespeare has placed the man whom his ally Douglas expressly calls "the king of honour"—a figure as firmly moulded and as great as the Achilles of the Greeks or Donatello's Italian St. George—"the Hotspur of the North," an English national hero quite as much as the young Prince.

The chronicle and the ballad of Douglas and Percy gave Shakespeare no more than the name and the dates of a couple of battles. He seized upon the name Harry Percy, and although its bearer was not historically of the same age as Prince Henry, but as old as his father, the King, he docked him of a score of years, with the poetical design of opposing to the hero of the play a rival who should be his peer, and should at first seem to outshine him.

Percy is above everything and every one avid of honour. It is he who would have found it easy to pluck down honour from the moon or drag it up from the depths of the sea. But he is of an open, confiding, simple nature, with nothing of the diplomatist about him. He is hasty and impetuous; his spur is never cold until he is dead. Under the mistaken impression that women cannot keep their counsel, he is reticent towards his wife, in whom he might quite well confide, since she adores him, and calls him "the miracle of men." On the other hand, he suffers himself to be driven by the King's sour suspiciousness into foolhardy rebellion, and he is so simple-minded as to trust to his father and his uncle Worcester, one of whom deserts him in the hour of need, while the other plays a double game with him.

Shakespeare has thrown himself so passionately into the creation of this character that he has actually painted for us Hotspur's exterior, giving him a peculiar walk and manner of speech. The warmth of the poet's sympathy has rendered his hero irresistibly attractive, and made him, in his manliness, a pattern for the youth of the whole country.

Henry Percy enters (ii. 3) with a letter in his hand, and reads:—

"—'But, for mine own part, my lord, I could be well contented to be there, in respect of the love I bear your house.'—He could be contented,—why is he not then? In respect of the love he bears our house:—he shows in this, he loves his own barn better than he loves our house. Let me see some more. 'The purpose you undertake is dangerous;'—why, that's certain: 'tis dangerous to take a cold, to sleep, to drink; but I tell you, my lord fool, out of this nettle, danger, we pluck this flower, safety. 'The purpose you undertake, is dangerous; the friends you have named, uncertain; the time itself unsorted, and your whole plot too light for the counterpoise of so great an opposition.' —Say you so, say you so? *I say unto you again, you are a shallow, cowardly hind, and you lie.* What a lack-brain is this! By the Lord, our plot is as good a plot as ever was laid; our friends true and constant: a good plot, good friends, and full of expectation; an excellent plot, very good friends. . . . O! I could divide myself and go to buffets, for moving such a dish of skimmed milk with so honourable an action. Hang him! let him tell the King; we are prepared. I will set forward to-night."

We can see him before our eyes, and hear his voice. He strides up and down the room as he reads, and we can hear in the rhythm of his speech that he has a peculiar gait of his own. Not for nothing is Henry Percy called Hotspur; whether on foot or on horseback, his movements are equally impetuous. Therefore his wife says of him after his death (II. *Henry IV.*, ii. 3):—

"He was, indeed, the glass
Wherein the noble youth did dress themselves.
He had no legs, that practised not his gait."

Everything is here consistent, the bodily movements and the tone of speech. We can hear in Hotspur's soliloquy how his sentences stumble over each other; how, without giving himself time to articulate his words, he stammers from sheer impatience, and utters no phrase that does not bear the stamp of his choleric temperament:—

"And speaking thick, which nature made his blemish,
Became the accents of the valiant;

> For those that could speak low, and tardily,
> Would turn their own perfection to abuse,
> To seem like him: so that, in speech, in gait,
> In diet, in affections of delight,
> In military rules, humours of blood,
> He was the mark and glass, copy and book,
> That fashion'd others."

Shakespeare found no hint of these external traits in the chronicle. He bodied forth Hotspur's idiosyncrasy with such ardour that everything, down to his outward habit, shaped itself accordantly. Hotspur speaks in impatient ejaculations; he is absent and forgetful out of sheer passionateness. His characteristic impetuousness shows itself in such little traits as his inability to remember the names he wants to cite. When the rebels are portioning out the country between them, he starts up with an oath because he has forgotten his map. When he has something to relate, he is so absorbed in the gist of his matter, and so impatient to get at it, that the intermediate steps escape his memory (i. 3):—

> "Why, look you, I am whipp'd and scourg'd with rods,
> Nettled, and stung with pismires, when I hear
> Of this vile politician, Bolingbroke.
> *In Richard's time,—what do ye call the place?—
> A plague upon 't—it is in Glostershire:—
> 'T was where the madcap Duke his uncle kept,
> His uncle York*,—where I first bow'd my knee
> Unto this king of smiles, this Bolingbroke."

When another person speaks to him, he listens for a moment, but presently his thoughts are away on their own affairs; he forgets where he is and what is said to him; and when Lady Percy has finished her long and moving appeal (ii. 3) with the words—

> "Some heavy business hath my lord in hand,
> And I must know it, else he loves me not,"

all the reply vouchsafed her is:—

> "*Hotspur.* What, ho!
>
> *Enter Servant.*
> Is Gilliams with the packet gone?

Serv. He is, my lord, an hour ago.
Hot. Hath Butler brought those horses from the sheriff?" &c.

Perpetually baulked of an answer, she at last cannot help coming out with this caressing menace, which gives us in one touch the whole relation between the pair of married lovers:—

> "In faith, I'll break thy little finger, Harry,
> An if thou wilt not tell me all things true."

And this absence of mind of Percy's is so far from being accidental or momentary that it is the very trait which Prince Henry seizes upon to characterise him (ii. 4):—

> "I am not yet of Percy's mind, the Hotspur of the North; he that kills me some six or seven dozen of Scots at a breakfast, washes his hands, and says to his wife,—'Fie upon this quiet life! I want work.' 'O my sweet Harry,' says she, 'how many hast thou killed to-day?' 'Give my roan horse a drench,' says he, and answers, 'Some fourteen,' an hour after; 'a trifle, a trifle.'"

Shakespeare has put forth all his poetic strength in giving to Percy's speeches, and especially to his descriptions, the most graphic definiteness of detail, and a naturalness which raises into a higher sphere the racy audacity of Faulconbridge. Hotspur sets about explaining (i. 3) how it happened that he refused to hand over his prisoners to the King, and begins his defence by describing the courtier who demanded them of him:—

> "When I was dry with rage and extreme toil,
> Breathless and faint, leaning upon my sword,
> Came there a certain lord, neat, trimly dress'd,
> Fresh as a bridegroom; and his chin, new reap'd,
> Show'd like a stubble-land at harvest-home.
> He was perfumed like a milliner."

But he is not content with a general outline, or with relating what this personage said with regard to the prisoners; he gives an example even of his talk:—

> "He made me mad,
> To see him shine so brisk, and smell so sweet,
> And talk so like a waiting-gentlewoman .
> Of guns, and drums, and wounds, God save the mark!

And telling me, the sovereign'st thing on earth
Was parmacity for an inward bruise;
And that it was great pity, so it was,
That villainous saltpetre should be digg'd
Out of the bowels of the harmless earth."

Why this spermaceti? Why this dwelling upon so trivial and ludicrous a detail? Because it is a touch of reality and begets illusion. Precisely because we cannot at first see the reason why Percy should recall so trifling a circumstance, it seems impossible that the thing should be a mere invention. And from this insignificant word all the rest of the speech hangs as by a chain. If this be real, then all the rest is real, and Henry Percy stands before our eyes, covered with dust and blood, as on the field of Holmedon. We see the courtier at his side holding his nose as the bodies are carried past, and we hear him giving the young commander his medical advice and irritating him to the verge of frenzy.

With such solicitude, with such minute attention to tricks, flaws, whims, humours, and habits, all deduced from his temperament, from the rapid flow of his blood, from his build of body, and from his life on horseback and in the field, has Shakespeare executed this heroic character. Restless gait, stammering speech, forgetfulness, absence of mind, he overlooks nothing as being too trivial. Hotspur portrays himself in every phrase he utters, without ever saying a word directly about himself; and behind his outward, superficial peculiarities, we see into the deeper and more significant characteristics from which they spring. These, too, are closely interwoven; these, too, reveal themselves in his lightest words. We hear this same hero whom pride, sense of honour, spirit of independence, and intrepidity inspire with the sublimest utterances, at other times chatting, jesting, and even talking nonsense. The jests and nonsense are an integral part of the real human being; in them, too, one side of his nature reveals itself (iii. 1):—

"*Hotspur.* Come, Kate, I'll have your song too.

Lady Percy. Not mine, in good sooth.

Hot. Not yours, in good sooth! 'Heart! you swear like a comfit-maker's wife. 'Not you, in good sooth;' and, 'As true as I live;' and, 'As God shall mend me;' and, 'As sure as day:'

. . . . . .

Swear me, Kate, like a lady as thou art,
A good mouth-filling oath; and leave 'in sooth,'
And such protest of pepper-gingerbread,
To velvet-guards, and Sunday-citizens."

In a classical tragedy, French, German, or Danish, the hero is too solemn to talk nonsense and too lifeless to jest.

In spite of his soaring energy and ambition, Hotspur is sober, rationalistic, sceptical. He scoffs at Glendower's belief in spirits and pretended power of conjuring them up (iii. 1). His is to the inmost fibre a truth-loving nature :—

"*Glend.* I can call spirits from the vasty deep.
Hot. Why, so can I, or so can any man;
But will they come, when you do call for them?
Glend. Why, I can teach you, cousin, to command the devil.
Hot. And I can teach thee, coz, to shame the devil,
By telling truth: tell truth, and shame the devil."

There is a militant rationalism in these words which was rare, very rare, in Shakespeare's time, to say nothing of Hotspur's own.

He has also, no doubt, the defects of his qualities. He is contentious, quarrels the moment he is thwarted over the division of booty that has yet to be won, and then, having gained his point, gives up his share in the spoils. He is jealous in his ambition, cannot bear to hear any one else praised, and would like to see Harry of Monmouth poisoned with a pot of ale, so tired is he of hearing him spoken of. He judges hastily, according to appearances; he has the profoundest contempt for the Prince of Wales on account of the levity of his life, and does not divine what lies behind it. He of course lacks all æsthetic faculty. He is a bad speaker, and sentiment is as foreign to him as eloquence. He prefers his dog's howling to music, and declares that the turning of brass candlesticks does not set his teeth on edge so much as the rhyming of balladmongers.

Yet, with all his faults, he is the greatest figure of his time. Even the King, his enemy, becomes a poet when he speaks of him (iii. 2). :—

" Thrice hath this Hotspur, Mars in swathing-clothes,
This infant warrior, in his enterprises
Discomfited great Douglas: ta'en him once,
Enlarged him, and made a friend of him."

The King longs daily that he could exchange his son for Northumberland's; Hotspur is worthier than Prince Henry to be heir to the throne of England.

From first to last, from top to toe, Hotspur is the hero of the feudal ages, indifferent to culture and polish, faithful to his brother-in-arms to the point of risking everything for his sake, caring neither for state, king, nor commons; a rebel, not for the sake of any political idea, but because independence is all in all to him; a proud, self-reliant, unscrupulous vassal, who, himself a sort of sub-king, has deposed one king, and wants to depose the usurper he has exalted, because he has not kept his promises. Clothed in renown, and ever more insatiate of military honour, he is proud from independence of spirit and truthful out of pride. He is a marvellous figure as Shakespeare has projected him, stammering, absent, turbulent, witty, now simple, now magniloquent. His hauberk clatters on his breast, his spurs jingle at his heel, wit flashes from his lips, while he moves and has his being in a golden nimbus of renown.

Individual as he is, Shakespeare has embodied in him the national type. From the crown of his head to the sole of his foot, Hotspur is an Englishman. He unites the national impetuosity and bravery with sound understanding; he is English in his ungallant but cordial relation to his wife; in the form of his chivalry, which is Northern, not Romanesque; in his Viking-like love of battle for battle's and honour's sake, apart from any sentimental desire for a fair lady's applause.

But Shakespeare's especial design was to present in him a master-type of manliness. He is so profoundly, so thoroughly a man that he forms the one counterpart in modern poetry to the Achilles of the Greeks. Achilles is the hero of antiquity, Henry Percy of the Middle Ages. The ambition of both is entirely personal and regardless of the common weal. For the rest, they are equally noble and high-spirited. The one point on which Hotspur is inferior to the Greek demigod is that of free naturalness. His soul has been cramped and hardened by being strapped into the harness of the feudal ages. Hero as he is, he is at the same time a soldier, obliged and accustomed to be over-bold, forced to restrict his whole activity to feuds and fights. He cannot weep like Achilles, and he would be ashamed of himself if he could. He cannot play the lyre like Achilles, and he would think himself bewitched if he could be brought to admit that music sounded sweeter in his ears than the baying of a dog or the mewing of a cat.[1] He compensates for these deficiencies by the unyielding, restless, untiring energy of his character, by the spirit of enterprise in his manly soul, and by his healthy and amply justified pride. It is in virtue of these qualities that he can, without shrinking, sustain comparison with a demigod.

So deep are the roots of Hotspur's character. Eccentric in externals, he is at bottom typical. The untamed and violent spirit of feudal nobility, the reckless and adventurous activity of the English race, the masculine nature itself in its uncompromising genuineness, all those vast and infinite forces which lie deep under the surface and determine the life of a whole period, a whole people, and one half of humanity, are at work in this character. Elaborated to infinitesimal detail, it yet includes the immensities into which thought must plunge if it would seek for the conditions and ideals of a historic epoch.

But in spite of all this, Henry Percy is by no means the hero of the play. He is only the foil to the hero, throwing into relief the young Prince's unpretentious nature, his careless sporting with rank and dignity, his light-hearted contempt for all conventional honour, all show and appearance. Every garland with which Hotspur wreathes his helm is destined in the end to deck the brows of Henry of Wales. The answer to Hotspur's question

---

[1] " And Achilles at last
Brake suddenly forth into weeping, and turned from his comrades aside,
And sat by the cold grey sea, looking forth o'er the harvestless tide."
Iliad, i. 348.

" So when to the tents and the ships of the Myrmidon host they had won,
They found him delighting his soul as rang to the sweep of his hand
His beautiful rich-wrought lyre with a silver cross-bar spanned,
Which he chose from the spoils of the war when he smote Eetion's town.
Sweetly it rang as he sang old deeds of hero-renown."
Iliad, ix. 185.

So Greek and so musical is he who can yet give this answer to the dying Hector's appeal :—
"' Knee me no knees, thou dog, neither prate of my parents to me!
Would God my spirit within me would leave my fury free
To carve the flesh of thee raw, and devour, for the deeds thou hast done.' "
Iliad, xxii. 345.

(Translated by Arthur S. Way.)

as to what has become of the madcap Prince of Wales and his comrades, shows what colours Shakespeare has held in reserve for the portraiture of his true hero. Even Vernon, an enemy of the Prince, thus depicts his setting forth on the campaign (iv. 1):

> "All furnished, all in arms,
> All plum'd like estridges that wing the wind;
> Bated like eagles having lately bath'd;
> Glittering in golden coats, like images;
> As full of spirit as the month of May,
> And gorgeous as the sun at midsummer;
> Wanton as youthful goats, wild as young bulls.
> I saw young Harry, with his beaver on,
> His cuisses on his thighs, gallantly arm'd,
> Rise from the ground like feather'd Mercury,
> And vaulted with such ease into his seat,
> As if an angel dropp'd down from the clouds,
> To turn and wind a fiery Pegasus,
> And witch the world with noble horsemanship."

XXIV

PRINCE HENRY — THE POINT OF DEPARTURE FOR SHAKESPEARE'S IMAGINATION—A TYPICAL ENGLISH NATIONAL HERO — THE FRESHNESS AND PERFECTION OF THE PLAY

HENRY V. was, in the popular conception, the national hero of England. He was the man whose glorious victories had brought France under English rule. His name had a ring like that of Valdemar in Denmark, bringing with it memories of a time of widespread dominion, which the weakness of his successors had suffered to shrink again. As a matter of history, Henry had been a soldier almost from his boyhood, had been stationed on the Welsh borders from his sixteenth to his one-and-twentieth year, and had afterwards, in London, enjoyed the full confidence of his father and of the Parliament. But there was some hint in the old chronicles of his having, in his youth, frequented bad company and led a wild life which gave no foretaste of his coming greatness. This hint had been elaborated in the old and worthless play, *The Famous Victories;* and no more was needed to set Shakespeare's imagination to work, and render it productive. He revelled in the idea of representing the young Prince of Wales roistering among drunkards and demireps, only to rise all the more brilliantly and superbly into the irreproachable sovereign, the greatest soldier among England's kings, the humiliator of France, the victor of Agincourt.

No doubt Shakespeare's imagination here started from a basis of personal experience. As a young player and poet, he in all probability lived a Bohemian life in London, not, indeed, of debauchery, but full of such passions and dissipations as his vigorous temperament, his overflowing vitality, and his position beyond the pale of staid and respectable citizenship, would tend to throw in his way. The Sonnets, which speak so plainly of vehement and fateful emotions on his part, also hint at temptations which he did not resist. We read, for instance, in Sonnet cxix. :—

> "What potions have I drunk of Siren tears,
> Distill'd from limbecks foul as hell within,
> Applying fears to hopes, and hopes to fears,
> Still losing when I saw myself to win!
> What wretched errors hath my heart committed,
> Whilst it hath thought itself so blessed never!
> How have mine eyes out of their spheres been fitted,
> In the distraction of this madding fever!"

And again in Sonnet cxxix. :—

> "The expense of spirit in a waste of shame
> Is lust in action; and till action, lust
> Is perjur'd, murderous, bloody, full of blame,
> Savage, extreme, rude, cruel, not to trust;
> Enjoy'd no sooner but despised straight;
> Past reason hunted; and no sooner had,
> Past reason hated, as a swallow'd bait,
> On purpose laid to make the taker mad:
> . . . .
> All this the world well knows; yet none knows well
> To shun the heaven that leads men to this hell."

This is the philosophy of the morrow, of the reaction. But Shakespeare had also, no doubt, his hours of light-hearted enjoyment, when such moralising reflections were far enough from his mind. We have evidence of this in more than one anecdote. In the diary of John Manningham, of the Middle Temple, the following entry occurs, under the date March 13, 1602 :—

"Upon a tyme when Burbidge played Rich. 3, there was a Citizen grone soe farr in liking with him, that before shee went from the play shee appointed him to come that night vnto hir by the name of Ri: the 3. Shakespeare ouerhearing their conclusion went before, [and] was intertained . . . ere Burbidge came. Then message being brought that Rich. the 3[d] was at the dore, Shakespeare caused returne to be made that William the Conquerour was before Rich. the 3. Shakespere's name was William."

Aubrey, who, however, did not write until 1680, is the authority, supported by several others (Pope, Oldys, &c.), for the legend that Shakespeare, on his yearly journeys from London to Stratford-on-Avon and back, by way of Oxford and Woodstock, used to alight at the "Crown" tavern, kept by one Davenant in Oxford, and there won the heart of his hostess, the buxom and merry Mrs. Davenant, who "used much to delight in his pleasant company." According to this tradition, the young William Davenant, afterwards a poet of note, commonly passed in Oxford for Shakespeare's son, and was said to bear some resemblance to him. Sir William himself was not unwilling to have it believed that he was "more than a poetic child only" of Shakespeare's.[1]

Be this as it may, Shakespeare had certainly sufficient personal experience to enable him to sympathise with this princely youth, who, despite the consciousness of his high aims, revels in his freedom, shuns the court life and ceremonial which await him, throws his dignity to the winds, riots in reckless high spirits, boxes the ears of the Lord Chief-Justice, and has yet self-command enough to suffer arrest without resistance, takes part in a tourney with a common wench's glove in his helm—in short, does everything that most conflicts with his people's sense of propriety and his father's doctrines of prudence, but does it without coarseness, with a certain innocence, and without ever having to reproach himself with any actual self-degradation. Henry IV. misunderstands his son as completely as Frederick William of Prussia misunderstood the young Frederick the Great.

We see him, indeed, plunging into the most boyish and thoughtless diversions, in company with topers, tavern-wenches, and pot-boys; but we see, also, that he is magnanimous, and full of profound admiration for Harry Percy, that admiration for a rival of which Percy himself was incapable. And he rises, ere long, above this world of triviality and make-believe to the true height of his nature. His alert self-esteem, his immovable self-confidence, can early be traced in minor touches. When Falstaff asks him if "his blood does not thrill" to think of the alliance

[1] This tradition seems in no way improbable, and its probability is not diminished by the fact that an anecdote connected with it has been shown by Halliwell-Phillips to be an old Joe Miller, merely adapted to the case in point. "One day an old townsman, observing the boy running homeward almost out of breath, asked him whither he was posting in that heat and hurry. He answered to see his *god*father Shakespeare. 'There is a good boy,' said the other; 'but have a care that you don't take *God's* name in vain'" (*Oldys*).

between three such formidable foes as Percy, Douglas, and Glendower, he dismisses with a smile all idea of fear. A little later, he plays upon his truncheon of command as upon a fife. He has the great carelessness of the great natures; he does not even lose it when he feels himself unjustly suspected. At bottom he is a good brother, a good son, a great patriot; and he has the makings of a great ruler. He lacks Hotspur's optimism (which sees some advantage even in his father's desertion), nor has he his impetuous pugnacity; yet we see outlined in him the daring, typically English conqueror, adventurer, and politician, unscrupulous, and, on occasion, cruel, undismayed though the enemy outnumber him tenfold—the prototype of the men who, a century and a half after Shakespeare's death, achieved the conquest of India.

It is a pity that Shakespeare could find no other way of displaying his military superiority to Percy than simply to make him a better swordsman and let him kill his rival in single combat. This is a return to the Homeric conception of martial prowess. It was by such traits as this that Shakespeare repelled Napoleon. These things appeared to him childish. He found more "politics" in Corneille.

With complete magnanimity, Prince Henry leaves to Falstaff the honour of having slain Hotspur, that honour whose true nature forms the central theme of the whole play, although the idea is nowhere formulated in any individual speech. But after Henry Percy's death, Shakespeare, strangely enough, sometimes actually transfers to Henry Plantagenet his fallen rival's characteristics. He says, for example (*Henry V.*, iv. 3), "If it be a sin to covet honour, I am the most offending soul alive." He declares that he understands neither rhyme nor metre. He woos his bride as ungallantly as Hotspur talks to his Kate, and he answers the challenges of the French with a boastfulness that throws Hotspur's into the shade. In *Henry V.* Shakespeare strikes the key of pure panegyric. The play is a National Anthem in five acts.

We must remember that Shakespeare from the first could not treat this character with perfect freedom. There is a touch of reverence, of patriotic religion in his tone, even where he shows the Prince given over to wild and wanton frolics. At the close of the Second Part of *Henry IV.* he is already transformed by his sense of responsibility; and he develops, as Henry V., a sincerely religious frame of mind, based on personal humility and on the consciousness of his father's defective right to the throne, which no one could ever have divined in the light-hearted Prince Hal.

These later plays, however, are not to be compared with this First Part of *Henry IV.*, which in its day made so great and well-deserved a success. It presented life itself in all its fulness and variety, great typical creations and figures of racy reality, which, without standing in symmetrical antithesis or parallelism to each other, moved freely over the boards where a never-to-be-forgotten history was enacted. Here no fundamental idea held tyrannical sway, forcing every word that was spoken into formal relation to the whole; here nothing was abstract. No sooner has the rebellion been hatched in the royal palace than the second act opens with a scene in an inn-yard on the Dover road. It is just daybreak; some carriers cross the yard with their lanterns, going to the stable to saddle their horses; they hail each other, gossip, and tell each other how they have passed the night. Not a word do they say about Prince Henry or Falstaff; they talk of the price of oats, and of how "this house is turned upside down since Robin ostler died." Their speeches have nothing to do with the action; they merely sketch its locality and put the audience in tune for it; but seldom in poetry has so much been effected in so few words. The night sky, with Charles's Wain "over the new chimney," the flickering gleam of the lanterns in the dirty yard, the fresh air of the early dawn, the misty atmosphere, the mingled odour of damp peas and beans, of bacon and ginger, all comes straight home to our senses. The situation takes hold of us with all the irresistible force of reality.

Shakespeare must have written this drama with a feeling of almost infallible inspiration and triumphant ease. We understand in reading it what his contemporaries say of his manuscripts: he did not blot a single line.

The political developments arising from Henry IV.'s wrongful seizure of the throne of Richard II. afford the groundwork of the play.

The King, situated partly like Louis Philippe, partly like Napoleon III., does all he can to obliterate the memory of his usurpation. But he does not succeed. Why not? Shakespeare gives a twofold answer. First there is the natural, human reason: the relation of characters and circumstances.

The King has risen by the "fell working" of his friends; he is afraid of falling again before their power. His position forces him to be mistrustful, and his mistrust repels every one from him, first Mortimer, then Percy, then, as nearly as possible, his own son. Secondly, we have the prescribed religious reason: that wrong avenges itself, that punishment follows upon the heels of guilt—in a word, the so-called principle of "poetic justice." If only to propitiate the censorship and the police, Shakespeare could not but do homage to this principle. It was bad enough that the theatres should be suffered to exist at all; if they so far forgot themselves as to show vice unpunished and virtue unrewarded, the playwright would have to be sternly brought to his senses.

The character of the King is a masterpiece. He is the shrewd, mistrustful, circumspect ruler, who has made his way to the throne by dint of smiles and pressures of the hand, has employed every artifice for making an impression, has first ingratiated himself with the populace by his affability, and has then been sparing of his personal presence. Hence those words of his which so deeply impressed Sören Kierkegaard,[1] who despised and acted in direct opposition to the principle they formulated (Pt. i. iii. 2):—

> " Had I so lavish of my presence been,
> So common-hackney'd in the eyes of men,
> So stale and cheap to vulgar company,
> Opinion, that did help me to the crown,
> Had still kept loyal to possession,
> And left me in reputeless banishment,
> A fellow of no mark, nor likelihood.
> By being seldom seen, I could not stir,
> But like a comet I was wonder'd at."

He thus illustrates, from the point of view of an old diplomatist, the injury his son does himself by flaunting it among his disreputable associates.

Yet the son is not so unlike the father as the father believes. Shakespeare has made him, in his own way, adopt a scarcely less diplomatic policy: that of establishing a false opinion about

---

[1] A Danish ethical and theological thinker, a Northern Pascal, said to have in some measure suggested to Ibsen the character of Brand.

himself, letting himself pass for a frivolous debauchee, in order to make all the deeper impression by his firmness and energy as soon as an opportunity offers of showing what is in him. Even in his first soliloquy (i. 2) he lays down this line of policy with a definiteness which is psychologically feeble :—

> " I know you all, and will awhile uphold
> The unyok'd humour of your idleness.
> Yet herein will I imitate the sun,
> Who doth permit the base contagious clouds
> To smother up his beauty from the world,
> That when he please again to be himself,
> Being wanted, he may be more wondered at."

This self-consciousness on Henry's part was to some extent imposed upon Shakespeare. Without it, he could scarcely have brought upon the stage, in such questionable company, a prince who had become a national hero. Yet if the Prince had acted with the cut-and-dried deliberation of purpose which he here attributes to himself, we should have to write him down an unmitigated charlatan.

Here, as in a former instance of psychological crudity— Richard III.'s description of himself as a villain—we must allow for Shakespeare's use of the soliloquy. He frequently regards it as an indispensable stage-convention, which does not really reveal the inmost thoughts of the speaker, but only serves to place the hearer at a certain point of view, and to give him information which he needs. Furthermore, such a soliloquy as this ought to be spoken with a good deal of sophistical self-justification on the Prince's part, or else, as the German actor, Josef Kainz, treats it, in a tone of gay raillery. Finally, it is to be regarded as a first hint—rather a broad one, it must be admitted—which Shakespeare gives us thus early in order to get rid of the improbability he found in the Chronicle, where the Prince is instantaneously and miraculously transformed through a single resolve. The soliloquy is introduced at this point to ensure the coherence of his character, lest the spectator should feel that the Prince's conversion to a totally different manner of life was mechanically tacked on and had no root in his inner nature. And it must have been one of the chief attractions of the theme for Shakespeare to show precisely this conversion.

No doubt he enjoyed depicting his hero's gay and thoughtless life, at war with all the morality which is founded on mere social convention; but at least as great must have been the pleasure he took, as a man of ripe experience, in vindicating that morality which he now felt to be the determining factor in human life—the morality of voluntary self-reform and self-control, without which there can be no concentration of purpose or systematic activity. When the new-crowned king will no longer recognise Falstaff, when he repulses him with the words :—

"How ill white hairs become a fool and jester. . . .
Reply not to me with a fool-born jest;
Presume not that I am the thing I was,"

he speaks out of Shakespeare's own soul. Behind the words there glows a new-born warmth of feeling. The calm sense of justice of the island king makes haste to express itself, and to refuse all further dallying with evil. He grants Falstaff a maintenance and banishes him from his presence. Shakespeare's hero is at this point a living embodiment of that earnestness and sense of responsibility which the poet, whom one of his greatest and ablest admirers (Taine) has represented as being devoid of moral feeling, held to be the indispensable condition of all high endeavour.

XXV

"KING HENRY IV.," SECOND PART—OLD AND NEW CHARACTERS IN IT—DETAILS—"HENRY V.," A NATIONAL DRAMA—PATRIOTISM AND CHAUVINISM—THE VISION OF A GREATER ENGLAND

THE Second Part of *Henry IV.*, which must have been written in 1598, since Justice Silence is mentioned in Ben Jonson's *Every Man out of his Humour*, acted in 1599, abounds, no less than the First Part, in poetic power, but is only a dramatised chronicle, not a drama. In its serious scenes, the play is more faithful to history than the First Part, and it is not Shakespeare's fault that the historical characters are here of less interest. In the comic scenes, which are very amply developed, Shakespeare has achieved the feat of bringing Falstaff a second time upon the stage without giving us the least sense of anticlimax. He is incomparable as ever in his scenes with the Lord Chief-Justice and with the women of the tavern; and when he goes down into Gloucestershire in his character of recruiting-officer, he is still at the height of his genius. As new comrades and foils to him, Shakespeare has here created the two contemptible country Justices, Shallow and Silence. Shallow is a masterpiece, a compact of mere stupidity, foolishness, boastfulness, rascality, and senility; yet he appears a genius in comparison with the ineffable Silence. Here, as in the First Part, the poet evidently drew his comic types from the life of his own day. Another very amusing new personage, who, like Falstaff, was much imitated by the minor dramatists of the time, is Falstaff's Ancient, the braggart Pistol, whose talk is an anthology of playhouse bombast. This inept affectation not only makes him a highly comic personage, but gives Shakespeare an opportunity of girding at the robustious style of the earlier tragic poets, which had become repulsive to him. He parodies Marlowe's *Tamburlaine* in Pistol's outburst (ii. 4):—

> "Shall packhorses,
> And hollow pamper'd jades of Asia,
> Which cannot go but thirty miles a-day,
> Compare with Cæsars and with Cannibals,
> And Trojan Greeks?"

The passage in *Tamburlaine* (Second Part, ii. 4) runs thus:—

> "Holla, ye pamper'd jades of Asia,
> What? can ye draw but twenty miles a day?"

He makes fun of Peele's *Turkish Mahomet and Hyren the fair Greek*, when Pistol, alluding to his sword, exclaims, "Have we not Hiren here?" And again it is George Peele who is aimed at when Pistol says to the hostess:—

> "Then feed and be fat, my fair Calipolis;
> Come, give's some sack."

In *The Battle of Alcazar* (see above, p. 39), Muley Mahomet brings his wife some flesh on the point of his sword and says—

> "Hold thee, Calipolis, feed and faint no more!"

But Falstaff himself is, and must ever remain, the chief attraction of the comic scenes. Never was the Fat Knight wittier than when he answers the Lord Chief-Justice, who has told him that his figure bears "all the characters of age" (i. 2):—

"My Lord, I was born about three of the clock in the afternoon, with a white head, and something a round belly. For my voice, I have lost it with hollaing and singing of anthems. To approve my youth further, I will not: the truth is, I am only old in judgment and understanding; and he that will caper with me for a thousand marks, let him lend me the money, and have at him."

The play is a mere bundle of individual passages, but each of these passages is admirable. A great example is King Henry's soliloquy which opens the third act, the profoundly imaginative apostrophe to sleep:—

> "O thou dull god! why liest thou with the vile,
> In loathsome beds, and leav'st the kingly couch,
> A watch-case, or a common 'larum bell?

> Wilt thou upon the high and giddy mast
> Seal up the ship-boy's eyes, and rock his brains
> In cradle of the rude imperious surge,
> And in the visitation of the winds,
> Who take the ruffian billows by the top,
> Curling their monstrous heads, and hanging them
> With deaf'ning clamours in the slippery clouds,
> That with the hurly death itself awakes?
> Canst thou, O partial sleep! give thy repose
> To the wet sea-boy in an hour so rude;
> And in the calmest and most stillest night,
> With all appliances and means to boot,
> Deny it to a king? Then, happy low, lie down!
> Uneasy lies the head that wears a crown."

Throughout this Second Part, the King, besieged by cares and living in the shadow of death, is richer in thought and wisdom than ever before. What he says, and what is said to him, seems drawn by the poet from the very depths of his own experience, and addressed to men of the like experience and thought. Every word of that first scene of the third act is in the highest degree significant and admirable. It is here that the King turns to what we now call geology (see above, p. 114) for an image of the historical mutability of all things. When he mournfully reminds his attendants that Richard II., whom he displaced, prophesied a Nemesis to come from those who had helped him to the throne, and that this Nemesis has now overtaken him, Warwick answers with the profound and astonishingly modern reflection that history is apparently governed by laws, and that each man's life—

> "Figures the nature of the times deceas'd;
> The which observ'd, a man may prophesy,
> With a near aim, of the main chance of things
> As yet not come to life."

To this the King returns the no less philosophical answer:—

> "Are these things, then, necessities?
> Then let us meet them like necessities."

But it is at the close of the fourth act, where news of the total defeat of the rebels is brought to the dying King, that he utters what is perhaps his most profoundly pessimistic speech, complaining that Fortune never comes with both hands full, but "writes her fair words still in foulest letters," so that life is like a feast at which either the food or the appetite [or the guests] are always lacking.

From the moment of King Henry's death, Shakespeare concentrates all his poetical strength upon the task of presenting in his great son the pattern and ideal of English kingship. In all the earlier Histories the King had grave defects; Shakespeare now applies himself, with warm and undisguised enthusiasm, to the portrayal of a king without a flaw.

His *Henry V.* is a glorification of this national ideal. The five choruses which introduce the acts are patriotic pæans, Shakespeare's finest heroic lyrics; and the play itself is an epic in dialogue, without any sort of dramatic structure, development, or conflict. It is an English ἐγκώμιον, a dramatic monument, as was the *Persæ* of Æschylus for ancient Athens. As a work of creative art, it cannot be compared with the two preceding Histories, to which it forms a supplement. Its theme is English patriotism, and its appeal is to England rather than to the world.

The allusion to Essex's command in Ireland in the prologue to the fifth act gives us beyond a doubt the date of its first performance. Essex was in Ireland from the 15th of April 1599 to the 28th of September in the following year. As we find the play alluded to by other poets in 1600, it must in all probability have been produced in 1599.

How strongly Shakespeare was impressed by the greatness of his theme appears in his reiterated expressions of humility in approaching it. He begins, like the epic poets of antiquity, with an invocation of the Muse; he implores forgiveness, not only for the imperfection of his scenic apparatus, but for the "flat unraised spirits" in which he treats so mighty a theme. And in the prologue to the fourth act he returns to the subject of his unworthiness and the pitiful limitations of the stage. Throughout the choruses, he has done his utmost, by dint of vivid imagery and lyric impetus and splendour, to make up for the sacrifice of unity and cohesion involved in his faithfulness to history. Shakespeare was evidently unconscious of the naïveté of the lecture on the Salic law, establishing Henry's claim to the crown of France, with which the Archbishop opens the play; no doubt he thought it absolutely imposed upon him.

For he here strives to make Henry an epitome of all the virtues he himself most highly values. Even in the last act of the Second Part of *Henry IV.* he had endowed him with traits of irreproachable kingly magnanimity. Henry confirms in his office the Chief-Justice, who, in the execution of his duty, had arrested the Prince of Wales, addresses him with the deepest respect, and even calls him "father." In reality this Chief-Justice was dismissed at the King's accession. *Henry V.* completes the evolution of the royal butterfly from the larva and chrysalis stages of the earlier plays. Henry is at once the monarch who always thinks royally, and never forgets his pride as the representative of the English people; the man with no pose or arrogance, who bears himself simply, talks modestly, acts energetically, and thinks piously; the soldier who endures privations like the meanest of his followers, is downright in his jesting and his wooing, and enforces discipline with uncompromising strictness, even as against his own old comrades; and finally, the citizen who is accessible alike to small and great, and in whom the youthful frolicsomeness of earlier days has become the humourist's relish for a practical joke, like that which he plays off upon Williams and Fluellen. Shakespeare shows him, like a military Haroun Al Raschid, seeking personally to insinuate himself into the thoughts and feelings of his followers; and—what is very unlike him—he manifests no disapproval where the King sinks far below the ideal, as when he orders the frightful massacre of all the French prisoners taken at Agincourt. Shakespeare tries to pass the deed off as a measure of necessity.

The reason of this is that the spirit which here prevails is not pure patriotism, but in many points a narrow Chauvinism. King Henry's two speeches before Harfleur (iii. 1 and iii. 3) are bombastic, savage, and threatening to the point of frothy bluster; and wherever Frenchmen and Englishmen are brought into contrast, the French, even if they at that time showed themselves inferior soldiers, are treated with obvious injustice. With his sharp eye for national, as for personal peculiarities, Shakespeare has of course seized upon certain weaknesses of the French character; but for the most part his Frenchmen are mere caricatures for the diversion of the gallery. Quite childish is the way in which he makes the Frenchmen mix fragments of French in their speeches. But it is consistent enough with the national and popular design of the play that not a little of it should seem to be addressed to the common, uneducated public—for instance, the scene in which the miserable blusterer Pistol makes prisoner a French nobleman whom he has succeeded in overawing, and that in which the young Princess Katherine of France takes lessons in English from one of her ladies-in-waiting. This passage (iii. 4) and the wooing scene between King Henry and the Princess (v. 2) are incidentally interesting as giving us a good idea of Shakespeare's acquaintance with French. No doubt he could read French, but he must have spoken it very imperfectly. He is perhaps not to blame for such blunders as *le possession* and *à les anges*. On the other hand, it was doubtless he who placed in the mouth of the Princess such comically impossible expressions as these when Henry has kissed her hand:—

"*Je ne veux point que vous abbaissez vostre grandeur, en baisant le main d'une vostre indigne serviteur.*"

And this :—

"*Les dames, et damoiselles, pour estre baisées devant leur nopces, il n'est pas le costume de France.*"

According to his custom, and in order to preserve continuity of style with the foregoing plays, Shakespeare has interspersed *Henry V.* with comic figures and scenes. Falstaff himself does not appear, his death being announced at the beginning of the play; but the members of his gang wander around, as living and ludicrous mementos of him, until they disappear one by one by way of the gallows, so that nothing may survive to recall the great king's frivolous youth. To console us for their loss, we are here introduced to a new circle of comic figures—soldiers from the different English-speaking countries which make up what we now call the United Kingdom. Each of them speaks his own dialect, in which resides much of the comic effect for English ears. We have a Welshman, a Scot, and an Irishman. The Welshman is intrepid, phlegmatic, somewhat pedantic, but all fire and flame for discipline and righteousness; the Scot is immovable in his equilibrium, even-tempered, sturdy, and trustworthy; the Irishman is a true Celt, fiery, passionate, quarrelsome and apt at misunderstanding. Fluellen, the Welshman, with his comic phlegm and manly severity, is the most elaborate of these figures.

But in placing on the stage these representatives of the different English-speaking peoples, Shakespeare had another and deeper purpose than that of merely amusing his public with a medley of dialects. At that time the Scots were still the hereditary enemies of England, who always attacked her in the rear whenever she went to war, and the Irish were actually in open rebellion. Shakespeare evidently dreamed of a Greater England, as we nowadays speak of a Greater Britain. When he wrote this play, King James of Scotland was busily courting the favour of the English, and the question of the succession to the throne, when the old Queen should die, was not definitely settled. Shakespeare clearly desired that, with the coming of James, the old national hatred between the Scotch and the English should cease. Essex, in Ireland, was at this very time carrying out the policy which was to lead to his destruction—that, namely, of smoothing away hatred by means of leniency, and trying to come to an arrangement with the leader of the Catholic rebellion. Southampton was with him in Ireland as his Master of the Horse, and we cannot doubt that Shakespeare's heart was in the campaign. Bates in this play (iv. 1) probably expresses Shakespeare's own political ideas when he says—

"Be friends, you English fools, be friends: we have French [Spanish] quarrels enow, if you could tell how to reckon."

Henry V. is not one of Shakespeare's best plays, but it is one of his most amiable. He here shows himself not as the almost superhuman genius, but as the English patriot, whose enthusiasm is as beautiful as it is simple, and whose prejudices, even, are not unbecoming. The play not only points backward to the greatest period of England's past, but forward to King James, who, as the Protestant son of the Catholic Mary Stuart, was to put an end to religious persecutions, and who, as a Scotchman and a supporter of the Irish policy of Essex, was for the first time to show the world not only a sturdy England, but a powerful Great Britain.

XXVI

ELIZABETH AND FALSTAFF—THE MERRY WIVES OF WINDSOR—THE PROSAIC AND BOURGEOIS TONE OF THE PIECE—THE FAIRY SCENES

SHAKESPEARE must have written *The Merry Wives of Windsor* immediately after *Henry V.*, probably about Christmas 1599; for Sir Thomas Lucy, on whom the poet here takes his revenge, died in 1600, and it is improbable that Shakespeare would have cared to gird at him after his death. He almost certainly did not write the piece of his own motive, but at the suggestion of one whose wish was a command. There is the strongest internal evidence for the truth of the tradition which states that the play was written at the request of Queen Elizabeth. The first Quarto of 1602 has on its title-page the words, "As it hath been divers times acted by the right honourable my Lord Chamberlain's servants. Both before Her Majesty, and elsewhere." A century later (1702), John Dennis, who published an adaptation of the play, writes, "I know very well that it had pleased one of the greatest queens that ever was in the world. . . . This comedy was written at her command and by her direction, and she was so eager to see it acted, that she commanded it to be finished in fourteen days." A few years later (1709) Rowe writes, "She was so well pleased with that admirable character of Falstaff in the two parts of *Henry IV.*, that she commanded him to continue it for one play more and show him in love. This is said to be the occasion of his writing *The Merry Wives*. How well she was obeyed, the play itself is an admirable proof."

Old Queen Bess can scarcely have been a great judge of art, or she would not have conceived the extravagant notion of wanting to see Falstaff in love; she would have understood that if there was anything impossible to him it was this. She would also have realised that his figure was already a rounded whole and could not be reproduced. It is true that in the Epilogue to *Henry IV*. (which, however, is probably not by Shakespeare) a continuation of the history is promised, in which, "for anything I know, Falstaff shall die of a sweat, unless already he be killed with your hard opinions;" but no such continuation is to be found in *Henry V.*, evidently because Shakespeare felt that Falstaff had played out his part. Neither is *The Merry Wives* the promised continuation, for Falstaff does not die, and the action is conceived as an earlier episode in his life, though it is entirely removed from its historical setting and brought forward into the poet's own time, so unequivocally that there is even in the fifth act a direct mention of "our radiant queen" in Windsor Castle.

The poet must have set himself unwillingly to the fulfilment of the "radiant queen's" barbarous wish, and tried to make the best of a bad business. He was compelled entirely to ruin his inimitable Falstaff, and degrade the fat knight into an ordinary avaricious, wine-bibbing, amatory old fool. Along with him, he resuscitated the whole merry company from *Henry V.*, who had all come to an unpleasant end—Bardolph, Pistol, Nym, and Dame Quickly—making the men repeat themselves with a difference, endowing Pistol with the splendid phrase "The world's mine oyster, which I with sword will open," and giving to Dame Quickly softened and more commonplace lineaments. From the Second Part of *Henry IV.*, too, he introduces Justice Shallow, placing him in a less friendly relation to Falstaff, and giving him a highly comic nephew, Slender, who, in his vanity and pitifulness, is like a first sketch for Sir Andrew Aguecheek in *Twelfth Night*.

His task was now to entertain a queen and a court "with their hatred of ideas, their insensibility to beauty, their hard, efficient manners, and their demand for impropriety."[1] As it amused the London populace to see kings and princes upon the stage, so it entertained the Queen and her court to have a glimpse into the daily life of the middle classes, so remote from their own, to look into their rooms, and hear their chat with the doctor and the parson, to see a picture of the prosperity and contentment which flourished at Windsor right under the windows of the Queen's summer residence, and to witness the downright virtue and merry humour of the red-cheeked, buxom townswomen.

[1] Dowden: *Shakspere—his Mind and Art*, p. 370.

Thus was the keynote of the piece determined. Thus it became more prosaic and bourgeois than any other play of Shakespeare's. *The Merry Wives* is indeed the only one of his works which is almost entirely written in prose, and the only one of his comedies in which, the scene being laid in England, he has taken as his subject the contemporary life of the English middle classes. It is not quite unlike the more farcical of Molière's comedies, which also were often written with an eye to royal and courtly audiences. All the more significant is the fact that Shakespeare has found it impossible to content himself with thus dwelling on the common earth, and has introduced at the close a fairy-dance and fairy-song, as though from the *Midsummer Night's Dream* itself, executed, it is true, by children and young girls dressed up as elves, but preserving throughout the air and style of genuine fairy scenes.

Shakespeare had just been trying his hand in *Henry V.* at writing the broken English spoken by a Welshman and by a Frenchman. He knew that at court, where people prided themselves on the purest pronunciation of their mother-tongue, he would find an audience exceedingly alive to the comic effects thus obtained, and he therefore, while he was in the vein, introduced into this hasty and occasional production two not unkindly caricatures—the Welsh priest, Sir Hugh Evans, in whom he perhaps immortalised one of his Stratford schoolmasters, and the French Doctor Caius, a thoroughly farcical eccentric, who pronounces everything awry.

The hurry with which Shakespeare wrote this comedy has led him into some confusion as to the process of time. In Act iii. 4, when Dame Quickly is sent to Falstaff to make a second appointment with him, it is the afternoon of the second day; in the following scene, when she comes to him, it is the morning of the third day. But this haste has also given the play an unusually dramatic swing and impetus; it is quite free from the episodes in which the poet is at other times apt to loiter.

Nevertheless Shakespeare has here woven together no fewer than three different actions—Falstaff's advances to the two Merry Wives, Mrs. Ford and Mrs. Page, and all the consequences of his ill-timed rendezvous; the rivalry between the foolish doctor, the imbecile Slender, and young Fenton for the hand of fair Anne Page; and finally, the burlesque duel between the Welsh priest and the French doctor, which is devised and set afoot by the jovial Windsor innkeeper.

Shakespeare has himself invented much more than usual of the complicated intrigue. But Falstaff's concealment in the buck-basket was suggested by a similar incident in Fiorentino's *Il Pecorone*, from which Shakespeare had already borrowed in the *Merchant of Venice;* and the idea of making Falstaff incessantly confide his designs and his rendezvous to the husband of the lady in question came from another Italian story by Straparola, which had been published some ten years earlier, under the title of *Two Lovers of Pisa*, in Tarlton's *News of Purgatory*.

The invention is not always very happy. For instance, it is a highly unpleasing and improbable touch that Ford, as Master Brook, should bribe Falstaff to procure him possession of the woman (his own wife) whom he affects to desire, and whom Falstaff also is pursuing. Ford's jealousy, moreover, is altogether too stupid and crude in its manifestations. But we have especially to deplore that the nature of the intrigue and the moral tendency to be impressed on the play should have made Falstaff, who used to be quickness and ingenuity personified, so preternaturally dense that his incessant defeats afford his opponents a very poor triumph.

He is ignorant of everything it would have been his interest to know, and he is perpetually committing afresh the same inconceivable blunders. It is foolish enough, in the first place, to write two identical love-letters to two women in the same little town, who, as he ought to know, are bosom friends. It is incredibly stupid of him to walk three times in succession straight into the coarse trap which they set for him; in doing so he betrays such a monstrous vanity that we find it impossible to recognise in him the ironical Falstaff of the Histories. It is inexpressibly guileless of him never to conceive the slightest suspicion of "Master Brook," who, being his only confidant, is therefore the only man who can have betrayed him to the husband. And finally, it is not only childish, but utterly inconsistent with the keen understanding of the earlier Falstaff, that he should believe in the supernatural nature of the beings who pinch him and burn him by night in the park.

On the other hand, the old high spirits and the old wit now and again flame forth in him, and a few of his speeches to Shallow, to Pistol, to Bardolph and others are exceedingly amusing. He shows a touch of his old self when, after having been soused in the water along with the foul linen, he protests that drowning is "a death that I abhor, for the water swells a man, and what a thing should I have been when I had been swelled!" And he has a highly humorous outburst in the last act (v. 5) when he declares, "I think the devil will not have me damned, lest the oil that is in me should set hell on fire." But what are these little flashes in comparison with the inexhaustible whimsicality of the true Falstaff!

The play is more consistently farcical than any earlier comedy of Shakespeare's, *The Taming of the Shrew* not excepted. The graceful and poetical passages are few. We have in Mr. and Mrs. Page a pleasant English middle-class couple; and though the young lovers, Fenton and Anne Page, have only one short scene together, they display in it some attractive qualities. Anne Page is an amiable middle-class girl of Shakespeare's day, one of the healthy and natural young women whom Wordsworth has celebrated in the nineteenth century. Fenton, who is said (though we cannot believe it) to have been at one time a comrade of Prince Hal and Poins, is certainly attached to her; but it is very characteristic that Shakespeare, with his keen sense for the value of money, sees nothing to object to in the fact that Fenton, as he frankly confesses, was first attracted to Anne by her wealth. This is the same trait which we found in another wooer, Bassanio, of a few years earlier.

Finally, there is real poetry in the short fairy scene of the last act. The poet here takes his revenge for the prose to which he has so long been condemned. It is full of the aromatic wood-scents of Windsor Park by night. What is altogether most valuable in *The Merry Wives* is its strong smack of the English soil. The play appeals to us, in spite of the drawbacks inseparable from a work hastily written to order, because the poet has here for once remained faithful to his own age and his own country, and has given us a picture of the contemporary middle-class, in its sturdy and honest worth, which even the atmosphere of farce cannot quite obscure.

XXVII

SHAKESPEARE'S MOST BRILLIANT PERIOD—THE FEMININE TYPES BELONGING TO IT—WITTY AND HIGHBORN YOUNG WOMEN—MUCH ADO ABOUT NOTHING—SLAVISH FAITHFULNESS TO HIS SOURCES—BENEDICK AND BEATRICE—SPIRITUAL DEVELOPMENT—THE LOW-COMEDY FIGURES

SHAKESPEARE now enters upon the stage in his career in which his wit and brilliancy of spirit reach a perfection hitherto unattained. It seems as though these years of his life had been bathed in sunshine. They certainly cannot have been years of struggle, and still less of sorrow; there must have been a sort of lull in his existence—a tranquil zone, as it were, in the troubled waters of life. He seems for a short time to have revelled in his own genius with a sort of pensive happiness, to have drunk exhilarating draughts of his own inspiration. He heard the nightingales warbling in the sacred grove of his spirit. His whole nature burst into flower.

In the Republican Calendar one of the months was named Floréal. There is such a flower-month in almost every human life; and this is Shakespeare's.

He was doubtless in love at this time—as he had probably been all his life through—but his love was not an overmastering passion like Romeo's, nor did it depress him with that half-despairing feeling of the unworthiness of its object which he betrays in his Sonnets; nor, again, was it the airy ecstasy of youthful imagination that ran riot in *A Midsummer Night's Dream*. No, it was a happy love, which filled his head as well as his heart, accompanied with joyous admiration for the wit and vivacity of the beloved one, for her graciousness and distinction. Her coquetry is gay, her heart is excellent, and her intelligence so quick that she seems to be wit incarnate in the form of a woman.

In his early years he had presented not a few unamiable, mannish women in his comedies, and not a few ambitious, bloodthirsty, or corrupt women in his serious plays—figures such as Adriana and the shrewish Katharine on the one hand, Tamora and Margaret of Anjou on the other hand, who have all a stiff-necked will, and a certain violence of manners. In the later years of his ripe manhood he displays a preference for young women who are nothing but soul and tenderness, silent natures without wit or sparkle, figures such as Ophelia, Desdemona, and Cordelia.

Between these two strongly-marked groups we come upon a bevy of beautiful young women, who all have their heart in the right place, but whose chief attraction lies in their sparkling quickness of wit. They are often as lovable as the most faithful friend can be, and witty as Heinrich Heine himself, though with another sort of wit. We feel that Shakespeare must have admired with all his heart the models from whom he drew these women, and must have rejoiced in them as one brilliant mind rejoices in another. These types of delicate and aristocratic womanhood cannot possibly have had plebeian models.

In his first years in London, Shakespeare, as an underling in a company of players, can have had no opportunity of associating with other women than, firstly, those who sat for his Mistress Quickly and Doll Tearsheet; secondly, those passionate and daring women who make the first advances to actors and poets; and, thirdly, those who served as models for his " Merry Wives," with their sound bourgeois sense and not over delicate gaiety. But the ordinary citizen's wife or daughter of that day offered the poet no sort of spiritual sustenance. They were, as a rule, quite illiterate. Shakespeare's younger daughter could not even write her own name.

But he was presently discovered by men like Southampton and Pembroke, cordially received into their refined and thoroughly cultivated circle, and in all probability presented to the ladies of these noble families. Can we doubt that the tone of conversation among these aristocratic ladies must have enchanted him, that he must have rejoiced in the nobility and elegance of their manners, and that their playful freedom of speech must have afforded him an object for imitation and idealisation?

The great ladies of that date were exceedingly accomplished. They had been educated as highly as the men, spoke Italian, French, and Spanish fluently, and were not infrequently acquainted with Latin and Greek. Lady Pembroke, Sidney's sister, the mother of Shakespeare's patron, was regarded as the most intellectual woman of her time, and was equally celebrated as an author and as a patroness of authors. And these ladies were not oppressed by their knowledge or affected in their speech, but natural, rich in ideas as in acquirements, free in their wit, and sometimes in their morals; so that we can easily understand how a daring, high-bred, womanly intelligence should have been, for a series of years, the object which it most delighted Shakespeare to portray. He supplements this intellectual superiority, in varying measures, with independence, goodness of heart, pride, humility, tenderness, the joy of life; so that from the central conception there radiates a fan-like semicircle of different personalities. It was of such women that he had dreamt when he sketched his Rosaline in *Love's Labour's Lost*. Now he knew them, as he had already shown in Portia, the first of the group.

In spite of his latent melancholy, he is now highly-favoured and happy, this young man of thirty-five; the sun of his career is in the sign of the Lion; he feels himself strong enough to sport with the powers of life, and he now writes nothing but comedies. He does not take the trouble to invent them; he employs his old method of carving a play out of this or that mediocre romantic novel, or he revises inferior old pieces. As a rule, he goes thus to work: he retains without a qualm those traits in his fable which are fantastic, improbable, even repulsive to a more delicate taste—such points are always astonishingly unimportant in his eyes; he sometimes transfers to his play undigested masses of the material before him, with no care for psychological plausibility; but he seizes upon some leading situation in the novel, or upon some single character in the earlier play, and he animates this situation or this character, or (it may be) added characters of his own invention, with the whole fervour of his soul, until the speeches shine forth as in letters of fire, and sparkle with wit or glow with passion.

Thus, in *Much Ado about Nothing*, he retains a fable which offers almost insuperable difficulties to satisfactory poetical treatment, and nevertheless produces, partly outside of its framework, poetical values of the first order.

The play was entered in the Stationers' Register on the 4th of August 1600, and appeared in the same year under the title:

Much Adoe about Nothing. As it hath been sundrie times publikely acted by the Right Honourable the Lord Chamberlaine his Servants. Written by William Shakespeare. It must thus have been written in 1599 or 1600; and we find, too, in its opening scene, certain allusions that accord with this date. Thus Leonato's speech, "A victory is twice itself when the achiever brings home full numbers," and Beatrice's "You had musty victual," are both thought to point to Essex's campaign in Ireland.

Shakespeare has taken the details of his plot from several Italian sources. From the first book of Ariosto's *Orlando Furioso* (the story of Ariodante and Genevra), which was translated in 1591, and had already provided the material for a play performed before the Queen in 1582, he borrowed the idea of a malevolent nobleman persuading a youthful lover that his lady is untrue to him, and suborning a waiting-woman to dress like her mistress, and receive a nocturnal visit by means of a ladder placed against her lady's window, so that the bridegroom, watching the scene from a distance, may accept it as proof of the calumny, and so break off the match. All the other details he took from a novel of Bandello's, the story of Timbreo of Cardona. Timbreo is represented by Claudio; through the medium of a friend, he woos the daughter of Leonato, a nobleman of Messina. The intrigue which separates the young pair is woven by Girondo (in Shakespeare, Don John) just as in the play, but with a more adequate motive, since Girondo himself is in love with the lady. She faints when she is accused, is given out to be dead, and there is a sham funeral, as in the play. But in the story it is represented that the whole of Messina espouses her cause, and believes in her innocence, while in the play Beatrice alone remains true to her young kinswoman. The truth is discovered and the engagement renewed, just as in Shakespeare.

Only for a much cruder habit of mind than that which prevails among people of culture in our days can this story provide the motive for a comedy. The very title indicates a point of view quite foreign to us. The implication is that since Hero was innocent, and the accusation a mere slander; since she was not really dead, and the sorrow for her loss was therefore groundless; and since she and Claudio are at last married, as they might have been at first—therefore the whole thing has been much ado about nothing, and resolves itself in a harmony which leaves no discord behind.

The ear of the modern reader is otherwise attuned. He recognises, indeed, that Shakespeare has taken no small pains to make this fable dramatically acceptable. He appreciates the fact that here again, in the person of Don John, the poet has depicted mere unmixed evil, and has disdained to supply a motive for his vile action in any single injury received, or desire unsatisfied. Don John is one of the sour, envious natures which suck poison from all sources, because they suffer from the perpetual sense of being unvalued and despised. He is, for the moment, constrained by the forbearance with which his victorious brother has treated him, but "if he had his mouth he would bite." And he does bite, like the cur and coward he is, and makes himself scarce when his villainy is about to be discovered. He is an ill-conditioned, base, and tiresome scoundrel; and, although he conscientiously does evil for evil's sake, we miss in him all the defiant and brilliantly sinister qualities which appear later on in Iago and in Edmund. There is little to object to in Don John's repulsive scoundrelism; at most we may say that it is a strange motive-power for a comedy. But to Claudio we cannot reconcile ourselves. He allows himself to be convinced, by the clumsiest stratagem, that his young bride, in reality as pure and tender as a flower, is a faithless creature, who deceives him the very day before her marriage. Instead of withdrawing in silence, he prefers, like the blockhead he is, to confront her in the church, before the altar, and in the hearing of every one overwhelm her with coarse speeches and low accusations; and he induces his patron, the Prince Don Pedro, and even the lady's own father, Leonato, to join him in heaping upon the unhappy bride their idiotic accusations. When, by the advice of the priest, her relatives have given her out as dead, and the worthy old Leonato has lied up hill and down dale about her hapless end, Claudio, who now learns too late that he has been duped, is at once taken into favour again. Leonato only demands of him—in accordance with the mediæval fable—that he shall declare himself willing to marry whatever woman he (Leonato) shall assign to him. This he promises, without a word or thought about Hero; whereupon she is placed in his arms. The original spectators, no doubt, found this solution satisfactory; a modern audience is exasperated by it, very much as Nora, in

A Doll's House, is exasperated on finding that Helmer, after the danger has passed away, regards all that has happened in their souls as though it had never been, merely because the sky is clear again. If ever man was unworthy a woman's love, that man is Claudio. If ever marriage was odious and ill-omened, this is it. The old taleteller's invention has been too much even for Shakespeare's art.

When we moderns, however, think of *Much Ado about Nothing,* it is not this distasteful story that rises before our mind's eye. It is Benedick and Beatrice, and the intrigue in which they are involved. The light from these figures, and especially from that of Beatrice, irradiates the play, and we understand that Shakespeare was forced to make Claudio so contemptible, because by that means alone could the enchanting personality of Beatrice shine forth in its fullest splendour.

Beatrice is a great lady of the Renaissance in her early youth, overflowing with spirits and energy, brightly, defiantly virginal, inclined, in the wealth of her daring wit, to a somewhat aggressive raillery, and capable of unabashed freedom of speech, astounding to our modern taste, but permitted by their education to the foremost women of that age. Her behaviour to Benedick, whom she cannot help perpetually twitting and teasing, is as headstrong and refractory as Katharine's treatment of Petruchio.

Her diction is marvellous, glittering with unrestrained fantasy. For instance, after she has assured her uncle (ii. 1) that she "is on her knees every morning and evening" to be spared the infliction of a husband, since a man with a beard and a man without one would be equally intolerable to her, she proceeds—

"*Beatrice.* . . . Therefore I will even take sixpence in earnest of the bear-ward, and lead his apes into hell.

"*Leonato.* Well, then, go you into hell?

"*Beat.* No; but to the gate; and there will the devil meet me, like an old cuckold, with horns on his head, and say, 'Get you to heaven, Beatrice, get you to heaven; here's no place for you maids:' so deliver I up my apes, and away to Saint Peter for the heavens; he shows me where the bachelors sit, and there live we as merry as the day is long."

She holds that—

"Wooing, wedding, and repenting, is as a Scotch jig, a measure, and a cinque-pace: the first suit is hot and hasty, like a Scotch jig, and

full as fantastical: the wedding, mannerly modest, as a measure, full
of state and ancientry; and then comes repentance, and with his bad
legs falls into the cinque-pace faster and faster, till he sink into his
grave.

Therefore she exclaims with roguish irony—

"Good Lord, for alliance!—Thus goes every one to the world but
I, and I am sun-burnt. I may sit in a corner, and cry heigh-ho for a
husband!"

In her battles with Benedick she outdoes him in fantasy, both
congruous and incongruous, or burlesque. Here, again, Shakespeare has evidently taken Lyly as his model, and has tried to
reproduce the polished facets of his dialogue, while at the same
time correcting its unnaturalness, and giving it fresh life. And
Beatrice follows up her victory over Benedick, even when he is
no longer her interlocutor, with a freedom which is now-a-days
unthinkable in a young girl:—

"*D. Pedro.* You have put him down, lady; you have put him
down.

"*Beat.* So I would not he should do me, my lord, lest I should
prove the mother of fools."

But this unbridled whimsicality conceals the energetic virtues of
a firm and noble character. When her poor cousin is falsely
accused and cruelly put to shame; when those who should have
been her natural protectors fall away from her, and even outside
spectators like Benedick waver and lean to the accuser's side;
then it is Beatrice alone who, unaffected even for an instant by
the slander, indignantly and passionately takes up her cause,
and shows herself faithful, high-minded, right-thinking, far-seeing,
superior to them all—a pearl of a woman.

By her side Shakespeare has placed Benedick, a Mercutio
redivivus; a youth who is the reverse of amatory, opposed to a
maiden who is the reverse of tender. He abhors betrothal and
marriage quite as vehemently as she, and is, from the man's
point of view, no less scornful of all sentimentality than she,
from the woman's; so that he and she, from the first, stand on
a warlike footing with each other. In virtue of a profound and
masterly psychological observation, Shakespeare presently makes
these two fall suddenly in love with each other, over head and

ears, for no better reason than that their friends persuade Benedick that Beatrice is secretly pining for love of him, and Beatrice that Benedick is mortally enamoured of her, accompanying this information with high-flown eulogies of both. Their thoughts were already occupied with each other; and now the amatory fancy flames forth in both of them all the more strongly, because it has so long been banked down. And here, where everything was of his own invention and he could move quite freely, Shakespeare has with delicate ingenuity brought the pair together, not by means of empty words, but in a common cause, Beatrice's first advance to Benedick taking place in the form of an appeal to him for chivalrous intervention in behalf of her innocent cousin.

The reversal in the mutual relations of Benedick and Beatrice is, moreover, highly interesting in so far as it is probably the first instance of anything like careful character-development which we have as yet encountered in any single play of Shakespeare's. In the earlier comedies there was nothing of the kind, and the chronicle-plays afforded no opportunity for it. The characters had simply to be brought into harmony with the given historical events, and in every case Shakespeare held firmly to the character-scheme once laid down. Neither *Richard III.* nor *Henry V.* presents any spiritual history; both kings, in the plays which take their names from them, are one and the same from first to last. Enough has already been said of Henry's change of front with respect to Falstaff in *Henry IV.;* we need only remark further that here the old play of *The Famous Victories*[1] unmistakably pointed the way to Shakespeare. But this melting of all that is hard and frozen in the natures of Benedick and Beatrice is without a parallel in any earlier work, and is quite

---

[1] In this play the king says:—

"Ah, Tom, your former life greeves me,
And makes me to abandon and abolish your company for ever,
And therefore not upon pain of death to approach my presence
By ten miles' space, then if I heare well of you,
It may be I will do somewhat for you."

In Shakespeare:—

"Till then I banish thee on pain of death
As I have done the rest of my misleaders,
Not to come near our person by ten mile.
For competence of life I will allow you."

plainly executed *con amore*. And the real substance of the play lies not in the plot from which it takes its name, but in the relation between these two characters, freely invented by Shakespeare.

Some other characters Shakespeare has added, and they are among the most admirable of his comic creations: the peace-officer Dogberry, and his subordinate Verges. Dogberry is a country constable, simple as a child, and vain as a peacock—a well-meaning, timid, honest, good-natured blockhead. To show that, in those days, such functionaries were almost as helpless in real life as they are here represented, Henrik Schück has cited a letter from Elizabeth's Prime Minister, Lord Burghley, in which he relates how, in 1586, on a journey from London into the country, he found at the gate of every town ten or twelve persons armed with long poles. On inquiring, he learned that they were stationed there to seize three young men, unknown. Asked what description they had received of the malefactors, they replied that one of them was said to have a crooked nose. "And have you no other mark to recognise them by?" "No," was the answer. Moreover, they always stood so openly in a body, that no criminal could fail to give them a wide berth.

Dogberry is still less formidable than this detective force. Here are the wise and wary instructions which he gives to his watchmen:—

"*Dogberry*. If you meet a thief, you may suspect him, by virtue of your office, to be no true man; and, for such kind of men, the less you meddle or make with them, why, the more is for your honesty.

"2 *Watch*. If we know him to be a thief, shall we not lay hands on him?

"*Dogb*. Truly, by your office you may; but, I think, they that touch pitch will be defiled. The most peaceable way for you, if you do take a thief, is, to let him show himself what he is, and steal out of your company."

XXVIII

THE INTERVAL OF SERENITY — AS YOU LIKE IT — THE ROVING SPIRIT—THE LONGING FOR NATURE—JAQUES AND SHAKESPEARE—THE PLAY A FEAST OF WIT

NEVER had Shakespeare produced with such rapidity and ease as in this bright and happy interval of two or three years. It is positively astounding to note all that he accomplished in the year 1600, when he stood, not exactly at the height of his poetical power, for that steadily increased, but at the height of his poetical serenity. Among the exquisite comedies he now writes, *As You Like It* is one of the most exquisite.

The play was entered in the Stationers' Register, along with *Much Ado About Nothing*, on the 4th of August 1600, and must in all probability have been written in that year. Meres does not mention it, in 1598, in his list of Shakespeare's plays; it contains (as already noted, page 36) a quotation from Marlowe's *Hero and Leander*, published in 1598—

"Who ever lov'd, that lov'd not at first sight?"

a quotation, by the way, which sums up the matter of the comedy; and we find in Celia's words (i. 2), "Since the little wit that fools have was silenced," an allusion to the public and judicial burning of satirical publications which took place on the 1st of June 1599. As there does not seem to be room in the year 1599 for more works than we have already assigned to it, *As You Like It* must be taken as dating from the first half of the following year.

As usual, Shakespeare took from another poet the whole material of this enchanting comedy. His contemporary, Thomas Lodge (who, after leaving Oxford, became first a player and playwright in London, then a lawyer, then a doctor and writer on medical subjects, until he died of the plague in the year 1625), had in 1590 published a pastoral romance, with many poems interspersed, entitled *Euphues golden Legacie, found after his death in his Cell at Silexedra*,[1] which he had written, as he sets forth in his Dedication to Lord Hunsdon, "to beguile the time" on a voyage to the Canary Islands. The style is laboured and exceedingly diffuse, a true pastoral style; but Lodge had that gift of mere external invention in which Shakespeare, with all his powers, was so deficient. All the different stories which the play contains or touches upon are found in Lodge, and likewise all the characters, with the exception of Jaques, Touchstone, and Audrey. Very remarkable to the attentive reader is Shakespeare's uniform passivity with regard to what he found in his sources, and his unwillingness to reject or alter anything, combined as it is with the most intense intellectual activity at the points upon which he concentrates his strength.

We find in *As You Like It*, as in Lodge, a wicked Duke who has expelled his virtuous brother, the lawful ruler, from his domains. The banished Duke, with his adherents, has taken refuge in the Forest of Arden, where they live as free a life as Robin Hood and his merry men, and where they are presently sought out by the Duke's daughter Rosalind and her cousin Celia, the daughter of the usurper, who will not let her banished friend wander forth alone. In the circle of nobility subordinate to the princes, there is also a wicked brother, Oliver, who seeks the life of his virtuous younger brother, Orlando, a hero as modest and amiable as he is brave. He and Rosalind fall in love with each other the moment they meet, and she makes sport with him throughout the play, disguised as a boy. These scenes should probably be acted as though he half recognised her. At last all ends happily. The wicked Duke most conveniently repents; the wicked brother is all of a sudden converted (quite without rhyme or reason) when Orlando, whom he has persecuted, kills a lioness—a lioness in the Forest of Arden! —which is about to spring upon him as he lies asleep. And the caitiff is rewarded (no less unreasonably), either for his villainy or for his conversion, with the hand of the lovely Celia.

This whole story is perfectly unimportant; Shakespeare, that is to say, evidently cared very little about it. We have here no attempt at a reproduction of reality, but one long festival of gaiety and wit, a soulful wit that vibrates into feeling.

First and foremost, the play typifies Shakespeare's longing,

[1] Reprinted in Hazlitt's Shakespeare's Library, ed. 1875, part i. vol. ii.

the longing of this great spirit, to get away from the unnatural city life, away from the false and ungrateful city folk, intent on business and on gain, away from flattery and falsehood and deceit, out into the country, where simple manners still endure, where it is easier to realise the dream of full freedom, and where the scent of the woods is so sweet. There the babble of the brooks has a subtler eloquence than any that is heard in cities; there the trees and even the stones say more to the wanderer's heart than the houses and streets of the capital; there he finds " good in everything."

The roving spirit has reawakened in his breast—the spirit which in bygone days sent him wandering with his gun through Charlcote Park—and out yonder in the lap of Nature, but in a remoter, richer Nature than that which he has known, he dreams of a communion between the best and ablest men, the fairest and most delicate women, in ideal fantastic surroundings, far from the ugly clamours of a public career, and the oppression of everyday cares. A life of hunting and song, and simple repasts in the open air, accompanied with witty talk; and at the same time a life full to the brim with the dreamy happiness of love. And with this life, the creation of his roving spirit, his gaiety and his longing for Nature, he animates a fantastic Forest of Arden.

But with this he is not content. He dreams out the dream, and feels that even such an ideal and untrammelled life could not satisfy that strange and unaccountable spirit lurking in the inmost depths of his nature, which turns everything into food for melancholy and satire. From this rib, then, taken from his own side, he creates the figure of Jaques, unknown to the romance, and sets him wandering through his pastoral comedy, lonely, retiring, self-absorbed, a misanthrope from excess of tenderness, sensitiveness, and imagination.

Jaques is like the first light and brilliant pencil-sketch for Hamlet. Taine, and others after him, have tried to draw a parallel between Jaques and Alceste—of all Molière's creations, no doubt, the one who contains most of his own nature. But there is no real analogy between them. In Jaques everything wears the shimmering hues of wit and fantasy, in Alceste everything is bitter earnest. Indignation is the mainspring of Alceste's misanthropy. He is disgusted at the falsehood around him, and outraged to see that the scoundrel with whom he is at law, although despised by every one, is nevertheless everywhere received with open arms. He declines to remain in bad company, even in the hearts of his friends; therefore he withdraws from them. He loathes two classes of people:

> "Les uns parcequ'ils sont méchants et malfaisants,
> Et les autres pour être aux méchants complaisants."

These are the accents of Timon of Athens, who hated the wicked for their wickedness, and other men for not hating the wicked.

It is, then, in Shakespeare's Timon, of many years later, that we can alone find an instructive parallel to Alceste. Alceste's nature is keenly logical, classically French; it consists of sheer uncompromising sincerity and pride, without sensibility and without melancholy.

The melancholy of Jaques is a poetic dreaminess. He is described to us (ii. 1) before we see him. The banished Duke has just been blessing the adversity which drove him out into the forest, where he is exempt from the dangers of the envious court. He is on the point of setting forth to hunt, when he learns that the melancholy Jaques repines at the cruelty of the chase, and calls him in that respect as great a usurper as the brother who drove him from his dukedom. The courtiers have found him stretched beneath an oak, and dissolved in pity for a poor wounded stag which stood beside the brook, and "heaved forth such groans That their discharge did stretch his leathern coat Almost to bursting." Jaques, they continue, "moralised this spectacle into a thousand similes:"—

> "Then, being there alone,
> Left and abandon'd of his velvet friends;
> ''Tis right,' quoth he; 'thus misery doth part
> The flux of company.' Anon, a careless herd,
> Full of the pasture, jumps along by him,
> And never stays to greet him. 'Ay,' quoth Jaques,
> 'Sweep on, you fat and greasy citizens;
> 'Tis just the fashion: wherefore do you look
> Upon that poor and broken bankrupt there?'"

His bitterness springs from a too tender sensibility, a sensibility like that of Sakya Mouni before him, who made tenderness to animals part of his religion, and like that of Shelley after him, who, in his pantheism, realised the kinship between his own soul and that of the brute creation.

Thus we are prepared for his entrance. He introduces himself into the Duke's circle (ii. 7) with a glorification of the fool's motley. He has encountered Touchstone in the forest, and is enraptured with him. The motley fool lay basking in the sun, and when Jaques said to him, "Good morrow, fool!" he answered, "Call me not fool till heaven have sent me fortune." Then this sapient fool drew a dial from his pocket, and said very wisely—

"'It is ten o'clock:
Thus may we see,' quoth he, 'how the world wags:
'Tis but an hour ago since it was nine,
And after one hour more 'twill be eleven;
And so from hour to hour we ripe and ripe,
And then from hour to hour we rot and rot,
And thereby hangs a tale.'"

"O noble fool!" Jaques exclaims with enthusiasm. "A worthy fool! Motley's the only wear."

In moods of humorous melancholy, it must have seemed to Shakespeare as though he himself were one of these jesters, who had the privilege of uttering truths to great people and on the stage, if only they did not blurt them out directly, but disguised them under a mask of folly. It was in a similar mood that Heinrich Heine, centuries later, addressed to the German people these words: "Ich bin dein Kunz von der Rosen, dein Narr."

Therefore it is that Shakespeare makes Jaques exclaim—

"O, that I were a fool!
I am ambitious for a motley coat."

When the Duke answers, "Thou shalt have one," he declares that it is the one thing he wants, and that the others must "weed their judgments" of the opinion that he is wise:—

"I must have liberty
Withal, as large a charter as the wind,
To blow on whom I please; for so fools have:
And they that are most galled with my folly,
They most must laugh.

.   .   .   .   .

Invest me in my motley: give me leave
To speak my mind, and I will through and through
Cleanse the foul body of the infected world,
If they will patiently receive my medicine."

It is Shakespeare's own mood that we hear in these words. The voice is his. The utterance is far too large for Jaques: he is only a mouthpiece for the poet. Or let us say that his figure dilates in such passages as this, and we see in him a Hamlet *avant la lettre*.

When the Duke, in answer to this outburst, denies Jaques' right to chide and satirise others, since he has himself been "a libertine, As sensual as the brutish sting itself," the poet evidently defends himself in the reply which he places in the mouth of the melancholy philosopher:—

"Why, who cries out on pride,
That can therein tax any private party?
Doth it not flow as hugely as the sea,
Till that the weary very means do ebb?
What woman in the city do I name,
When that I say, the city-woman bears
The cost of princes on unworthy shoulders?
Who can come in, and say that I mean her,
When such a one as she, such is her neighbour?"

This exactly anticipates Holberg's self-defence in the character of Philemon in *The Fortunate Shipwreck*. The poet is evidently rebutting a common prejudice against his art. And as he makes Jaques an advocate for the freedom which poetry must claim, so also he employs him as a champion of the actor's misjudged calling, in placing in his mouth the magnificent speech on the Seven Ages of Man. Alluding, no doubt, to the motto of *Totus Mundus Agit Histrionem*, inscribed under the Hercules as Atlas, which was the sign of the Globe Theatre, this speech opens with the words:—

"All the world's a stage,
And all the men and women merely players;
They have their exits and their entrances;
And one man in his time plays many parts."

Ben Jonson is said to have inquired, in an epigram against the motto of the Globe Theatre, where the spectators were to be found if all the men and women were players? And an epigram attributed to Shakespeare gives the simple answer that all are players and audience at one and the same time. Jaques' survey of the life of man is admirably concise and impressive. The last line—

"Sans teeth, sans eyes, sans taste, sans everything"—

with its half French equivalent for "without," is imitated from the *Henriade* of the French poet Garnier, which was not translated, and which Shakespeare must consequently have read in the original.

This same Jaques, who gives evidence of so wide an outlook over human life, is in daily intercourse, as we have said, nervously misanthropic and formidably witty. He is sick of polite society, pines for solitude, takes leave of a pleasant companion with the words: "I thank you for your company; but, good faith, I had as lief have been myself alone." Yet we must not take his melancholy and his misanthropy too seriously. His melancholy is a comedy-melancholy, his misanthropy is only the humourist's craving to give free vent to his satirical inspirations.

And there is, as aforesaid, only a certain part of Shakespeare's inmost nature in this Jaques, a Shakespeare of the future, a Hamlet in germ, but not that Shakespeare who now bathes in the sunlight and lives in uninterrupted prosperity, in growing favour with the many, and borne aloft by the admiration and goodwill of the few. We must seek for this Shakespeare in the interspersed songs, in the drollery of the fool, in the lovers' rhapsodies, in the enchanting babble of the ladies. He is, like Providence, everywhere and nowhere.

When Celia says (i. 2), "Let us sit and mock the good housewife, Fortune, from her wheel, that her gifts may henceforth be bestowed equally," she strikes, as though with a tuning-fork, the keynote of the comedy. The sluice is opened for that torrent of jocund wit, shimmering with all the rainbows of fancy, which is now to rush seething and swirling along.

The Fool is essential to the scheme: for the Fool's stupidity is the grindstone of wit, and the Fool's wit is the touchstone of character. Hence his name.

The ways of the real world, however, are not forgotten. The good make enemies by their very goodness, and the words of the old servant Adam (Shakespeare's own part) to his young master Orlando (ii. 3), sound sadly enough:—

> " Your praise is come too swiftly home before you.
> Know you not, master, to some kind of men
> Their graces serve them but as enemies?
> No more do yours: your virtues, gentle master,
> Are sanctified, and holy traitors to you.
> O, what a world is this, when what is comely
> Envenoms him that bears it!"

But soon the poet's eye is opened to a more consolatory life-philosophy, combined with an unequivocal contempt for school-philosophy. There seems to be a scoffing allusion to a book of the time, which was full of the platitudes of celebrated philosophers, in Touchstone's speech to William (v. 1), "The heathen philosopher, when he had desire to eat a grape, would open his lips when he put it into his mouth, meaning thereby that grapes were made to eat and lips to open;" but no doubt there also lurks in this speech a certain lack of respect for even the much-belauded wisdom of tradition. The relativity of all things, at that time a new idea, is expounded with lofty humour by the Fool in his answer to the question what he thinks of this pastoral life (iii. 2):—

"Truly, shepherd, in respect of itself it is a good life, but in respect that it is a shepherd's life, it is naught. In respect that it is solitary, I like it very well; but in respect that it is private, it is a very vile life. Now, in respect it is in the fields, it pleaseth me well; but in respect it is not in the court, it is tedious. As it is a spare life, look you, it fits my humour well; but as there is no more plenty in it, it goes much against my stomach. Hast any philosophy in thee, shepherd?"

The shepherd's answer makes direct sport of philosophy, in the style of Molière's gibe, when he accounts for the narcotic effect of opium by explaining that the drug possesses a certain *facultas dormitativa:*—

"*Corin.* No more, but that I know, the more one sickens, the worse at ease he is; and that he that wants money, means, and content, is without three good friends; that the property of rain is to wet, and fire to burn; that good pasture makes fat sheep, and that a great cause of the night is lack of the sun. . . .

"*Touchstone.* Such a one is a natural philosopher."

This sort of philosophy leads up, as it were, to Rosalind's sweet gaiety and heavenly kindness.

The two cousins, Rosalind and Celia, seem at first glance like variations of the two cousins, Beatrice and Hero, in the play Shakespeare has just finished. Rosalind and Beatrice in particular are akin in their victorious wit. Yet the difference between them is very great; Shakespeare never repeats himself. The wit of Beatrice is aggressive and challenging; we see, as it were, the gleam of a rapier in it. Rosalind's wit is gaiety without a sting; the gleam in it is of "that sweet radiance" which Oehlenschläger attributed to Freia; her sportive nature masks the depth of her love. Beatrice can be brought to love because she is a woman, and stands in no respect apart from her sex; but she is not of an amatory nature. Rosalind is seized with a passion for Orlando the instant she sets eyes on him. From the moment of Beatrice's first appearance she is defiant and combative, in the highest of spirits. We are introduced to Rosalind as a poor bird with a drooping wing; her father is banished, she is bereft of her birthright, and is living on sufferance as companion to the usurper's daughter, being, indeed, half a prisoner in the palace, where till lately she reigned as princess. It is not until she has donned the doublet and hose, appears in the likeness of a page, and wanders at her own sweet will in the open air and the greenwood, that she recovers her radiant humour, and roguish merriment flows from her lips like the trilling of a bird.

Nor is the man she loves, like Benedick, an overweening gallant with a sharp tongue and an unabashed bearing. This youth, though brave as a hero and strong as an athlete, is a child in inexperience, and so bashful in the presence of the woman who instantly captivates him, that it is she who is the first to betray her sympathy for him, and has even to take the chain from her own neck and hang it around his before he can so much as muster up courage to hope for her love. So, too, we find him passing his time in hanging poems to her upon the trees, and carving the name of Rosalind in their bark. She amuses herself, in her page's attire, by making herself his confidant, and pretending, as it were in jest, to be his Rosalind. She cannot bring herself to confess her passion, although she can think and talk (to Celia) of no one but him, and although his delay of a few minutes in keeping tryst with her sets her beside herself with impatience. She is as sensitive as she is intelligent, in this differing from Portia, to whom, in other respects, she bears some resemblance, though she lacks her persuasive eloquence, and is, on the whole, more tender, more virginal. She faints when Oliver, to excuse Orlando's delay, brings her a handkerchief stained with his blood; yet has sufficient self-mastery to say with a smile the moment she recovers, "I pray you tell your brother how well I counterfeited." She is quite at her ease in her male attire, like Viola and Imogen after her. The fact that female parts were played by youths had, of course, something to do with the frequency of these disguises.

Here is a specimen of her wit (iii. 2). Orlando has evaded the page's question what o'clock it is, alleging that there are no clocks in the forest.

"*Rosalind.* Then, there is no true lover in the forest; else sighing every minute, and groaning every hour, would detect the lazy foot of Time as well as a clock.

"*Orlando.* And why not the swift foot of Time? had not that been as proper?

"*Ros.* By no means, sir. Time travels in divers paces with divers persons. I'll tell you, who Time ambles withal, who Time trots withal, who Time gallops withal, and who he stands still withal.

"*Orl.* I pr'ythee, who doth he trot withal?

"*Ros.* Marry, he trots hard with a young maid, between the contract of her marriage, and the day it is solemnised: if the interim be but a se'nnight, Time's pace is so hard that it seems the length of seven years.

"*Orl.* Who ambles Time withal?

"*Ros.* With a priest that lacks Latin, and a rich man that hath not the gout; for the one sleeps easily, because he cannot study; and the other lives merrily, because he feels no pain. . . .

"*Orl.* Who doth he gallop withal?

"*Ros.* With a thief to the gallows; for though he go as softly as foot can fall, he thinks himself too soon there.

"*Orl.* Who stays it still withal?

"*Ros.* With lawyers in the vacation; for they sleep between term and term, and then they perceive not how Time moves."

She is unrivalled in vivacity and inventiveness. In every answer she discovers gunpowder anew, and she knows how to use it to boot. She explains that she had an old uncle who warned her against love and women, and, from the vantage-ground of her doublet and hose, she declares—

"I thank God, I am not a woman, to be touched with so many giddy offences, as he hath generally taxed their whole sex withal.

"*Orl.* Can you remember any of the principal evils that he laid to the charge of women?

"*Ros.* There were none principal: they were all like one another, as half-pence are; every one fault seeming monstrous, till its fellow fault came to match it.

"*Orl.* I pr'ythee, recount some of them.

"*Ros.* No; I will not cast away my physic but on those that are sick. There is a man haunts the forest, that abuses our young plants with carving Rosalind on their barks; hangs odes upon hawthorns, and elegies on brambles; all, forsooth, deifying the name of Rosalind: if I could meet that fancy-monger, I would give him some good counsel, for he seems to have the quotidian of love upon him."

Orlando admits that he is the culprit, and they are to meet daily that she may exorcise his passion. She bids him woo her in jest, as though she were indeed Rosalind, and answers (iv. 1):—

"*Ros.* Well, in her person, I say—I will not have you.

"*Orl.* Then, in mine own person, I die.

"*Ros.* No, 'faith, die by attorney. The poor world is almost six thousand years old, and in all this time there was not any man died in his own person, *videlicet*, in a love-cause. Troilus had his brains dashed out with a Grecian club; yet he did what he could to die before, and he is one of the patterns of love. Leander, he would have lived many a fair year, though Hero had turned nun, if it had not been for a hot midsummer night; for, good youth, he went but forth to wash him in the Hellespont, and, being taken with the cramp, was drowned, and the foolish chroniclers of that age found it was—Hero of Sestos. But these are all lies: men have died from time to time, and worms have eaten them, but not for love."

What Rosalind says of women in general applies to herself in particular: you will never find her without an answer until you find her without a tongue. And there is always a bright and merry fantasy in her answers. She is literally radiant with youth, imagination, and the joy of loving so passionately and being so passionately beloved. And it is marvellous how thoroughly feminine is her wit. Too many of the witty women in books written by men have a man's intelligence. Rosalind's wit is tempered by feeling.

She has no monopoly of wit in this Arcadia of Arden. Every one in the play is witty, even the so-called simpletons. It is a festival of wit. At some points Shakespeare seems to have followed no stricter principle than the simple one of making each interlocutor outbid the other in wit (see, for example, the conversation between Touchstone and the country wench whom he befools). The result is that the piece is bathed in a sunshiny humour. And amid all the gay and airy wit-skirmishes, amid the cooing love-duets of all the happy youths and maidens, the poet intersperses the melancholy solos of his Jaques :—

"I have neither the scholar's melancholy, which is emulation; nor the musician's, which is fantastical; nor the courtier's, which is proud; nor the soldier's, which is ambitious; nor the lawyer's, which is politic; nor the lady's, which is nice; nor the lover's, which is all these; but it is a melancholy of mine own, compounded of many simples, extracted from many objects."

This is the melancholy which haunts the thinker and the great creative artist; but in Shakespeare it as yet modulated with ease into the most engaging and delightful merriment.

XXIX

*CONSUMMATE SPIRITUAL HARMONY—TWELFTH NIGHT—
JIBES AT PURITANISM—THE LANGUISHING CHARAC-
TERS—VIOLA'S INSINUATING GRACE—FAREWELL TO
MIRTH*

IF the reader would picture to himself Shakespeare's mood during this short space of time at the end of the old century and beginning of the new, let him recall some morning when he has awakened with the sensation of complete physical well-being, not only feeling no definite or indefinite pain or uneasiness, but with a positive consciousness of happy activity in all his organs: when he drew his breath lightly, his head was clear and free, his heart beat peacefully: when the mere act of living was a delight: when the soul dwelt on happy moments in the past and dreamed of joys to come. Recall such a moment, and then conceive it intensified an hundredfold—conceive your memory, imagination, observation, acuteness, and power of expression a hundred times multiplied—and you may divine Shakespeare's prevailing mood in those days, when the brighter and happier sides of his nature were turned to the sun.

There are days when the sun seems to have put on a new and festal splendour, when the air is like a caress to the cheek, and when the glamour of the moonlight seems doubly sweet; days when men appear manlier and wittier, women fairer and more delicate than usual, and when those who are disagreeable and even odious to us appear, not formidable, but ludicrous—so that we feel ourselves exalted above the level of our daily life, emancipated and happy. Such days Shakespeare was now passing through.

It is at this period, too, that he makes sport of his adversaries the Puritans without bitterness, with exquisite humour. Even in *As You Like It* (iii. 2), we find a little allusion to them, where Rosalind says, " O most gentle Jupiter !—what tedious homily of love have you wearied your parishioners withal, and never cried, 'Have patience, good people!'" In his next play, the typical, solemn, and self-righteous Puritan is held up to ridicule in the Don-Quixote-like personage of the moralising and pompous Malvolio, who is launched upon a billowy sea of burlesque situations. Of course the poet goes to work with the greatest circumspection. Sir Toby has made some inquiry about Malvolio, to which Maria answers (ii. 3):—

"*Maria.* Marry, sir, sometimes he is a kind of Puritan.

"*Sir Andrew.* O! if I thought that, I'd beat him like a dog.

"*Sir Toby.* What, for being a Puritan? thy exquisite reason, dear knight?

"*Sir And.* I have no exquisite reason for't, but I have reason good enough.

"*Mar.* The devil a Puritan that he is, or anything constantly but a time-pleaser; an affectioned ass, that cons state without book, and utters it by great swarths."

Not otherwise does Molière expressly insist that Tartuffe is not a clergyman, and Holberg that Jacob von Tyboe is not an officer.

A forged letter, purporting to be written by his noble mistress, is made to fall into Malvolio's hands, in which she begs for his love, and instructs him, as a sign of his affection towards her, always to smile, and to wear cross-gartered yellow stockings. He "smiles his face into more lines than are in the new map [of 1598] with the augmentation of the Indies;" he wears his preposterous garters in the most preposterous fashion. The conspirators pretend to think him mad, and treat him accordingly. The Clown comes to visit him disguised in the cassock of Sir Topas the curate. "Well," says the mock priest (not without intention on the poet's part), when Maria gives him the gown, "I'll put it on, and I will dissemble myself in't; and I would I were the first that ever dissembled in such a gown."

It is to Malvolio, too, that the merry and mellow Sir Toby, amid the applause of the Clown, addresses the taunt :—

"*Sir Toby.* Dost thou think, because thou art virtuous, there shall be no more cakes and ale?

"*Clown.* Yes, by Saint Anne; and ginger shall be hot i' the mouth too."

In these words, which were one day to serve as a motto to Byron's *Don Juan*, there lies a gay and daring declaration of rights.

Twelfth Night, or What you Will, must have been written in 1601, for in the above-mentioned diary kept by John Manningham, of the Middle Temple, we find this entry, under the date February 2, 1602: "At our feast wee had a play called Twelve Night, or what you will, much like the commedy of errores, or Menechmi in Plautus, but most like and neere to that in Italian called *Inganni*. A good practise in it to make the steward beleeve his lady widdowe was in love with him," &c. That the play cannot have been written much earlier is proved by the fact that the song, "Farewell, dear heart, since I must needs be gone," which is sung by Sir Toby and the Clown (ii. 3), first appeared in a song-book (*The Booke of Ayres*) published by Robert Jones, London, 1601. Shakespeare has altered its wording very slightly. In all probability *Twelfth Night* was one of the four plays which were performed before the court at Whitehall by the Lord Chamberlain's company at Christmastide, 1601-2, and no doubt it was acted for the first time on the evening from which it takes its name.

Among several Italian plays which bore the name of *Gl' Inganni* there is one by Curzio Gonzaga, published in Venice in 1592, in which a sister dresses herself as her brother and takes the name of Cesare—in Shakespeare, Cesario—and another, published in Venice in 1537, the action of which bears a general resemblance to that of *Twelfth Night*. In this play, too, passing mention is made of one "Malevolti," who may have suggested to Shakespeare the name Malvolio.

The matter of the play is found in a novel of Bandello's, translated in Belleforest's *Histoires Tragiques*; and also in Barnabe Rich's translation of Cinthio's *Hecatomithi*, published in 1581, which Shakespeare appears to have used. The whole comic part of the action, and the characters of Malvolio, Sir Toby, Sir Andrew Aguecheek, and the Clown, are of Shakespeare's own invention.

There occurs in Ben Jonson's *Every Man out of his Humour* a speech which seems very like an allusion to *Twelfth Night;* but as Jonson's play is of earlier date, the speech, if the allusion be not fanciful, must have been inserted later.[1]

---

[1] There is some (ironic) discussion of a possible criticism that might be brought against a playwright: "That the argument of his comedy might have been of some other nature, as of a duke to be in love with a countess, and that countess to be in love with the duke's son, and the son to love the lady's waiting-maid; some such cross wooing, with a clown to their servingman. . . ."

As was to be expected, *Twelfth Night* became exceedingly popular. The learned Leonard Digges, the translator of Claudian, enumerating in his verses, "Upon Master William Shakespeare" (1640), the poet's most popular characters, mentions only three from the comedies, and these from *Much Ado* and *Twelfth Night*. He says:—

"Let but *Beatrice*
And *Benedicke* be seene, loe in a trice
The Cockpit, Galleries, Boxes, all are full
To hear *Malvoglio*, that crosse garter'd Gull."

Twelfth Night is perhaps the most graceful and harmonious comedy Shakespeare ever wrote. It is certainly that in which all the notes the poet strikes, the note of seriousness and of raillery, of passion, of tenderness, and of laughter, blend in the richest and fullest concord. It is like a symphony in which no strain can be dispensed with, or like a picture veiled in a golden haze, into which all the colours resolve themselves. The play does not overflow with wit and gaiety like its predecessor; we feel that Shakespeare's joy of life has culminated and is about to pass over into melancholy; but there is far more unity in it than in *As You Like It*, and it is a great deal more dramatic.

A. W. Schlegel long ago made the penetrating observation that, in the opening speech of the comedy, Shakespeare reminds us how the same word, "fancy," was applied in his day both to love and to fancy in the modern sense of the term; whence the critic argued, not without ingenuity, that love, regarded as an affair of the imagination rather than of the heart, is the fundamental theme running through all the variations of the play. Others have since sought to prove that capricious fantasy is the fundamental trait in the physiognomy of all the characters. Tieck has compared the play to a great iridescent butterfly, fluttering through pure blue air, and soaring in its golden glory from the many-coloured flowers into the sunshine.

Twelfth Night, in Shakespeare's time, brought the Christmas festivities of the upper classes to an end; among the common people they usually lasted until Candlemas. On Twelfth Night all sorts of sports took place. The one who chanced to find a bean baked into a cake was hailed as the Bean King, chose himself a Bean Queen, introduced a reign of unbridled frivolity, and issued whimsical commands, which had to be punctually obeyed. Ulrici has sought to discover in this an indication that the play represents a sort of lottery, in which Sebastian, the Duke, and Maria chance to win the great prize. The bibulous Sir Toby, however, can scarcely be regarded as a particularly desirable prize for Maria; and the second title of the play, *What you Will*, indicates that Shakespeare did not lay any stress upon the *Twelfth Night*.

This comedy is connected by certain filaments with its predecessor, *As You Like It*. The passion which Viola, in her male attire, awakens in Olivia, reminds us of that with which Rosalind inspires Phebe. But the motive is quite differently handled. While Rosalind gaily and unfeelingly repudiates Phebe's burning love, Viola is full of tender compassion for the lady whom her disguise has led astray. In the admirably worked-up confusion between Viola and her twin brother Sebastian, an effect from the *Comedy of Errors* is repeated; but the different circumstances and method of treatment make this motive also practically new.

With a careful and even affectionate hand, Shakespeare has elaborated each one of the many characters in the play.

The amiable and gentle Duke languishes, sentimental and fancy-sick, in hopeless enamourment. He is devoted to the fair Countess Olivia, who will have nothing to say to him, and whom he none the less besieges with his suit. An ardent lover of music, he turns to it for consolation; and among the songs sung to him by the Clown and others, there occurs the delicate little poem, of wonderful rhythmic beauty, "Come away, come away, death." It exactly expresses the soft and melting mood in which his days pass, lapped in a nerveless melancholy. To the melody abiding in it we may apply the lovely words spoken by Viola of the melody which preludes it:—

"It gives a very echo to the seat
Where love is throned."

In his fruitless passion, the Duke has become nervous and excitable, inclined to violent self-contradictions. In one and the same scene (ii. 4) he first says that man's love is

"More giddy and unfirm,
More longing, wavering, sooner lost and worn"

than woman's; and then, a little further on, he says of his own love—

"There is no woman's sides
Can bide the beating of so strong a passion
As love doth give my heart; no woman's heart
So big to hold so much: they lack retention."

The Countess Olivia forms a pendant to the Duke; she, like him, is full of yearning melancholy. With an ostentatious exaggeration of sisterly love, she has vowed to pass seven whole years veiled like a nun, consecrating her whole life to sorrow for her dead brother. Yet we find in her speeches no trace of this devouring sorrow; she jests with her household, and rules it ably and well, until, at the first sight of the disguised Viola, she flames out into passion, and, careless of the traditional reserve of her sex, takes the most daring steps to win the supposed youth. She is conceived as an unbalanced character, who passes at a bound from exaggerated hatred for all worldly things to total forgetfulness of her never-to-be-forgotten sorrow. Yet she is not comic like Phebe; for Shakespeare has indicated that it is the Sebastian type, foreshadowed in the disguised Viola, which is irresistible to her; and Sebastian, we see, at once requites the love which his sister had to reject. Her utterance of her passion, moreover, is always poetically beautiful.

Yet while she is sighing in vain for Viola, she necessarily appears as though seized with a mild erotic madness, similar to that of the Duke: and the folly of each is parodied in a witty and delightful fashion by Malvolio's entirely ludicrous love for his mistress, and vain confidence that she returns it. Olivia feels and says this herself, where she exclaims (iii. 4)—

"Go call him hither.—I am as mad as he
If sad and merry madness equal be."

Malvolio's figure is drawn in very few strokes, but with incomparable certainty of touch. He is unforgetable in his turkey-like pomposity, and the heartless practical joke which is played off upon him is developed with the richest comic effect. The inimitable love-letter, which Maria indites to him in a handwriting like that of the Countess, brings to light all the lurking vanity in his nature, and makes his self-esteem, which was patent enough before, assume the most extravagant forms. The scene in which he approaches Olivia, and triumphantly quotes the expressions in the letter, "yellow stockings," and "cross-gartered," while every word confirms her in the belief that he is mad, is one of the most effective on the comic stage. Still more irresistible is the scene (iv. 2) in which Malvolio is imprisoned as a madman in a dark room, while the Clown outside now assumes the voice of the Curate, and seeks to exorcise the devil in him, and again, in his own voice, converses with the supposed Curate, sings songs, and promises Malvolio to carry messages for him. We have here a comic *jeu de théâtre* of the first order.

In harmony with the general tone of the play, the Clown is less witty and more musical than Touchstone in *As You Like It*. He is keenly alive to the dignity of his calling: "Foolery, sir, does walk about the orb like the sun: it shines everywhere." He has many delightful sayings, as for example, "Many a good hanging prevents a bad marriage," or the following demonstration (v. 1) that one is the better for one's foes, and the worse for one's friends:—

"Marry, sir, my friends praise me, and make an ass of me; now, my foes tell me plainly I am an ass: so that by my foes, sir, I profit in the knowledge of myself, and by my friends I am abused: so that, conclusions to be as kisses, if your four negatives make your two affirmatives, why then, the worse for my friends, and the better for my foes."

Shakespeare even departs from his usual practice, and, as though to guard against any misunderstanding on the part of his public, makes Viola expound quite dogmatically that it "craves a kind of wit" to play the fool (iii. 1):—

"He must observe their mood on whom he jests,
The quality of persons, and the time,
And, like the haggard, check at every feather
That comes before his eye. This is a practice
As full of labour as a wise man's art."

The Clown forms a sort of connecting-link between the serious characters and the exclusively comic figures of the play—the pair of knights, Sir Toby Belch and Sir Andrew Aguecheek, who are entirely of Shakespeare's own invention. They are sharply contrasted. Sir Toby, sanguine, red-nosed, burly, a practical joker, always ready for "a hair of the dog that bit him," a figure after the style of Bellman;[1] Sir Andrew, pale as though with the ague, with thin, smooth, straw-coloured hair, a wretched little nincompoop, who values himself on his dancing and fencing, quarrelsome and chicken-hearted, boastful and timid in the same breath, and grotesque in his every movement. He is a mere echo and shadow of the heroes of his admiration, born to be the sport of his associates, their puppet, and their butt; and while he is so brainless as to think it possible he may win the love of the beautiful Olivia, he has at the same time an inward suspicion of his own stupidity which now and then comes in refreshingly: "Methinks sometimes I have no more wit than a Christian or an ordinary man has; but I am a great eater of beef, and, I believe, that does harm to my wit" (i. 3). He does not understand the simplest phrase he hears, and is such a mere reflex and parrot that "I too" is, as it were, the watchword of his existence. Shakespeare has immortalised him once for all in his reply when Sir Toby boasts that Maria adores him (ii. 3), "I was adored once too." Sir Toby sums him up in the phrase:

"For Andrew, if he were opened, and you find so much blood in his liver as will clog the foot of a flea, I'll eat the rest of the anatomy."

The central character in *Twelfth Night* is Viola, of whom her brother does not say a word too much when, thinking that she has been drowned, he exclaims, "She bore a mind that envy could not but call fair."

Shipwrecked on the coast of Illyria, her first wish is to enter the service of the young Countess; but learning that Olivia is inaccessible, she determines to dress as a page (a eunuch) and approach the young unmarried Duke, of whom she has heard her father speak with warmth. He at once makes the deepest impression upon her heart, but being ignorant of her sex, does not dream of what is passing within her; so that she is perpetually placed in the painful position of being employed as a messenger from the man she loves to another woman. She gives utterance to her love in carefully disguised and touching words (ii. 4):—

> "My father had a daughter lov'd a man,
> As it might be, perhaps, were I a woman,
> I should your lordship.

---

[1] See *ante*, p. 219.

Duke. And what's her history?
Vio. A blank, my lord. She never told her love,—
But let concealment, like a worm i' the bud,
Feed on her damask cheek: she pin'd in thought:
And, with a green and yellow melancholy,
She sat like Patience on a monument,
Smiling at grief."

But the passion which possesses her makes her a more eloquent messenger of love than she designs to be. To Olivia's question as to what she would do if she loved her as her master does, she answers (i. 5):—

"Make me a willow cabin at your gate,
And call upon my soul within the house;
Write loyal cantons of contemned love,
And sing them loud even in the dead of night;
Holla your name to the reverberate hills,
And make the babbling gossip of the air
Cry out, Olivia! O! you should not rest
Between the elements of air and earth,
But you should pity me."

In short, if she were a man, she would display all the energy which the Duke lacks. No wonder that, against her own will, she awakens Olivia's love. She herself, as a woman, is condemned to passivity; her love is wordless, deep, and patient. In spite of her sound understanding, she is a creature of emotion. It is a very characteristic touch when, in the scene (iii. 5) where Antonio, taking her for Sebastian, recalls the services he has rendered, and begs for assistance in his need, she exclaims that there is nothing, not even "lying vainness, babbling drunkenness, or any taint of vice," that she hates so much as ingratitude. However bright her intelligence, her soul from first to last outshines it. Her incognito, which does not bring her joy as it does to Rosalind, but only trouble and sorrow, conceals the most delicate womanliness. She never, like Rosalind or Beatrice, utters an audacious or wanton word. Her heart-winning charm more than makes up for the high spirits and sparkling humour of the earlier heroines. She is healthful and beautiful, like these her somewhat elder sisters; and she has also their humorous eloquence, as she proves in her first scene with Olivia. Yet there rests upon her lovely figure a tinge of melancholy. She is an impersonation of that "farewell to mirth" which an able English critic discerns in this last comedy of Shakespeare's brightest years.[1]

[1] "It is in some sort a farewell to mirth, and the mirth is of the finest quality, an incomparable ending. Shakespeare has done greater things, but he has never done anything more delightful."—*Arthur Symons*.

XXX

THE REVOLUTION IN SHAKESPEARE'S SOUL—THE GROWING MELANCHOLY OF THE FOLLOWING PERIOD—PESSIMISM, MISANTHROPY

FOR the time is now approaching when mirth, and even the joy of life, are extinguished in his soul. Heavy clouds have massed themselves on his mental horizon—their nature we can only divine—and gnawing sorrows and disappointments have beset him. We see his melancholy growing and extending; we observe its changing expressions, without knowing its causes. This only we know, that the stage which he contemplates with his mind's eye, like the material stage on which he works, is now hung with black. A veil of melancholy descends over both.

He no longer writes comedies, but sends a train of gloomy tragedies across the boards which so lately echoed to the laughter of Beatrice and Rosalind.

From this point, for a certain period, all his impressions of life and humanity become ever more and more painful. We can see in his Sonnets how even in earlier and happier years a restless passionateness had been constantly at war with the serenity of his soul, and we can note how, at this time also, he was subject to accesses of stormy and vehement unrest. As time goes on, we can discern in the series of his dramas how not only what he saw in public and political life, but also his private experience, began to inspire him, partly with a burning compassion for humanity, partly with a horror of mankind as a breed of noxious wild animals, partly, too, with loathing for the stupidity, falsity, and baseness of his fellow-creatures. These feelings gradually crystallise into a large and lofty contempt for humanity, until, after a space of eight years, another revolution occurs in his prevailing mood. The extinguished sun glows forth afresh, the black heaven has become blue again, and the kindly interest in everything human has returned. He attains peace at last in a sublime and melancholy clearness of vision. Bright moods, sunny dreams from the days of his youth, return upon him, bringing with them, if not laughter, at least smiles. High-spirited gaiety has for ever vanished; but his imagination, feeling itself less constrained than of old by the laws of reality, moves lightly and at ease, though a deep earnestness now underlies it, and much experience of life.

But this inward emancipation from the burthen of earthly life does not occur, as we have said, until about eight years after the point which we have now reached.

For a little time longer the strong and genial joy of life is still dominant in his mind. Then it begins to darken, and, after a short tropical twilight, there is night in his soul and in all his works.

In the tragedy of *Julius Cæsar* there still reigns only a manly seriousness. The theme seems to have attracted him on account of the analogy between the conspiracy against Cæsar and the conspiracy against Elizabeth. Despite the foolish precipitancy of their action, the leaders of this conspiracy, men like Essex and his comrade Southampton, had Shakespeare's full personal sympathy; and he transferred some of that sympathy to Brutus and Cassius. He created Brutus under the deeply-imprinted conviction that unpractical magnanimity, like that of his noble friends, is unfitted to play an effective part in the drama of history, and that errors of policy revenge themselves at least as sternly as moral delinquencies.

In *Hamlet* Shakespeare's growing melancholy and bitterness take the upper hand. For the hero, as for the poet, youth's bright outlook upon life has been overclouded. Hamlet's belief and trust in mankind have gone to wreck. Under the disguise of apparent madness, the melancholy life-lore which Shakespeare, at his fortieth year, had stored up within him, here finds expression in words of spiritual profundity such as had not yet been thought or uttered in Northern Europe.

We catch a glimpse at this point of one of the subsidiary causes of Shakespeare's melancholy. As actor and playwright he stands in a more and more strained relation to the continually growing Free Church movement of the age, to Puritanism, which he comes to regard as nothing but narrow-mindedness and hypocrisy. It was the deadly enemy of his calling; it secured, even in his lifetime, the prohibition of theatrical performances in the provinces, a prohibition which after his death was extended to the capital. From *Twelfth Night* onwards, an unremitting war against Puritanism, conceived as hypocrisy, is carried on through *Hamlet*, through the revised version of *All's Well that Ends Well*, and through *Measure for Measure*, in which his wrath rises to a tempestuous pitch, and creates a figure to which Molière's Tartuffe can alone supply a parallel.

What struck him so forcibly in these years was the pitifulness of earthly life, exposed as it is to disasters, not allotted by destiny, but brought about by a conjunction of stupidity with malevolence.

It is especially the power of malevolence that now looms large before his eyes. We see this in Hamlet's astonishment that it is possible for a man "to smile and smile and be a villain." Still more strongly is it apparent in *Measure for Measure* (v. 1):—

> " Make not impossible
> That which but seems unlike. 'Tis not impossible,
> But one, the wicked'st caitiff on the ground,
> May seem as shy, as grave, as just, as absolute,
> As Angelo; even so may Angelo,
> In all his dressings, characts, titles, forms,
> Be an arch-villain."

It is this line of thought that leads to the conception of Iago, Goneril, and Regan, and to the wild outbursts of Timon of Athens.

Macbeth is Shakespeare's first attempt, after *Hamlet*, to explain the tragedy of life as a product of brutality and wickedness in conjunction—that is, of brutality multiplied and raised to the highest power by wickedness. Lady Macbeth poisons her husband's mind. Wickedness instils drops of venom into brutality, which, in its inward essence, may be either weakness, or brave savagery, or stupidity of manifold kinds. Whereupon brutality falls a-raving, and becomes terrible to itself and others.

The same formula expresses the relation between Othello and Iago.

Othello was a monograph. *Lear* is a world-picture. Shakespeare turns from *Othello* to *Lear* in virtue of the artist's need to supplement himself, to follow up every creation with its counterpart or foil.

Lear is the greatest problem Shakespeare had yet proposed to himself, all the agonies and horrors of the world compressed into five short acts. The impression of *Lear* may be summed up in the words: a world-catastrophe. Shakespeare is no longer minded to depict anything else. What is echoing in his ears, what is filling his mind, is the crash of a ruining world.

This becomes even clearer in his next play, *Antony and Cleopatra*. This subject enabled him to set new words to the music within him. In the history of Mark Antony he saw the deep downfall of the old world-republic—the might of Rome, austere and rigorous, collapsing at the touch of Eastern luxury.

By the time Shakespeare had written *Antony and Cleopatra*, his melancholy had deepened into pessimism. Contempt becomes his abiding mood, an all-embracing scorn for mankind, which impregnates every drop of blood in his veins, but a potent and creative scorn, which hurls forth thunderbolt after thunderbolt. *Troilus and Cressida* strikes at the relation of the sexes, *Coriolanus* at political life; until all that, in these years, Shakespeare has endured and experienced, thought and suffered, is concentrated into the one great despairing figure of Timon of Athens, "misanthropos," whose savage rhetoric is like a dark secretion of clotted blood and gall, drawn off to assuage pain.

BOOK SECOND

I

INTRODUCTION—THE ENGLAND OF ELIZABETH IN SHAKESPEARE'S YOUTH

EVERYTHING had flourished in the England of Elizabeth while Shakespeare was young. The sense of belonging to a people which, with great memories and achievements behind it, was now making a decisive and irresistible new departure—the consciousness of living in an age when the glorious culture of antiquity was being resuscitated, and when great personalities were vindicating for England a lofty and assured position, alike in the practical and in the intellectual departments of life—these feelings mingled in his breast with the vernal glow of youth itself. He saw the star of his fatherland ascending, with his own star in its train.

It seemed to him as though men and women had in that day richer abilities, a more daring spirit, and fuller powers of enjoyment than they had possessed in former times. They had more fire in their blood, more insatiable longings, a keener appetite for adventure, than the men and women of the past. They knew how to rule with courage and wisdom, like the Queen and Lord Burghley; how to live nobly and fight gloriously, to love with passion and sing with enthusiasm, like the beautiful hero of the younger generation, Sir Philip Sidney, who found an early Achilles-death. They were bent on enjoying existence with all their senses, comprehending it with all their powers, revelling in wealth and splendour, in beauty and wit; or they set forth to voyage round the world, to see its marvels, conquer its treasures, give their names to new countries, and display the flag of England on unknown seas.

Statesmanship and generalship were represented among them by the men who, in these years, had humbled Spain, rescued Holland, held Scotland in awe. They were sound and vigorous natures. Although they all had the literary proclivities of the Renaissance, they were before everything practical men, keen observers of the signs of the times, firm and wary in adversity, in prosperity prudent and temperate.

Shakespeare had seen Spenser's faithful friend, Sir Walter Raleigh, next to himself and Francis Bacon the most brilliant and interesting Englishman of his day, after covering himself with renown as a soldier, a viking, and a discoverer, win the favour of Elizabeth as a courtier, and the admiration of the people as a hero and poet. Shakespeare no doubt laid to heart these lines in his elegy on Sidney:—

"England doth hold thy limbs, that bred the same;
Flanders thy valour, where it last was tried;
The camp thy sorrow, where thy body died:
Thy friends thy want; the world thy virtues' fame."

For Raleigh, too, was a poet, as well as an orator and historian. "We picture him to ourselves," says Macaulay, "sometimes reviewing the Queen's guard, sometimes giving chase to a Spanish galleon, then answering the chiefs of the country party in the House of Commons, then again murmuring one of his sweet love-songs too near the ears of her Highness's maids of honour, and soon after poring over the Talmud, or collating Polybius with Livy."[1]

And Shakespeare had seen the young Robert Devereux, Earl of Essex, who in 1577, when only ten years old, had made a sensation at court by wearing his hat in the Queen's presence and denying her request for a kiss; at the age of eighteen win renown for himself as a cavalry general under Leicester in the Netherlands, and at the age of twenty depose Raleigh from the highest place in Elizabeth's favour. He played "cards or one game or another with her . . . till birds' sing in the morning." She shut herself up with him in the daytime, while the Venetian and French ambassadors, who had already learnt to wait at locked doors in the time of his step-father, Leicester, jested with each other in the anteroom as to whether mounting guard in this

[1] Macaulay, *Essays*—"Burleigh and his Times."

fashion ought to be called *tener la mula* or *tenir la chandelle*. And Essex demanded that Raleigh should be sacrificed to his youthful devotion. As captain of the guard, Raleigh had to stand at the door with a drawn sword, in his brown and orange uniform, while the handsome youth whispered to the spinster Queen of fifty-four things which set her heart beating. He made all the mischief he could between her and Raleigh. She assured him that he had no reason to "disdain" a man like that. But Essex asked her—so he himself writes—"Whether he could have comfort to give himself over to the service of a mistress that was in awe of such a man;" "and," he continues, "I think he, standing at the door, might very well hear the worst I spoke of him."

This impetuosity characterised Essex throughout his career; but he soon developed great qualities, of which his first appearances gave no promise; and when Shakespeare made his acquaintance, probably in the year 1590, his personality must have been extremely winning. Himself a poet, he no doubt knew how to value *A Midsummer Night's Dream*, and its author. In all probability, Shakespeare even at this time found a protector in the young nobleman, and afterwards made acquaintance through him with his kinsman Southampton, six years younger than himself. Essex had already distinguished himself as a soldier. In May 1589 he had been the first Englishman to wade ashore upon the coast of Portugal, and in the lines before Lisbon he had challenged any of the Spanish garrison to single combat in honour of his queen and mistress. In July 1591 he joined the standard of Henry of Navarre with an auxiliary force of 4000 men; he shared all the hardships of the common soldiers; during the siege of Rouen he challenged the leader of the enemy's forces to single combat; and then by his incapacity he dissipated all the results of the campaign. His army melted away to almost nothing.

He was at home during the following years, when Shakespeare probably came to know him well, and to appreciate his chivalrous nature, his courage and talent, his love of poetry and science, and his helpfulness towards men of ability, such as Francis Bacon and others. He therefore, no doubt, followed with more than the ordinary patriotic interest the expedition of the English fleet to Cadiz in 1596, in which the two old antagonists, Raleigh and Essex, were to fight side by side. Raleigh here won a brilliant victory over the great galleons of the Spanish fleet, burning them all except two, which he captured; while on the following day, when a severe wound in the leg prevented Raleigh from taking part in the action, Essex, at the head of his troops, stormed and sacked the town of Cadiz. In his despatches to Elizabeth, Raleigh praised Essex for this exploit. He became the hero of the day; his name was in every mouth, and he was even eulogised from the pulpit of St. Paul's.

It was indeed a great age. England's world-wide power was founded at the expense of defeated and humiliated Spain; England's world-wide commerce and industry came into existence. Before Elizabeth came to the throne, Antwerp had been the metropolis of commerce; during her reign, London took that position. The London Exchange was opened in 1571; and twenty years later, English merchants all the world over had appropriated to themselves the commerce which had formerly been almost entirely in the hands of the Hanseatic Towns. London urchins hung about the wharves of the Thames, listening to the marvels related by seamen who had made the voyage round the Cape of Good Hope to Hindostan. Sunburnt, scarred, and bearded men haunted the taverns; they had crossed the ocean, lived in the Bermuda Islands, and brought negroes and Red Indians and great monkeys home with them. They told tales of the golden Eldorado, and of real and imaginary perils in distant quarters of the globe.

This peaceful development of commerce and industry had taken place simultaneously with the development of naval and military power. And the scientific and poetical culture of England advanced with equal strides. While mariners had brought home tidings of many an unknown shore, scholars also had made voyages of discovery in Greek and Roman letters; and while they praised and translated authors unheard of before, dilettanti brought forward and interpreted Italian and Spanish poets who served as models of invention and delicacy. The world, which had hitherto been a little place, had suddenly grown vast; the horizon, which had been narrow, widened out all of a sudden, and every mind was filled with hopes for the days to come.

It had been a vernal season, and it was a vernal mood that

had uttered itself in the songs of the many poets. In our days, when the English language is read by hundreds of millions, the poets of England may be quickly counted. In those days the country possessed something like three hundred lyric and dramatic poets, who, with potent productivity, wrote for a reading public no larger than that of Denmark to-day; for of the six millions of the population, four millions could not read. But the talent for writing verses was as widespread among the Englishmen of that time as the talent for playing the piano among German ladies of to-day. The power of action and the gift of song did not exclude each other.

But the blossoming springtide had been short, as springtide always is.

II

ELIZABETH'S OLD AGE

AT the dawn of the new century the national mood had already altered.

Elizabeth herself was no longer the same. There had always been a dark side to her nature, but it had passed almost unnoticed in the splendour which national prosperity, distinguished men, great achievements and fortunate events had shed around her person. Now things were changed.

She had always been excessively vain; but her coquettish pretences to youth and beauty reached their height after her sixtieth year. We have seen how, when she was sixty, Raleigh, from his prison, addressed a letter to Sir Robert Cecil, intended for her eyes, in which he sought to regain her favour by comparing her to Venus and Diana. When she was sixty-seven, Essex's sister, in a supplication for her brother's life, wrote of that brother's devotion to "her beauties," which did not merit so hard a punishment, and of her "excellent beauties and perfections," which "ought to feel more compassion." In the same year the Queen took part, masked, in a dance at Lord Herbert's marriage; and she always looked for expressions of flattering astonishment at the youthfulness of her appearance.

When she was sixty-eight, Lord Mountjoy wrote to her of her "faire eyes," and begged permission to "fill his eyes with their onely deere and desired object." This was the style which every one had to adopt who should have the least prospect of gaining, preserving, or regaining her favour.

In 1601 Lord Pembroke, then twenty-one years old, writes to Cecil (or, in other words, to Elizabeth, in her sixty-eighth year) imploring permission once more to approach the Queen, "whose incomparable beauty was the onely sonne of my little world."

When Sir Roger Aston, about this time, was despatched with

letters from James of Scotland to the Queen, he was not allowed to deliver them in person, but was introduced into an ante-chamber from which, through open door-curtains, he could see Elizabeth dancing alone to the music of a little violin,—the object being that he should tell his master how youthful she still was, and how small the likelihood of his succeeding to her crown for many a long day.[1] One can readily understand, then, how she stormed with wrath when Bishop Rudd, so early as 1596, quoted in a sermon Kohélet's verses as to the pains of age, with unmistakable reference to her.

She was bent on being flattered without ceasing and obeyed without demur. In her lust of rule, she knew no greater pleasure than when one of her favourites made a suggestion opposed to one of hers, and then abandoned it. Leicester had employed this means of confirming himself in her favour, and had bequeathed it to his successors. So strong was her craving to enjoy incessantly the sensation of her autocracy, that she would intrigue to set her courtiers up in arms against each other, and would favour first one group and then the other, taking pleasure in their feuds and cabals. In her later years her court was one of the most corrupt in the world. The only means of prospering in it were those set forth in Roger Ascham's distich:

> "Cog, lie, flatter and face
> Four ways in court, to win men grace."

The two main parties were those of Cecil and Essex. Whoever gained the favour of one of these great lords, be his merits what they might, was opposed by the other party with every weapon in their power.

In some respects, however, Elizabeth in her later years had made progress in the art of government. So weak had been her faith in the warlike capabilities of her country, and so potent, on the other hand, her avarice, that she had neglected to make preparation for the war with Spain, and had left her gallant seamen inadequately equipped; but after the victory over the Spanish Armada she ungrudgingly devoted all the resources of her treasury to the war, which survived her and extended well

---

[1] Arthur Weldon: *The Court and Character of King James*, 1650; quoted by Drake, ii. 149.

ATTITUDE OF ELIZABETH TO RELIGION   291

into the following century. This war had forced Elizabeth to take a side in the internal religious dissensions of the country. She was the head of the Church, regarded ecclesiastical affairs as subject to her personal control, and, so far as she was able, would suffer no discussion of religious questions in the House of Commons. Like her contemporary Henri Quatre of France, she was in her heart entirely indifferent to religion, had a certain general belief in God, but thought all dogmas mere cobwebs of the brain, and held one rite neither better nor worse than another. They both regarded religious differences exclusively from the political point of view. Henry ended by becoming a Catholic and assuring his former co-religionists freedom of conscience. Elizabeth was of necessity a Protestant, but tolerance was an unknown doctrine in England. It was an established principle that every subject must accept the religion of the State.

Authoritarian to her inmost fibre, Elizabeth had a strong bent towards Catholicism. The circumstances of her life had placed her in opposition to the Papal power, but she was fond of describing herself to foreign ambassadors as a Catholic in all points except subjection to the Pope. She did not even make any secret of her contempt for Protestantism, whose head she was, and whose support she could not for a moment dispense with. She felt it a humiliation to be regarded as a co-religionist of the French, Scotch, or Dutch heretics. She looked down upon the Anglican Bishops whom she had herself appointed, and they, in their worldliness, deserved her scorn. But still deeper was her detestation of all sectarianism within the limits of her Church, and especially of Puritanism in all its forms. If she did not in the first years of her reign indulge in open persecution of the Puritans, it was only because she was as yet dependent on their support; but as soon as she felt herself firmly seated on her throne, she established, in spite of the stiff-necked opposition of Parliament, the jurisdiction of the Bishops on all matters of ecclesiastical politics, and suffered Puritan writers to be condemned to death or life-long imprisonment for free but quite innocent expressions of opinion regarding the relation of the State to religion.

Her greatness had mainly reposed upon the insight she had shown in the choice of her counsellors and commanders. But the most distinguished of those who had shed glory on her throne died one after the other in the last decade of the century. The first to die was Walsingham, one of her most disinterested servants, whom she had repaid with black ingratitude. He had done her great and loyal services, and had saved her life at the time of the last conspiracy, which led to the execution of Mary Stuart. Then she lost such notable members of her Council as Lord Hunsdon and Sir Francis Knowles; then Lord Burghley himself, the true ruler of England during her reign; and finally, Sir Francis Drake, the great naval hero of the war with Spain. She felt herself lonely and deserted. She no longer took any pleasure in the position of power to which England had attained under her rule. In spite of all she could do to conceal it, she began to feel the oppression of age, and to see how little real affection those men felt for her who were always posing in the light of adorers. She was the last of her line, and the thought of her successor was so intolerable to her, that she deferred his final nomination until she lay on her death-bed. But it availed her nothing; she knew very well that her ministers and courtiers, during the last years of her life, were in constant and secret communication with James of Scotland. They would kneel in the dust as she passed with exclamations of enchantment at her youthful appearance, and then rise, brush the dust from their knees, and write to James that the Queen looked ghastly and could not possibly last long. They did all they possibly could to conceal from her their Scotch intrigues; but she divined what went on behind her back, even if she did not realise the extent to which it was carried, or know definitely which of her most trusted servants were shrinking from nothing that could assure them the favour of James. For example, she did not suspect Robert Cecil of the double game he was carrying on, at the very time when he was doing his best to drive Essex to desperation and secure his punishment for an act of disobedience scarcely more heinous in the Queen's eyes than his own underhand dealings. But she felt herself isolated in the midst of a crowd of courtiers impatiently awaiting the new era that was to dawn after her death. She realised that the men who still flattered her had never been attached to her for her own sake, and she specially resented the fact that they no longer seemed even to fear her.

ELIZABETH AND SOUTHAMPTON

One result of this deep dejection was that she gave her tyrannical tendencies a freer course than before, and became less and less inclined to forbearance or mercy towards those who had once been dear to her but had fallen into disgrace.

She had always taken it very ill when one of her favourites showed any inclination towards matrimony, and they had therefore always been forced to marry secretly, though that did not in the end save them from her displeasure. Now her despotism rose to such a pitch that she wanted to control the marriages even of those courtiers who had never enjoyed her favour.

One of the things which Shakespeare doubtless took most to heart at the end of the old century and beginning of the new was the hard fate which overtook his distinguished and highly valued patron Southampton. This nobleman had fallen in love with Essex's cousin, the Lady Elizabeth Vernon. The Queen forbade him to marry her, but he would not relinquish his bride. He was hot-headed and high-spirited. Young as he was, he had boarded and taken a Spanish ship of war in the course of the expedition commanded by his friend Essex. Once, in the palace itself, when Southampton, Raleigh, and another courtier had been laughing and making a noise over a game of primero, the captain of the guard, Ambrose Willoughby, called them to order because the Queen had gone early to bed; whereupon Southampton struck this high official in the face and actually had a bout of fisticuffs with him. Such being his character, we cannot wonder that he contracted a private marriage in spite of the prohibition (August 1598). Elizabeth sent him to pass his honeymoon in the Tower, and thenceforth viewed him with high disfavour.

His close relationship to Essex led to a new outburst of the Queen's displeasure. When Essex took command of the army in Ireland in 1599, he appointed Southampton his General of Horse; but simply out of resentment for Southampton's disobedience in the matter of his marriage, the Queen forced Essex to rescind the appointment.

One must bear in mind, among other things, this attitude of the Queen towards Shakespeare's first patron in order to understand the evident coolness of his feeling towards Elizabeth. He did not, for example, join in the threnodies of the other English poets on her death, and even after Chettle had expressly urged him,[1] refrained from writing a single line in her praise. He probably read her character much as Froude did in our own day.

Froude admits that she was "supremely brave," and was turned aside from her purposes by no care for her own life, though she was "perpetually a mark for assassination." He admits, too, that she lived simply, worked hard, and ruled her household with economy. "But her vanity was as insatiable as it was commonplace. . . . Her entire nature was saturated with artifice. Except when speaking some round untruths, Elizabeth never could be simple. Her letters and her speeches were as fantastic as her dress, and her meaning as involved as her policy. She was unnatural even in her prayers, and she carried her affectations into the presence of the Almighty. . . . Obligations of honour were not only occasionally forgotten by her, but she did not seem to understand what honour meant."[2]

At the point we have now reached in Shakespeare's life, the event occurred which, of all external circumstances of his time, seems to have made the deepest impression upon his mind: the ill-starred rebellion of Essex and Southampton, the execution of the former, and the latter's condemnation to imprisonment for life.

[1] "Nor doth the silver-tongued *Melicert*
Drop from his honied muse one sable teare
To mourne her death that graced his desert,
And to his laies opend her Royall eare.
Shepheard, remember our *Elizabeth*,
And sing her Rape, done by that *Tarquin*, Death."

[2] Froude: *History of England*, vol. xii. Conclusion.

III

ELIZABETH, ESSEX, AND BACON

IN order rightly to understand these events a short retrospect is necessary.

We have seen how Essex in 1587 ousted Raleigh from the Queen's favour. From the very first he united with the insinuating tone of the adorer the domineering attitude of the established favourite. This was new to her, and for a considerable time obviously impressed more than it irritated her.

Here is an instance, from the early days of their relationship. Essex's sister, Penelope, had, against her will, been married to Lord Rich. She was adored by Sir Philip Sidney, who sang of her as his Stella, and their mutual passion was an open secret. The Maiden Queen, who was always very strict as to the moral purity of those around her, during a visit which she paid with Essex to the Earl of Warwick at North Hall in 1587, took offence at the presence of Lady Rich, and insisted that she should leave the house. Essex declared that the Queen subjected him and his sister to this insult "only to please that knave Raleigh," and left the house at midnight along with Lady Rich. He wanted to join the army in the Netherlands, but the Queen, finding that she could not do without him, had him brought back again.

At the time of the Armada, therefore, the Queen kept him at court, much against his own will. Nor would he have been allowed to take part in the war of 1589 if he had not secretly made his escape from England, leaving behind him a letter to the Queen and Council to the effect that "he would return alive at no one's bidding." An angry letter from Elizabeth forced him, however, to come back after he had distinguished himself before Lisbon. They were then reconciled, but the practical-minded Queen immediately demanded of him the repayment of a sum of £3000 which she had lent him, so that he was forced to sell his mansion of Keyston. He received in return "the farm of sweet wines," a very lucrative monopoly, the withdrawal of which many years afterwards led to the boiling over of his discontent.

We have seen how his secret marriage in 1590 enraged the Queen, who at once vented her wrath upon his bride. Presently, however, he was once more in favour, and in the middle of the French campaign of 1591, Elizabeth recalled him to England for a week, which was passed in all sorts of festivities. She wept when he returned to the army, and laid upon him an injunction, to which he paid very little heed, that he must on no account incur any personal danger.

During the subsequent four years which Essex passed in England, occupied with his plans of ambition, it became clear to him that Burghley's son, Sir Robert Cecil, was the chief obstacle to his advancement. All of those, therefore, who for one reason or another hated the house of Cecil, cast in their lot with Essex. Thus it happened that Cecil's cousin, Francis Bacon, who had in vain besought first the father and then the son for some profitable office, became a close personal adherent of Essex. It was necessary to make choice of one party or the other if you were to hope for any preferment. In the years 1593 and 1594, accordingly, we find Essex again and again importuning Elizabeth for offices for Bacon. She had no very great confidence in Bacon, and bore him a grudge, moreover, because he had incautiously spoken in Parliament against a Government measure; so that Essex, to his great annoyance and disgust, met with a refusal to all his applications. As a consolation to his client, he made him a present of land to the value of not less than £1800. That was the price for which Bacon sold the property; Essex had believed it to be worth more.[1] This gift, we see, was nearly twice as large as that which Southampton is reported to have made to Shakespeare (see above, p. 181).

Henceforward Bacon is to be regarded as an attentive and officious adherent of Essex, while Essex makes it a point of honour to obtain for him every recognition, preferment, and advantage. Again and again Bacon places his pen at the dis-

---

[1] James Spedding: *Letters and Life of Francis Bacon*, i. 371.

posal of Essex. There are extant three long letters from Essex to his young cousin Lord Rutland, dated 1596, giving him excellent advice as to how to reap most profit from his first Continental tour, on which he was then setting out. In many passages of these letters we recognise Bacon's ideas, and in some his style, his acknowledged writings containing almost identical parallels. The probability is that in these, as in many subsequent instances, Bacon supplied Essex with the ideas and the first draft of the letters. Well knowing that the Queen's dissatisfaction with Essex arose chiefly from his desire for military glory and the popularity which follows in its train— well knowing, too, that Essex's enemies at court were always representing this ambition to the Queen as a hindrance to the peace with Spain, which nevertheless must one day be concluded —Bacon thought it a good move for his protector to display unequivocally his care for the occupations of peace, the acquisition of useful knowledge, and other unmilitary advantages, in letters which, although private, were likely enough to come into her Majesty's hands.

Francis Bacon's brother, Anthony, about the same time attached himself closely (and more faithfully) to Essex. Through him the Earl established communications with all the foreign courts, so that for a time his knowledge of European affairs rivalled that of the Foreign Ministry itself.

The zeal which Essex had displayed in unravelling Doctor Roderigo Lopez's suspected plot against Elizabeth (see above, p. 191) had placed him very high in her renewed favour. His heroic exploits at Cadiz ought to have strengthened his position; but his adversary, Robert Cecil, had during his absence acquired new power, and the rapacious Elizabeth complained of the smallness of the booty (it amounted to £13,000). As a matter of fact, Essex alone had wanted to follow up the advantage gained, and to seize the Indian fleet, which was allowed to escape: he had been out-voted in the council of war.

In order to overcome this new resentment on the Queen's part, Bacon, who regarded his fate as bound up in that of the Earl, wrote a letter to Essex (dated October 4, 1596), full of good advice with respect to the attitude he ought to adopt towards Elizabeth, especially in order to disabuse her mind of the idea that his disposition was ungovernable—advice which

Bacon himself, with his courtier temperament, might easily enough have followed, but which was too hard for the downright Essex, who had no sooner made humble submission than his pride again brought arrogant expressions to his lips.

At the close of the year 1596 Bacon's protector was accused by his client's mother, Lady Bacon, of misconduct with one of the ladies of the court. He denied the charge, but confessed to "similar errors."

In 1597 Essex, who had been longing for a new command, undertook an expedition to the Azores with twenty ships and 6000 men—an enterprise which, largely owing to his inexperience and unfortunate leadership, was entirely unsuccessful. On his return he was very coldly received by the Queen, especially on the ground that towards the end of the expedition he had behaved ill to Raleigh, his colleague in command. In order to make his peace with Elizabeth, he sent her insinuating letters; but he was mortally offended when the eminent services of the old Lord Howard were rewarded by the appointment of Lord High Admiral. As the victor of Cadiz, he regarded himself as the one possible man for this distinction, which gave Howard precedence over him. He bemoaned his fate, however, to such purpose that he soon after secured the appointment of Earl Marshal of England, which in turn gave him precedence over Howard. He received a very valuable present—worth £7000—and for the first and last time induced the Queen to grant an audience to his mother, Lady Lettice, whose marriage with Leicester, twenty-three years before, was not yet forgiven, although in 1589, at the age of forty-nine, she had married a third husband, Sir Christopher Blount.

But Essex was not long at peace with the Queen and Court. In 1598 he was accused of illicit relations with no fewer than four ladies of the court (Elizabeth Southwell, Elizabeth Brydges, Mrs. Russell, and Lady Mary Howard), and the charge seems to have been well founded. At the same time violent dissensions broke out as to whether an attempt should or should not be made to bring the war with Spain to a close. Essex carried the day, and it was continued. It was at this time that he wrote a pamphlet defending himself warmly from the charge of desiring war at any price. It was not published until 1602, under the title: *An apology of the Earle of Essex against those which jealously and maliciously tax him to be the hinderer of the peace and quiet of his country.*

To the Queen's birthday of this year (November 17, 1598) belongs an anecdote which shows what ingenuity Essex displayed in annoying his rival. As was the custom of the day, the leading courtiers tilted at the ring in honour of her Majesty, and each knight was required to appear in some disguise. It was known, however, that Sir Walter Raleigh would ride in his own uniform of orange-tawny medley, trimmed with black budge of lamb's wool. Essex, to vex him, came to the lists with a body-guard of two thousand retainers all dressed in orange-tawny, so that Raleigh and his men seemed only an insignificant division of Essex's splendid retinue.[1]

No later than June or July 1598 there occurred a new scene between Essex and the Queen in the Council, the most unpleasant and grotesque passage which had yet taken place between them. The occasion was trifling, being nothing more than the choice of an official to be despatched to Ireland. Essex was in the habit of permitting himself every liberty towards Elizabeth; and it was now, or soon after, that, as Raleigh relates, he told her "that her conditions were as crooked as her carcase." Certain it is that, on this occasion, he turned his back to her with an expression of contempt. She retorted by giving him a box on the ear and bidding him "Go and be hanged." He laid his hand upon his sword-hilt, declared that he would not have suffered such an insult from Henry the Eighth himself, and held aloof from the court for months.

Not till October was Essex forgiven, and even then with no heartiness or sincerity. The Irish rebellion, however, had to be put down, so a truce was called to all trivial quarrels. O'Neil, Earl of Tyrone, had got together an army, as he had often done before, and the whole island was in revolt. Public opinion, for no sufficient reason, pointed to Essex as the only man who could deal with the rebels. He, on his part, was by no means eager to accept the mission. It was of the utmost importance for every courtier, and especially for the head of a party, not to be out of the Queen's sight more than was imperatively necessary. There was every reason to fear that his enemies of the opposite party would avail themselves of his absence in order so to blacken

[1] Gosse: *Raleigh*, p. 113.

him in the eyes of his omnipotent mistress that he would never regain her favour. Elizabeth, at this juncture, like Louis XIV. in the following century, was monarch and constitution in one. Her displeasure meant ruin, her favour was the only source of prosperity. Therefore Essex did all he could to secure permission to return from the front whenever he pleased, in order to report personally to the Queen; and it was therefore that, in the following year, when he was forbidden to leave his post, he threw caution to the winds, and defied the prohibition. He knew that he was lost unless he could speak to Elizabeth face to face.

In March 1599 Essex took the command of the English troops; he was to suppress the rebellion and grant Tyrone his life only on condition of his complete surrender. But instead of carrying out his orders, which were to attack the rebels in their stronghold, Ulster, Essex remained for long inactive, and at last marched into Munster. One of his subordinate officers, Sir Henry Harington, suffered a disgraceful defeat, partly through his own incompetence, partly through the cowardice of his officers and men. He was tried by court-martial in Dublin, and he himself, and every tenth man of his command, were shot. The summer slipped away, and in its course the 16,000 men with whom Essex had come to Ireland were reduced by sickness and desertion to a quarter of their original number. Under these circumstances, Essex again deferred his march upon Ulster, so that the Queen, who was excessively displeased, expressly forbade him to return from Ireland without her permission.

When at last, in the beginning of September 1599, he confronted with his shrunken forces Tyrone's unbreathed army, which had taken up a strong position to await the coming of the English, he abandoned his plan of attack, invited Tyrone to a parley, had half an hour's conversation with him on the 6th of September, and concluded a fourteen weeks' armistice, to be renewed every six weeks until the 1st of May. According to his own account, he promised Tyrone that this treaty should not be placed in writing, lest it should fall into the hands of the Spaniards and be used against him.

This was certainly not what Elizabeth had expected of the Irish campaign, which had opened with such a flourish of trumpets, and we cannot wonder that her anger was fierce

FALL OF ESSEX 301

and deep-seated. No sooner had she received the intelligence, than she forbade the conclusion of any treaty whatsoever.

Convinced that his enemies now had the entire ear of the Queen, Essex sought safety in once more disobeying Elizabeth's express command. With a train of only six followers, which in the indictment against him afterwards grew into a body of 200 picked men, he crossed to England to attempt his own justification, rode direct to Nonsuch Palace, where Elizabeth then was, forced all the doors, and, travel-stained as he was, threw himself on his knees before the Queen, whom he surprised in her bed-chamber, with her hair undressed, at ten o'clock in the morning of the 28th of September.

It is a strong proof of the power which his personality still retained over Elizabeth, that at the first moment she felt nothing but pleasure in seeing him. As soon as he had changed his clothes, he was admitted to an audience, which lasted an hour and a half. As yet all seemed well. He dined at the Queen's table and told her about Ireland and its people. But in the evening he was "commanded to keep his chamber" until the lords of the Council should have spoken with him; and a few days later he was confined to York House, with his friend the Lord Keeper, however, for his gaoler.

He presently fell ill, when it appeared that the Queen had by no means forgotten her former tenderness for him. In the middle of December she sent eight physicians to consult as to his case. They despaired of his life, but he recovered.

While matters thus looked very black for Essex, his nearest friends also were, of course, in disgrace. In a letter from Rowland Whyte to Sir Robert Sidney (dated October 11, 1599), we find the following significant statement: "My Lord *Southhampton*, and Lord *Rutland* come not to the court; the one doth but very seldome; they pass away the Tyme in *London* merely in going to Plaies euery day."[1] Southampton had married a cousin of Essex, and Rutland a daughter of Lady Essex by her first marriage with Sir Philip Sidney; so that both were in the same boat with their more distinguished kinsman.

On the 5th of June 1600, Essex was brought to trial—not before the Star Chamber, but, by particular favour, before a

---

[1] A. Collins: *Letters and Memorials of State*, ii. 132.

special court, consisting of four earls, two barons, and four judges, which assembled at the Lord Keeper's residence, York House, the general public being excluded. The procedure was mainly dictated by the Queen's wish to justify the arrest of Essex in the face of public opinion, which idolised him and regarded him as a martyr.

IV

THE FATE OF ESSEX AND SOUTHAMPTON

THE indictment did not press too severely upon Essex, did not as yet seek to discover treasonable motives for his inactivity in Ireland, but simply dwelt upon his disobedience to the Queen's commands, and the dangerous and dishonourable agreement with Tyrone. Francis Bacon had not been allotted any part in the proceedings; but on his writing to the Queen and expressing his desire to serve her in this conjuncture, he was assigned the quite subordinate task of calling Essex to account for his indiscretion in accepting the dedication, in unbefitting terms, of a political pamphlet written by a certain Dr. Hayward. Bacon exceeded his instructions by dwelling at length on certain passionate expressions in a letter from Essex to the Lord Keeper, in which he had spoken of the hardness of the Queen's heart and compared her princely wrath to a tempest. A man who was less nervously anxious to retain the Queen's favour would have declined this commission on the ground of his close relations with Essex; Bacon begged for it, went farther than it required him to go, and is scarcely to be believed when he afterwards, in his *Apology*, represents himself as actuated by the wish ultimately to be of service to Essex with the Queen. Still, he evidently had not ceased to regard a reconciliation between Elizabeth and Essex as the most probable result, and he may perhaps have done his best in private conversations to soften the Queen's resentment.

The sentence passed by the Lord Keeper was the not very severe one that Essex should, in the meantime, be deprived of all his offices, and remain a prisoner in Essex House "till it shall please her Majesty to release both this and all the rest."

Bacon, who still did not think Essex irretrievably lost, now tried, in a carefully worded letter to him, to explain his attitude, and at once received from his magnanimous friend a forgiveness which was scarcely deserved. Bacon declared that, next to the interests of the Queen and the country, those of Essex always lay nearest his heart; and he now composed two documents: first, a very judicious letter, which Essex was partly to re-write and then to send to the Queen, and next a fictitious letter, a masterpiece of diplomacy, purporting to have been written by his brother, Anthony Bacon, Essex's faithful adherent, to Essex himself. This letter, and Essex's reply to it, which prove to admiration Bacon's talent for reproducing the styles of two such different men, were to be copied by them respectively, and to be brought to the knowledge of the Queen, on whom they would no doubt produce the desired impression. With Machiavellian subtlety, these letters are carefully framed so as to place Francis Bacon himself in the light which should most appeal to the Queen: Essex is represented as regarding him as entirely won over to her side, and Anthony expresses the hope that she will show him the favour he has deserved "for that he hath done and suffered."

Bacon did not succeed in inducing Elizabeth to restore Essex to his former position in her favour. In August, a couple of months after the date of the sentence, he was placed at full liberty; but access to Elizabeth's person was denied him, and he was bidden to regard himself as still in disgrace. The consequence was that few now came about him except the members of his own family. Add to this, that he was over head and ears in debt, and that his monopoly of sweet wines, which had been his chief source of income, and on the renewal of which his financial rescue depended, ran out in the following month.

He wavered between fear and hope, and was for ever "shifting from sorrow and repentance to rage and rebellion so suddenly, as well proveth him devoid of good reason as of right mind." At one moment he is appealing to the Queen with the deepest humility in flattering letters, and at the next he is speaking of her—so his friend Sir John Harington reports—as "became no man who had *mens sana in corpore sano.*"

Then came the catastrophe. His sources of income were cut off, and his hope of the Queen's relenting was broken. He was convinced—without reason, as it appears—that his enemies at court, who had deprived him of his wealth, had now laid a plot to deprive him of his life as well. He imagined, too, that Sir

Robert Cecil was weaving intrigues to bring about the nomination of the Infanta of Spain as Elizabeth's successor; and in his desperation he began to nurse the illusion that it was as necessary for the welfare of the state as for his own that he should gain forcible access to the Queen and secure the banishment from court of her present advisers. In his dread of being once more placed under arrest, and this time sent to the Tower, he determined, in February 1601, to carry out a plan he had been hatching, for taking the court by storm.

Southampton had at this time allowed the malcontents to make his residence, Drury House, their meeting-place for discussing the situation. Here the general plan was laid that they should seize upon Whitehall and that Essex should force his way into the Queen's presence; the time was to depend upon the arrival of the Scotch envoy. On the 5th of February, four or five of the Earl's friends presented themselves at the Globe Theatre, and promised the players eleven shillings more than they usually received if, on the 7th, they would perform the play of the deposition and death of King Richard II. (see above, p. 148). In the meantime, Essex had, in the beginning of February, assembled his adherents in his own residence, Essex House, and this induced the Government, which had heard with uneasiness of so large a concourse of people, to summon Essex before the Council. He received the summons on the 7th of February 1601, excused himself on the ground of indisposition, and at once called his friends together. On the same evening three hundred men were gathered at his house, although no real plan had as yet been determined upon. He informed them that his life was threatened by Cobham and Raleigh. On the morning of the 8th of February, the Lord Keeper with three other noblemen, commissioned by the Queen to inquire into what was going on, appeared at Essex House, and demanded to see the Earl. They told him that any complaints he might have to make to the Queen should receive attention, but that in the first place he must order his adherents to disperse.

Essex made only confused replies: his life was threatened, he was to be murdered in his bed, he had been treacherously dealt with, and so forth. In the meantime shouts arose from the crowd of his retainers, "Away, my lord; they abuse you, they betray you, they undo you; you lose time!" Essex led the noblemen into his house amid cries from his armed friends of "Kill them, kill them!" and "Shut them up! Keep them as pledges, cast the great seal out at the window!" He had them locked up in his library as prisoners or hostages. Then he came out again, and, amid cries of "To Court! to Court!" his party rushed through the gates. At the last moment, Essex learned that the Court was prepared, the watch was doubled, and every access to Whitehall was barred. They were therefore forced to attempt, in the first place, to stir up an insurrection in the city. But in order to pass through the streets horses were needed; they were sent for, but there was delay in procuring them. So impatient was every one by this time, that instead of awaiting their arrival, several hundred men, headed by Essex, Southampton, Rutland, Blount, and other gentlemen, but without any real leader or effective plan of action, set off for the city. Essex nowhere made any speech to the populace, but merely shouted, as though beside himself, that an attempt had been made to murder him. A good many people, indeed, appeared to join him, but none of them were armed, and they were in reality no more than onlookers. In the meantime, the Government despatched high officials on horseback to different quarters of the town to proclaim Essex a traitor; whereupon many of his following deserted him. Troops, too, were despatched against him, so that he, with the remainder of his band, with difficulty made their way by water back to Essex House, which was immediately besieged and fired upon. In the evening Essex and Southampton opened negotiations, and about ten o'clock surrendered with their little force, on the understanding that they should be courteously treated and accorded an honourable trial. The prisoners were taken to the Tower.

Francis Bacon now again plays a part, and this time a decisive one, in Essex's history. There was no need for him to take any share in the trial; and even if his office had imposed it upon him, he ought in common decency to have refrained. He was neither Attorney-General nor Solicitor, but only one of the "Learned Counsel." The very fact of his close friendship with Essex, however, made the Government anxious that he should appear in the case. He was at once advocate and witness, and was not summoned as one of the learned counsel, but expressly as "friend to the accused."

On the 19th February, Essex and Southampton were brought

before a court consisting of twenty-five peers and nine judges. Already, on the 17th, Thomas Leigh, a captain in Essex's Irish army, for trying to gain access to the palace on the 8th February, had been beheaded in the Tower. Now that Essex's cause was irreparably lost, Bacon had no other thought than to make himself useful to the party in power and prove his devotion to the Queen. The purport of his first speech against Essex was to prove that the plan of exciting an insurrection in the city, which was in reality an inspiration of the moment, had been the result of three months' deliberation. He represented as false and hypocritical Essex's assurance that he was driven to action by dread of the machinations of powerful enemies. He compared Essex to Cain, the first murderer, who also sought excuses for his deed, and to Pisistratus, who wounded himself and ran through the streets of Athens, crying that an attempt had been made upon his life. The Earl of Essex, he said, in reality had no enemies.

Essex rejoined that he could "call forth Mr. Bacon against Mr. Bacon." Bacon, "being a daily courtier," had promised to plead his cause with the Queen. He had with great address composed a letter to her, to be signed by Essex. He had also written another letter in his brother Anthony's name, and an answer to it from Essex, both of which he was to show to the Queen; and in these "he laid down the grounds of my discontent, and the reasons I pretend against mine enemies, pleading as orderly for me as I could do myself."

This rejoinder told sensibly against Bacon, and drove him in his reply to launch against his benefactor a new and much more malignant and dangerous comparison. He likened him to a renowned contemporary, also a nobleman and a rebel, the Duke of Guise: "It was not the company you carried with you, but the assistance you hoped for in the City which you trusted unto. The Duke of Guise thrust himself into the streets of Paris on the day of the Barricados in his doublet and hose, attended only with eight gentlemen, and found that help in the city which (thanks be to God) you failed of here. And what followed? The King was forced to put himself into a pilgrim's weeds, and in that disguise to steal away to scape their fury."

In view of Essex's persistent denial that he had aspired to the throne or sought to do the Queen any injury, this parallel was a terrible one for him.

Both he and Southampton were found guilty and condemned to death.

The trial of Shakespeare's protector, Southampton, and his signed confession, have a special interest for us. In a private letter from John Chamberlain, dated the 24th February, we read: "The Earl of Southampton spake very well (but methought somewhat too much, as well as the other), and as a man that would fain live, pleaded hard to acquit himself; but all in vain, for it could not be: whereupon he descended to entreaty and moved great commiseration, and though he were generally well liked, yet methought he was somewhat too low and submiss, and seemed too loath to die before a proud enemy."

Southampton, in his own confession, admits that immediately after his arrival in Ireland, he became aware of Essex's letter to King James of Scotland, urging that, for his own sake, he ought not to permit the government of England to remain in the hands of his and Essex's common enemies, proposing that he should, at a fitting opportunity, assemble an army, and promising that Essex, in so far as his duty to her Majesty permitted, should support the King with his Irish troops. James replied evasively, and nothing came of the plan, in which Southampton soon regretted that he had taken share. After losing his post in Ireland, he went to the Netherlands, and had no other desire than to regain the favour of the Queen, when Essex, his kinsman and friend, summoned him to London and requested his support in the plan he had formed for seeking access to her Majesty. With a heavy heart, he had consented, and engaged in the enterprise, not from any treachery or disrespect towards her Majesty, but solely on account of his affection for Essex. He repents and abhors his action, and promises on his knees to consecrate to the Queen's service every day that remains to him, if she will but spare his life.

Southampton impresses us as a man of fiery but yielding character, entirely under the influence of a stronger personality; but he is never betrayed into a single unworthy word with respect to his kinsman and friend, whose cause he of course knew to be hopeless. His sentence was commuted to imprisonment for life.

Essex himself, at the end, endured with less resolution the cruel ordeal to which he was subjected. Finding himself con-

DEATH OF ESSEX 309

demned to death, and knowing that many of his closest friends had confessed to the Drury House discussions and designs, he lost all balance during the last days of his life, entirely forgot his dignity, and overwhelmed those around him, his sister, his friends, his secretary, and himself, with a torrent of reproaches.

In the meantime his enemies were not idle. Even Raleigh, on whose proud nature one is sorry to find such a stain, impelled, of course, not only by their old enmity, but by Essex's recent assertions that he was plotting against his life, wrote to Cecil, in his uneasiness lest Essex should be pardoned, and urged him "not to relent," but to see that the sentence was carried out.

Elizabeth had first signed the death-warrant, and then recalled it. On the 24th February she signed it a second time, and on the 25th February 1601, Essex's head was severed by three blows of the axe.

The populace could not be persuaded of their favourite's guilt. They loathed his executioner, and detested those men who, like Bacon and Raleigh, had, by their malice, contributed to his downfall.

In order to justify itself, the Government issued an official *Declaration touching the Treasons of the late Earl of Essex and his complices*, in the composition of which Bacon bore a large part. It is very untrustworthy. James Spedding, indeed, one of Bacon's best biographers, has tried to reconcile it with the facts; but he has not succeeded in explaining away the damnatory circumstance that everything is omitted which tended at the trial to establish Essex's intention to use no violence, and to prove how entirely unpremeditated was the attempt to raise an insurrection in the city. Where passages of this nature occur in the records, all of which are preserved, we find the letters *om*. (meaning, of course, "to be omitted") written in the margin, sometimes in Bacon's hand, sometimes in that of the Attorney-General, Coke.[1]

Bacon, with his brilliant intellectual equipment and his consciousness of his great powers, is not to be set down as simply a bad man. But his heart was cold, and he had no greatness of soul. He was absorbed, to a quite unworthy degree, in the pursuit

---

[1] Compare *Dictionary of National Biography*, Robert Devereux; Spedding, *Letters and Life of Francis Bacon*, ii. 190-374; Edwin Abbott, *Francis Bacon, an Account of his Life and Works*, pp. 53-82; Macaulay, *Lord Bacon*; Gosse, *Raleigh*.

of worldly prosperity. Always deeply in debt, he coveted above everything fine houses and gardens, massive plate, great revenues, and, as essential preliminaries, high offices and employments, titles and distinctions, which he might well have left to men of meaner worth. He passed half his life in the character of an office-seeker, met with one humiliating refusal after another, and returned humble thanks for the gracious denial. Once and once only, in his early days in Parliament, did he display some independence and rectitude; but when he saw that it gave offence in the highest places, he repented as bitterly as though he had been guilty of a sin against all political morality, and besought her Majesty's forgiveness in terms that might have befitted a detected thief. With the like baseness and pusillanimity he now turned against Essex. He had often cited the maxim, which even Cicero criticised in the *De Amicitia*: "Love as if you should hereafter hate, and hate as if you should hereafter love." He had never loved Essex otherwise. His excuse, if there can be any, for seeking advancement at all costs, must be found in the fact that he had the highest conception of his own value to science, and thought that it would be to the honour and advantage of learning that he, its high-priest, should be highly placed.

If we examine Essex's portrait, with its regular beauty, its air of distinction and gentleness, the high forehead, the curly hair, and the carefully combed long light beard, we can readily understand that such a man, surrounded by a halo of adventurous renown, must become the idol of the populace, and that the military incompetence which he had twice displayed should not greatly affect the high esteem in which the people held him. He was in reality as little of a statesman as of a general; he was simply a free-speaking, passionate man, innocent of diplomacy, a brave soldier without an idea of tactics. He misunderstood his influence over Elizabeth, and did not realise that the Queen, while she felt the charm of his personality, contemned his political counsels. There was a good deal of the poet in his composition; he wrote pretty sonnets, was a patron of writers no less than of fighters, showed himself generous to profusion towards his friends and clients, and found, perhaps, his sincerest and most convinced admirers among the authors and poets of the day. Innumerable are the books which are dedicated to him.

There is no doubt that after his melancholy death, a marked

decline was apparent in the Queen's courage and spirits. The legend, however, that it was the fact of his execution which she took so much to heart, is scarcely to be believed, and the story about Essex's ring, which was conveyed to her too late, is unquestionably a fable. It is certain, on the other hand— for the Duc de Biron, the envoy of Henri IV., had no motive for telling a falsehood—that on the 12th September 1601, after a conversation about Essex in which she jested over her departed favourite, Elizabeth opened a box and took out of it Essex's skull, which she showed to Biron. Ten months later, this favourite of the French king — whose name Shakespeare had borrowed for the hero of his first comedy—met with the very fate of Essex, and for a similar crime.

Bacon, no doubt, mourned Essex's disappearance even less than did the Queen. After Elizabeth's death, however, when the friends of Essex stood in the highest favour with the new King, he was shameless enough to send a letter to Southampton (who, though not yet released from the Tower, was already regarded as a power in the land), in which, after having expressed his fear of being met with distrust, he concludes thus: "It is as true as a thing that God knoweth, that this great change hath wrought in me no other change towards your Lordship than this, that I may safely be now that which I was truly before."

The circumstances of Essex's condemnation were of course not known in the London of those days so minutely as we now know them. But we see, as already indicated, that public opinion turned vehemently against Bacon, regarding and despising him as the traitor to his lord who, more than any one else, had brought about his unhappy end. We see that Raleigh, in spite of his greatness, now became one of the most unpopular men in England; and we observe that, notwithstanding all that was done to disparage him in the general regard, Essex's memory continued to be idolised by the great mass of the people.

If we now inquire in what relation Shakespeare stood to these events which so absorbed the English people, it seems more than probable that he, who had so recently been so intimately associated with Southampton, and cannot therefore have been very far from Essex, followed the accused with his sympathy, felt a lively resentment towards their enemies, and took their fate much to heart. And when we observe that just at this juncture a revolution occurs in Shakespeare's hitherto cheerful habit of mind, and that he begins to take ever gloomier views of human nature and of life, we cannot but recognise the probability that grief for the fate which had overtaken Essex, Southampton, and their fellows, was one of the sources of his growing melancholy.

V

THE YEAR 1601—THE SONNETS AND PEMBROKE

THE turning-point in Shakespeare's prevailing mood must be placed in or about the year 1601. We naturally looked for one source of his henceforth deepening melancholy in outward events, in the political drama which in that year reached its crisis and catastrophe; but it is still more imperative that we should look into his private and personal experiences for the ultimate cause of the revolution in his soul. We must therefore inquire what light his works throw upon his private circumstances and state of mind during this fateful year.

Now, we find among Shakespeare's works one which, more than any other, enables us to look into his inmost soul; and this work, as the latest and most penetrating of his students and critics have established, must date from about 1601—I mean his Sonnets. It is to these remarkable poems that we must mainly address ourselves for the information we require. Public events may, indeed, cast a certain measure of light or shadow over a man's inward world of thought and feeling; but they are never the efficient factors in determining the happiness or melancholy of his fundamental mood. If he has personal reasons for feeling that fate is against him, the utmost serenity in the political atmosphere will not dissipate his gloom; and, conversely, if a deep joy abides within him, and he has personal reasons for feeling himself favoured by fortune, then public discontent will be powerless to disturb the harmony in his soul. But his depression will, of course, be doubly severe if public events and private experiences combine to cast a gloom over his mind.

Shakespeare's "sugred Sonnets" are first mentioned in the well-known passage in Meres's *Palladis Tamia* (1598), where they are spoken of as passing from hand to hand "among his private friends." In the following year the two important Sonnets now numbered cxxxviii. and cxliv. were printed (with readings subsequently revised) in a collection of poems named *The Passionate Pilgrim*, dishonestly published, and falsely attributed to Shakespeare, by a bookseller named Jaggard. For the next ten years we find no mention of Sonnets by Shakespeare, until, in 1609, a bookseller named Thomas Thorpe issued a quarto book entitled *Shakespeares Sonnets. Neuer before Imprinted*—an edition which the poet himself certainly cannot have revised for the press, but which may possibly have been printed from an authentic manuscript.

To this first edition is prefixed a dedication, written by the bookseller in the most contorted style, which has given rise to theories and conjectures without number. It runs as follows:—

TO . THE . ONLIE . BEGETTER . OF
THESE . INSVING . SONNETS .
MR . W . H . ALL . HAPPINESSE .
AND . THAT . ETERNITIE .
PROMISED .
BY .
OVR . EVER-LIVING . POET .
WISHETH .
THE . WELL-WISHING .
ADVENTVRER . IN .
SETTING .
FORTH .

T . T .

The meaning of the signature is clear enough, since "A booke called Shakespeare's Sonnets" was entered in the Stationers' Register on May 20, 1609, under the name of Thomas Thorpe. On the other hand, throughout this century and the last, there has been no end to the discussion as to what is meant by "onlie begetter" (only producer, or only procurer, or only inspirer?); and numberless have been the attempts to identify the "Mr. W. H." who is so designated. While the far-fetched expression "begetter" has been subjected to equally far-fetched interpretations, the most impossible guesses have been hazarded as to the initials W. H., and the most incredible conjectures put forward as to the person to whom the Sonnets are addressed.

Strange as it may seem, it is nevertheless the fact, that during the first eighty years of the eighteenth century the Sonnets were taken as being all addressed to one woman, all written in honour of Shakespeare's mistress. It was not till 1780 that Malone and his friends declared that more than one hundred of the poems were addressed to a man. This view of the matter, however, did not even then command general assent, and so late as 1797 Chalmers seriously maintained that all the Sonnets were addressed to Queen Elizabeth, who was also, he believed, the inspirer of Spenser's famous *Amoretti*, in reality addressed to the lady who afterwards became his wife. Not until the beginning of this century did people in general understand, what Shakespeare's contemporaries can certainly never have doubted, that the first hundred and twenty-six Sonnets are directed to a young man.

It now followed almost of necessity that this young man should be identified with the "Mr. W. H." who is described as the "onlie begetter" of the poems. The second group, indeed, is addressed to a woman; but the first group is much the larger, and follows immediately upon the dedication.

Some have taken the word "begetter" to signify the man who procured the manuscript for the bookseller, and have conjectured that the initials are those of William Hathaway, a brother-in-law of Shakespeare's (Neil, Elze). Dr. Farmer last century advanced the claims of William Hart, the poet's nephew, who, as was afterwards discovered, was not born until 1600. The mere fact that, by a whim or oversight of which there are many other examples in the first edition, the word "hues," in Sonnet xx., is printed in italics with a capital and spelt *Hews*, led Tyrwhitt to assume the existence of an otherwise unknown Mr. William Hughes, to whom he supposed the Sonnets to have been addressed. People have even been found to maintain that "Mr. W. H." referred to Shakespeare himself, some taking the "H." to be a mere misprint for "S.," others holding that the initials meant "Mr. William Himself" (Barnstorff).

Serious and competent critics for a long time inclined to the opinion that the "W. H." was a transposition of "H. W.," and represented none other than Henry Wriothesley, Earl of Southampton, whose close relation to the poet had long been known, and to whom his two narrative poems had been dedicated. This theory was held by Drake and Gervinus. But so early as 1832, Boaden advanced some strong objections to this view, which in our days has become quite untenable. There can be no doubt that the poet's friend whom the Sonnets celebrate bore the Christian name of William (see Sonnets cxxxv., cxxxvi., cxliii.), whereas Southampton's Christian name was Henry. Southampton, moreover, never possessed the personal beauty incessantly dwelt upon in these poems. Finally, the Sonnets fit neither his age, nor his character, nor his history, full of movement, activity, and adverse fortune, to which no smallest allusion appears.

In the year 1601, when, as we shall presently see, Sonnets c. to cxxvi. must have been written, Southampton was twenty-eight years old, and consequently could not be the "lovely boy" addressed in Sonnet cxxvi., and compared in Sonnet cxiv. to a "cherubin."

There is only one person whose name, age, history, appearance, virtues, and vices accord in every respect with those of the "Mr. W. H." to whom the Sonnets are dedicated and addressed, and that is the young William Herbert, who in 1601 became Earl of Pembroke. Born on April 8, 1580, he came to London in the autumn of 1597 or spring of 1598, and very soon, in all probability, made the acquaintance of Shakespeare, with whom he doubtless remained on terms of friendship until the poet's death. The first folio of 1623 is dedicated by the editors to him and his brother, on the ground that they have "prosequuted" both the plays, "and their Authour liuing, with so much fauour." We see, too, that since Bright in 1819, and Boaden in 1832, had independently of each other put forward the theory that Pembroke was the hero of the Sonnets, this view has gradually made its way, and is now shared by the best critics (such as Dowden), while it has received, as it were, its final confirmation in the acute and often convincing critical observations contained in Mr. Thomas Tyler's book on the Sonnets, published in 1890.

The way by which we arrive at William Herbert is this: Shakespeare's Sonnets are not isolated poems. We very soon discern that they stand in an intimate relation to each other, a thought or motive suggested in one being developed more at length in the next or one of the subsequent Sonnets. The grouping proves to be by no means arbitrary, as was once thought to be the case; on the contrary, it is so careful that all attempts to alter it have only rendered the poems more obscure. The first seventeen Sonnets, for example, form a closely interwoven group; in all of them the friend is exhorted not to die unmarried, but to leave the world an heir to his beauty, which must otherwise fade and perish with him. Sonnets c.–cxxvi., which are inseparably connected, turn on the reunion of the two friends after a coldness or misunderstanding has for a time severed them. Finally, Sonnets cxxvii.–clii. are all addressed, not to the friend, but to a mistress, the Dark Lady whose relation to the two friends has already formed the subject of earlier Sonnets.

Sonnet cxliv.—one of the most interesting, inasmuch it depicts in straightforward terms the poet's situation between friend and mistress—had already appeared, as above mentioned, in *The Passionate Pilgrim* (1599). It characterises the friend as the poet's "better angel," the mistress as his "worser spirit," and expresses the painful suspicion that the friend is entangled in the Dark Lady's toils—

"I guess one angel in another's hell;"

so that both at once are lost to him, he through her and she through him.

But precisely the same theme is treated in Sonnet xl., which turns on the fact that the friend has robbed Shakespeare of his "love." These two Sonnets must thus be of the same date; and from Sonnet xxxiii., which relates to the same circumstances, we see that the friendship had existed only a very short time when it was overshadowed by the intrigue between the friend and the mistress :—

"But out, alack! he was but one hour mine."

At what time, then, did the friendship begin? The date may be determined with some confidence, even apart from the question as to who the friend was. We know that Shakespeare must have written sonnets before 1598, since Meres published in that year his often-quoted words about the "sugred Sonnets"; but we cannot possibly determine which Sonnets these were, or whether we possess them at all, since those which passed from hand to hand "among his private friends" may very possibly have disappeared. If they are included in our collection, we may take them to be those in which we find frequent parallels to lines in *Venus and Adonis* and the early comedies, though these coincidences are by no means sufficient, as Hermann Conrad[1] would have us

[1] Hermann Conrad in *Preussische Jahrbücher*, February 1895. Under the pseudonym of Hermann Isaac in *Jahrbuch der Deutschen Shakespeare-Gesellschaft*, vol. xix. p. 176.

believe, finally to establish the date of the Sonnets in which they occur. On the other hand, Thomas Tyler has conclusively demonstrated that the passage in Meres's book influenced the conception and expression of one of Shakespeare's Sonnets. It cannot reasonably be doubted that Shakespeare saw *Palladis Tamia;* the author perhaps sent him a copy; and in any case he could not but read with interest the warm and sincere commendation there bestowed upon him. Now there occurs in Meres's book a passage in which, after quoting Ovid's

> " Jamque opus exegi, quod nec Jovis ira, nec ignis,
> Nec poterit ferrum, nec edax abolere vetustas,"

and Horace's

> " Exegi momentum aere perennius,"

the critic goes on to apply these words to his contemporaries Sir Philip Sidney, Spenser, Daniel, Drayton, Shakespeare, and Warner, and then winds up with a Latin eulogy of the same writers, composed by himself, partly in prose and partly in verse. But on reading attentively Shakespeare's Sonnet lv., whose resemblance to the well-known lines of Horace must have struck every reader, we find several expressions from this passage in *Palladis Tamia*, and even from the lines written by Meres himself, reappearing in it. The Sonnet must thus have been written at earliest in the end of 1598—Meres's book was entered in the Stationers' Register in September—and possibly not till the beginning of 1599. Since, then, the following Sonnet (lvi.), which must date from about the same time, speaks of the friendship as newly formed—

> "Let this sad interim like the ocean be
> Which parts the shores, where *two contracted new*
> Come daily to the banks "—

we may confidently assign to the year 1598 the first contract of amity between the poet and his friend.

The historical allusions in Sonnets c.–cxxvi., which form a continuous poem, are not, indeed, by any means clear or easy to interpret; but Sonnet civ. dates the whole group definitely enough, in the statement that three years have elapsed since the first meeting of the friends :—

"Three winters cold
Have from the forests shook three summers' pride ;
Three beauteous springs to yellow autumn turn'd
In process of the seasons have I seen ;
Three April perfumes in three hot Junes burn'd,
Since first I saw you fresh, which yet are green."

Thus we must assign this important group to the year 1601; and this being so, it must also appear probable that the line—

"The mortal moon hath her eclipse endured"—

alludes to the fact that Elizabeth (for whom, in the mode of the day, the moon was the accepted symbol) had come unharmed through the dangers of Essex's rebellion—the more so as the beautiful lines—

"Now with the drops of this most balmy time
My love looks fresh"—

show that the poem was written in the spring. It would be unreasonable to infer from this allusion any ill-will on the poet's part towards Essex and his comrades. Still less can we follow Tyler, when, by the aid of a complex scaffolding of hypotheses built up, in German rather than in English fashion, around Sonnets cxxiv. and cxxv., he laboriously works up to the air-drawn conjecture that Shakespeare is here expressing himself offensively towards his former patron Southampton, now a prisoner in the Tower, and even that Southampton is aimed at in the line about those "who have lived for crime." Equally baseless, of course, is the corollary which would find in Sonnet cxxv. Shakespeare's defence against an accusation of faithlessness towards the man to whom he had written, seven years earlier, in the dedication of *Lucrece*, "The love I dedicate Your Lordship is without end." Nor do we need all this fantastic and unpleasing romance, constructed on the basis of a single obscure phrase, in order to make us accept the theory of which it is supposed to supply further confirmation—namely, that these Sonnets date from 1601.

Turning now from the poems to the person to whom they are believed to have been addressed, this is what we learn of him :—

William Herbert, son of Henry Herbert and his third wife, the celebrated Mary Sidney, had for his tutor as a boy the poet

Samuel Daniel; entered at Oxford in 1593, where he remained for two years; received permission in April 1597, when he was seventeen years old, to live in London, but, as we gather from letters of the period, does not seem to have come up to town until the spring of 1598.

In August 1597, negotiations were conducted by letter between his parents and Lord Burghley with a view to his marriage with Burghley's grand-daughter Bridget Vere, a daughter of the Earl of Oxford. It is true that she was only thirteen, but William Herbert was quite prepared to enter upon the engagement. He was to travel abroad before the marriage. Although his mother, the Countess of Pembroke, perhaps divining her son's too inflammable nature, and therefore wanting to see him married betimes, was much in favour of this project, and although the Earl of Oxford was pleased with the young man and praised his "many good partes," difficulties arose of which we have no record, and the plan came to nothing.

In London, young Herbert lived at Baynard's Castle, close to the Blackfriars Theatre, and may thus have been brought in contact with the players. It is more probable, however, that so brilliant a woman as "Sidney's sister, Pembroke's mother," should have aroused his interest in Shakespeare; and in that case the poet, in all probability, made the acquaintance of this distinguished and discerning patroness of art and artists as early as 1598. Herbert's father, who died soon afterwards, was already an invalid.

It appears that in August 1599 Herbert "followed the camp" at the annual musters, attending her Majesty with two hundred horse, and " swaggering it among the men of war."

He is from the first described as a bad courtier. Rowland Whyte writes of him at this time: " He was much blamed for his cold and weeke Maner of pursuing her Majesties favour, having had soe good steps to lead him unto it. There is want of Spirit and Courage laid to his charge, and that he is a melancholy young man." We may gather from this what fiery devotion every handsome and well-born young man was expected to pay to the elderly Queen. Soon after, however, it appears from a letter from his father to Elizabeth that she must have expressed herself highly satisfied with the young man, and we also learn that he was "exceedingly beloued at Court of all Men." He appears to have been very handsome, and to have possessed all the fascination which so often belongs to an amiable *mauvais sujet*. Clarendon says of him, in the first book of his *History of the Rebellion*, that "he was immoderately given up to women," and that "he indulged himself in pleasures of all kind, almost in all excesses." Clarendon remarks, however, what is of particular interest for us, that the young Pembroke possessed a good deal of self-control: "He retained such a power and jurisdiction over his very appetite, that he was not so much transported with beauty and outward allurements as with those advantages of the mind as manifested an extraordinary wit, and spirit, and knowledge, and administered great pleasure in the conversation. To these he sacrificed himself, his precious time, and much of his fortune."

In November 1599, Herbert had an hour's private audience with Elizabeth. Whyte, who relates this, remarks that he now stands high in the Queen's favour, "but he greatly wants advise." He passed the rest of the winter in the country, suffering from an illness which seems to have taken the form of ague, with incessant headaches.

Tyler is inclined, not without reason, to assign Sonnets xc.-xcvi. to this period. Shakespeare's complaints of his friend's "desertion" may refer to his life at Court; the expressions in Sonnet xci. as to horses, hawks, and hounds, perhaps point to the young man's absorption in sport. The following Sonnets dwell unequivocally upon discreditable rumours as to the friend's life and conduct. Here appears the above-quoted (p. 203) line :—

"Lilies that fester smell far worse than weeds."

Here occurs the couplet :—

"How like Eve's apple doth thy beauty grow,
If thy sweet virtue answer not thy show!"

And, in spite of all the loving forbearance which the poet manifests towards his friend, he seems to imply that the ugly rumours were not unfounded :—

"How sweet and lovely dost thou make the shame,
Which, like a canker in the fragrant rose,
Doth spot the beauty of thy budding name!
O, in what sweets dost thou thy sins enclose!

That tongue that tells the story of thy days,
(Making lascivious comments on thy sport,)
Cannot dispraise but in a kind of praise;
Naming thy name blesses an ill report."

There was an improvement in the health of Herbert's father during the year 1600, yet Lord and Lady Pembroke were absent from London all summer, remaining at their country seat, Wilton. In the month of May, Herbert, accompanied by Sir Charles Danvers, went to Gravesend to pay his respects to Lady Rich and Lady Southampton. This visit proves clearly that there was not, as Tyler's above-mentioned interpretation of certain Sonnets would lead us to assume, any coolness between Herbert and the houses of Essex and Southampton. It is also worth noting that his companion on this excursion was so intimately associated with the chiefs of the malcontent party, that in the following year he had to pay with his life for his share in the rebellion.

In the accounts of a splendid and very much talked-of wedding, between a Lord Herbert and one of the Queen's ladies, which took place at Blackfriars in June 1600, we for the first time come upon William Herbert's name in company with that of the lady who seems to be the heroine of Shakespeare's Sonnets. The bride, Mrs. Ann Russell, was conducted to church by William Herbert and Lord Cobham. After supper there was a masque, in which eight splendidly dressed ladies executed a new and unusual dance. Among these are mentioned Mrs. Fitton, and two of the ladies-in-waiting whose names had shortly before been coupled with that of Essex (Mrs. Southwell and Mrs. Bess Russell). Each had "a skirt of Cloth of Siluer, a Mantell of Carnacion Taffete cast vnder the Arme, and their Haire loose about their Shoulders, curiously knotted and interlaced." The leader of this double quadrille was Mrs. Fitton. She approached the Queen and "woed her to dawnce; her Majestie asked what she was; '*Affection*,' she said. '*Affection!*' said the Queen, '*affection* is false.' Yet her Majestie rose and dawnced."

Later in the year Whyte remarks in his letters that Herbert shows no "disposition to marry"; and we find him in September and October 1600 vigorously training at Greenwich for a Court tournament.

On January 19, 1601, his father's death made William Herbert Earl of Pembroke. Very soon afterwards (the matter is mentioned in a letter from Robert Cecil so early as February 5) he got into deep disgrace over a love affair—evidently that which forms the subject of Shakespeare's Sonnets. He had for some time carried on a secret intrigue with the aforesaid Mary Fitton, a maid-of-honour who stood high in the Queen's good graces; and the secret now came to light. "Mistress Fitton," writes Cecil, "is proved with child, and the Earl of Pembroke, being examined, confesseth a fact, but utterly renounceth all marriage. I fear they will both dwell in the Tower awhile, for the Queen hath vowed to send them thither." In another contemporary letter it is stated that "in that tyme when that M^{res} Fytton was in great fauor . . . and duringe the time yt the Earle of Pembrooke fauord her, she would put off her head tire and tucke vp her clothes and take a large white cloake, and march as though she had bene a man to meete the said Earle out of the Courte."

Mary Fitton gave birth to a still-born son; Pembroke lay for a month in the Fleet Prison, and was banished from Court. He shortly afterwards applied through Cecil for leave to travel abroad. The Queen's displeasure, he says, is "a hell" to him; he hopes the Queen will not carry her resentment so far as to bind him to the country which has now become "hateful to him of all others." The permission to travel seems to have been given and then revoked. In the middle of June he writes that imploring letter to Cecil in which the reference to "her whose Incomparable beauty was the onely sonne of my little world," was designed to touch Elizabeth's hard heart; for Pembroke, it is plain, had now realised that what had offended her Majesty was not so much his intrigue with Mary Fitton as the fact of his having overlooked her own much higher perfections. But the compliments came too late. Elizabeth, as we have already seen in the case of Essex, knew how to make the objects of her resentment suffer in that most sensitive point—the pocket. The "patent of the Forest of Dean," which had been held by the late Lord Pembroke, expired with him, and the son expected, according to use and wont, to have it renewed in his favour; but it was assigned to Pembroke's rival, Sir Edward Winter, and not until seven years later, under James, did Pembroke recover it.

Pembroke continued in disgrace, his renewed applications for permission to travel were persistently refused, and he was ordered to regard himself as banished from Court, and to "keep house in the country." It is this overshadowing of Pembroke's fortunes in 1601 which explains the temporary breaking-off of his relations with Shakespeare in London, indicated by the "Envoy" with which Sonnet cxxvi. ends the series addressed to the Friend.

The close and affectionate relation between them was no doubt revived under James. This appears clearly enough from the Dedication of the First Folio. Let us now cast a rapid glance over the remainder of Pembroke's career.

His father's death placed him in possession of a large fortune, but the irregularity of his life left him seldom free from money embarrassments. In 1604 he married Lady Mary, the seventh daughter of Lord Talbot, and the marriage was celebrated with a tournament. His wife brought him a large property, but it was thought at the time that he paid very dear for it in having to take her into the bargain. The marriage was far from happy.

Pembroke shared the love of literature which had distinguished his mother and his uncle, Sir Philip Sidney. According to Aubrey, he was "the greatest Mæcenas to learned men of any peer of his time or since." Among his "learned" friends were the poets Donne, and Daniel, and Massinger, who was the son of his father's steward. Ben Jonson composed a eulogistic epigram in his honour, as well he might, for every New Year Pembroke sent Ben £20 to buy books with. Inigo Jones is said to have visited Italy at his expense, and was frequently employed by him. Davison's *Poetical Rhapsody* and numerous other books are dedicated to him. Chapman, who was among his intimates, inscribed a sonnet to him at the close of his translation of the *Iliad*. This fact is of particular interest to us, because Chapman (as Professor Minto succeeded in establishing) is clearly the rival poet who paid court to Pembroke, won his goodwill and admiration, and thereby aroused jealousy and melancholy self-criticism in Shakespeare's breast, as we read in Sonnets lxxviii.–lxxxvi.[1]

It is especially on Sonnet lxxxvi. that Minto bases his identification of the rival poet with Chapman. The very opening line, referring to the "proud full sail of his great verse," suggests at once the fourteen-syllable measure in which Chapman translated

[1] I do not find that Mr. G. A. Leigh has succeeded in identifying the rival poet with Tasso (*Westminster Review*, February 1897).

the *Iliad*. Chapman was full of a passionate enthusiasm for the art of poetry, which he lost no opportunity of glorifying; and he laid claim to supernatural inspiration. In the Dedication to his poem *The Shadow of the Night* (1594), he speaks with severe contempt of the presumption of those who "think Skill so mightily pierced with their loves that she should prostitutely show them her secrets, when she will scarcely be looked upon by others but with invocation, fasting, watching—yea, not without having drops of their souls, *like a heavenly familiar.*" Hence Shakespeare's lines—

"Was it his spirit, by spirits taught to write
Above a mortal pitch that struck me dead?"

and the expression—

"He, nor that affable familiar ghost
Which nightly gulls him with intelligence."

After the accession of James, Pembroke immediately took a high position at the new Court. Before the year 1603 was out, he was a Knight of the Garter, and had entertained the King at Wilton. He rose from one high post to another, until in 1615 he became Lord Chamberlain; but he continued to the last the dissipated life of his youth. He devoted large sums of money to the exploration and colonisation of America. Places were named after him in the Bermudas and Virginia. In 1614, moreover, he became a member of the East India Company.

He opposed the Spanish Alliance, and was no friend to the King's foreign policy. He is thought to have instigated in some measure the attack on the Mexico fleet for which Raleigh paid so dear. He was an opponent of Bacon as Lord Chancellor, and in 1621 advocated an inquiry into the charges of corruption which were brought against him; but afterwards, like Southampton, displayed great moderation, and spoke strongly against the proposal to deprive Bacon of his peerage.

He stood by the King's deathbed in March 1625, had a serious illness in 1626, and died in April 1630 "of an apoplexy after a full and cheerful supper." Donne in 1660 published some poems of his among a collection by several other hands. Here is a specimen of his work:—

"Yet when unto our Eyes
Abscense denyes

> Each others sight
> And makes to us a constant night
> When others change to light;
>
> O give no waye to griefe,
> But let beliefe
> Of mutuall loue
> This wonder to the vulgar proue,
> Our bodies, not we, moue.
>
> Let not thy wit beweepe
> Wounds but sense deepe,
> For while we misse,
> By distance, our lipp-ioyning blisse,
> Even then our soules shall kisse."

Tyler has pointed out certain resemblances of thought and expression between this poem and several of Shakespeare's Sonnets (xxii., lxii., xliii., xxvii.). No wonder that Pembroke as a poet should have shown himself a pupil of Shakespeare's.

VI

THE "DARK LADY" OF THE SONNETS— MARY FITTON

IN speaking of *Love's Labour's Lost*, I remarked that it was not difficult to distinguish the original text of the comedy from the portions added and altered during the revision of 1598; and I cited (p. 47) several instances in which the distinction was clear. Especial emphasis was laid on the fact that Biron's (or, as the context shows, Biron-Shakespeare's) rapturous panegyrics of love in the fourth act belong to the later date.

At another place (p. 100) it was pointed out that the two Rosalines of *Love's Labour's Lost* (end of the third act) and of *Romeo and Juliet* (ii. 4) were in all probability drawn from the same model, since she is in both places described as a blonde with black eyes. In the original text of *Love's Labour's Lost* (Act iii.) she is expressly called—

"A whitely wanton with a velvet brow,
With two pitch balls stuck in her face for eyes."

All the more surprising must it seem that during the revision the poet quite obviously had before his eyes another model, repeatedly described as "black," whose dark complexion indeed, so uncommon and un-English that it was apt to be thought ugly, is insisted upon as strongly as that of the "Dark Lady" in the Sonnets. Immediately before Biron bursts forth into his great hymn to Eros, in which Shakespeare so clearly makes him his mouthpiece, the King banters him as to the murky hue of the object of his adoration :—

"*King.* By heaven, thy love is black as ebony.
Biron. Is ebony like her ? O wood divine !
A wife of such wood were felicity.

> O! who can give an oath? where is a book?
> That I may swear beauty doth beauty lack,
> If that she learn not of her eye to look:
> No face is fair, that is not full so black.
>   *King.* O paradox! Black is the badge of hell,
> The hue of dungeons, and the scowl of night;
> And beauty's crest becomes the heavens well."

Biron's answer to this is highly remarkable; for it is exactly what Shakespeare himself says, in Sonnet cxxvii., to the advantage of his dark beauty:—

> "*Biron.* Devils soonest tempt, resembling spirits of light.
> O! if in black my lady's brows be deck'd,
> It mourns, that painting, and usurping hair,
> Should ravish doters with a false aspect;
> And therefore is she born to make black fair.
> Her favour turns the fashion of the days;
> For native blood is counted painting now,
> And therefore red, that would avoid dispraise,
> Paints itself black, to imitate her brow."

The Sonnet runs thus:—

> "In the old age black was not counted fair,
>   Or if it were, it bore not beauty's name;
> But now is black beauty's successive heir,
>   And beauty slander'd with a bastard shame;
> For since each hand hath put on nature's power,
> Fairing the foul with art's false borrow'd face,
> Sweet beauty hath no name, no holy bower,
> But is profan'd, if not lives in disgrace.
> Therefore my mistress' eyes are raven black,
>   Her eyes so suited, and they mourners seem
> At such, who, not born fair, no beauty lack,
>   Slandering creation with a false esteem:
>   Yet so they mourn, becoming of their woe,
>   That every tongue says, beauty should look so."

It appears, then, that the dark beauty in *Love's Labour's Lost* must also have had a living model; and when we observe that the revision, as the title-page tells us, took place when the comedy was to be presented before her Highness at Christmas 1597, and further, that the dark Rosaline in the play is maid-of-honour to a princess who is called, in words strongly suggesting a passing compliment to the Queen, "a gracious moon"—we can scarcely avoid the conclusion that the beautiful brunette must have been one of the Queen's ladies, and that the whole end of the fourth act was addressed to her over the heads of the uninitiated spectators. Who she was, moreover, we can now conjecture with tolerable security. We know quite well which of the Queen's ladies brought Pembroke into disgrace, and we are no less certain that the lady who enthralled Pembroke was the black-eyed brunette whom Shakespeare, in his own words, loved to "distraction" and to "madding fever."

There still exists on the monument of Mary Fitton's mother in Gawsworth Church, in Cheshire, a highly coloured bust of Mary Fitton herself.[1] The colours are so well preserved that it is clear she must have been a marked brunette. It is true that the bust cannot give us a very accurate idea of her appearance in the year 1600, since it was executed in 1626, when she was forty-eight; but so much is certain, that the complexion was dark, the high-piled hair and the large eyes black, the features not beautiful, but the whole form and expression of the face such as might quite well have been highly attractive, and might even have exercised a certain sensual-spiritual fascination. Shakespeare has made it abundantly clear in his Sonnets that the lady was no beauty. He says in Sonnet cxxx., which seems, however, to be mainly a satire upon the conventional similes employed by bad poets:—

> "My mistress' eyes are nothing like the sun;
> Coral is far more red than her lips' red;
> If snow be white, why then her breasts are dun;
> If hairs be wires, black wires grow on her head.
> I have seen roses damask'd, red and white,
> But no such roses see I in her cheeks;
> And in some perfumes is there more delight
> Than in the breath that from my mistress reeks.
> I love to hear her speak, yet well I know
> That music hath a far more pleasing sound:
> I grant I never saw a goddess go;
> My mistress, when she walks, treads on the ground:
> And yet, by Heaven, I think my love as rare
> As any she belied with false compare."

---

[1] Reproduced in Tyler's *Shakespeare's Sonnets*.

Still more interesting is Sonnet cxli., where the poet, oddly enough, declares himself dissatisfied with her voice, which, in the last-quoted Sonnet, he "loved to hear:"—

> "In faith, I do not love thee with mine eyes,
> For they in thee a thousand errors note;
> But 'tis my heart that loves what they despise,
> Who in despite of view is pleas'd to dote.
> Nor are mine ears with thy tongue's tune delighted;
> Nor tender feeling to base touches prone,
> Nor taste, nor smell, desire to be invited
> To any sensual feast with thee alone:
> But my five wits nor my five senses can
> Dissuade one foolish heart from serving thee,
> Who leaves unsway'd the likeness of a man,
> Thy proud heart's slave and vassal wretch to be:
>   Only my plague thus far I count my gain,
>   That she that makes me sin awards me pain."

The Rev. W. A. Harrison has discovered a family tree from which it appears that Mary Fitton, born June 24, 1578, became a maid-of-honour to Elizabeth in 1595, at the age of seventeen. Thus she was nineteen years old when, at the Court festivities of 1597, Shakespeare's company acted *Love's Labour's Lost*, with the panegyric of the dark beauty, Rosaline. She must have made the acquaintance of the poet and player, then thirty-three years old, at earlier Court entertainments. Who can doubt that it was she, with her high position and daring spirit, who made the first advances?

That the Dark Lady did not live with Shakespeare appears clearly enough in the Sonnets—for instance, in Sonnet cxliv. ("but being both from me"). It may be gathered from Sonnet cli., with the expressions "triumphant prize," "proud of this pride," that she was greatly his superior in rank and station, so that her conquest for some time filled him with a sense of triumph. Tyler even holds, no doubt rightly, that there is an actual allusion to her name in Sonnet cli., which, as a whole, abounds in such daring equivoques as would be impossible in modern poetry. Puns upon names were much in vogue among the verse-writers of that period—Sonnets cxxxv., cxxxvi., and cxliii., for example, are for ever playing on "Will" and "will." The similarity of sound between the name *Fitton* and *fit one* was thought so interesting and taken so seriously that it was emphasised even in the inscription on the family monument, which ends with the lines :—

> " Whose sovle's and body's beavties sentence them,
> *Fittons*, to weare a heavenly Diadem."

Shakespeare seems to have had the same word-play in his mind, though to less pious purpose, when he wrote in Sonnet cli. :—

> " Flesh stays no farther reason;
> But rising *at thy name* doth point out thee
> As his triumphant prize."

Similarly, in one of his Sonnets to Stella (Lady Penelope Rich), Sir Philip Sidney had made use of a pun upon the word *rich* in order to express his contempt for her husband.

It has been thought surprising that in Sonnet clii., in which Shakespeare calls himself forsworn because he loves his lady although married to another, he also states expressly that she too is married, calling her " twice forsworn," since she has not only broken her " bed-vow," but broken her " new faith " to Shakespeare himself. It seemed difficult to reconcile this with the fact that Mrs. Fitton (" Mistress " in those days being applicable to unmarried no less than to married women) was always called by her father's name. From a letter, however, addressed by her father to Sir Robert Cecil on January 29, 1599 (Tyler, p. 86), it is inferred that she had already been married at the age of sixteen. Performed, perhaps, by some accommodating cleric, and without the parents' consent, the ceremony would not be entirely valid, and measures would be taken as quickly as possible to have it annulled. Thus, although she figured at Court as a maid-of-honour, and did not bear her husband's name, she was no inexperienced girl at the time when she made Shakespeare's acquaintance.

From the genealogical tree preserved in the Fitton family it appears that her first husband was a Captain Lougher; and from this document, confirmed by the will of her grand-uncle, Sir Francis Fitton, we learn that (probably in 1607) she was married a second time to a Captain Polwheele. It is further noted in the genealogical table that she "had one bastard by Wm. E. of Pembroke, and two bastards by Sir Richard Leveson, Kt." The picture suggested by these curt data cannot be said to conflict in any way with the portrait painted in the Sonnets. As, however, another version of the pedigree makes Captain Polwheele her first husband, the question of her different marriages remains somewhat obscure.

The Dark Lady must have been a woman in the extremest sense of the word, a daughter of Eve, alluring, ensnaring, greedy of conquest, mendacious and faithless, born to deal out rapture and torment with both hands, the very woman to set in vibration every chord in a poet's soul.

There can be no reasonable doubt that in the early days of his relation with the young maid-of-honour, Shakespeare felt himself a favourite of fortune, intoxicated with love and happiness, exalted above his station, honoured and enriched. She must at first have been to him what Maria Fiammetta, the natural daughter of a king, was to Boccaccio. She must have brought a breath from a higher world, an aroma of aristocratic womanhood, into his life. He must have admired her wit, her presence of mind and her daring, her capricious fancy and her quickness of retort. He must have studied, enjoyed, and adored in her—and that in the closest intimacy—the well-bred ease, the sportive coquetry, the security, elegance, and gaiety of the emancipated lady. Who can tell how much of her personality has been transferred to his brilliant young Beatrices and Rosalinds?

First and foremost he must have owed to her the rapture of feeling his vitality intensified—a main element in the happiness which, in the first years of their communion, finds expression in the sparkling love-comedies we have just reviewed. Let it not be objected that the Sonnets do not dwell upon this happiness. The Sonnets date from the period of storm and stress, when he had ascertained what at first, no doubt, he had but vaguely suspected, that his mistress had ensnared his friend; and in composing them he no doubt antedated many of the passionate and distracted moods which overwhelmed him at the crisis, when he not only realised the fact of their intrigue, but saw it dragged to the light of day. He then felt as though, doubly betrayed, he had irrevocably lost them both. Thus the picture of his mistress drawn in the Sonnets shows her, not as she appeared to him in earlier years, but as he saw her during this later period.

Yet he also depicts moments, and even hours, when his whole nature must have been lapped in tenderness and harmony. The scene, for instance, so melodiously portrayed in Sonnet cxxviii. is steeped in an atmosphere of happy love—the scene in which, seated at the virginals, the lady, whom the poet addresses as "my music," lets her delicate aristocratic fingers wander over the keys, enchanting with their concord the listener who longs to press her fingers and her lips to his. He envies the keys that "kiss the tender inward of her hand," and concludes:—

> "Since saucy jacks so happy are in this,
> Give them thy fingers, me thy lips to kiss."

It is only natural, however, that the morbidly passionate, complaining, and accusing Sonnets should be in the majority.

Again and again he reverts to her faithlessness and laxity of conduct. In Sonnet cxxxvii. he speaks of his love as "anchored in the bay where all men ride." Sonnet cxxxviii. begins:—

> "When my love swears that she is made of truth,
> I do believe her, though I know she lies."

And in Sonnet clii. he reproaches himself with having sworn a host of false oaths in swearing to her good qualities:—

> "But why of two oaths' breach do I accuse thee,
> When I break twenty? I am perjur'd most;
> For all my vows are oaths but to misuse thee,
> And all my honest faith in thee is lost:
> For I have sworn deep oaths of thy deep kindness,
> Oaths of thy love, thy truth, thy constancy;
> And, to enlighten thee, gave eyes to blindness,
> Or made them swear against the thing they see."

In Sonnet cxxxix. he depicts her as carrying her thirst for admiration to such a pitch of wantonness that even in his presence she could not refrain from coquetting on every hand:—

> "Tell me thou lov'st elsewhere; but in my sight,
> Dear heart, forbear to glance thine eye aside:
> What need'st thou wound with cunning, when thy might
> Is more than my o'erpress'd defence can 'bide?"

She cruelly abuses her witchery over him. She is as tyrannical, he says in Sonnet cxxxi., "as those whose beauties proudly make them cruel," well-knowing that to his "dear-doting heart" she is "the finest and most precious jewel." There is actual magic in the power she exerts over him. He does not understand it himself, and exclaims in Sonnet cl. :—

> "Whence hast thou this becoming of things ill,
> That in the very refuse of thy deeds
> There is such strength and warrantise of skill,
> That in my mind thy worst all best exceeds?"

No French poet of the eighteen-thirties, not even Musset himself, has given more passionate utterance than Shakespeare to the fever and agony and distraction of love. See, for instance, Sonnet cxlvii. :—

> "My love is as a fever, longing still
> For that which longer nurseth the disease:
> Feeding on that which doth preserve the ill,
> The uncertain-sickly appetite to please.
> My reason, the physician to my love,
> Angry that his prescriptions are not kept,
> Hath left me, and I desperate now approve
> Desire is death, which physic did except.
> Past cure I am, now reason is past care,
> And frantic-mad with evermore unrest:
> My thoughts and my discourse as madmen's are,
> At random from the truth vainly express'd;
> For I have sworn thee fair, and thought thee bright,
> Who art as black as hell, as dark as night."

He depicts himself as a lover frenzied with passion. His eyes are dimmed with vigils and with tears. He no longer understands either himself or the world: "If that is fair whereon his false eyes dote, What means the world to say it is not so?" If it is not fair, then his love proves that a lover's eye is less trustworthy than that of the indifferent world (Sonnet cxlviii.).

And yet he well knows the seat of the witchery by which she holds him in thrall. It lies in the glow and expression of her exquisite "raven black" eyes (Sonnets cxxvii. and cxxxix.). He loves her soulful eyes, which, knowing the torments her disdain inflicts upon him—

> "Have put on black, and loving mourners be,
> Looking with pretty ruth upon my pain."
> —Sonnet cxxxii.

THE DARK LADY

Young as she is, her nature is all compounded of passion and will; she is ungovernable in her caprices, born for conquest and for self-surrender.

While we can guess that towards Shakespeare she made the first advances, we know that she did so in the case of his friend. In more than one sonnet she is expressly spoken of as "wooing him."[1] In Sonnet cxliii. Shakespeare uses an image which, in all its homeliness, is exceedingly graphic:—

> "Lo! as a careful housewife runs to catch
> One of her feather'd creatures broke away,
> Sets down her babe, and makes all swift despatch
> In pursuit of the thing she would have stay;
> Whilst her neglected child holds her in chase,
> Cries to catch her whose busy care is bent
> To follow that which flies before her face,
> Not prizing her poor infant's discontent:
> So runn'st thou after that which flies from thee,
> Whilst I, thy babe, chase thee afar behind;
> But if thou catch thy hope, turn back to me,
> And play the mother's part, kiss me, be kind:
> So will I pray that thou may'st have thy *Will*,
> If thou turn back, and my loud crying still."

The tenderness of feeling here apparent is characteristic of the poet's whole attitude of mind in this dual relation. Even when he cannot acquit his friend of all guilt, even when he mournfully upbraids him with having robbed the poor man of his one lamb, his chief concern is always lest any estrangement should arise between his friend and himself. See, for instance, the exquisitely melodious Sonnet xl.:—

> "Take all my loves, my love, yea, take them all:
> What hast thou then more than thou hadst before?
> No love, my love, that thou may'st true love call:
> All mine was thine before thou had'st this more.
> . . . .
> I do forgive thy robbery, gentle thief,
> Although thou steal thee all my poverty."

Shakespeare seems to have remembered, from time to time, that it was he himself who had brought these two together.

[1] "And when a woman *woos*, what woman's son will sourly leave her?" (Sonnet xli.). "*Wooing* his purity with her foul pride" (Sonnet cxliv.).

Sonnet cxxxiv. indicates, perhaps, that Pembroke first made the acquaintance of the dangerous fair one while acting as an emissary on the poet's behalf.[1] It is quite clear that Shakespeare consented to share her favour with his friend; his main anxiety was for the preservation of their friendship. Therefore we read (Sonnet cxxxiv.):—

> "So, now I have confess'd that he is thine,
> And I myself am mortgag'd to thy will,
> Myself I'll forfeit, so that other mine
> Thou wilt restore, to be my comfort still."

Noteworthy in this respect is Sonnet cxxxv., which plays upon the identity of Shakespeare's Christian name with Pembroke's:—

> "Whoever hath her wish, thou hast thy *Will*,
> And *Will* to boot, and *Will* in overplus:
> More than enough am I, that vex thee still,
> To thy sweet will making addition thus."

He proceeds in a strain of affectionate humility:—

> "The sea, all water, yet receives rain still,
> And in abundance addeth to his store;
> So thou, being rich in *Will*, add to thy *Will*
> One will of mine, to make thy large *Will* more."

He tries, by the aid of a sort of sophistry or word-juggling, to console himself with the reflection that when she speaks his name she includes both persons in one word:—

> "Think all but one, and me in that one *Will*."

The same tone of sentiment runs through the moving Sonnet xlii., which begins:—

> "That thou hast her, it is not all my grief,
> And yet it may be said, I loved her dearly;
> That she hath thee, is of my wailing chief,
> A loss in love that touches me more nearly."

---

[1] "Thou usurer, that put'st forth all to use
And sue a friend, came debtor for my sake;
So him I lose through my unkind abuse."

It closes with this somewhat vapid conceit:—

"But here's the joy: my friend and I are one;
Sweet flattery! then she loves but me alone."

All these expressions, taken together, point not only to the enormous value which Shakespeare attached to the young Pembroke's friendship, but also to the sensual and spiritual attraction which, in spite of everything, his fickle mistress continued to possess for him.

It is not impossible that a passage in Ben Jonson's *Bartholomew Fair* (1614) may contain a satirical allusion to the relation portrayed in the Sonnets (published in 1609). In act v. sc. 3 there is presented a puppet-show setting forth "The ancient modern history of Hero and Leander, otherwise called the Touchstone of true Love, with as true a trial of Friendship between Damon and Pythias, two faithful friends o' the Bankside." Hero is "a wench o' the Bankside," and Leander swims across the Thames to her. Damon and Pythias meet at her lodging, and abuse each other most violently when they find that they have but one love, only to finish up as the best friends in the world.[1]

It has thus been established, as clearly as anything of this kind can be established without the direct evidence of contemporaries, that Mrs. Mary Fitton and the Dark Lady were one and the same person. Some readers, perhaps, may still doubt the possibility of conceiving that an actor like Shakespeare could form any close intimacy with a woman of such high position as a maid-of-honour to the Queen. This objection is practically removed by a piece of evidence which pretty clearly brings her into connection with Shakespeare's company. A little book by the clown of the company, William Kemp, published in 1600

---

[1] "*Damon.* Whore-master in thy face;
Thou hast lain with her thyself, I'll prove it in this place.
"*Leatherhead.* They are whore-masters both, sir, that's a plain case.
"*Pythias.* Thou lie like a rogue.
"*Leatherhead.* Do I lie like a rogue?
"*Pythias.* A pimp and a scab.
"*Leatherhead.* A pimp and a scab!
I say, between you *you have both but one drab*.
"*Pythias and Damon.* Come, now we'll go together to breakfast to Hero.
"*Leatherhead.* Thus, gentles, you perceive without any denial
'Twixt Damon and Pythias here friendship's true trial."

under the title of "Nine Daies Wonder," was, as Mr. W. A. Harrison has shown, almost certainly dedicated to her. The actual wording of the dedication is to "Mistris Anne Fitton, Mayde of Honour to the most sacred Mayde, Royal Queene Elisabeth." But it is absolutely certain that neither in 1600 nor in the previous year was there any Anne Fitton among Elizabeth's maids-of-honour. Kemp must, therefore, have been mistaken as to the Christian name of his patroness, or the printer must have misread the name Marie and converted it into Anne, an error to which the handwriting of the period might easily give rise.

This little book gives us a most interesting glimpse into the English life of that age.

The most important duty of the clown was not to appear in the play itself, but to sing and dance his jig at the end of it, even after a tragedy, in order to soften the painful impression. The common spectator never went home without having seen this afterpiece, which must have resembled the comic "turns" of our variety-shows. Kemp's jig of *The Kitchen-Stuff Woman*, for instance, was a screaming farrago of rude verses, some spoken, others sung, of good and bad witticisms, of extravagant acting and dancing. It is of such a performance that Hamlet is thinking when he says of Polonius: "He's for a jig, or a tale of bawdry, or he sleeps."

As the acknowledged master of his time in the art of comic dancing, Kemp was immoderately loved and admired. He paid professional visits to all the German and Italian courts, and was even summoned to dance his Morrice Dance before the Emperor Rudolf himself at Augsburg. It was in his youth that he undertook the nine days' dance from London to Norwich which he describes in his book.

He started at seven o'clock in the morning from in front of the Lord Mayor's house, and half London was astir to see the beginning of the great exploit. His suite consisted of his "taberer," his servant, and an "overseer" or umpire to see that everything was performed according to promise. The journey was almost as trying to the "taberer" as to Kemp, for he had his drum hanging over his left arm and held his flageolet in his left hand while he beat the drum with his right. Kemp himself, on this occasion, contributed nothing to the music except the sound of the bells which were attached to his gaiters.

He reached Romford on the first day, but was so exhausted that he had to rest for two days. The people of Stratford-Langton, between London and Romford, had got up a bear-baiting show in his honour, knowing "how well he loved the sport"; but the crowd which had gathered to see him was so great that he himself only succeeded in hearing the bear roar and the dogs howl. On the second day he strained his hip, but cured the strain by dancing. At Burntwood such a crowd had gathered to see him that he could scarcely make his way to the tavern. There, as he relates, two cut-purses were caught in the act, who had followed with the crowd from London. They declared that they had laid a wager upon the dance, but Kemp recognised one of them as a noted thief whom he had seen tied to a post in the theatre. Next day he reached Chelmsford, but here the crowd which had accompanied him from London had dwindled away to a couple of hundred people.

In Norwich the city waits received him in the open market-place with an official concert in the presence of thousands. He was the guest of the town and entertained at its expense, received handsome presents from the mayor, and was admitted to the Guild of Merchant Venturers, being thereby assured a share in their yearly income, to the amount of forty shillings. The very buskins in which he had performed his dance were nailed to the wall in the Norwich Guild Hall and preserved in perpetual memory of the exploit.

So popular an artist as this must of course have felt himself at least Shakespeare's equal. He certainly assumed the right to address one of her Majesty's Maids-of-Honour with no slight familiarity. The tone in which he dedicates this catchpenny performance to Mrs. Fitton offers a remarkable contrast to the profoundly respectful tone in which professional authors couch their dedications to their noble patrons or patronesses:—

"In the waine of my little wit I am forst to desire your protection, else every Ballad-singer will proclaime me bankrupt of honesty. . . . To shew my duety to your honourable selfe, whose favours (among other bountifull friends) make me (dispight this sad world) iudge my hert Corke and my heeles feathers, so that me thinkes I could fly to Rome (at least hop to Rome, as the old Prouerb is) with a Morter on my head."

The free and confidential style of this dedication not only proves that one of the actor caste could approach a great lady like Mrs. Fitton without a too strict observance of the distance between them, but also affords conclusive proof that that emancipated young lady was intimately acquainted with members of the very company to which Shakespeare belonged.

VII

PLATONISM IN SHAKESPEARE'S AND MICHAEL ANGELO'S SONNETS—THE TECHNIQUE OF THE SONNETS

THE fact that the person to whom Shakespeare's Sonnets are dedicated is simply entitled "Mr. W. H." long served to divert attention from William Herbert, as it was thought that it would have been an impossible impertinence thus to address, without his title, a nobleman like the Earl of Pembroke. To us it is clear that this form of address was adopted precisely in order that Pembroke might not be exhibited to the great public as the hero of the conflict darkly adumbrated in the Sonnets. They were not, indeed, written quite without an eye to publication, as is proved by the poet's promises that they are to immortalise the memory of his friend's beauty. But it was not Shakespeare himself who gave them to the press, and bookseller Thorpe must have known very well that Lord Pembroke would not care to see himself unequivocally designated as the lover of the Dark Lady and the poet's favoured rival, especially as that dramatic episode of his youth ended in a manner which it can scarcely have been pleasant to recall.

The modern reader who takes up the Sonnets with no special knowledge of the Renaissance, its tone of feeling, its relation to Greek antiquity, its conventions and its poetic style, finds nothing in them more surprising than the language of love in which the poet addresses his young friend, the positively erotic passion for a masculine personality which here finds utterance. The friend is currently addressed as "my love." Sometimes it is stated in so many words that in the eyes of his admirer the friend combines the charms of man and woman ; for instance, in Sonnet xx. :—

"A woman's face, with Nature's own hand painted,
Hast thou, the master-mistress of my passion."

This Sonnet ends with a playful lament that the friend had not been born of the opposite sex; yet such is the warmth of expression in other Sonnets that one very well understands how the critics of last century supposed them to be addressed to a woman.[1]

This tone, however, is so characteristic a fashion of the age, that a number of writers, and especially those who have gone most deeply into contemporary English and Italian literature,[2] have found in it, and in other traits of mere convention, an argument for holding the circumstances set forth to be in the main imaginary, and denying to the Sonnets all direct autobiographical value.

It has been insisted that love for a beautiful youth, which the study of Plato had presented to the men of the Renaissance in its most attractive light, was a standing theme among English poets of that age, who, moreover, as in Shakespeare's case, were wont to praise the beauty of their friend above that of their mistress. The woman, too, as in this case, often enters as a disturbing element into the relation. It was an accepted part of the convention that the poet should represent himself as withered and wrinkled, whatever his real age might be; Shakespeare does so again and again, though he was at most thirty-seven. Finally, it was quite in accordance with use and wont that the fair youth should be exhorted to marry, so that his beauty might not die with him. Shakespeare had already placed such exhortations in the mouth of the Goddess of Love in *Venus and Adonis.*

Dr. Adolf Hansen, in his Danish translation of the Sonnets, has pointed out several other impersonal traits. Some of the weaker Sonnets, with their "wire-drawn and complicated imagery" (Sonnets xxiv., xlvi., xlvii.), so clearly bear the stamp of the age that they cannot be regarded as personally characteristic of Shakespeare; while others are such evident imitations that it is

---

[1] For instance, in Sonnet xxiii. :—

"O let my books be then the eloquence
And dumb presagers of my speaking breast,
Who plead for love, and look for recompense."

And in Sonnet xxvi. :—

"Lord of my love, to whom in vassalage
Thy merit hath my duty strongly knit."

[2] Such as Delius and Elze in Germany and Schück in Sweden.

impossible to accept them as individual utterances. Thus the theme of Sonnets xlvi. and xlvii. is precisely that of Watson's twentieth Sonnet in *The Tears of Fancie ;* Sonnets xviii. and xix. lead up to the same thought as that of Sonnet xxxix. in Daniel's *Delia ;* and Sonnets lv. and lxxxi. treat of precisely the same matter as Sonnet lxix. of Spenser's *Amoretti.* Finally, the story of the two friends, one of whom robs the other of his mistress, had already appeared in Lyly's *Euphues.*

All this is true, and yet there is no reasonable ground for doubting that the Sonnets stand in pretty close relation to actual facts.

The age, indeed, determines the tone, the colouring, of the expressions in which friendship clothes itself. In Germany and Denmark, at the end of the eighteenth century, friendship was a sentimental enthusiasm, just as in England and Italy during the sixteenth century it took the form of platonic love. We can clearly discern, however, that the different methods of expression answered to corresponding shades of difference in the emotion itself. The men of the Renaissance gave themselves up to an adoration of friendship and of their friend which is now unknown, except in circles where a perverted sexuality prevails. Montaigne's friendship for Estienne de la Boëtie, and Languet's passionate tenderness for the youthful Philip Sidney, are cases in point. Sir Thomas Browne writes in his *Religio Medici* (1642): "I never yet cast a true affection on a woman; but I have loved my friend as I do virtue, my soul, my God. . . . I love my friend before myself, and yet, methinks, I do not love him enough: some few months hence my multiplied affection will make me believe I have not loved him at all. When I am from him, I am dead till I be with him; when I am with him, I am not satisfied, but would still be nearer him." But the most remarkable example of a frenzied friendship in Renaissance culture and poetry is undoubtedly to be found in Michael Angelo's letters and sonnets.

Michael Angelo's relation to Messer Tommaso de' Cavalieri presents the most interesting parallel to the attitude which Shakespeare adopted towards William Herbert. We find the same expressions of passionate love from the older to the younger man; but here it is still more unquestionably certain that we have not to do with mere poetical figures of speech, since the letters are not a whit less ardent and enthusiastic than the sonnets. The expressions in the sonnets are sometimes so warm that Michael Angelo's nephew, in his edition of them, altered the word *Signiore* into *Signora*, and these poems, like Shakespeare's, were for some time supposed to have been addressed to a woman.[1]

On January 1, 1533, Michael Angelo, then fifty-seven years old, writes from Florence to Tommaso de' Cavalieri, a youth of noble Roman family, who afterwards became his favourite pupil: "If I do not possess the art of navigating the sea of your potent genius, that genius will nevertheless excuse me, and neither despise my inequality, nor demand of me that which I have it not in me to give; since that which stands alone in everything can in nothing find its counterpart. Wherefore your lordship, *the only light in our age vouchsafed to this world*, having no equal or peer, cannot find satisfaction in the work of any other hand. If, therefore, this or that in the works which I hope and promise to execute should happen to please you, I should call that work, not good, but fortunate. And if I should ever feel assured that—as has been reported to me—I have given your lordship satisfaction in one thing or another, I will make a gift to you of my present and of all that the future may bring me; and it will be a great pain to me to be unable to recall the past, in order to serve you so much the longer, instead of having only the future, which cannot be long, since I am all too old. There is nothing more left for me to say. Read my heart and not my letter, for my pen cannot approach the expression of my good will." [2]

Cavalieri writes to Michael Angelo that he regards himself as born anew since he has come to know the Master; who replies, "I for my part should regard myself as not born, born dead, or deserted by heaven and earth, if your letters had not brought me the persuasion that your lordship accepts with favour certain of my works." And in a letter of the following summer to Sebastian del Piombo, he sends a greeting to Messer Tommaso, with the

---

[1] Ludwig von Scheffler: *Michel Angelo. Eine Renaissancestudie*, 1892.
[2] "E se io non àrò l'arte del navicare per l'onde del mare del vostro valoroso ingegno, quello mi scuserà, nè si sdegnierà del mio disaguagliarsigli, nè desiderrà da me quello che in me non è: perchè chi è solo in ogni cosa, in cosa alcuna non può aver compagni. Però la vostra Signoria, luce del secol nostro unica al mondo, non puo sodisfarsi di opera d'alcuno altro, non avendo pari nè simile à sè," &c.

words: "I believe *I should instantly fall down dead* if he were no longer in my thoughts."[1]

Michael Angelo plays upon his friend's surname as Shakespeare plays upon his friend's Christian name. These are the last lines of the thirty-first sonnet :—

> "Se vint' e pres' i' debb' esser beato,
> Meraviglia non è se, nud' e solo,
> Resto prigion d'un *Cavalier* armato"

> "If only chains and bands can make me blest,
> No marvel if alone and bare I go
> An armed knight's captive and slave confessed."
>
> (*J. A. Symonds.*)

In other sonnets the tone is no less passionate than Shakespeare's—take, for example, the twenty-second :—

> "More tenderly perchance than is my due,
> Your spirit sees into my heart, where rise
> The flames of holy worship, nor denies
> The grace reserved for those who humbly sue.
> Oh blessèd day when you at last are mine!
> Let time stand still, and let noon's chariot stay;
> Fixed be that moment on the dial of heaven!
> That I may clasp and keep, by grace divine—
> Clasp in these yearning arms and keep for aye
> My heart's loved lord to me desertless given."[2]
>
> (*J. A. Symonds.*)

In comparison with Cavalieri, Michael Angelo could with justice call himself old. Some critics, on the other hand, have seen in the fact that Shakespeare was not really old at the time when the Sonnets were written, a proof of their conventional and unreal character. But this is to overlook the relativity of the term. As compared with a youth of eighteen, Shakespeare was in effect old, with his sixteen additional years and all his ex-

---

[1] "E io non nato, o vero nato morto mi reputerei, e direi in disgrazia del cielo e della terra, se per la vostra non avessi visto e creduto vostra Signoria accettare volentieri alcune delle opere mie." "Avete data la copia de' sopradetti Madrigali a messer Tomaso . . . che se m'uscissi della mente, credo che súbito cascherei morto."

[2] "Accio ch' i' abbi, e non già per mie merto,
Il desiato mio dolce signiore
Per sempre nell' indegnie e pronte braccia."

perience of life. And if we are right in assigning Sonnets lxiii. and lxxiii. to the year 1600 or 1601, Shakespeare had then reached the age of thirty-seven, an age at which (among his contemporaries) Drayton in his *Idea* dwells quite in the same spirit upon the wrinkles of age in his face, and at which, as Tyler has very aptly pointed out, Byron in his swan-song uses expressions about himself which might have been copied from Shakespeare's seventy-third Sonnet. Shakespeare says:—

> "That time of year thou mayst in me behold
> When *yellow leaves*, or none, or few, do hang
> Upon those boughs which shake against the cold
> Bare ruin'd choirs, where late the sweet birds sang."

Byron thus expresses himself:—

> "My days are in *the yellow leaf*,[1]
> The flowers and fruits of love are gone,
> The worm, the canker and the grief
> Are mine alone."

In Shakespeare we read:—

> "In me thou seest *the glowing of such fire*
> That on the ashes of his youth doth lie
> As the *death-bed* whereon it must expire,
> Consum'd with that which it was nourish'd by."

Byron's words are:—

> "*The fire that on my bosom preys*
> Is lone as some volcanic isle;
> No torch is kindled at its blaze—
> *A funeral pile.*"

Thus both poets liken themselves, at this comparatively early age, to the wintry woods with their yellowing leaves, and without blossom, fruit, or the song of birds; and both compare the fire which still glows in their soul to a solitary flame which finds no nourishment from without. The ashes of my youth become its death-bed, says Shakespeare. They are a funeral pile, says Byron.

[1] This line, however, is obviously suggested by the famous passage in *Macbeth* (Act v.)—

> "My way of life
> Is fall'n into the sere, the yellow leaf."

Nor is it possible to conclude, as Schück does, from the conventional style of the first seventeen Sonnets—for instance, from their almost verbal identity with a passage in Sidney's *Arcadia*— that they are quite devoid of relation to the poet's own life. We have seen that Pembroke's youth, which has been thought to render it improbable that these exhortations to marriage should have been addressed to him, in reality proves nothing to the purpose, since we have direct evidence of the fact that when he was only seventeen his parents were negotiating a marriage between him and Bridget Vere. Subsequently, when Pembroke had made the acquaintance of Mary Fitton, not only his mother but Shakespeare himself had a direct interest in seeing him married.

In short, the elements of temporary fashion and convention which appear in the Sonnets in no way prove that they were not genuine expressions of the poet's actual feelings.

They lay bare to us a side of his character which does not appear in the plays. We see in him an emotional nature with a passionate bent towards self-surrender in love and idolatry, and with a corresponding, though less excessive, yearning to be loved.

We learn from the Sonnets to what a degree Shakespeare was oppressed and tormented by his sense of the contempt in which the actor's calling was held. The scorn of ancient Rome for the mountebank, the horror of ancient Judea for whoever disguised himself in the garments of the other sex, and finally the age-old hatred of Christianity for theatres and all the temptations that follow in their train—all these habits of thought had been handed down from generation to generation, and, as Puritanism grew in strength and gained the upper hand, had begotten a contemptuous tone of public opinion under which so sensitive a nature as Shakespeare's could not but suffer keenly. He was not regarded as a poet who now and then acted, but as an actor who now and then wrote plays. It was a pain to him to feel that he belonged to a caste which had no civic status. Hence his complaint, in Sonnet xxix., of being "in disgrace with fortune and men's eyes." Hence, in Sonnet xxxvi., his assurance to his friend that he will not obtrude on others the fact of their friendship :—

> "I may not evermore acknowledge thee,
>   Lest my bewailèd guilt should do thee shame :

> Nor thou with public kindness honour me,
> Unless thou take that honour from thy name:
> But do not so; I love thee in such sort,
> As, thou being mine, mine is thy good report."

The bitter complaint in Sonnet lxxii. seems rather to refer to the writer's situation as a dramatist:—

> "For I am shamed by that which I bring forth,
> And so should you, to love things nothing worth."

The melancholy which fills Sonnet cx. is occasioned by the writer's profession and his nature as a poet and artist:—

> "Alas! 'tis true, I have gone here and there,
> And made myself a motley to the view;
> Gor'd mine own thoughts, sold cheap what is most dear,
> Made old offences of affections new:
> Most true it is, that I have look'd on truth
> Askance and strangely; but, by all above,
> These blenches gave my heart another youth,
> And worse essays prov'd thee my best of love."

Hence, finally, his reproach to Fortune, in Sonnet cxi., that she did not "better for his life provide Than public means which public manners breeds":—

> "Thence comes it that my name receives a brand;
> And almost thence my nature is subdu'd
> To what it works in, like the dyer's hand."

We must bear in mind this continual writhing under the prejudice against his calling and his art, and this indignation at the injustice of the attitude adopted towards them by a great part of the middle classes, if we would understand the high pressure of Shakespeare's feelings towards the noble youth who had approached him full of the art-loving traditions of the aristocracy, and the burning enthusiasm of the young for intellectual superiority. William Herbert, with his beauty and his personal charm, must have come to him like a very angel of light, a messenger from a higher world than that in which his lot was cast. He was a living witness to the fact that Shakespeare was not condemned to seek the applause of the multitude alone, but could win the favour of the noblest in the land, and was not

IDOLATRY IN FRIENDSHIP

excluded from a deep and almost passionate friendship which placed him on an equal footing with the bearer of an ancient name. Pembroke's great beauty no doubt made a deep impression upon the beauty-lover in Shakespeare's soul. It is very probable, too, that the young aristocrat, according to the fashion of the times, made the poet his debtor for solider benefactions than mere friendship; and Shakespeare must thus have felt doubly painful the situation in which he was placed by the intrigue between his mistress and his friend.[1]

In any case, the affection with which Pembroke inspired Shakespeare—the passionate attachment, leading even to jealousy of other poets admired by the young nobleman—had not only a vividness, but an erotic fervour such as we never find in our century manifested between man and man. Note such an expression as this in Sonnet cx. :—

> "Then give me welcome, next my heaven the best,
> Even to thy pure and most most loving breast."

This exactly corresponds to Michael Angelo's recently-quoted desire to "clasp in his yearning arms his heart's loved lord." Or observe such a line as this in Sonnet lxxv. :—

> "So are you to my thoughts as food to life."

We have here an exact counterpart to the following expressions in a letter from Michael Angelo to Cavalieri, dated July 1533 : "I would far rather forget the food on which I live, which wretchedly sustains the body alone, than your name, which sustains both body and soul, filling both with such happiness that I can feel neither care nor fear of death while I have it in my memory."[2]

The passionate fervour of this friendship on the Platonic model is accompanied in Shakespeare, as in Michael Angelo, by a submissiveness on the part of the elder friend towards the younger, which, in these two supreme geniuses, affects the modern reader

---

[1] Several passages in the Sonnets suggest that Pembroke must have conferred substantial gifts upon Shakespeare—for example, that expression "wealth" in Sonnet xxxvii., "your bounty" in Sonnet liii., and "your own dear-purchased right" in Sonnet cxvii.

[2] "Anzi posso prima dimenticare il cibo di ch'io vivo, che nutrisce solo il corpo infelicemente, che il nome vostro, che nutrisce il corpo e l'anima, riempiendo l'uno e l'altro di tanta dolcezza, che nè noia nè timor di morte, mentre la memoria mi vi serba, posso sentire."

painfully. Each had put off every shred of pride in relation to his idolised young friend. How strange it seems to find Shakespeare calling himself young Herbert's "slave," and assuring him that his time, more precious than that of any other man then living, is of no value, so that his friend may let him wait or summon him to his side as his caprice and fancy dictate. In Sonnet lviii. he speaks of "that God who made me first your slave." Sonnet lvii. runs thus:—

> "Being *your slave*, what should I do but tend
> Upon the hours and times of your desire?
> I have no precious time at all to spend,
> Nor services to do, till you require.
> Nor dare I chide the world-without-end hour,
> Whilst I, my sovereign, watch the clock for you,
> Nor think the bitterness of absence sour,
> When you have bid your servant once adieu;
> Nor dare I question with my jealous thought,
> Where you may be, or your affairs suppose;
> But, like a sad slave, stay and think of nought,
> Save, where you are how happy you make those."

Just as Michael Angelo spoke to Cavalieri of his works as though they were scarcely worth his friend's notice, so does Shakespeare sometimes speak of his verses. In Sonnet xxxii. he begs his friends to "re-survey" them when he is dead:—

> "And though they be outstripp'd by every pen,
> Reserve them for my love, not for their rhyme,
> Exceeded by the height of happier men."

This humility becomes quite despicable when a breach is threatened between the friends. Shakespeare then repeatedly promises so to blacken himself that his friend shall reap, not shame, but honour, from his faithlessness. In Sonnet lxxxviii.:—

> "With mine own weakness being best acquainted,
> Upon thy part I can set down a story
> Of faults concealed wherein I am attainted,
> That thou, in losing me, shalt win much glory."

Sonnet lxxxix. is still more strongly worded:—

> "Thou canst not, love, disgrace me half so ill,
> To set a form upon desirèd change,

As I'll myself disgrace : knowing thy will,
I will acquaintance strangle, and look strange ;
Be absent from thy walks ; and in my tongue
Thy sweet-belovèd name no more shall dwell,
Lest I (too much profane) should do it wrong,
And haply of our old acquaintance tell.
  For thee, against myself I'll vow debate,
  For I must ne'er love him whom thou dost hate."

We are positively surprised when, in a single passage, in Sonnet lxii., we come upon a forcible expression of self-love ; but it does not extend beyond the first half of the Sonnet ; in the second half this self-love is already regarded as a sin, and Shakespeare humbly effaces himself before his friend. All the more gladly does the reader welcome the few Sonnets (lv. and lxxxi.) in which the poet confidently predicts the immortality of these his utterances. It is true that Shakespeare is here greatly influenced by antiquity and by the fashion of his age ; and it is simply as records of his friend's beauty and amiability that his verses are to be preserved through all ages to come. But no poet without a sound and vigorous self-confidence could have written either these lines in Sonnet lv. :—

"Not marble, nor the gilded monuments
Of princes shall outlive this powerful rhyme"—

or these others in Sonnet lxxxi. :—

"Your monument shall be my gentle verse,
Which eyes not yet created shall o'erread ;
And tongues to be your being shall rehearse,
When all the breathers of this world are dead."

Yet, as we see, the first and last thought is always that of the friend, his beauty, worth, and fame. And as he will live in the future, so he has lived in the past. Shakespeare cannot conceive existence without him. In Sonnets which have no direct connection with each other (lix., cvi., cxxiii.) he returns again and again to that strange thought of a perpetual cycle or recurrence of events, which runs through the whole of the world's history, from the Pythagoreans and Kohélet to Friedrich Nietzsche. In view of such high-pitched idolatry, we can well understand that the friend's faithlessness, or, if you will, the mistress's conquest of the friend, and the sudden severance of the bond in 1601, must have made a deep impression upon Shakespeare's sensitive soul. The catastrophe left its mark upon him for many a long day.

And at the same time another and purely personal mortification was added to his troubles. Shakespeare's name was just then involved in a degrading scandal of one sort or another. He says so expressly in Sonnet cxii. :—

> "Your love and pity doth the impression fill
> Which vulgar scandal stamped upon my brow."

He here avers that he cares very little "to know his shames or praises" from the tongues of others, and that his friend's judgment is all in all to him; but in Sonnet cxxi., where he goes more closely into the matter, he confesses that some "frailty" in him has given rise to these malignant rumours, and we see that for this frailty his "sportive blood" was to blame. He does not deny the accusation, but asks—

> "Why should others' false adulterate eyes
> Give salutation to my sportive blood?
> Or on my frailties why are frailer spies,
> Which in their wills count bad what I think good?"

The details of this scandal are unknown to us. We can only conclude that it referred to Shakespeare's alleged relation to some woman, or implication in some amorous adventure. In discussing this point, Tyler has aptly cited two passages in contemporary writings, though of course without absolutely proving that they have any bearing on the matter. The first is the above-quoted anecdote in John Manningham's Diary for March 13, 1601 (New Style, 1602), as to Shakespeare's forestalling Burbadge in the graces of a citizen's wife, and announcing himself as "William the Conqueror"—an anecdote which seems to have been widely current at the time, and no doubt arose from more or less recent events. The second passage occurs in *The Returne from Pernassus*, dating from December 1601, in which (iv. 3) Burbadge and Kemp are introduced, and these words are placed in the mouth of Kemp: "O that *Ben Jonson* is a pestilent fellow, he brought vp *Horace* giuing the Poets a pill, but our fellow *Shakespeare* hath giuen him a purge that made him beray his credit." The allusion is evidently to the feud between Ben Jonson on the

FORM OF THE SONNETS

one hand and Marston and Dekker on the other, which culminated in 1601 with the appearance of Ben Jonson's *Poetaster*, in which Horace serves as the poet's mouthpiece. Dekker and Marston retorted in the same year with *Satiromastix, or the Untrussing of the Humorous Poet*. As Shakespeare took no direct part in this quarrel, we can only conjecture what is meant by the above allusion. Mr. Richard Simpson has suggested that King William Rufus, in whose reign the action of *Satiromastix* takes place, and who "presides over the untrussing of the humorous poet," may be intended for William Shakespeare. Rufus, in the play, is by no means a model of chastity, and carries off Walter Terrill's bride very much as "William the Conqueror" in Manningham's anecdote carries off "Richard the Third's" mistress. Simpson thinks it probable that the spectators would have little difficulty in recognising the William the Conqueror of the anecdote in the William Rufus of the play, whose nickname, indeed, might be taken as referring to Shakespeare's complexion. If we accept this interpretation, we find in *Satiromastix* a further proof of the notoriety of the anecdote. Whether it be this scandal or another of the same kind to which the Sonnets refer, Shakespeare seems to have taken greatly to heart the besmirching of his name.

It remains that we should glance at the form of the Sonnets and say a word as to their poetic value.

As regards the form, the first and most obvious remark is that, in spite of their name, these poems are not in reality sonnets at all, and have, indeed, nothing in common with the sonnet except their fourteen lines. In the structure of his so-called Sonnets Shakespeare simply followed the tradition and convention of his country.

Sir Thomas Wyatt, the leading figure in the earlier English school of lyrists, travelled in Italy in the year 1527, familiarised himself with the forms and style of Italian poetry, and introduced the sonnet into English literature. A somewhat younger poet, Henry, Earl of Surrey, soon followed in his footsteps; he, too, travelled in Italy, and cultivated the same poetic models. Not until after the death of both poets were their sonnets published in the collection known as *Tottel's Miscellany* (1557). Neither of the poets succeeded in keeping to the Petrarchan model—an octave and a sestett. Wyatt, it is true, usually preserves the octave, but breaks up the sestett and finishes with a couplet.

Surrey departs still more widely from his model's strict and difficult form: his "Sonnet" consists, like Shakespeare's after him, of three quatrains and a couplet, the rhymes of which are in nowise interwoven. Sidney, again, preserved the octave, but broke up the sestett. Spenser attempted a new rhyme-scheme, interweaving the second and third quatrain, but keeping to the final couplet. Daniel, who is Shakespeare's immediate predecessor and master, returns to Surrey's really formless form. The chief defect in Shakespeare's Sonnets as a metrical whole consists in the appended couplet, which hardly ever keeps up to the level of the beginning, hardly ever presents any picture to the eye, but is, as a rule, merely reflective, and often brings the burst of feeling which animates the poem to a feeble, or at any rate more rhetorical than poetic, issue.

In actual poetic value the Sonnets are extremely uneven. The first group undoubtedly stands lowest in the scale, with its seventeen times repeated and varied exhortation to the friend to leave the world a living reproduction of his beauty. They necessarily express but little of the poet's personal feeling; and though, as we have shown, there is no reason why they should not have been addressed to William Herbert in 1598, it is also quite possible, as their many resemblances in thought and expression to *Venus and Adonis*, *Romeo and Juliet*, and others of the poet's early works would indicate, that they may have been written at a considerably earlier date.

The last two Sonnets in the collection (cliii. and cliv.), dealing with a conventional theme borrowed from the antique, are likewise entirely impersonal. W. Hertzberg, having been put on the track by Herr von Friesen, in 1878 discovered the Greek original of these two Sonnets in the ninth book of the Palatine Anthology.[1] The poem which Shakespeare has adapted, and in Sonnet cliv. almost translated, was written by the Byzantine scholar Marianus, probably in the fifth century after Christ; it was published in Latin, among other epigrams, at Basle in 1529, was retranslated several times before the end of the sixteenth century, and must have become known to Shakespeare in one or other of these different forms.

Next in order stand the Sonnets of merely conventional inspiration, those in which the eye and heart go to law with each

[1] *Jahrbuch der deutschen Shakespeare-Gesellschaft*, Band xiii. S. 158.

other, or in which the poet plays upon his own name and his friend's. These cannot possibly claim any high poetic value.

But the poems thus set apart form but a small minority of the collection. In all the others the waves of feeling run high, and it may be said in general that the deeper the sentiment and the stronger the emotion they express, the more admirable is their force of diction and their marvellous melody. There are Sonnets whose musical quality is unsurpassed by any of the songs introduced into the plays, or even by the most famous and beautiful speeches in the plays themselves. The free and lax form he had adopted was of evident advantage to Shakespeare. The triple and quadruple rhymes, which in Italian involve scarcely any difficulty or constraint, would have proved very hampering in English. As a matter of fact, Shakespeare has been able to follow out every inspiration unimpeded by the shackles of an elaborate rhyme-scheme, and has achieved a rare combination of terseness and harmony in the expression of sorrow, melancholy, anguish, and resignation. Nothing can be more melodious than the opening of Sonnet xl., quoted above, or these lines from Sonnet lxxxvi. :—

> " Was it the proud full sail of his great verse,
> Bound for the prize of all-too-precious you,
> That did my ripe thoughts in my brain inhearse,
> Making their tomb the womb wherein they grew?"

And how moving is the earnestness of Sonnet cxvi., on faith in love :—

> " Let me not to the marriage of true minds
> Admit impediments. Love is not love
> Which alters when it alteration finds,
> Or bends with the remover to remove :
> O, no ! it is an ever-fixèd mark,
> That looks on tempests, and is never shaken ;
> It is the star to every wandering bark,
> Whose worth's unknown, although his height be taken."

Shakespeare's Sonnets are for the general reader the most inaccessible of his works, but they are also the most difficult to tear oneself away from. "With this key Shakespeare unlocked his heart," says Wordsworth ; and some people are repelled from them by the *Menschliches*, or, as they think, *Allzumenschliches*, which is there revealed. They at any rate hold Shakespeare diminished by his openness. Browning, for example, thus retorts upon Wordsworth :—

> "'With this same key
> Shakespeare unlocked his heart' once more!
> Did Shakespeare? If so, the less Shakespeare he."

The reader who can reconcile himself to the fact that great geniuses are not necessarily models of correctness will pass a very different judgment. He will follow with eager interest the experiences which rent and harrowed Shakespeare's soul. He will rejoice in the insight afforded by these poems, which the crowd ignores, into the tempestuous emotional life of one of the greatest of men. Here, and here alone, we see Shakespeare himself, as distinct from his poetical creations, loving, admiring, longing, yearning, adoring, disappointed, humiliated, tortured. Here alone does he enter the confessional. Here more than anywhere else can we, who at a distance of three centuries do homage to the poet's art, feel ourselves in intimate communion, not only with the poet, but with the man.

VIII

JULIUS CÆSAR—ITS FUNDAMENTAL DEFECT

IT is afternoon, a little before three o'clock. Whole fleets of wherries are crossing the Thames, picking their way among the swans and the other boats, to land their passengers on the south bank of the river. Skiff after skiff puts forth from the Blackfriars stair, full of theatre-goers who have delayed a little too long over their dinner and are afraid of being too late; for the flag waving over the Globe Theatre announces that there is a play to-day. The bills upon the street-posts have informed the public that Shakespeare's *Julius Cæsar* is to be presented, and the play draws a full house. People pay their sixpences and enter; the balconies and the pit are filled. Distinguished and specially favoured spectators take their seats on the stage behind the curtain. Then sound the first, the second, and the third trumpet-blasts, the curtain parts in the middle, and reveals a stage entirely hung with black.

Enter the tribunes Flavius and Marullus; they scold the rabble and drive them home because they are loafing about on a week-day without their working-clothes and tools—in contravention of a London police regulation which the public finds so natural that they (and the poet) can conceive it as in force in ancient Rome. At first the audience is somewhat restless. The groundlings talk in undertones as they light their pipes. But the Second Citizen speaks the name of Cæsar. There are cries of "Hush! hush!" and the progress of the play is followed with eager attention.

It was received with applause, and soon became very popular. Of this we have contemporary evidence. Leonard Digges, in the poem quoted above (p. 273), vaunts its scenic attractiveness at the expense of Ben Jonson's Roman plays:—

"So have I seene, when Cesar would appeare,
And on the Stage at halfe-sword parley were

> *Brutus* and *Cassius :* oh how the Audience
> Were ravish'd, with what new wonder they went thence,
> When some new day they would not brooke a line
> Of tedious (though well laboured) *Catiline*."

The learned rejoiced in the breath of air from ancient Rome which met them in these scenes, and the populace was entertained and fascinated by the striking events and heroic characters of the drama. A quatrain in John Weever's *Mirror of Martyrs, or The Life and Death of Sir Iohn Oldcastle Knight, Lord Cobham*, tells how

> "The many-headed multitude were drawne
> By *Brutus* speech, that *Cæsar* was ambitious,
> When eloquent *Mark Antonie* had showne
> His vertues, who but *Brutus* then was vicious?"

There were, indeed, numerous plays on the subject of Julius Cæsar—they are mentioned in Gosson's *Schoole of Abuse*, 1579, in *The Third Blast of Retraite from Plaies*, 1580, in Henslowe's Diary, 1594 and 1602, in *The Mirrour of Policie*, 1598, &c.—but Weever's words do not apply to any of those which have come down to us. It can therefore scarcely be doubted that they refer to Shakespeare's drama; and as the poem appeared in 1601, it affords us almost decisive evidence as to the date of *Julius Cæsar*. In all probability, it was in the same year that the play was written and produced. Weever, indeed, says in his dedication that his poem was "some two yeares agoe made fit for print;" but even if this be true, the lines above quoted may quite well have been inserted later. There are several reasons for believing that *Julius Cæsar* can scarcely have been produced earlier than 1601. The years 1599 and 1600 are already so full of work that we can scarcely assign to them this great tragedy as well; and internal evidence indicates that the play must have been written about the same time as *Hamlet*, to which its style offers so many striking resemblances.

The immediate success of the play is proved by this fact, among others, that it at once called forth a rival production on the same theme. Henslow notes in his diary that in May 1602, on behalf of Lord Nottingham's company, he paid five pounds for a drama called *Cæsar's Fall* to the poets Munday,

Drayton, Webster, Middleton, and another. It was evidently written to order. And as *Julius Cæsar*, in its novelty, was unusually successful, so, too, we find it still reckoned one of Shakespeare's greatest and profoundest plays, unlike the English " Histories " in standing alone and self-sufficient, characteristically composed, forming a rounded whole in spite of its apparent scission at the death of Cæsar, and exhibiting a remarkable insight into Roman character and the life of antiquity.

What attracted Shakespeare to this theme ? And, first and foremost, what *is* the theme ? The play is called *Julius Cæsar*, but it was obviously not Cæsar himself that attracted Shakespeare. The true hero of the piece is Brutus; he it is who has aroused the poet's fullest interest. We must explain to ourselves the why and wherefore.

The answer is to be found in the point of time at which the play was written. It was that eventful year when Shakespeare's earliest friends among the great, Essex and Southampton, had set on foot their foolhardy conspiracy against Elizabeth, and when their attempted insurrection had ended in the death of the one, the imprisonment of the other. He had seen how proud and nobly-disposed characters might easily be seduced into political error, and tempted to rebellion, on the plea of independence. It is true that there was little enough resemblance of detail between the mere palace-revolution designed by Essex, which should free him from his subjection to the Queen's incalculable caprices, and the attempt of the Roman patricians to liberate an aristocratic republic, by assassination, from the yoke of a newly-founded despotism. The point of resemblance lay in the mere fact of the imprudent and ill-starred attempt to effect a subversion of public order.

Add to this the fact that Shakespeare, in the present stage of his career, displays a certain preference for characters who, in spite of noble qualities, have fortune against them and are unable to bring their projects to a successful issue. While he himself was still fighting for his position, Henry V., the man of practical genius, the born victor and conqueror, had been his ideal ; now that he stood on firm ground, and was soon to reach the height of his reputation, he seems to have turned with a sort of melancholy predilection to characters like Brutus and Hamlet, who, in spite of the highest endowments, proved unequal to the tasks proposed to them.[1] They appealed to him as profound dreamers and high-minded idealists. He found something of their nature, too, in his own.

A good score of years earlier, in 1579, North's version of Plutarch's parallel biographies had been published, not translated from the original, but from the French translation of Amyot. In this book Shakespeare found his material.

His method of using this material differs considerably from his treatment of his other authorities. From a chronicler like Holinshed he, as a rule, takes nothing but the course of events, the outline of the leading personages and such anecdotes as suit his purpose. From novelists like Bandello or Cinthio he takes the main lines of the action, but relies almost entirely on his own invention for the characters and the dialogue. From the earlier plays, which he adapts or re-casts, such as *The Taming of a Shrew*, *King John*, *The Famous Victories* of Henry V., and *King Leir* (the original *Hamlet* is unfortunately not preserved), he transfers into his own work every scene and speech that is worth anything; but in the cases in which we can make the comparison, there is little enough that he finds available. Here, on the other hand, we find a curious and instructive example of his method of work when he most faithfully followed his original. We realise that the more developed the art and the more competent the psychology of the writer before him, the more closely did Shakespeare tread in his footsteps.

Here for the first time he found himself in touch with a wholly civilised spirit—not seldom childlike in his antique simplicity, but still no mean artist. Jean Paul, with some exaggeration, yet not quite extravagantly, has called Plutarch the biographical Shakespeare of world-history.

The whole drama of *Julius Cæsar* may be read in Plutarch. Shakespeare had before him three Lives—those of Cæsar, Brutus, and Mark Antony. Read them consecutively, and you find in them every detail of *Julius Cæsar*.

Let us take some examples from the first act of the play. It begins with the tribunes' jealousy of the favour in which Cæsar stands with the common people; and everything down to the minutest trait is taken from Plutarch. The same with what follows: Mark Antony's repeated offer of the crown to Cæsar at the

---

[1] Compare Dowden, *Shakspere*, p. 280.

feast of the Lupercal, and his unwilling refusal of it. So too with
Cæsar's suspicions of Cassius; Cæsar's speech on his second
entrance—
> "Let me have men about me that are fat,
> Sleek-headed men, and such as sleep o' nights :
> Yond Cassius has a lean and hungry look ;
> He thinks too much ; such men are dangerous,"—

occurs word for word in Plutarch ; the anecdote, indeed, made
such an impression on him that he has repeated it three times in
different Lives. We find, furthermore, in the Greek historian,
how Cassius gradually involves Brutus in the conspiracy; how
papers exhorting Brutus to action are thrown into his house; the
deliberations as to whether Antony is to die along with Cæsar,
and Brutus's mistaken judgment of Antony's character; Portia's
complaint at being excluded from her husband's confidence; the
proof of courage which she gives by plunging a knife into her
thigh ; all the omens and prodigies that precede the murder ; the
sacrificial ox without a heart ; the fiery warriors fighting in the
clouds ; Calphurnia's warning dream ; Cæsar's determination not
to go to the Senate on the Ides of March; Decius [Decimus]
Brutus's endeavour to change his purpose ; the fruitless efforts of
Artemidorus to restrain him from facing the danger, &c., &c. It
is all in Plutarch, point for point.

Here and there we find small and subtle divergences from the
original, which may be traced now to Shakespeare's temperament,
now to his view of life, and again to his design in the play.
Plutarch, for example, has not Shakespeare's contempt for the
populace, and does not make them so senselessly fickle. Then,
again, he gives no hint for Brutus's soliloquy before taking the
final resolution (II. 1). For the rest, wherever it is possible,
Shakespeare employs the very words of North's translation. Nay,
more, he accepts the characters, such as Brutus, Portia, Cassius,
just as they stand in Plutarch. His Brutus is absolutely the same
as Plutarch's ; his Cassius is a man of somewhat deeper character.

In dealing with the great figure of Cæsar, which gives the
play its name, Shakespeare follows faithfully the detached, anec-
dotic indications of Plutarch ; but he, strangely enough, seems
altogether to miss the remarkable impression we receive from
Plutarch of Cæsar's character, which, for the rest, the Greek historian himself was not in a position fully to understand. We

must not forget the fact, of which Shakespeare of course knew nothing, that Plutarch, who was born a century after Cæsar's death, at a time when the independence of Greece was only a memory, and the once glorious Hellas was part of a Roman province, wrote his comparative biographies to remind haughty Rome that Greece had a great man to oppose to each of her greatest sons. Plutarch was saturated with the thought that conquered Greece was Rome's lord and master in every department of the intellectual life. He delivered Greek lectures in Rome and could not speak Latin, while every Roman spoke Greek to him and understood it as well as his native tongue. Significantly enough, Roman literature and poetry do not exist for Plutarch, though he incessantly cites Greek authors and poets. He never mentions Virgil or Ovid. He wrote about his great Romans as an enlightened and unprejudiced Pole might in our days write about great Russians. He, in whose eyes the old republics shone transfigured, was not specially fitted to appreciate Cæsar's greatness.

Shakespeare, having so arranged his drama that Brutus should be its tragic hero, had to concentrate his art on placing him in the foreground, and making him fill the scene. The difficulty was not to let his lack of political insight (in the case of Antony), or of practical sense (in his quarrel with Cassius), detract from the impression of his superiority. He had to be the centre and pivot of everything, and therefore Cæsar was diminished and belittled to such a degree, unfortunately, that this matchless genius in war and statesmanship has become a miserable caricature.

We find in other places clear indications that Shakespeare knew very well what this man was and was worth. Edward's young son, in *Richard III.*, speaks with enthusiasm of Cæsar as that conqueror whom death has not conquered; Horatio, in the almost contemporary *Hamlet*, speaks of "mightiest Julius" and his death; and Cleopatra, in *Antony and Cleopatra*, is proud of having been the mistress of Cæsar. It is true that in *As You Like It* the playful Rosalind uses the expression, "Cæsar's thrasonical brag," with reference to the famous *Veni, vidi, vici*, but in an entirely jocose context and acceptation.

But here! here Cæsar has become in effect no little of a braggart, and is compounded, on the whole, of anything but attractive characteristics. He produces the impression of an

CHARACTER OF CÆSAR

invalid. His liability to the "falling sickness" is emphasised. He is deaf of one ear. He has no longer his old strength. He faints when the crown is offered to him. He envies Cassius because he is a stronger swimmer. He is as superstitious as an old woman. He rejoices in flattery, talks pompously and arrogantly, boasts of his firmness and is for ever wavering. He acts incautiously and unintelligently, and does not realise what threatens him, while every one else sees it clearly.

Shakespeare dared not, says Gervinus, arouse too great interest in Cæsar; he had to throw into relief everything about him that could account for the conspiracy; and, moreover, he had Plutarch's distinct statement that Cæsar's character had greatly deteriorated shortly before his death. Hudson practically agrees with this, holding that Shakespeare wished to present Cæsar as he appeared in the eyes of the conspirators, so that "they too might have fair and equal judgment at our hands;" admitting, for the rest, that "Cæsar was literally too great to be seen by them," and that "Cæsar is far from being himself in these scenes; hardly one of the speeches put in his mouth can be regarded as historically characteristic." Thus Hudson arrives at the astonishing result that "there is an undertone of irony at work in the ordering and tempering of this composition," explaining that, "when such a shallow idealist as Brutus is made to overtop and outshine the greatest practical genius the world ever saw," we are bound to assume that the intention is ironical.

This is the emptiest cobweb-spinning. There is no trace of irony in the representation of Brutus. Nor can we fall back upon the argument that Cæsar, after his death, becomes the chief personage of the drama, and as a corpse, as a memory, as a spirit, strikes down his murderers. How can so small a man cast so great a shadow! Shakespeare, of course, intended to show Cæsar as triumphing after his death. He has changed Brutus's evil genius, which appears to him in the camp and at Philippi, into Cæsar's ghost; but this ghost is not sufficient to rehabilitate Cæsar in our estimation.

Nor is it true that Cæsar's greatness would have impaired the unity of the piece. Its poetic value, on the contrary, suffers from his pettiness. The play might have been immeasurably richer and deeper than it is, had Shakespeare been inspired by a feeling of Cæsar's greatness.

Elsewhere in Shakespeare one marvels at what he has made out of poor and meagre material. Here, history was so enormously rich, that his poetry has become poor and meagre in comparison with it.

Just as Shakespeare (if the portions of the first part of *Henry VI.* which deal with La Pucelle are by him) represented Jeanne d'Arc with no sense for the lofty and simple poetry that breathed around her figure—national prejudice and old superstition blinding him—so he approached the characterisation of Cæsar with far too light a heart, and with imperfect knowledge and care. As he had made Jeanne d'Arc a witch, so he makes Cæsar a braggart. Cæsar!

If, like the schoolboys of later generations, he had been given Cæsar's *Gallic War* to read in his childhood, this would not have been possible to him. Is it conceivable that, in what he had heard about the Commentaries, he had naïvely seized upon and misinterpreted the fact that Cæsar always speaks of himself in the third person, and calls himself by his name?

Let us compare for a moment this posing self-worshipper of Shakespeare's with the picture of Cæsar which the poet might easily have formed from his Plutarch alone, thus explaining Cæsar's rise to the height of autocracy on which he stands at the beginning of the play, and at the same time the gradual piling up of the hatred to which he succumbed. On the very second page of the life of Cæsar he must have read the anecdote of how Cæsar, when quite a young man, on his way back from Bithynia, was taken prisoner by Cilician pirates. They demanded a ransom of twenty talents (about £4000). He answered that they clearly did not know who their prisoner was, promised them fifty talents, sent his attendants to different towns to raise this sum, and remained with only a friend and two servants among these notoriously bloodthirsty bandits. He displayed the greatest contempt for them, and freely ordered them about; he made them keep perfectly quiet when he wanted to sleep; for the thirty-eight days he remained among them he treated them as a prince might his bodyguard. He went through his gymnastic exercises, and wrote poems and orations in the fullest security. He often assured them that he would certainly have them hanged, or rather crucified. When the ransom arrived from Miletus, the first use he made of his liberty was to fit out some ships, attack the pirates, take them

CHARACTER OF CÆSAR

all prisoners, and seize upon their booty. Then he carried them before the Prætor of Asia, Junius, whose business it was to punish them. Junius, out of avarice, replied that he would take time to reflect what should be done with the prisoners; whereupon Cæsar returned to Pergamos, where he had left them in prison, and kept his word by having them all crucified.

What has become of this masterfulness, this grace, and this iron will, in Shakespeare's Cæsar?

> "I fear him not:
> Yet if my name were liable to fear,
> I do not know the man I should avoid
> So soon as that spare Cassius.
> . . . .
> I rather tell thee what is to be fear'd
> Than what I fear, for always I am Cæsar."

It is well that he himself makes haste to say so, otherwise one would scarcely believe it. And does one believe it, after all?

As Shakespeare conceives the situation, the Republic which Cæsar overthrew might have continued to exist but for him, and it was a criminal act on his part to destroy it.

But the old aristocratic Republic had already fallen to pieces when Cæsar welded its fragments into a new monarchy. Sheer lawlessness reigned in Rome. The populace was such as even the rabble of our own great cities can give no conception of: not the brainless mob, for the most part tame, only now and then going wild through mere stupidity, which in Shakespeare listens to the orations over Cæsar's body and tears Cinna to pieces; but a populace whose innumerable hordes consisted mainly of slaves, together with the thousands of foreigners from all the three continents, Phrygians from Asia, Negroes from Africa, Iberians and Celts from Spain and France, who flocked together in the capital of the world. To the immense bands of house-slaves and field-slaves, there were added thousands of runaway slaves who had committed theft or murder at home, lived by robbery on the way, and now lay hid in the purlieus of the city. But besides foreigners with no means of support and slaves without bread, there were swarms of freedmen, entirely corrupted by their servile condition, for whom freedom, whether combined with helpless poverty or with new-made riches, meant only the freedom to do harm. Then there were troops of gladiators, as indifferent to the lives of others as to their own, and entirely at the beck and call of whoever would pay them. It was from ruffians of this class that a man like Clodius had recruited the armed gangs who surrounded him, divided like regular soldiers into decuries and centuries under duly appointed commanders. These bands fought battles in the Forum with other bands of gladiators or of herdsmen from the wild regions of Picenum or Lombardy, whom the Senate imported for its own protection. There was practically no street police or fire-brigade. When public disasters happened, such as floods or conflagrations, people regarded them as portents and consulted the augurs. The magistrates were no longer obeyed; consuls and tribunes were attacked, and sometimes even killed. In the Senate the orators covered each other with abuse, in the Forum they spat in each other's faces. Regular battles took place on the Campus Martius at every election, and no man of position ever appeared in the streets without a bodyguard of gladiators and slaves. "If we try to conceive to ourselves," wrote Mommsen in 1857, "a London with the slave population of New Orleans, with the police of Constantinople, with the non-industrial character of the modern Rome, and agitated by politics after the fashion of the Paris of 1848, we shall acquire an approximate idea of the republican glory, the departure of which Cicero and his associates in their sulky letters deplore."[1]

Compare with this picture Shakespeare's conception of an ambitious Cæsar striving to introduce monarchy into a well-ordered republican state!

What enchanted every one, even his enemies, who came in contact with Cæsar, was his good-breeding, his politeness, the charm of his personality. These characteristics made a doubly strong impression upon those who, like Cicero, were accustomed to the arrogance and coarseness of Pompey, so-called the Great. However busy he might be, Cæsar had always time to think of his friends and to jest with them. His letters are gay and amiable. In Shakespeare, when he is not familiar, he is pompous.

For the space of twenty-five years, Cæsar, as a politician, had by every means in his power opposed the aristocratic party in Rome. He had early resolved to make himself, without the

---

[1] Mommsen, *History of Rome*, translated by W. P. Dickson, ed. 1894, vol. v. p. 371. Gaston Boissier, *Cicéron et ses Amis*, p. 224.

employment of force, the master of the then known world, assured as he was that the Republic would fall to pieces of its own accord. Not until his prætorship in Spain had he displayed ability as a soldier and administrator outside the every-day round of political life. Then suddenly, when everything seems to be prospering with him, he breaks away from it all, leaves Rome, and passes into Gaul. At the age of forty-four, he enters upon his military career, and becomes perhaps the greatest commander known to history, an unrivalled conqueror and organiser, revealing, in middle life, a whole host of unsuspected and admirable qualities. Shakespeare conveys no idea of the wealth and many-sidedness of his gifts. He makes him belaud himself with unceasing solemnity (II. 2):—

> "Cæsar shall forth : the things that threaten'd me
> Ne'er look'd but on my back ; when they shall see
> The face of Cæsar, they are vanishèd."

Cæsar had nothing of the stolid pomposity and severity which Shakespeare attributes to him. He united the rapid decision of the general with the man of the world's elegance and lofty indifference to trifles. He liked his soldiers to wear glittering weapons and to adorn themselves. "What does it matter," he said, "though they use perfumes? They fight none the worse for that." And soldiers who under other leaders did not surpass the average became invincible under him.

He, who in Rome had been the glass of fashion, was so careless of his comfort in the field that he often slept under the open sky, and ate rancid oil without so much as a grimace; but richly-decked tables always stood in his tents, and all the golden youth, for whom Gaul was at that time what America became in the days of the first discoverers, made their way from Rome to his camp. It was the most wonderful camp ever seen, crowded with men of elegance and learning, young writers and poets, wits and thinkers, who, in the midst of the greatest and most imminent dangers, busied themselves with literature, and sent regular reports of their meetings and conversations to Cicero, the acknowledged arbiter of the literary world of Rome. During the brief space of Cæsar's expedition into Britain, he writes two letters to Cicero. Their relation, in its different phases, in some ways reminds us of the relation between Frederick the Great and

Voltaire. What a paltry picture does Shakespeare draw of Cicero as a mere pedant!—

"*Cassius.* Did Cicero say anything?
"*Casca.* Ay, he spoke Greek.
"*Cassius.* To what effect?
"*Casca.* Nay, an I tell you that, I'll ne'er look you in the face again: but those that understood him smiled at one another, and shook their heads; but, for mine own part, it was Greek to me."

Amid labours of every sort, his life always in danger, incessantly fighting with warlike enemies, whom he beats in battle after battle, Cæsar writes his grammatical works and his Commentaries. His dedication to Cicero of his work *De Analogia* is a homage to literature no less than to him: "You have discovered all the treasures of eloquence and been the first to employ them. . . . You have achieved the crown of all honours, a triumph the greatest generals may envy; for it is a nobler thing to remove the barriers of the intellectual life than to extend the boundaries of the Empire." These are the words of the man who has just beaten the Helvetii, conquered France and Belgium, made the first expedition into Britain, and so effectually repelled the German hordes that they were for long innocuous to the Rome which they had threatened with destruction.

How little does this Cæsar resemble the pompous and high-flown puppet of Shakespeare:—

"Danger knows full well
That Cæsar is more dangerous than he.
We are two lions litter'd in one day,
And I the elder and more terrible."

Cæsar could be cruel at times. In his wars, he never shrank from taking such revenges as should strike terror into his enemies. He had the whole senate of the Veneti beheaded. He cut the right hand off every one who had borne arms against him at Uxellodunum. He kept the gallant Vercingetorix five years in prison, only to exhibit him in chains at his triumph and then to have him executed.

Yet, where severity was unnecessary, he was tolerance and mildness itself. Cicero, during the civil war, went over to the camp of Pompey, and after the defeat of that party sought and received forgiveness. When he afterwards wrote a book in honour of Cæsar's mortal enemy Cato, who killed himself so as not to have to obey the dictator, and thereby became the hero of all the republicans, Cæsar wrote to Cicero: "In reading your book, I feel as though I myself had become more eloquent." And yet in his eyes Cato was only an uncultured personage and a fanatic for an obsolete order of things. When a slave, out of tenderness for his master, refused to hand Cato his sword wherewith to kill himself, Cato gave him such a furious blow in the face that his hand was dyed with blood. Such a trait must have spoiled for Cæsar the impressiveness of this suicide.

Cæsar was not content with forgiving almost all who had borne arms against him at Pharsalia; he gave many of them, and among the rest Brutus and Cassius, an ample share of his power. He tried to protect Brutus before the battle and heaped honours upon him after it. Again and again Brutus came forward in opposition to Cæsar, and even, in his conscientious quixotism, took part against him with Pompey, although Pompey had had his father assassinated. Cæsar forgave him this and everything else; he was never tired of forgiving him. He had, it appears, transferred to Brutus the love of his youth for Brutus's mother Servilia, Cato's sister, who had been passionately and faithfully devoted to Cæsar. Voltaire, in his *Mort de César*, makes Cæsar hand to Brutus a letter just received from the dying Servilia, in which she begs Cæsar to watch well over their son. Plutarch relates that on one occasion, at the time of Catiline's conspiracy, a letter was brought to Cæsar in the Senate. Cato, seeing him rise and go apart to read it, gave open utterance to the suspicion that it was a missive from the conspirators. Cæsar laughingly handed him the letter, which contained declarations of love from his sister; whereupon Cato, enraged, burst out with the epithet "Drunkard!"—the direst term of abuse a Roman could employ. (Ben Jonson has introduced this anecdote in his *Catiline*, v. 6.)

Brutus inherited his uncle Cato's hatred for Cæsar. A certain brutality was united with a noble stoicism in these two last Roman republicans of the time of the Republic's downfall. The rawness of antique Rome survived in Cato's nature, and Brutus, in his conduct towards the towns of the Asiatic provinces, was nothing but a bloodthirsty usurer, who, in the name of a man of straw (Scaptius) extorted from them his exorbitant interests with threats of fire and sword. He had lent to the inhabitants of the town of Salamis a sum of money at 48 per cent. On their failure to pay, he kept their Senate so closely besieged by a squadron of cavalry that five senators died of starvation. Shakespeare, in his ignorance, attributes no such vices to Brutus, but makes him simple and great, at Cæsar's expense.

Cæsar as opposed to Cato—and afterwards as opposed to Brutus—is the many-sided genius who loves life and action and power, in contradistinction to the narrow Puritan who hates such emancipated spirits, partly on principle, partly from instinct.

What a strange misunderstanding that Shakespeare—himself a lover of beauty, intent on a life of activity, enjoyment, and satisfied ambition, who always stood to Puritanism in the same hostile relation in which Cæsar stood—should out of ignorance take the side of Puritanism in this case, and so disqualify himself from extracting from the rich mine of Cæsar's character all the gold contained in it. In Shakespeare's Cæsar we find nothing of the magnanimity and sincerity of the real man. He never assumed a hypocritical reverence towards the past, not even on questions of grammar. He grasped at power and seized it, but did not, as in Shakespeare, pretend to reject it. Shakespeare has let him keep the pride which he in fact displayed, but has made it unbeautiful, and eked it out with hypocrisy.

This further trait, too, in Cæsar's character Shakespeare has failed to understand. When at last, after having conquered on every side, in Africa as in Asia, in Spain as in Egypt, he held in his hands the sovereign power which had been the object of his twenty years' struggle, it had lost its attraction for him. Knowing that he was misunderstood and hated by those whose respect he prized the most, he found himself compelled to make use of men whom he despised, and contempt for humanity took possession of his mind. He saw nothing around him but greed and treachery. Power had lost all its sweetness for him, life itself was no longer worth living, worth preserving. Hence his answer when he was besought to take measures against his would-be assassins: "Rather die once than tremble always!" and he went to the Senate on the 15th of March without arms and without a guard. In the tragedy, the motives which ultimately lure him thither are the hope of a title and a crown, and the fear of being esteemed a coward.

Those foolish persons who attribute Shakespeare's works to Francis Bacon argue, amongst other things, that such an insight into Roman antiquity as is manifested in *Julius Cæsar* could be attained by no one who did not possess Bacon's learning. On the contrary, this play is obviously written by a man whose learning was in no sense on a level with his genius, so that its faults, no less than its merits, afford a proof, however superfluous, that Shakespeare himself was the author of Shakespeare's works. Bunglers in criticism never realise to what an extent genius can supply the place of book-learning, and how vastly greater is its importance. But, on the other hand, one is bound to declare unequivocally that there are certain domains in which no amount of genius can compensate for reconstructive insight and study of recorded fact, and where even the greatest genius falls short when it tries to create out of its own head, or upon a scanty basis of knowledge.

Such a domain is that of historical drama, when it deals with periods and personalities in regard to which recorded fact surpasses all possible imagination. Where history is stranger and more poetic than any poetry, more tragic than any antique tragedy, there the poet requires many-sided insight in order to rise to the occasion. It was because of Shakespeare's lack of historical and classical culture that the incomparable grandeur of the figure of Cæsar left him unmoved. He depressed and debased that figure to make room for the development of the central character in his drama—to wit, Marcus Brutus, whom, following Plutarch's idealising example, he depicted as a stoic of almost flawless nobility.

IX

THE MERITS OF JULIUS CÆSAR—BRUTUS

NONE but a naïve republican like Swinburne can believe that it was by reason of any republican enthusiasm in Shakespeare's soul that Brutus became the leading character. He had assuredly no systematic political conviction, and manifests at other times the most loyal and monarchical habit of mind.

Brutus was already in Plutarch the protagonist of the Cæsar tragedy, and Shakespeare followed the course of history as represented by Plutarch, under the deep impression that an impolitic revolt, like that of Essex and his companions, can by no means stem the current of the time, and that practical errors revenge themselves quite as severely as moral sins—nay, much more so. The psychologist was now awakened in him, and he found it a fascinating task to analyse and present a man who finds a mission imposed upon him for which he is by nature unfitted. It is no longer outward conflicts like that in *Romeo and Juliet* between the lovers and their surroundings, or in *Richard III.*, between Richard and the world at large, that fascinate him in this new stage of his development, but the inner processes and crises of the spiritual life.

Brutus has lived among his books and fed his mind upon Platonic philosophy; therefore he is more occupied with the abstract political idea of republican freedom, and the abstract moral conception of the shame of enduring a despotism, than with the actual political facts before his eyes, or the meaning of the changes which are going on around him. This man is vehemently urged by Cassius to place himself at the head of a conspiracy against his fatherly benefactor and friend. The demand throws his whole nature into a ferment, disturbs its harmony, and brings it for ever out of equilibrium.

On Hamlet also, who is at the same time springing to life in

CHARACTER OF BRUTUS

Shakespeare's mind, the spirit of his murdered father imposes the duty of becoming an assassin, and the claim acts as a stimulus, a spur to his intellectual faculties, but as a solvent to his character; so close is the resemblance between the situation of Brutus, with his conflicting duties, and the inward strife which we are soon to find in Hamlet.

Brutus is at war with himself, and therefore forgets to show others attention and the outward signs of friendship. His comrades summon him to action, but he hears no answering summons from within. As Hamlet breaks out into the well known words:—

"The time is out of joint:—O, cursed spite
That ever I was born to set it right!"

so also Brutus shrinks with horror from his task. He says (I. 2):—

"Brutus had rather be a villager
Than to repute himself a son of Rome
Under these hard conditions as this time
Is like to lay upon us."

His noble nature is racked by these doubts and uncertainties.

From the moment Cassius has spoken to him, he is sleepless. The rugged Macbeth becomes sleepless after he has killed the King—"Macbeth has murdered sleep." Brutus, with his delicate, reflective nature, bent on obeying only the dictates of duty, is calm after the murder, but sleepless before it. His preoccupation with the idea has altered his whole manner of being; his wife does not know him again. She tells how he can neither converse nor sleep, but strides up and down with his arms folded, sighing and lost in thought, does not answer her questions, and, when she repeats them, waves her off with rough impatience.

It is not only his gratitude to Cæsar that keeps Brutus in torment; it is especially his uncertainty as to what Cæsar's intentions really are. Brutus sees him, indeed, idolised by the people and endowed with supreme power; but as yet Cæsar has never abused it. He concurs with Cassius's view that when Cæsar declined the crown he in reality hankered after it; but, after all, they have nothing to go upon but his supposed desire:—

"To speak truth of Cæsar,
I have not known when his affections sway'd
More than his reason. But 'tis a common proof
That lowliness is young ambition's ladder."

If Cæsar is to be slain, then, it is not for what he has done, but for what he may do in the future. Is it permissible to commit a murder upon such grounds?

In Hamlet we find this variant of the difficulty: Is it certain that the king murdered Hamlet's father? May not the ghost have been a hallucination, or the devil himself?

Brutus feels the weakness of his basis of action the more clearly the more he leans towards the murder as a political duty. And Shakespeare has not hesitated to attribute to him, high-minded as he is, that doctrine of expediency, so questionable in the eyes of many, which declares that a necessary end sanctifies impure means. Two separate times, once when he is by himself, and once in addressing the conspirators, he recommends political hypocrisy as judicious and serviceable. In the soliloquy he says (II. 1):—

> "And, since the quarrel
> Will bear no colour for the thing he is,
> Fashion it thus: that what he is, augmented,
> Would run to these and these extremities."

To the conspirators his words are:—

> "And let our hearts, as subtle masters do,
> Stir up their servants to an act of rage,
> And after seem to chide 'em."

That is to say, the murder is to be carried out with as much decency as possible, and the murderers are afterwards to pretend that they deplore it.

As soon as the murder is resolved upon, however, Brutus, assured of the purity of his motives, stands proud and almost unconcerned in the midst of the conspirators. Far too unconcerned, indeed; for though he has not shrunk in principle from the doctrine that one cannot will the end without willing the means, he yet shrinks, upright and unpractical as he is, from employing means which seem to him either too base or too unscrupulous. He will not even suffer the conspirators to be bound by oath: "Swear priests and cowards and men cautelous." They are to trust each other without the assurance of an oath, and to keep their secret unsworn. And when it is proposed that Antony shall be killed along with Cæsar, a necessary step, to which, as a politician, he was bound to consent, he rejects it, in

Shakespeare as in Plutarch, out of humanity : " Our course will seem too bloody, Caius Cassius." He feels that his will is as clear as day, and suffers at the thought of employing the methods of night and darkness :

"O Conspiracy!
Sham'st thou to show thy dangerous brow by night,
When evils are most free? O, then, by day
Where wilt thou find a cavern dark enough
To mask thy monstrous visage?"

Brutus is anxious that a cause which is to be furthered by assassination should achieve success without secrecy and without violence. Goethe has said: "Only the man of reflection has a conscience." The man of action cannot have one while he is acting. To plunge into action is to place oneself at the mercy of one's nature and of external powers. One acts rightly or wrongly, but always upon instinct—often stupidly, sometimes, it may be, brilliantly, never with full consciousness. Action implies the inconsiderateness of instinct, or egoism, or genius; Brutus, on the other hand, is bent on acting with every consideration.

Kreyssig, and after him Dowden, have called Brutus a Girondin, in opposition to his brother-in-law, Cassius, a sort of Jacobin in antique dress. The comparison is just only in regard to the lesser or greater inclination to the employment of violent means; it halts when we reflect that Brutus lives in the rarefied air of abstractions, face to face with ideas and principles, while Cassius lives in the world of facts; for the Jacobins were quite as stiff-necked theorists as any Girondin. Brutus, in Shakespeare, is a strict moralist, excessively cautious lest any stain should mar the purity of his character, while Cassius does not in the least aspire to moral flawlessness. He is frankly envious of Cæsar, and openly avows that he hates him; yet he is not base; for envy and hatred are in his case swallowed up by political passion, strenuous and consistent. And, unlike Brutus, he is a good observer, looking right through men's words and actions into their souls. But as Brutus is the man whose name, birth, and position as Cæsar's intimate friend, point him out to be the head of the conspiracy, he is always able to enforce his impolitic and short-sighted will.

When we find that Hamlet, who is so full of doubts, never for a moment doubts his right to kill the king, we must remember that Shakespeare had just exhausted this theme in his characterisation of Brutus.

Brutus is the ideal whom Shakespeare, like all men of the better sort, cherished in his soul—the man whose pride it is before everything to keep his hands clean and his mind high and free, even at the cost of failure in his undertakings and the wreck of his tranquillity and of his fortunes.

He does not care to impose an oath upon the others; he is too proud. If they want to betray him, let them! These others, it is true, may be moved by their hatred of the great man, and eager to quench their malice in his blood; he, for his part, admires him, and will sacrifice, not butcher him. The others fear the consequences of suffering Antony to address the people; but Brutus has explained to the people his reasons for the murder, so Antony may now eulogise Cæsar as much as he pleases. Did not Cæsar deserve eulogy? Does not he himself desire that Cæsar shall lie honoured, though punished, in his grave? He is too proud to keep a watch upon Antony, who has approached him in friendly fashion, though at the same time in the character of Cæsar's friend; therefore he leaves the Forum before Antony begins his speech. Such moods are familiar to many. Many another has acted in this apparently unwise way, proudly reckless of consequences, moved by the dislike of the magnanimous man for all that savours of base cautiousness. Many a one, for example, has told the truth where it was stupid to do so, or has let slip an opportunity of revenge because he despised his enemy too much to seek compensation for his injuries, though he thereby neglected to render him innocuous for the future. An intense realisation of the necessity for confidence, or, on the other hand, of the untrustworthiness of friends and the contemptibleness of enemies, may easily lead one to despise every measure of prudence.

It was upon the basis of an intense feeling of this nature that Shakespeare created Brutus. With the addition of humour and a touch of genius he would be Hamlet, and he becomes Hamlet. With the addition of despairing bitterness and misanthropy he would be Timon, and he becomes Timon. Here he is the man of uncompromising character and principle, who is too proud to be prudent and too bad an observer to be practical; and this man is so situated that not only the life and death of another and of himself, but the welfare of the State, and even, as it appears, that of the whole civilised world, depend upon the resolution at which he arrives.

At Brutus's side Shakespeare places the figure which forms his female counterpart, the kindred spirit who has become one with him, his cousin and wife, Cato's daughter married to Cato's disciple. He has here, and here alone, given us a picture of the ideal marriage as he conceived it.

In the scene between Brutus and Portia the poet takes up afresh a motive which he has handled once before—the anxious wife beseeching her husband to initiate her into his great designs. It first appears in *Henry IV.*, Part I., where Lady Percy implores her Harry to let her share his counsels. (See above, p. 222.) The description which she gives of Hotspur's manner and conduct exactly corresponds to Portia's description of the transformation which has taken place in Brutus. Both husbands, indeed, are nursing a similar project. But Lady Percy learns nothing. Her Harry no doubt loves her, loves her now and then, between two skirmishes, briskly and gaily; but there is no sentiment in his love for her, and he never dreams of any spiritual communion between them.

When Portia, in this case, begs her husband to tell her what is weighing on his mind, he at first, indeed, replies with evasions about his health; but on her vehemently declaring that she feels herself degraded by this lack of confidence (Shakespeare has but slightly softened the antique frankness of the words which Plutarch places in her mouth), Brutus answers her with warmth and beauty. And when (again as in Plutarch) she tells of the proof she has given of her steadfastness by thrusting a knife into her thigh and never complaining of the "voluntary wound," he bursts forth with the words which Plutarch places in his mouth:—

"O ye gods,
Render me worthy of this noble wife,"

and promises to tell her everything.

Neither Shakespeare nor Plutarch, however, regards his facile communicativeness as a mark of prudence. For it is not Portia's fault that it does not betray everything. When it comes to the point, she can neither hold her tongue nor control herself. She betrays her anxiety and uneasiness to the boy Lucius, and herself exclaims:—

"I have a man's mind, but a woman's might.
How hard it is for women to keep counsel!"

This reflection is obviously not Portia's, but an utterance of Shakespeare's own philosophy of life, which he has not cared to keep to himself. In Plutarch she even falls down as though dead, and the news of her death surprises Brutus just before the time appointed for the murder of Cæsar, so that he needs all his self-control to save himself from breaking down.

From the character with which Shakespeare has thus endowed Brutus spring the two great scenes which carry the play.

The first is the marvellously-constructed scene, the turning-point of the tragedy, in which Antony, speaking with Brutus's consent over the body of Cæsar, stirs up the Romans against the murderers of the great imperator.

Even Brutus's own speech Shakespeare has moulded with the rarest art. Plutarch relates that when Brutus wrote Greek he cultivated a "compendious" and laconic style, of which the historian adduces a string of examples. He wrote to the Samians: "Your councels be long, your doings be slow; consider the end." And in another epistle: "The Xanthians, despising my good wil, haue made a graue of dispaire; and the Patareians, that put themselves into my protection, have lost no iot of their liberty: and therefore whilst you haue libertie, either chuse the iudgement of the Patareians or the fortune of the Xanthians." See now, what Shakespeare has made out of these indications:—

"Romans, countrymen, and lovers! hear me for my cause, and be silent, that you may hear: believe me for mine honour, and have respect to mine honour, that you may believe. . . . If there be any in this assembly, any dear friend of Cæsar's, to him I say, that Brutus' love to Cæsar was no less than his. If, then, that friend demand, why Brutus rose against Cæsar, this is my answer:—Not that I loved Cæsar less, but that I loved Rome more."

And so on, in this style of laconic antithesis. Shakespeare has made a deliberate effort to assign to Brutus the diction he had cultivated, and, with his inspired faculty of divination, has, as it were, reanimated it:—

"As Cæsar loved me, I weep for him; as he was fortunate, I rejoice at it; as he was valiant, I honour him: but, as he was ambitious, I slew him."

With ingenious and yet noble art the speech culminates in the question, "Who is here so vile that will not love his country! If any, speak; for him have I offended." And when the crowd answers, "None, Brutus, none," he chimes in with the serene assurance, "Then none have I offended."

The still more admirable oration of Antony is in the first place remarkable for the calculated difference of style which it displays. Here we have no antitheses, no literary eloquence; but a vernacular eloquence of the most powerful demagogic type. Antony takes up the thread just where Brutus has dropped it, expressly assures his hearers at the outset that this is to be a speech over Cæsar's bier, but not to his glory, and emphasises to the point of monotony the fact that Brutus and the other conspirators are all, all honourable men. Then the eloquence gradually works up, subtle and potent in its adroit crescendo, and yet in truth exalted by something which is not subtlety: glowing enthusiasm for Cæsar, scathing indignation against his assassins. The contempt and anger are at first masked, out of consideration for the mood of the populace, which has for the moment been won over by Brutus; then the mask is raised a little, then a little more and a little more, until, with a wild gesture, it is torn off and thrown aside.

Here again Shakespeare has utilised in a masterly fashion the hints he found in Plutarch, scanty as they were:—

"Afterwards, when Cæsar's body was brought into the market-place, Antonius, making his funeral oration in praise of the dead, according to the aunciente custome of Rome, and perceiuing that his words moued the common people to compassion: he framed his eloquence to make their harts yerne the more."

Mark what Shakespeare has made of this:—

"Friends, Romans, countrymen, lend me your ears:
I come to bury Cæsar, not to praise him.
The evil that men do lives after them,
The good is oft interred with their bones;
So let it be with Cæsar. The noble Brutus
Hath told you, Cæsar was ambitious:

> If it were so, it was a grievous fault,
> And grievously hath Cæsar answered it.
> Here, under leave of Brutus and the rest,
> (For Brutus is an honourable man,
> So are they all, all honourable men),
> Come I to speak in Cæsar's funeral.
> He was my friend, faithful and just to me :
> But Brutus says he was ambitious;
> And Brutus is an honourable man."

Then Antony goes on to insinuate doubts as to Cæsar's ambition, and tells how he rejected the kingly diadem, rejected it three times. Was this ambition ? Thereupon he suggests that Cæsar, after all, was once beloved, and that there is no reason why he should not be mourned. Then with a sudden outburst :—

> "O judgment! thou art fled to brutish beasts,
> And men have lost their reason !—Bear with me;
> My heart is in the coffin there with Cæsar,
> And I must pause till it come back to me."

Next comes an appeal to their pity for this greatest of men, whose word but yesterday might have stood against the world, and who now lies so low that the poorest will not do him reverence. It would be wrong to make his speech inflammatory, a wrong towards Brutus and Cassius "who—as you know—are honourable men" (mark the jibe in the parenthetic phrase); no, he will rather do wrong to the dead and to himself. But here he holds a parchment—he assuredly will not read it—but if the people came to know its contents they would kiss dead Cæsar's wounds, and dip their handkerchiefs in his sacred blood. And then, when cries for the reading of the will mingle with curses upon the murderers, he stubbornly refuses to read it. Instead of doing so, he displays to them Cæsar's cloak with all the rents in it.

What Plutarch says here is :—

"To conclude his Oration, he unfolded before the whole assembly the bloudy garments of the dead, thrust through in many places with their swords, and called the malefactors cruell and cursed murtherers."

Out of these few words Shakespeare has made this miracle of invective :—

" You all do know this mantle! I remember
The first time ever Cæsar put it on :
'Twas on a summer's evening, in his tent,
That day he overcame the Nervii.
Look ! in this place ran Cassius' dagger through :
See, what a rent the envious Casca made :
Through this, the well-beloved Brutus stabb'd ;
And, as he pluck'd his cursed steel away,
Mark how the blood of Cæsar followed it,
As rushing out of doors, to be resolv'd
If Brutus so unkindly knock'd. or no ;
For Brutus, as you know, was Cæsar's angel.
Judge, O you gods, how dearly Cæsar lov'd him !
This was the most unkindest cut of all ;
For when the noble Cæsar saw him stab,
Ingratitude, more strong than traitors' arms,
Quite vanquish'd him : then burst his mighty heart ;
And, in his mantle muffling up his face,
Even at the base of Pompey's statua,
Which all the while ran blood, great Cæsar fell.
O, what a fall was there, my countrymen !
Then I, and you, and all of us fell down,
Whilst bloody treason flourish'd over us.
O ! now you weep ; and, I perceive, you feel
The dint of pity : these are gracious drops.
Kind souls ! what, weep you, when you but behold
Our Cæsar's vesture wounded ? Look you here,
Here is himself, marr'd, as you see, with traitors."

He uncovers Cæsar's body ; and not till then does he read the will, overwhelming the populace with gifts and benefactions. This climax is of Shakespeare's own invention.

No wonder that even Voltaire was so struck with the beauty of this scene, that for its sake he translated the first three acts of the play. At the end of his own *Mort de César*, too, he introduced a feeble imitation of the scene ; and he had it in his mind when, in his *Discours sur la Tragédie*, dedicated to Bolingbroke, he expressed so much enthusiasm and envy for the freedom of the English stage.

In the last two acts, Brutus is overtaken by the recoil of his deed. He consented to the murder out of noble, disinterested and patriotic motives ; nevertheless he is struck down by its consequences, and pays for it with his happiness and his life. The declining action of the last two acts is—as is usual with Shakespeare—less effective and fascinating than the rising action which fills the first three; but it has one significant, profound, and brilliantly constructed and executed scene—the quarrel and reconciliation between Brutus and Cassius in the fourth act, which leads up to the appearance of Cæsar's ghost.

This scene is significant because it gives a many-sided picture of the two leading characters—the sternly upright Brutus, who is shocked at the means employed by Cassius to raise the money without which their campaign cannot be carried on, and Cassius, a politician entirely indifferent to moral scruples, but equally unconcerned as to his own personal advantage. The scene is profound because it presents to us the necessary consequences of the law-defying, rebellious act: cruelty, unscrupulous policy, and lax tolerance of dishonourable conduct in subordinates, when the bonds of authority and discipline have once been burst. The scene is brilliantly constructed because, with its quick play of passion and its rising discord, which at last passes over into a cordial and even tender reconciliation, it is dramatic in the highest sense of the word.

The fact that Brutus was in Shakespeare's own mind the true hero of the tragedy appears in the clearest light when we find him ending the play with the eulogy which Plutarch, in his life of Brutus, places in the mouth of Antony; I mean the famous words:—

> " This was the noblest Roman of them all:
> All the conspirators, save only he,
> Did that they did in envy of great Cæsar;
> He only, in a general honest thought
> And common good to all, made one of them.
> His life was gentle; and the elements
> So mixed in him that Nature might stand up,
> And say to all the world, ' This was a man!'"

The resemblance between these words and a celebrated speech of Hamlet's is unmistakable. Everywhere in *Julius Cæsar* we feel the proximity of *Hamlet*. The fact that Hamlet hesitates so long before attacking the King, finds so many reasons to hold his hand, is torn with doubts as to the act and its consequences,

TRANSITION FROM BRUTUS TO HAMLET 383

and insists on considering everything even while he upbraids himself for considering so long—all this is partly due, no doubt, to the circumstance that Shakespeare comes to him directly from Brutus. His Hamlet has, so to speak, just seen what happened to Brutus, and the example is not encouraging, either with respect to action in general, or with respect to the murder of a stepfather in particular.

It is not difficult to conceive that Shakespeare may at this period have been subject to moments of scepticism, in which he could scarcely understand how any one could make up his mind to act, to assume responsibility, to set in motion the rolling stone which is the type of every action. If we once begin to brood over the incalculable consequences of an action and all that circumstance may make of it, all action on a great scale becomes impossible. Therefore it is that very few old men understand their youth; they dare not and could not act again as, in their recklessness of consequences, they acted then. Brutus forms the transition to Hamlet, and Hamlet no doubt grew up in Shakespeare's mind during the working out of *Julius Cæsar*.

The stages of transition are perhaps these: the conspirators, in egging Brutus on to the murder, are always reminding him of the elder Brutus, who pretended madness and drove out the Tarquins. This may have led Shakespeare to dwell upon his character as drawn by Livy, which had always been exceedingly popular. But Brutus the elder is an antique Hamlet; and the very name of Hamlet, as he found it in the older play and in Saxo, seems always to have haunted Shakespeare. It was the name he had given to the little boy whom he lost so early.

X

BEN JONSON AND HIS ROMAN PLAYS

IN precisely the same year as Shakespeare, his famous brother-poet, Ben Jonson, made his first attempt at a dramatic presentation of Roman antiquity. His play, *The Poetaster*, was written and acted in 1601. Its purpose is the literary annihilation of two playwrights, Marston and Dekker, with whom the author was at feud; but its action takes place in the time of Augustus; and Jonson, in spite of his satire on contemporaries, no doubt wanted to utilise his thorough knowledge of ancient literature in giving a true picture of Roman manners. As Shakespeare's *Julius Cæsar* was followed by two other tragedies of antique Rome, *Antony and Cleopatra* and *Coriolanus*, so Ben Jonson also wrote two other plays on Roman themes, the tragedies of *Sejanus* and *Catiline*. It is instructive to compare his method of treatment with Shakespeare's; but a general comparison of the two creative spirits must precede this comparison of artistic processes in a single limited field.

Ben Jonson was nine years younger than Shakespeare, born in 1573, a month after the death of his father, the son of a clergyman whose forefathers had belonged to "the gentry." He was a child of the town, while Shakespeare was a child of the country; and the fact is not without significance, though town and country were not then so clearly opposed to each other as they are now. When Ben was two years old, his mother married a worthy master-bricklayer, who did what he could to procure his stepson a good education, so that, after passing some years at a small private school, he was sent to Westminster. Here the learned William Camden, his teacher, introduced him to the two classical literatures, and seems, moreover, to have exercised a not altogether fortunate influence upon his subsequent literary habits; for it was Camden who taught him first to write out in prose whatever he wanted to express in verse. Thus the foundation was laid at school, not only of his double ambition to shine as a scholar and a poet, or rather as a scholar-poet, but also of his heavy and rhetorically emphatic verse.

In spite of his worship of learning, his dislike to all handicraft, and his unfitness for practical work, he was forced by poverty to break off his studies in order to enter the employment of his bricklayer stepfather—a fact which, in his subsequent literary feuds, always procured him the nickname of "the bricklayer." He could not long endure this occupation, went as a soldier to the Netherlands, killed one of the enemy in single combat, under the eyes of both camps, returned to London and married—almost as early as Shakespeare—at the age of only nineteen. Twenty-six years later, in his conversations with Drummond, he called his wife "a shrew, yet honest." He seems to have been an affectionate father, but had the misfortune to survive his children.

He was strong and massive in body, racy and coarse, full of self-esteem and combative instincts, saturated with the conviction of the scholar's high rank and the poet's exalted vocation, full of contempt for ignorance, frivolity, and lowness, classic in his tastes, with a bent towards careful structure and leisurely development of thought in all that he wrote, and yet a true poet in so far as he was not only irregular in his life and quite incapable of saving any of the money he now and then earned, but was, moreover, subject to hallucinations: once saw Carthaginians and Romans fighting on his great toe, and, on another occasion, had a vision of his son with a bloody cross on his brow, which was supposed to forbode his death.

Like Shakespeare, he sought to make his bread by entering the theatre and appearing as an actor. To him, as to Shakespeare, old pieces of the repertory were entrusted to be rewritten, expanded, and furbished up. Thus as late as 1601-2 he made a number of very able additions, in the style of the old play, to that *Spanish Tragedy* of Kyd's, which must in many ways have been in Shakespeare's mind during the composition of *Hamlet*.

He did this work on the commission of Henslow, for whose company, which competed with Shakespeare's, he worked regularly from 1597 onwards. He collaborated with Dekker in a tragedy, and had a hand in other plays; in short, he made himself useful to the theatre as best he could, but did not, like Shakespeare, acquire a share in the enterprise, and thus never became a man of substance. He was to the end of his life forced to rely for his income upon the liberality of royal and noble patrons.

The end of 1598 is doubly significant in Ben Jonson's life. In September he killed in a duel another of Henslow's actors, a certain Gabriel Spencer (who seems to have challenged him), and was therefore branded on the thumb with the letter T (Tyburn). A couple of months later, this occurrence having evidently led to a break in his connection with Henslow's company, his first original play, *Every Man in his Humour*, was acted by the Lord Chamberlain's men. According to a tradition preserved by Rowe, and apparently trustworthy, the play had already been refused, when Shakespeare happened to see it and procured its acceptance. It met with the success it deserved, and henceforward the author's name was famous.

Even in the first edition of this play he makes Young Knowell speak with warm enthusiasm of poetry, of the dignity of the sacred art of invention, and express that hatred for every profanation of the Muses which appears so frequently in later works, finding, perhaps, its most vehement utterance in *The Poetaster*, where the young Ovid eulogises his art in opposition to the scorn of his father and others. From the first, too, he made no concealment of his strong sense of being at once a high-priest of art, and, in virtue of his learning, an Aristarchus of taste. He not only scorned all attempts to tickle the public ear, but, with the firm and superior attitude of a teacher, he again and again imprinted on spectators and readers what Goethe has expressed in the well-known words: "Ich schreibe nicht, Euch zu gefallen; Ihr sollt was lernen." Again and again he claimed for his own person the sanctity and inviolability of art, and attacked his inferior rivals unsparingly, with ferocious rather than witty satire. His prologues and epilogues are devoted to a self-acclamation which was entirely foreign to Shakespeare's nature. Asper in *Every Man out of his Humour* (1599), Crites in *Cynthia's Revels* (1600), and Horace in *The Poetaster* (1601), are so many pieces of self-idolising self-portraiture.

All who, in his judgment, degrade art are made to pay the penalty in scathing caricatures. In *The Poetaster*, for example, his taskmaster, Henslow, is presented under the name of Histrio as a depraved slave-dealer, and his colleagues Marston and Dekker are held up to ridicule under Roman names, as intrusive and despicable scribblers. Their attacks upon the admirable poet Horace, whose name and personality the extremely dissimilar Ben Jonson has arrogated to himself, spring from contemptible motives, and receive a disgraceful punishment.

This whole warfare must not be taken too seriously. The worthy Ben could be at the same time an indignant moralist and a genial boon-companion. We presently find him taking service afresh with the very Henslow whom he has just treated with such withering contempt; and though his attack of 1601 had been met by a most malicious retort in Marston and Dekker's *Satiromastix*, he, three years afterwards, accepts the dedication of Marston's *Malcontent*, and in 1605 collaborates with this lately-lampooned colleague and with Chapman in the comedy of *Eastward Ho!* One could not but think of the German proverb, " Pack schlägt sich, Pack verträgt sich," were it not that Jonson's action at this juncture reveals him in anything but a vulgar light. Marston and Chapman having been thrown into prison for certain gibes at the Scotch in this play, which had come to the notice of the King, and being reported to be in danger of having their noses and ears cut off, Ben Jonson, of his own free will, claimed his share in the responsibility and joined them in prison. At a supper which, after their liberation, he gave to all his friends, his mother clinked glasses with him, and at the same time showed him a paper, the contents of which she had intended to mix with his drink in prison if he had been sentenced to mutilation. She added that she herself would not have survived him, but would have taken her share of the poison. She must have been a mother worthy of such a son.

While Ben lay in durance on account of his duel, he had been converted to Catholicism by a priest who attended him— a conversion at which his adversaries did not fail to jeer. He does not seem, however, to have embraced the Catholic dogma with any great fervour, for twelve years later he once more changes his religion and returns to the Protestant Church. Equally characteristic of Ben and of the Renaissance is his own statement, preserved for us by Drummond, that at his first communion after his reconciliation with Protestantism, in token of his sincere return to the doctrine which gave laymen as well as priests access to the chalice, he drained at one draught the whole of the consecrated wine.

Not without humour, moreover—to use Jonson's own favourite word—is his story of the way in which Raleigh's son, to whom he acted as governor during a tour in France (while Raleigh himself was in the Tower), took a malicious pleasure in making his mentor dead drunk, having him wheeled in a wheelbarrow through the streets of Paris, and showing him off to the mob at every street corner. Ben's strong insistence on his spiritual dignity was not infrequently counterbalanced by an extreme carelessness of his personal dignity.

With all his weaknesses, however, he was a sturdy, energetic, and high-minded man, a commanding, independent, and very comprehensive intelligence; and from 1598, when he makes his first appearance on Shakespeare's horizon, throughout the rest of his life, he was, so far as we can see, the man of all his contemporaries whose name was oftenest mentioned along with Shakespeare's. In after days, especially outside England, the name of Ben Jonson has come to sound small enough in comparison with the name of solitary greatness with which it was once bracketed; but at that time, although Jonson was never so popular as Shakespeare, they were commonly regarded in literary circles as the dramatic twin-brethren of the age. For us it is still more interesting to remember that Ben Jonson was one of the few with whom we know that Shakespeare was on terms of constant familiarity, and, moreover, that he brought to this intercourse a set of definite artistic principles, widely different from Shakespeare's own. Though his society may have been somewhat fatiguing, it must nevertheless have been both instructive and stimulating to Shakespeare, since Ben was greatly his superior in historical and linguistic knowledge, while as a poet he pursued a totally different ideal.

Ben Jonson was a great dramatic intelligence. He never, like the other poets of his time, took this or that novel and dramatised it as it stood, regardless of its more or less incoherent structure, its more or less flagrant defiance of topographical, geographical, or historical reality. With architectural solidity—was he not the step-son of a master-builder?—he built up his dramatic plan out of his own head, and, being a man of great learning, he did his best to avoid all incongruities of local colour. If he is now and then negligent in this respect —if the characters in *Volpone* now and then talk as if they were in London, not in Venice, and those in *The Poetaster* as if they were in England, not in Rome—it is because of his satiric purpose, and not at all by reason of the indifference to such considerations which characterises all other dramatists of the time, Shakespeare not the least.

The fundamental contrast between them can be most shortly expressed in the statement that Ben Jonson accepted the view of human nature set forth in the classic comedies and the Latin tragedies. He does not represent it as many-sided, with inward developments and inconsistencies, but fixes character in typical forms, with one dominant trait thrown into high relief. He portrays, for example, the crafty parasite, or the eccentric who cannot endure noise, or the braggart captain, or the depraved anarchist (Catiline), or the stern man of honour (Cato)—and all these personalities are neither more nor less than the labels imply, and act up to their description always and in all circumstances. The pencil with which he draws is hard, but he wields it with such power that his best outlines subsist through the centuries, unforgettable, despite their occasional oddity of design, in virtue of the indignation with which wickedness and meanness are branded, and the racy merriment with which the caricatures are sketched, the farces worked out.

Some of Molière's farces may now and then remind us of Jonson's, but, as regards the pitiless intensity of the satire, we shall find no counterpart to his *Volpone* until we come in our own times to Gogol's *Revisor*.

The Graces stood by Shakespeare's cradle, not by Jonson's; and yet this heavy-armed warrior has now and then attained to grace as well—has now and then given a holiday to his sound systematic intelligence and his solidly-constructed logic, and, like a true poet of the Renaissance, soared into the rarer atmosphere of pure fantasy.

He shows himself very much at home in the allegorical masques which were performed at court festivals; and in the pastoral play *The Sad Shepherd*, which seems to have been written upon his death-bed, he proved that even in the purely romantic style he could challenge comparison with the best writers of his day. Yet it is not in this sphere that he displays his true originality. It is in his keen and faithful observation of the conditions and manners of his time, which Shakespeare left on one side, or depicted only incidentally and indirectly. The London of Elizabeth lives again in Jonson's plays; both the lower and higher circles, but especially the lower: the haunters of taverns and theatres, the men of the riverside and the markets, rogues and vagabonds, poets and players, watermen and jugglers, bear-leaders and hucksters, rich city dames, Puritan fanatics and country squires, English oddities of every class and kind, each speaking his own language, dialect, or jargon. Shakespeare never kept so close to the life of the day.

It is especially Johnson's scholarship that must have made his society full of instruction for Shakespeare. Ben's acquirements were encyclopædic, and his acquaintance with the authors of antiquity was singularly complete and accurate. It has often been remarked that he was not content with an exhaustive knowledge of the leading writers of Greece and Rome. He knows not only the great historians, poets, and orators, such as Tacitus and Sallust, Horace, Virgil, Ovid, and Cicero, but sophists, grammarians, and scholiasts, men like Athenæus, Libanius, Philostratus, Strabo, Photius. He is familiar with fragments of Æolic lyrists and Roman epic poets, of Greek tragedies and Roman inscriptions; and, what is still more remarkable, he manages to make use of all his knowledge. Whatever in the ancients he found beautiful or profound or stimulating, that he wove into his work. Dryden says of him in his "Essay of Dramatic Poesy":—

"The greatest man of the last age (Ben Jonson) was willing to give place to the ancients in all things: he was not only a professed imitator of Horace, but a learned plagiary of all the others; you track him everywhere in their snow. If Horace, Lucan, Petronius Arbiter, Seneca, and Juvenal had their own from him, there are few serious thoughts which are new in him. . . . But he has done his robberies so openly, that one may see he fears not to be taxed by any law. He invades authors like a monarch; and what would be theft in other poets is only victory in him."

Certain it is that an uncommon learning and an extraordinary memory supplied him with an immense store of small touches, poetical and rhetorical details, which he could not refrain from incorporating in his plays.

Yet his mass of learning was not of a merely verbal or rhetorical nature; he knew things as well as words. Whatever subject he treats of, be it alchemy, or witchcraft, or cosmetics in the time of Tiberius, he handles it with competence and has its whole literature at his fingers' ends. He thus becomes universal like Shakespeare, but in a different way. Shakespeare knows, firstly, all that cannot be learnt from books, and in the second place, whatever can be gleaned by genius from a casual utterance, an intelligent hint, a conversation with a man of high acquirements. Besides this, he knows the literature which was at that time within the reach of a quick-witted and studious man without special scholarship. Ben Jonson, on the other hand, is a scholar by profession. He has learnt from books all that the books of his day—for the most part, of course, the not too numerous survivals of the classic literatures—could teach a man who made scholarship his glory. He not only possesses knowledge, but he knows whence he has acquired it; he can cite his authorities by chapter and paragraph, and he sometimes garnishes his plays with so many learned references that they bristle with notes like an academic thesis.

Colossal, coarse-grained, vigorous, and always ready for the fray, with his gigantic burden of learning, he has been compared by Taine to one of those war-elephants of antiquity which bore on their backs a whole fortress, with garrison, armoury, and munitions, and under the weight of this panoply could yet move as quickly as a fleet-footed horse.

It must have been intensely interesting for their comrades at the Mermaid to listen to the discussions between Jonson and Shakespeare, to follow two such remarkable minds, so differently organised and equipped, when they debated, in jest or earnest, this or that historic problem, this or that moot point in æsthetics; and no less interesting is it for us, in our days, to compare their almost contemporaneous dramatic treatment of Roman antiquity. We might here expect Shakespeare to have the worst of it, since he, according to Jonson's well-known phrase, had "small Latine and less Greek;" while Ben was as much at home in ancient Rome as in the London of his day, and, with his altogether masculine talent, could claim a certain kinship with the Roman spirit.

And yet even here Shakespeare stands high above Jonson, who, with all his learning and industry, lacks his great contemporary's sense for the fundamental element in human nature, to which the terms good and bad do not apply, and has, besides, very few of those unforeseen inspirations of genius which constitute Shakespeare's strength, and make up for all the gaps in his knowledge. Jonson, moreover, could not modulate into the minor key, and is thus unable to depict the inmost subtleties of feminine character.

None the less would it be unjust to make Jonson, as the Germans are apt to do, nothing but a foil to Shakespeare. We must, in mere equity, bring out the points at which he attains to real greatness.

Although the scene of *The Poetaster* is laid in Rome in the days of Augustus, the play eludes comparison with Shakespeare's Roman dramas in so far as its costume is partly a mere travesty under which Ben Jonson defends himself against his contemporaries Marston and Dekker, who also figure, of course, in a Roman disguise. Even here, however, he has done his best to give an accurate picture of antique Roman manners, and has applied to the task all his learning, with rather too little aid, perhaps, from his fancy. His comic figures, for instance, the intrusive Crispinus and the foolish singer Hermogenes, are taken bodily from Horace's Satires (Book i. Satires 3 and 9); but both these pleasant caricatures are executed with vigour and life.

Ben Jonson has in this play woven together three different actions, one only of which has a symbolic meaning outside the frame of the picture. In the first place, he presents Ovid's struggle for leave to follow his poetic vocation, his suspected love-affair with Augustus's daughter, Julia, and his banishment from the court when Augustus discovers the intrigue between the young poet and his child. In the second place, he introduces us into the house of the rich bourgeois Albius, who has been ill-advised enough to marry one of the emancipated great ladies of the period, Chloe by name, and who, by her help, obtains admission to court society. Chloe's house is a meeting-place for all the love-poets of the period, Tibullus, Propertius, Ovid, Cornelius Gallus, and the ladies who favour them; and Jonson has succeeded very fairly in suggesting the free tone of conversation prevalent in those circles, which was doubtless reproduced in many circles of London life during the Renaissance. Finally, we have a representation — Jonson's chief object in writing the play — of the conspiracy of the bad and envious poets against Horace, which culminates in a formal impeachment. The Emperor himself, and the famous poets of his court, form a sort of tribunal before which the case is tried. Horace is acquitted on every count, and the accusers are sentenced to a punishment entirely in the spirit of the Aristophanic comedy—so foreign to Shakespeare—Crispinus being forced to take a pill of hellebore, which makes him vomit up all the affected or merely novel words he has used, which appear to Ben Jonson ridiculous. Some of them—for example the first two, "retrograde" and "reciprocal"—have nevertheless survived in modern English. In spite of its allegorical character, the episode is not deficient in an almost too pungent realism.

The most Roman of all these scenes are doubtless those in which the gallantry between the young men and the ladies, and the snobbery which forces its way into Augustus's court, are freely represented. Less Roman, by reason of their too palpable tendency, are the scenes in which Augustus appears in the circle of his court poets. No serious attempt is made to portray the Emperor's character, and the speeches placed in the mouths of the poets are very clearly designed simply for the glorification of poetry in general, and Ben Jonson in particular.

The sins of which his enemies were always accusing him were "self-love, arrogancy, impudence, and railing," together with "filching by translation." As he explains in the defensive dialogue which he appended to his play, it was his purpose—

> "To show that Virgil, Horace, and the rest
> Of those great master-spirits, did not want
> Detractors then, or practisers against them."

He makes foolish persons find injurious allusions to themselves, and even insults to the Emperor, in entirely innocent poems of Horace's, and shows how the Emperor orders them to be whipped as backbiters. Horace's literary relation to the Greeks, be it noted, was not unlike that of Ben Jonson himself to the Latin writers.

A special interest attaches for us to the passage in the fifth act, where, immediately before Virgil's entrance, the different poets, at the suggestion of the Emperor, express their judgment of his genius, and where Horace, after warmly protesting against the common belief that one poet is necessarily envious of another, joins in the general eulogy of his great rival. There is this remarkable circumstance about the encomiums on Virgil, here placed in the mouths of Gallus, Tibullus, and Horace, that while some of them are appropriate enough to the real Virgil (else all verisimilitude would have been sacrificed), others seem unmistakably to point away from Virgil towards one or other famous contemporary of Jonson's own. Look for a moment at these speeches (v. 1):—

> "*Tibullus.* That which he hath writ
> Is with such judgment labour'd, and distill'd
> Through all the needful uses of our lives,
> That could a man remember but his lines,
> He should not touch at any serious point,
> But he might breathe his spirit out of him.
> *Augustus.* You mean, he might repeat part of his works
> As fit for any conference he can use?
> *Tibullus.* True, royal Cæsar.
> *Horace.* His learning savours not the school-like gloss
> That most consists in echoing words and terms,
> And soonest wins a man an empty name;
> Nor any long or far-fetch'd circumstance
> Wrapp'd in the curious generalties of arts,
> But a direct and analytic sum
> Of all the worth and first effects of arts.
> And for his poesy, 'tis so ramm'd with life,
> That it shall gather strength of life, with being,
> And live hereafter more admired than now."

Can we conceive that Ben Jonson had not Shakespeare in his eye as he wrote these speeches, which apply better to him than to any one else? It is true that a Shakespeare scholar of such authority as the late C. M. Ingleby, the compiler of *Shakespeare's Centurie of Prayse*, has declared against this theory, together with Nicholson and Furnivall. But none of them has brought forward any conclusive argument to prevent us from following Ben Jonson's admirer, Gifford, and his impartial critic, John Addington Symonds, in accepting these speeches as allusions to Shakespeare. It is useless to be for ever citing the passage in *The Return from Parnassus*, as to the "purge" Shakespeare has given Ben Jonson, in proof that there was an open feud between them, when, in fact, there is no evidence whatever of any hostility on Shakespeare's part; and the very stress laid on the assertion that Horace, as a poet, is innocent of envy towards a famous and popular colleague, makes it unreasonable to take the eulogies as applying solely to the real Virgil, whom they fit so imperfectly. Of course it by no means follows that we are to conceive every word of these eulogies as unreservedly applied to Shakespeare; the speeches seem to have been purposely left somewhat vague, so that they might at once point to the ancient poet and suggest the modern. But out of the mists of the characterisation certain definite contours stand forth; and the physiognomy which they form, the picture of the great teacher in all earthly affairs, rich, not in book-learning, but in the wisdom of life, whose poetry is so vital that it will live through the ages with an ever-intenser life—this portrait we know and recognise as that of the genius with the great, calm eyes under the lofty brow.

Ben Jonson's *Sejanus*, which dates from 1603, only two years after *The Poetaster*, is a historical tragedy of the time of Tiberius, in which the poet, without any reference to contemporary personalities, sets forth to depict the life and customs of the imperial court. It is as an archæologist and moralist, however, that he depicts them, and his method is thus very different from Shakespeare's. He not only displays a close acquaintance with the life of the period, but penetrates through the outward forms to its spirit. He is animated, indeed, by a purely moral indignation against the turbulent and corrupt protagonist of his tragedy, but his wrath does not prevent him from giving a careful delineation of the figure of Sejanus in relation to its surroundings, by means of thoughtfully-designed and even imaginative individual scenes. Jonson does not, like Shakespeare, display from within the character of this unscrupulous and audacious man, but he shows the circumstances which have produced it, and its modes of action.

The difference between Jonson's and Shakespeare's method is not that Jonson pedantically avoids the anachronisms which swarm in *Julius Cæsar*. In both plays, for instance, watches are spoken of.[1] But Ben, on occasion, can paint a scene of Roman life with as much accuracy as we find in a picture by Alma Tadema or a novel by Flaubert. For example, when he depicts an act of worship and sacrifice in the Sacellum or private chapel of Sejanus's house (v. 4), every detail of the ceremonial is correct. After the Herald (Præco) has uttered the formula, "Be all profane far hence," and horn and flute players have performed their liturgical music, the priest (Flamen) exhorts all to appear with "pure hands, pure vestments, and pure minds;" his acolytes intone the complementary responses; and while the trumpets are again sounded, he takes honey from the altar with his finger, tastes it, and gives it to the others to taste; goes through the same process with the milk in an earthen vessel; and then sprinkles milk over the altar, "kindleth his gums," and goes with the censer round the altar, upon which he ultimately places it, dropping "branches of poppy" upon the smouldering incense. In justification of these traits, Jonson gives no fewer than thirteen footnotes, in which passages are cited from a very wide range of Latin authors. Kalisch has counted the notes appended to this play, and finds 291 in all. The ceremonial is here employed to introduce a scene in which "great Mother Fortune," to whom the libation is made, averts her face from Sejanus, and thereby portends his fall; whereupon, in an access of fury, he overturns her statue and altar.

Another scene, constructed with quite as much learning, and far more able and remarkable, is that which opens the second Act. Livia's physician, Eudemus, has been suborned by Sejanus to procure him a meeting with the princess, and, moreover, to concoct a potent poison for her husband. In the act of assisting his mistress to rouge her cheek, and recommending her an effective "dentrifice" and a "prepared pomatum to smooth the skin," he answers her casual questions as to who is to present the poisoned cup to Drusus and induce him to drink it. Here, again, Ben Jonson's mastery of detail displays itself. Eudemus's remark, for example, that the "ceruse" on Livia's cheeks has faded in the sun, is supported by a reference to an epigram of Martial, from which

---

[1] "Observe him as his watch observes his clock."—*Sejanus*, i. 1.

it appears that this cosmetic was injured by heat. But here all these details are merged in the potent general impression produced by the dispassionate and business-like calmness with which the impending murder is arranged in the intervals of a disquisition upon those devices of the toilet which are to enchain the contriver of the crime.

Ben Jonson possesses the undaunted insight and the vigorous pessimism which render it possible to represent Roman depravity and wild-beast-like ferocity under the first Emperors without extenuation and without declamation. He cannot, indeed, dispense with a sort of chorus of honourable Romans, but they express themselves, as a rule, pithily and without prolixity; and he has enough sense of art and of history never to let his ruffians and courtesans repent.

Now and then he even attains to a Shakespearian level. The scene in which Sejanus approaches Eudemus first with jesting talk, and then, with wily insinuations, worms himself into his acquaintance and makes him his creature, while Eudemus, with crafty servility, shows that he can take a half-spoken hint, and, without for a moment committing himself, offers his services as pander and assassin—this passage is in no way inferior to the scene in Shakespeare's *King John* in which the King suggests to Hubert the murder of Arthur.

The most remarkable scene, however, is that (v. 10) in which the Senate is assembled in the Temple of Apollo to hear messages from Tiberius in his retreat at Capri. The first letter confers upon Sejanus "the tribunitial dignity and power," with expressions of esteem, and the Senate loudly acclaims the favourite. Then the second letter is read. It is expressed in a strangely contorted style, begins with some general remarks on public policy, hypocritical in tone, then turns, like the first, to Sejanus, and, to the astonishment of all, dwells with emphasis upon his low origin and the rare honours to which he has been preferred. Already the hearers are alarmed; but the impression is obliterated by new sentences of flattery. Then unfavourable opinions and judgments regarding the favourite are cited and dwelt upon with a certain complacency; then they are refuted with some vehemence; finally, they are brought forward again, and this time in a manner unmistakably hostile to Sejanus. Immediately the senators who have swarmed around him withdraw from his neighbourhood, leaving him in the centre of an empty space; and the reading continues until Laco enters with the guards who are to arrest the hitherto all-powerful favourite and lead him away. We can find no parallel to this reading of the letter and the vacillations it produces among the cringing senators, save in Antony's speech over the body of Cæsar and the consequent revulsion in the attitude and temper of the Roman mob. Shakespeare's scene is more vividly projected, and shines with the poet's humour; Jonson's scene is elaborated with grim energy, and worked out with the moralist's bitterness. But in the dramatic movement of the moralist's scene, no less than of the poet's, antique Rome lives again.

Jonson's *Catiline*, written some time later, appeared in 1611, and was dedicated to Pembroke. Although executed on the same principles, it is on the whole inferior to *Sejanus;* but it is better fitted for comparison with *Julius Cæsar* in so far as its action belongs to the same period, and Cæsar himself appears in it. The second act of the tragedy is in its way a masterpiece. As soon as Jonson enters upon the political action proper, he transcribes endless speeches from Cicero, and becomes intolerably tedious; but so long as he keeps to the representation of manners, and seeks, as in his comedies, to paint a quite unemotional picture of the period, he shows himself at his best.

This second act takes place at the house of Fulvia, the lady who, according to Sallust, betrayed to Cicero the conspirators' secret. The whole picture produces an entirely convincing effect. She first repels with unfeeling coldness an intrusive friend and protector, Catiline's fellow-conspirator, Curius; but when he at last turns away in anger, telling her that she will repent her conduct when she finds herself excluded from participation in an immense booty which will fall to the share of others, she calls him back, full of curiosity and interest, becomes suddenly friendly, and even caressing, and wrings from him his secret, instantly recognising, however, that Cicero will pay for it without stint, and that this money is considerably safer than the sum which might fall to her share in a general revolution. Her visit to Cicero, with his craftily friendly interrogatory, first of her, and then of her lover Curius, whom he summons and converts into one of his spies, deserves the highest praise. These scenes contain the concentrated essence of Sallust's *Catiline* and of Cicero's Orations and Letters. The Cicero of this play rises high above the Cicero to whom Shakespeare has assigned a few speeches. Cæsar, on the other hand, comes off no better at Ben Jonson's hands than at Shakespeare's. The poet was obviously determined to show a certain independence of judgment in the way in which he has treated Sallust's representation both of Cæsar and of Cicero. Sallust, whom Jonson nevertheless follows in the main, is hostile to Cicero and defends Cæsar. The worthy Ben, on the other hand, was, as a man of letters, a sworn admirer of Cicero, while in Cæsar he sees only a cold, crafty personage, who sought to make use of Catiline for his own ends, and therefore joined forces with him, but repudiated him when things went wrong, and was so influential that Cicero dared not attack him when he rooted out the conspiracy. Thus the great Caius Julius did not touch Jonson's manly heart any more than Shakespeare's. He appears throughout in an extremely unsympathetic light, and no speech, no word of his, portends his coming greatness.

Of this greatness Jonson had probably no deep realisation. It is surprising enough to note that the scholars and poets of the Renaissance, in so far as they took sides in the old strife between Cæsar and Pompey, were all on Pompey's side. Even in the seventeenth century, in France, under a despotism more absolute than Cæsar's, the men who were familiar with antique history, and who, for the rest, vied with each other in loyalty and king-worship, were unanimously opposed to Cæsar. Strange as it may seem, it is not until our century, with its hostility to despotism and its continuous advance in the direction of democracy, that Cæsar's genius has been fully appreciated, and the benefits his life conferred on humanity have been thoroughly understood.

The personal relation between Ben Jonson and Shakespeare is not to this day quite clearly ascertained. It was for long regarded as distinctly hostile, no one doubting that Jonson, during his great rival's lifetime, cherished an obstinate jealousy towards him. More recently, Jonson's admirers have argued with warmth that cruel injustice has been done him in this respect. So far as we can now judge, it appears that Jonson honestly recognised and admired Shakespeare's great qualities, but at the same time felt a displeasure he never could quite conquer at seeing him so much more popular as a dramatist, and—as was only natural—regarded his own tendencies in art as truer and better justified.

In the preface to *Sejanus* (edition of 1605) Jonson uses an expression which, as the piece was acted by Shakespeare's company, and Shakespeare himself appeared in it, was long interpreted as referring to him. Jonson writes:—

"Lastly, I would inform you that this book, in all numbers, is not the same with that which was acted on the public stage, wherein a second pen had good share; in place of which, I have rather chosen to put weaker, and, no doubt, less pleasing, of mine own, than to defraud so happy a genius of his right by my loathed usurpation."

The words "so happy a genius," in particular, together with the other circumstances, have directed the thoughts of commentators to Shakespeare. Mr. Brinsley Nicholson, however (in the *Academy*, Nov. 14th, 1874), has shown it to be far more probable that the person alluded to is not Shakespeare, but a very inferior poet, Samuel Sheppard. The marked politeness of Jonson's expressions may be due to his having inflicted on his collaborator a considerable disappointment, almost an insult, by omitting his portion of the work, and at the same time excluding his name from the title-page. It seems, at any rate, that Samuel Sheppard felt wounded by this proceeding, since, more than forty years later, he claimed for himself the honour of having collaborated in *Sejanus*, in a verse which is ostensibly a panegyric on Jonson.[1] Symonds, so late as 1888, nevertheless maintains in his *Ben Jonson* that the preface most probably refers to Shakespeare; but he

---

[1] He says of Jonson in *The Times Displayed in Six Sestyads*:—

> "So His, that Divine Plautus equalled,
> Whose Conmick vain Menander nere could hit,
> Whose tragic sceans shal be with wonder Read
> By after ages, for unto his wit
> My selfe gave personal ayd, *I* dictated
> To him when as *Sejanus* fall he writ,
> And yet on earth some foolish sots there bee
> That dare make Randolph his Rival in degree."

does not refute or even mention Nicholson's carefully-marshalled argument.

It is not, however, of great importance to decide whether a compliment in one of Jonson's prefaces is or is not addressed to Shakespeare, since we have ample evidence in the warm eulogy and mild criticism in his *Discoveries*, and in the enthusiastic poem prefixed to the First Folio, that the crusty Ben (who, moreover, is said to have been Shakespeare's boon companion on his last convivial evening) regarded him with the warmest feelings, at least towards the close of his life and after his death.

This does not exclude the probability that Jonson's radically different literary ideals may have led him to make incidental and sometimes rather tart allusions to what appeared to him weak or mistaken in Shakespeare's work.

There is no foundation for the theory which has sometimes been advanced, that the passage in *The Poetaster* ridiculing Crispinus's coat of arms is an allusion to Shakespeare. It is beyond all doubt that the figure of Crispinus was exclusively intended for Marston; he himself, at any rate, did not for a moment doubt it. For the rest, Jonson's ascertained or conjectured side-glances at Shakespeare are these :—

In the prologue to *Every Man in his Humour*, which can scarcely have been spoken when the play was performed by the Lord Chamberlain's company, not only is realistic art proclaimed the true art, in opposition to the romanticism which prevailed on the Shakespearian stage, but a quite definite attack is made on those who

"With three rusty swords,
And help of some few foot and half-foot words,
Fight over York and Lancaster's long jars."

And this is followed by a really biting criticism of the works of other playwrights, concluding—

"There's hope left then,
You, that have so graced monsters, may like men."

The possible jibe at *Twelfth Night* in *Every Man out of his Humour* (iii. 1) has already been mentioned (*ante*, p. 272). That, too, must be of late insertion, and is at worst extremely innocent.

Much has been made of the passage in *Volpone* (iii. 2) where Lady Politick Would-be, speaking of Guarini's *Pastor Fido*, says :—

"All our English writers
Will deign to steal out of this author, mainly :
Almost as much as from Montagnié."

This has been interpreted as an accusation of plagiarism, some pointing it at the well-known passage in *The Tempest*, where Shakespeare has annexed some lines from Montaigne's Essays; others at *Hamlet*, which has throughout many points of contact with the French philosopher. But *The Tempest* was undoubtedly written long after *Volpone*, and the relation of *Hamlet* to Montaigne is such as to render it scarcely conceivable that an accusation of plagiarism could be founded upon it. Here again Jonson seems to have been groundlessly suspected of malice.

Jacob Feis (*Shakespeare and Montaigne*, p. 183) would fain see in Nano's song about the hermaphrodite Androgyno a shameless attack upon Shakespeare, simply because the names Pythagoras and Euphorbus appear in it (*Volpone*, i. 1), as they do in the well-known passage in Meres; but this accusation is entirely fantastic. Equally unreasonable is it of Feis to discover an obscene besmirching of the figure of Ophelia in that passage of Jonson, Marston, and Chapman's *Eastward Ho!* (iii. 2) where there occur some passing allusions to *Hamlet*.

There remain, then, in reality, only one or two passages in *Bartholomew Fair*, dating from 1614. We have already seen (*ante*, p. 337) that there may possibly be a satirical allusion to the Sonnets in the introduced puppet-play, *The Touchstone of True Love*. The Induction contains an unquestionable jibe, both at *The Tempest* and *The Winter's Tale*, whose airy poetry the downright Ben was unable to appreciate.[1] Neither Caliban nor the element of enchantment in *The Tempest* appealed to him, and in *The Winter's Tale*, as in *Pericles*, it offended his classic taste and his Aristotelian theories that the action should

---

[1] "If there be never a servant-monster in the fair, who can help it, he says, nor a nest of antiques? He is loth to make Nature afraid in his plays, like those that beget tales, tempests, and such-like drolleries."

extend over a score of years, so that we see infants in one act reappear in the next as grown-up young women.

But these trifling intolerances and impertinences must not tempt us to forget that it was Ben Jonson who wrote of Shakespeare those great and passionate lines:—

> " Triumph, my Britain ! thou hast one to show
> To whom all scenes of Europe homage owe.
> He was not of an age, but for all time ! "

END OF VOL. I.

www.ingramcontent.com/pod-product-compliance
Lightning Source LLC
Chambersburg PA
CBHW022117290426
44112CB00008B/701